GREAT
SUMMER
OLYMPIC
MOMENTS

GREAT SUMMER OLYMPIC MOMENTS

Nate Aaseng

Lerner Publications Company
Minneapolis

Page 1: Jesse Owens, far right, crosses the finish line a stride ahead of his U.S. teammate, Ralph Metcalfe, in the 100-meter dash finals of the 1936 Olympics.
Page 2: Fanny Blankers-Koen wins the 200-meter dash at the 1948 Olympics to claim the third of her four gold medals.

Library of Congress Cataloging-in-Publication Data

Aaseng, Nate.
    Great summer Olympic moments / Nate Aaseng.

        p.   cm.
    Summary: Discusses unusual and memorable athletic performances
that have taken place in the history of the Summer Olympics.
    ISBN 0-8225-1536-9
    1. Olympics—History—Juvenile literature. [1. Olympics—
History.] I. Title.
GV721.5.A19   1990
796.48—dc20   90-32636
                                                       CIP
                                                       AC

Manufactured in the United States of America

1 2 3 4 5 6 7 8 9 10 99 98 97 96 95 94 93 92 91 90

Contents

After running from Marathon, Greece, to Athens, the Greek runner Spiridon Loues closes in on the finish line amid the cheers of his homeland fans in the stadium.

6

Introduction

For more than a thousand years, the ancient town of Olympia in western Greece was the gathering place for the greatest athletes of the world. Every four years, nations stopped their wars while men boxed, ran, jumped, and threw objects in the first Olympic stadium. First prize was a wreath of olive—and fame throughout the land. After the ancient Olympic games were banned by the Roman emperor in the year 394, the Olympian ideal of peaceful athletic competition among the nations became a distant memory. The stadium and temples of Olympia fell into ruin.

About 1,500 years later, in the 19th century, a group of German archaeologists began to dig in the area of Olympia. Many people around the world read about the ancient buildings that were being dug up. Scholars and students studied historical writings and learned how the ancient games had been organized. They even discovered the names of some of the great athletes who had competed in the games. Finally, in 1896,

a group of sports fans set out to bring the games back to life.

Most of the pieces for this noble experiment had already been assembled. The games had a tireless organizer (Baron Pierre de Coubertin), a host country (Greece), financing (courtesy of a wealthy Greek architect), and competitors (more than 300, from 13 different nations).

At first, the games failed to inspire. The athletic performances of the 1896 Athens Olympics seemed very ordinary compared to the stories of legendary heroes who had battled for Olympic honors in ancient Greece. As the games progressed, the failure of the host country to win any track and field events added to the disappointment of the fans. After lying dormant for 1,500 years, the Olympic games needed something extraordinary to bring them back to life.

Late in the competition, on April 10, 1896, a small group of men gathered at the Marathon Bridge. Marathon, a village north of Athens, was the site of an ancient

Greek victory over Persian invaders in 490 B.C. According to a story passed down through the years, a Greek messenger had run all the way from the battlefield to Athens with news of the victory. After giving his report, the runner had collapsed and died from exhaustion. In honor of this legend, Baron de Coubertin had introduced a new event called the marathon. The runners would follow the road from Marathon to Athens, an incredible 40 kilometers (about 25 miles) away.

Nearly 100,000 spectators gathered at the stadium to witness the finish. All afternoon they anxiously awaited reports of the race's progress. Unfortunately, the early news was no more promising for Greece than the results of any of the other events had been. A French athlete named Lermusiaux had dominated the early portion of the race. Unable to maintain his own pace, Lermusiaux slowed, gave up the lead to Edwin Flack of Australia, and soon collapsed. A subdued Greek crowd passed along the latest information—Flack was just a few miles away and holding on to his lead.

Four kilometers from the finish line, Flack, a gold medalist in the 800 meters, faltered. Soon after, a Greek army major charged into the stadium on horseback to deliver the latest bulletin to the king and queen of Greece: A Greek was in the lead!

The news spread rapidly throughout the stadium. Sports fans, who had been mildly curious onlookers, became excited and tried to will the Greek along to the finish. A long, resounding roar from outside the stadium signaled that the first runner was nearing the finish. When

Baron Pierre de Coubertin

the small form of Spiridon Loues appeared on the stadium track, the spectators leapt to their feet, shouting their delight. Loues crossed the finish line nearly seven minutes ahead of the next finisher and was practically drowned in a sea of congratulations.

This unexpected triumph by a poor man, who had finished no better than fifth in the Greek pre-Olympic trials, provided the spark that was needed to bring the Olympic games to life.

Years later, in 1968, the Olympic games in Mexico City followed a similar pattern. For 10 days of competition, the Mexican hosts politely applauded the victories of visiting athletes. In all that time, the Mexican athletes had faltered.

The host country's best prospect for a gold medal appeared to be in a swimming event, the 200-meter breaststroke. A 17-year-old named Felipe "Pepe" Muñoz had not only qualified for the finals but had also recorded the fastest time of the trial heats. Muñoz was still a long-shot to defeat Vladimir Kosinsky of the Soviet Union, who held the world record. But 8,000 Mexicans crowded the poolside bleachers to cheer his effort.

Halfway through the race, the Mexicans' hopes were evaporating. Muñoz, swimming in fourth place, appeared out of contention. Suddenly, the young swimmer surged forward. As he moved into third place, the hometown fans began cheering loudly. The inspired Muñoz continued to catch up to Kosinsky.

All spectators were on their feet as Muñoz touched the wall for the final turn just inches behind Kosinsky. Amid indescribable bedlam, the teenager caught the Soviet halfway down the final length and touched home half a second ahead of him to claim the gold medal.

In the celebration that followed, Muñoz was pulled out of the water and carried around the pool area. Spectators hugged and kissed each other. Television announcers wept openly. The Olympics had again provided hometown sports fans with an unforgettable experience.

Every four years, thousands of the world's greatest athletes gather to compete in the Olympic games. The grandeur and the massive scale of the Summer Olympics have made it the world's greatest showcase for what the human body and willpower can accomplish.

Paavo Nurmi leads his teammate, Ville Ritola, in the 5,000-meter race at the 1924 Olympics in Paris.

1

No Rest for the Flying Finn

Paavo Nurmi

Distance runners who tried to match strides with Paavo Nurmi felt as though they were racing against a machine. No matter how fierce the pace or how brutal the conditions, the best of the "Flying Finns" showed no sign of discomfort. He frequently announced before a race how fast he intended to run, kept to his schedule with the help of a stopwatch, and then walked off after his victory without a smile or a word to reporters. Nurmi's 1924 Olympic performance left his competition so far behind that he seemed superhuman.

Paavo Nurmi was born in Turku, Finland, in 1897. He was a quiet boy with few friends, and he became even more of a loner after the death of his father in 1909. As a teenager, Nurmi was one of many Finns who were inspired by the success of Johannes Kolehmainen in the 1912 Olympics. Kolehmainen had won gold medals in the 5,000-meter, 10,000-meter, and cross-country races.

Nurmi set out to follow the trail blazed by Kolehmainen, and he allowed few distractions to get in his way. Later, there were many rumors about the secret to his success. Some of them, such as his extremely low pulse rate, were true. Others, such as his supposed diet of black bread and fish, were not.

The key ingredient to his success was nothing magical—simply sheer determination. In an incredible display of self-discipline, Nurmi trained for two years before he entered his first race. While he served in the Finnish army during World War I, Nurmi would rise at 5 A.M. to work out. He studied the techniques and strategies of the best runners, then spent long hours developing his own training program and race tactics. Running was so important to

11

him that he spent his savings on a stopwatch to help him pace his workouts and races.

Nurmi first appeared in the Olympics at the 1920 games in Antwerp, Belgium, when he was 23. He set the pace in the 5,000-meter race and wore down all competitors except for Joseph Guillemot of France. The tiny Frenchman stayed with Nurmi throughout the race, then outsprinted him on the final straightaway for the win. Nurmi turned the tables on Guillemot in the 10,000 meters, however, passing Guillemot in the final lap to win in a world-record time of 31:45.8. Nurmi also captured gold medals in the cross-country individual and team races.

The victories were only a preview of what Nurmi would do in the 1924 Olympic games at Paris. The silent Finn had set his sights on capturing all the gold medals in distance running, from the 1,500 meters to the 10,000 meters.

In April of that year, Nurmi's plans were set back when he slipped on a patch of ice while running, injuring both of his knees. By the time of Finland's national Olympic trials that summer, Nurmi was still not up to full strength. Finnish officials decided that Nurmi would have to scale back his goals, so they withdrew him from the 10,000-meter contest. That still left Nurmi with an almost-impossible situation. Olympic officials had scheduled the 5,000-meter final to begin a half hour after the 1,500-meter final. No one could possibly run well against top competition with such a short period of rest. The Finns protested the schedule but succeeded only in increasing the time between the two events to 55 minutes.

Instead of fretting about the demanding schedule, Nurmi fumed that it was too easy! After learning the winning time posted by teammate Vilho "Ville" Ritola in the Olympic 10,000-meter race, Nurmi

Nurmi checks his stopwatch.

is said to have gone out to a track that same day and beaten Ritola's time.

Four days later, on July 10, he was ready to try for the 1,500-5,000 double. In the 1,500 meters, the expressionless Nurmi grabbed the lead immediately. Checking his ever-present stopwatch, he set a pace that was tough enough to exhaust the fast-finishing sprinters in the field. Nurmi checked his watch one last time, tossed it aside, sprinted to a commanding lead, and then coasted to victory in an Olympic-record time of 3:53.6.

Giving no indication that he heard the applause of the crowd, Nurmi trotted back to the locker room. Less than an hour later he was back at the starting line for the 5,000 meters. Not wanting to give Nurmi any time to recover, the other runners started off at a blistering pace. By the halfway mark, there were only two competitors able to stay with Ritola—Nurmi and Sweden's Edvin Wide. Nurmi soon grabbed the lead and, after checking his watch, forced the pace even faster. Wide quickly faded, but Ritola hung on grimly. When the challenger tried to pass in the final straightaway, Nurmi put on a burst of speed that carried him to a two-meter victory. Not only had Nurmi won both races with less than an hour's rest, he had also set Olympic records in both!

Impressive as this feat was, Nurmi topped it two days later in the 10,000-meter cross-country run. It was held on a sweltering day and the course, which ran through high weeds and over stone paths, was extremely rugged. Conditions were so brutal that only 15 of the 38 runners who started the race actually completed it. Several of those who staggered to the finish line collapsed and were carried away by medical officials. Yet while other runners were merely trying to finish the course on their feet, Paavo Nurmi showed few signs of discomfort at the end. He broke the finishing tape nearly a minute and a half ahead of the second-place runner.

When Nurmi showed up for the 3,000-meter team race the next day, competitors had given up their hopes that he would be slowed by fatigue. The tireless Finn breezed to a first-place finish, leading Finland to the team title. Nurmi finished the race looking so fresh that many experts believed he could have won the 10,000-meter race as well if Finnish team officials had not prevented him from entering. Despite winning five gold medals in distance running, an Olympic record that will probably never be equalled, there was no indication that Paavo Nurmi had even approached the limit of his endurance.

The 1936 games in Berlin opened with a lavish ceremony. The German team, marching through the stadium, was greeted with Nazi salutes from the crowd.

2

Exploding the Nazi Myth

Jesse Owens

In 1936 the United States was locked in a heated debate over whether or not to send a team to the Olympic games in Berlin, Germany. The German government formed by Adolf Hitler had made no secret of its contempt for Jews and blacks. The Nazis had mocked the United States for allowing "inferior" races to represent its country in international events. Germany itself had spent a great deal of money training athletes in an effort to prove that Northern Europeans were superior to all other people on Earth.

After gaining assurances that the 10 blacks and 2 Jews on the team would not be mistreated, the United States agreed to send its Olympic athletes to compete. So it was that Jesse Owens found himself on a cinder track in the middle of Nazi Germany, surrounded by 110,000 fans.

This son of sharecroppers was well aware of the Nazi theories on race. Although he was an established track star, having once set three world records and tied a fourth in less than an hour, he had never been able to conquer his nerves. As he settled into the starting blocks for his first heat of the 100-meter dash, the pressure he felt was overwhelming. Because of his nervousness, Owens was often the last runner out of the starting blocks.

Contrary to popular belief, Owens was not a heavy favorite in the 100-meter race. Until a few months before the Olympics, Ralph Metcalfe, a silver medalist in the 1932 games, had consistently beaten Owens at that distance. Both Owens and Metcalfe sailed through the preliminary heats without being challenged.

Once the final heat of the race started, Owens relaxed. He glided down the track in 10.3 seconds, tying the Olympic record and beating Metcalfe to the finish line by a meter. He did so with such grace and apparent ease that he immediately earned the admiration of the German crowd.

A day later, with his popularity growing among the German sports fans, Owens turned to the long jump. While taking a practice leap into the long jump pit, he was startled when the officials counted it as an attempt. Shaken by this surprise, Owens fouled on his second jump by stepping over the line. That meant that he had only one more chance to qualify for the finals. If he fouled again, or failed to jump 23 feet, 5½ inches, (7.15 meters) he was out of the competition.

While Owens awaited his last jump and desperately tried to regain his confidence, his German competitor, Luz Long, stepped in to help. He told Owens to aim for a line several inches behind the takeoff board so that he would be certain not to foul. Owens took the advice and qualified for the final round.

With that crisis over, Owens was able to relax. In the finals, he and Long staged a tremendous duel for the gold medal. First Owens set a new Olympic mark with a leap of 25 feet, 5½ inches (7.64 m). He then bettered his new record with a jump of 25 feet, 9¾ inches (7.87 m). On

Luz Long, above, and Jesse Owens competed for the gold medal in the long jump, but they became good friends during the 1936 Olympics. Long was later killed in battle during World War II.

his fifth jump, Long equaled that mark. As the crowd watched in tense silence, Owens uncorked a tremendous jump of 26 feet, 5½ inches (8.06 m). Going all out to beat Owens, Long fouled on his final attempt, and Owens had his second gold medal.

Jesse Owens breaks the tape in the 200-meter dash for his third gold medal. After the Olympics, Owens became a professional, running exhibition races and making speeches to earn money.

Owens' last scheduled event was the 200-meter race. There his toughest competition was expected to come from teammate Mack Robinson, the older brother of baseball's Jackie Robinson. Mack Robinson had matched Owens' Olympic record of 21.1 seconds that had been set in a preliminary round. As a gentle drizzle softened the track during the final, Robinson shot off to an early lead. Owens caught him in the middle of the turn, and by the time they hit the straightaway, he was pulling away to victory. By this time Owens' remarkable performances and warm personality had completely won over the German crowd. They roared their approval as he sped to a new Olympic record of 20.7 seconds.

Owens assumed that the Olympics were over for him. But at the last minute, he was inserted into the lineup for the 4 x 100-meter relay. Running the first leg, Owens staked his teammates to an early lead, which they held. Their finishing time of 39.8 seconds broke the world record and gave Owens his fourth gold medal.

Jesse Owens had captured four gold medals in track and field events, which no one had done before. More importantly, because of his gracious manner and outgoing personality, Owens was extremely popular with the Olympic crowd. He had shattered the Nazi myth about Northern European racial superiority in convincing fashion, and the common German people loved him.

3

Dutch Treat

Fanny Blankers-Koen

In the 1936 Olympics, an 18-year-old Dutch athlete named Francina "Fanny" Koen failed in her bid for medals in the high jump and the 4 x 100-meter relay. But she did not come home empty-handed. While in Berlin, she had gotten something nearly as valuable—an autograph from Jesse Owens. Twelve years later, married and the mother of two children, Fanny Blankers-Koen was the one signing autographs for wide-eyed youngsters. She had matched Owens' Olympic feats by winning four gold medals.

Many other female athletes have received more attention than Blankers-Koen (pronounced "Blankers Coon"). Babe Didrikson, who was fond of saying that she excelled at every game except dolls, is generally considered the finest all-around female athlete of all time. Modern female athletes receive far more

recognition than did Blankers-Koen. Yet the Olympic achievements of this woman from the Netherlands stand above all the rest. Even though she was past her prime as an athlete in 1948, Blankers-Koen won the 100-meter dash, the 80-meter hurdles, the 200-meter dash, and ran the last leg for the winning 4 x 100-meter relay team in the Olympics. Even more incredible is the fact that she held world records for two other events in which she did not compete during the Olympics!

Fanny Koen was a farm girl who discovered her athletic abilities at an early age. She could always outrun her four brothers and was equally adept at swimming. Undecided about which sport she should concentrate on, she finally took the advice of a coach, who told her that Netherlands had enough swimmers but could use some good track athletes.

While trying out for the Dutch Olympic team in 1936, Fanny Koen met track coach Jan Blankers. The two eventually married, and Jan became his wife's coach. When Blankers-Koen was in the prime of her athletic career, however, the Olympics were canceled because of World War II. The games were not held in 1940 nor in 1944. By 1948 Blankers-Koen was 30 years old. She still enjoyed running, however. She would go to the track each day, leaving her two children to play in a nearby sandbox while she worked out.

As the date of the Olympics approached, Blankers-Koen had a choice to make. She held the world record in six events: the 100-yard (91.44-m) dash, the 80-meter hurdles, the high jump, the long jump, and as part of two relay teams. According to the rules, she could enter only four events. The high jump was easy to eliminate. Although it had been her main event in the 1936 Olympics, she had never cared much for it. Also, there was only one relay event for women—the 4 x 100 relay. Blankers-Koen opted to skip the long jump and concentrate on the sprints. She was entered in the 100-meter dash, the 80-meter hurdles, the 4 x 100-meter relay, and the 200-meter dash, an event being offered to women in the Olympics for the first time.

The first final was the 100-meter dash, which was held in a driving rainstorm. Blankers-Koen, the oldest female runner in the Olympics that year, began pulling away from Dorothy Manley of Great Britain soon after the start. Churning through the mud, she won the race by three-tenths of a second, a comfortable margin for so short a race.

Two days later, she faced her toughest test, the 80-meter hurdles, in which she had to battle a confident teenager from Great Britain, Maureen Gardner. Affected by the tension, Blankers-Koen was the last runner out of the starting blocks in the final. Skimming over the hurdles with her long legs, the 5-foot, 9-inch Dutch woman caught up in the middle of the race, only to hit a hurdle. She was knocked off stride and cleared the last hurdles awkwardly, crossing the finish line at nearly the same time as Gardner. The contestants waited anxiously as the officials reviewed photographs of the finish. After a long delay, officials finally declared Blankers-Koen the winner, giving her a second gold medal.

The close call unnerved her. Everyone was expecting her to win a third gold medal in the 200 meters. Having come so close to losing in the hurdles, Blankers-Koen now feared failure so much that she begged to withdraw from the longer race. Only after some earnest coaxing was she persuaded to return to the track.

Fanny Blankers-Koen edges out Great Britain's Maureen Gardner at the finish line of the 80-meter hurdles.

Once the 200-meter dash began, it quickly became obvious that her fears were unfounded. Running in the ever-present mud of Wembley Stadium, Blankers-Koen left all rivals far behind with a time of 24.4. Second-place Audrey Williamson of Great Britain finished seven-tenths of a second behind the Dutch speedster.

Blankers-Koen saved her best for the last event, the 4 x 100-meter relay. By the time she received the handoff for the fourth and final leg, her team had fallen to fourth place. Blankers-Koen flew by the British and Canadian runners and set her sights on Australia's Joyce King, who was nearing the tape. Just before the finish, she drove past King to win another gold medal.

Following the Olympics, Blankers-Koen and her family were paraded through the streets of Amsterdam in a horse-drawn carriage. She never was comfortable with the celebrating. "All I have done is run fast," she said. "I don't see why people should make such a fuss."

Her fans were simply excited by Blankers-Koen's abilities. While she had been busy running away from her fellow sprinters and hurdlers, no one had challenged her world record of 5 feet, 7¼ inches (1.71 m) in the high jump, nor come within a foot and a half of her world-record long jump of 20 feet, 6¼ inches (6.25 m). At an age when most runners have retired, Fanny Blankers-Koen still had much of her ability, winning more gold medals in track and field during a single Olympics than any other woman in history.

Emil Zátopek takes the lead for good just after the final curve in the 5,000-meter run at the 1952 Olympics in Helsinki, Finland. Challenging Zátopek for the lead are Alain Mimoun of France and Herbert Schade of Germany. Christopher Chataway, who fell while trying to stay with the leaders, got up and managed to place fifth.

4

ZAT-O-PEK! ZAT-O-PEK!

Emil Zátopek

Paavo Nurmi and Emil Zátopek displayed such opposite extremes in style that had the two ever run against each other, the sight would have been comical. Unlike the silent, stoic Nurmi, who steadily drained opponents of their energy, Zátopek was a zany, lovable character who brought crowds to their feet with his dramatic antics.

Zátopek had unquestionably the worst form of any world-class distance runner in history. He lurched and chugged and grunted and flailed with his face twisted in agony. The "Beast of Prague," as he was called because of his unsightly running form, could nevertheless match Nurmi when it came to self-discipline. An officer in the Czech military, Zátopek ran between 10 and 25 miles (between 16 and 40.2 kilometers) each day, in rain or snow, and often in his heavy army boots. He never let the strain of this

effort dampen his cheerful spirits, however. Zátopek was witty, unpredictable, and so outgoing that he frequently held conversations with opponents in the middle of a race.

Zátopek, who was born in Koprivnice, Czechoslovakia, had to be forced into the sport of running. At the age of 16, he began working for a shoe factory. The company sponsored a road race, and young employees were expected to participate in the race. Although Zátopek pleaded that he was too weak for such strenuous activity, he was not excused. He did so well in the competition that he took up the sport permanently.

Zátopek first displayed his tortured running style to Olympic audiences in 1948. He wheezed and gasped through every step of the 10,000-meter race, seemingly determined to kill himself as well as all of his competitors. In spite of the muggy heat, he set such a fast pace that even world-record holder Viljo Heino of Finland had to drop out before the finish. Another fine Finnish runner, Evert Heinstrom, was led off the track in a daze. Zátopek lapped, or ran a lap ahead of, all but two runners on the 400-meter track and established an Olympic record of 29:59.6. He added a silver medal in the 5,000 meters.

Four years later and at his peak, Zátopek appeared in the 1952 Olympics in Helsinki, Finland, the homeland of several great distance runners from past Olympics. His first race was his specialty—the 10,000 meters. He started off slowly and did not gain the lead until 3,000 meters into the race. Then, with his face twisted in agony, he broke the will of one opponent after another with his bursts of speed. Still red-faced and grunting, Zátopek pulled away to a sizable lead with four laps to go and finished far ahead of the other runners.

A couple of days later, he set out to avenge the narrow defeat he had suffered in the 5,000-meter race during the 1948 Olympics. Not only did he plan to win, but he also intended to enjoy himself along the way. In a qualifying heat (to determine five of the runners who would be in the final heat) of the 5,000, Zátopek drifted back and forth from the leaders to the stragglers, resembling a shepherd herding a flock. After gaining the lead on the last lap, he slowed, waving another runner past him. As they came out of the last curve, a Swedish runner began to sprint from behind Zátopek. The Czech runner, fluent in five languages, hailed the fast-finishing Swede and chatted with him all the way to the finish, slowing just enough to let the Swede finish ahead of him.

In the finals, Zátopek took a far more serious attitude, for good reason. A strong field of contestants jockeyed for position throughout much of the race. Foremost among them was Germany's Herbert Schade, who had set an Olympic record of 14:15.4 in a qualifying heat. With two laps to go in the race, Zátopek tried to pull ahead of the pack but was unable to get a solid lead. Zátopek finally slowed down and was passed. When the bell sounded for the final lap, Zátopek had the lead, but Schade, Alain Mimoun of France, and Christopher Chataway of Great Britain shot past him in the backstretch.

In the words of sportswriter Red Smith, Zátopek seemed to be running "with his head in a noose." Clutching his sides as the other runners ran past, he also seemed to be out of the race. The Czech runner stayed with the leaders after they sprinted past. He entered the final curve and made a last effort, his head and arms

Zátopek leads the 10,000-meter race with Alain Mimoun of France close at his heels.

flopping like a marionette's. Zátopek veered over to the third lane. By the time he came out of the curve, he had regained the lead. He broke the tape in 14:06.6, less than a second ahead of Mimoun.

Like Nurmi, however, Zátopek was not content with merely mortal performances, outstanding though they were. After his wife, Dana, won a gold medal in the javelin throw, Zátopek joked with the media that he would have to win the marathon to restore some of his prestige in the family.

Zátopek had never run a marathon before. Concerned that there might be some subtle bits of strategy that he did not know about, he ran right behind someone who knew what he was doing— pre-race favorite Jim Peters of Great Britain. Peters set a fast pace, hoping to take some of the fight out of his rival. After a while, Zátopek asked Peters if he thought the pace was good enough. Hoping to intimidate him, Peters shook his head and said that the pace was actually too slow.

Zátopek merely shrugged and increased his speed. While trying to keep up, Peters ran himself into exhaustion and had to quit the race. Zátopek kept going. As Zátopek aproached the stadium, the crowd began chanting, "Zat-o-pek! Zat-o-pek!" Instead of his usual twisting and groaning, Zátopek actually smiled as he broke the tape in an Olympic-record time of 2:23:03.2. Unlike Nurmi, Zátopek stayed on the field after his victory, chatting and signing autographs. He allowed a Jamaican relay team to carry him around the track, then greeted the other runners as they finished the race. When asked his thoughts upon becoming the only person ever to win the three longest running races in the Olympics, Zátopek responded in the very human way that had made him such a favorite among fans. "The marathon is a very boring race," he declared.

Dawn Fraser stood head and shoulders above the runners-up during the awards ceremony for the 100-meter freestyle at Tokyo. The gold medal was Fraser's third in the same event.

5

Granny's Final Splash

Dawn Fraser

The sport of swimming is a cruel taskmaster. Most top female swimmers are so burned out by the intense workouts and the endless repetition of swimming laps, that they retire while still quite young. Dawn Fraser, though, was one young woman who refused to let the demands of the sport get the best of her.

Whenever practices became sheer drudgery, she simply climbed out of the swimming pool. Whenever her life as a swimmer became too dull, she created her own fun. When the rules were too confining, she broke them. As a result, Fraser ended up in more hot water than other swimmers. But she also competed longer and achieved more success than other swimmers. Even after a devastating accident, and at a time when she was so much older than her Australian teammates that they called her "Granny,"

Fraser refused to give in. Instead, she fought back and accomplished something no other swimmer had.

Fraser was born in a working-class suburb of Sydney, Australia, the youngest of eight children. She learned to swim at the age of five, but did so only for pleasure, not for competition. It was not until she was 14 that one of her brothers suggested she might want to take up swimming as a sport. A tall, powerful girl, Fraser improved rapidly. In early 1956, the 18-year-old broke the world record for the 100-meter freestyle—a record that had lasted for 20 years.

She did not have to travel far to find competition. Fellow Australian teenager Lorraine Crapp quickly topped Fraser's mark in the 100 meters and the two, along with a Dutch swimmer, took turns lowering the record during the next several months. By the time of the Olympics,

Crapp was the reigning world-record holder with a time of 1:02.4.

The Melbourne Olympics were Fraser's first international meet, and she suffered nightmares the night before the 100-meter freestyle finals. Despite her brash manner, she often battled the jitters during competition. (One time, she discovered she had reported to the starting area without a swimsuit under her warm-ups.)

Once the Olympic 100-meter freestyle race began, however, Fraser swam with confidence, building an early lead. After fighting off a late challenge by Crapp, she touched the wall in a world-record time of 1:02.0. Fraser added to her medal collection with a silver in the 400-meter freestyle, finishing behind Crapp.

Four years later, Fraser traveled to Rome to become the first female swimmer ever to defend her Olympic title. The Australian had little trouble holding off Chris Von Saltza of the United States for her second gold medal at 100 meters. The rest of the 1960 Olympics was a

Fraser, left, with teammate Lorraine Crapp

disaster for her, however. The day after her gold-medal performance, Fraser found herself in trouble with her teammates. Thinking she had the day off from competition, Fraser went shopping and ate a large lunch. No sooner had she finished eating than she was asked to swim a relay leg for the team in a qualifying heat. Fraser refused, and her teammates punished her by refusing to talk in her presence for the rest of the games. Fraser had also predicted she would win the 400-meter freestyle, but she finished only fifth.

Fraser overcame her problems with teammates, but became more insistent upon doing things her own way. In order to keep herself interested in swimming, she did not keep a rigid practice schedule but trained only when she felt like it. There were days when she put in exhausting three-hour workouts and others when she did nothing at all. Fraser frequently stayed out late in the evenings and enjoyed parties. Her unusual approach worked. In 1962 she became the first woman to swim 100 meters in less than a minute.

After Lorraine Crapp and the rest of Fraser's contemporaries had long since retired, Fraser busied herself preparing for her third Olympics. However, her long career seemed over when, in March of 1964, the car she was driving skidded out of control and smashed into a truck. Fraser's mother was killed, and the swimmer suffered injuries serious enough to put her in a neck cast for six weeks.

But Granny Fraser still loved to swim. When the 1964 Olympic games began in Tokyo, the 27-year-old free spirit was on the Australian team. Typically, she defied orders by attending the opening day parade and other festivities against the wishes of her coaches.

In the 100-meter finals, Fraser faced a strong challenge from Sharon Stouder, a 15-year-old U.S. swimmer. Stouder set out after the fast-starting Fraser and caught her with about 30 meters to go. Summoning a last burst of power, Fraser fought off her young rival and touched the wall in 59.5, a fraction of a second in front of Stouder.

It came as no surprise for those who knew her that the Dawn Fraser story did not end on such a peaceful note of triumph. Fraser's behavior in the days following her victory included leading a group of people who tried to steal a flag from the Japanese emperor's palace for a souvenir. She received a suspension from the Australian Swimming Union. Whether in the pool or out of it, the only athlete ever to win three Olympic gold medals in the same swimming event made plenty of waves.

6

Once More with Feeling

Al Oerter

For four straight Olympic games, from 1956 through 1968, there was only one name listed under Olympic gold medal winners in the men's discus: Al Oerter. Amazingly, during all that time, Oerter was a favorite in his event just once! Fighting through injuries, he outthrew the world-record holders in four consecutive Olympics. Oerter's incredible clutch performances made him one of the greatest Olympic competitors ever.

When the 20-year-old discus thrower from West Babylon, New York, arrived in Melbourne, Australia, for the 1956 Olympics, he seemed overwhelmed by the grandeur of the event. During practice he gaped in amazement at the soaring tosses of his teammate, world-record holder Fortune Gordien. Gordien

Left: Al Oerter picks up his first gold medal in the 1956 Olympics at Melbourne, Australia.

could hurl the discus well over 190 feet (57.9 m), while Oerter was only hoping to top 180 feet (54.9 m).

Not expecting to win, Oerter was able to relax and enjoy his turns in the discus circle. To his surprise, he uncorked a throw of 184 feet, 11 inches (56.36 m), on his first throw—the best of his life. Gordien's best throw for the Olympic games was 179 feet, 9 inches (54.79 m). The gold medal went to Oerter, the stunned sophomore from the University of Kansas.

The following year, Oerter was nearly killed in an automobile collision. He recovered and fulfilled his dream of returning to the Olympics by finishing second to Rink Babka in the United States Olympic trials. At the 1960 games in Rome, Oerter faced stiff competition from Babka and Edmund Piatkowski of Poland—the two athletes who shared

31

the world record in the discus. Even so, Oerter was considered a slight favorite to win the event.

Oerter threw better in practice than he ever had in his life, twice topping the world record. Rather than inspiring him, however, that feat almost unnerved Oerter. In the finals, Babka took an early lead with a throw of 190 feet, 4 inches (58.01 m). The pressure on Oerter to succeed was so great that he could hardly throw, and he failed to match Babka's best distance on any of the first four throws. Just before the fifth of Oerter's six allotted throws, Babka pointed out a flaw he had noticed in Oerter's throwing technique. Oerter corrected the mistake and hurled the discus 194 feet, 2 inches (59.18 m) for his second gold medal. Again, Oerter had made the best throw of his life in the Olympics, while others did not perform up to par.

Four years later, as the date for the Olympics approached, Oerter prepared for his third appearance in the games. The veteran of two Olympics admitted during the trials that he was more nervous than he had ever been in previous competition. He made the team, but Oerter's streak seemed certain to end. The world record had been pushed to 211 feet, 9 inches (64.54 m) by Czechoslovakia's Ludvik Daněk, who was unbeaten in 45 straight competitions.

Oerter competed in pain during the 1964 Olympics. Still, he managed to throw the discus almost 61 meters to claim his third gold medal in the event.

Oerter, meanwhile, had been sidelined for most of the year with a painful pinched nerve in his back. To keep the injury from getting worse, he wore a homemade neck brace, made of two towels wrapped around a belt, and took heat treatments. Six days before his scheduled event in the 1964 Tokyo games, Oerter suffered a crippling blow to his chances of winning: while practicing, he tore some cartilage in his rib cage.

Doctors told Oerter that the injury would take from four to six weeks to heal. But these were the Olympics— which Oerter lived for. He reported for the discus event with his midsection wrapped in surgical tape and ice packs. Fortunately, it took only one painful throw for the defending champion to qualify for the finals.

Going into the final round, Oerter hoped he could stand the pain long enough to make the one good throw that would win the gold medal. But his first throw was low and short. The pain from his injuries was terrible, and Oerter nearly quit to avoid embarrassing himself with more bad throws. He forced himself to try a second throw, but could not get the discus to travel high enough to go the maximum distance. Spurred on by his tremendous competitive desire, however, Oerter kept trying to beat the 195-foot, 11-inch (59.72-m) throw Daněk had made in the competition.

On his fifth throw, Oerter somehow let loose a tremendous toss before crumpling over in pain. The discus landed 200 feet, 1 inch (60.99 m) from the throwing circle. Winning his third gold medal seemed a fitting end to this master-discus thrower's career.

Oerter retired from competition after the 1964 Olympics. But in the fall of 1967, Oerter found himself preparing for yet another gold medal defense. He designed a 13-month training program that would get him back into top shape by the time of the Mexico City games.

Again, winning a gold medal seemed too tall an order for Oerter. The veteran Olympic star reported to the 1968 games 70 pounds (32 kilograms) heavier than the 220-pound (100-kg) weight at which he had won his first gold medal. During Oerter's brief retirement, other discus throwers had continued to increase the distance of their throws. United States star Jay Silvester had made a throw that was 17 feet (5.2 m) farther than Oerter's best.

Yet when the world's best discus throwers reported to the discus circle for the final, Oerter was among them. Rain had delayed the competition by one hour, and many of the discus throwers appeared unnerved. Few of

The University of Mexico Stadium in Mexico City was the site of the 1968 Olympics, where Oerter won his fourth gold medal in the discus throw.

them had performed up to their abilities. Gamely, the 32-year-old Oerter tried to stay with the young giants. After three rounds of throws, he was just out of medal range, in fourth place. Then, as if drawing superhuman strength from the tension of the Olympics, Oerter spun the discus past the 212-foot (64.62-m) mark—5 feet (1.5 m) farther than he had ever thrown before! The throw disheartened his competitors, and none was able to come close to Oerter's mark.

Al Oerter's fourth straight unexpected win had proved him, again, to be a true Olympic competitor.

7

Two Giant Leaps

Bob Beamon and Dick Fosbury

Within two days during the 1968 Olympics in Mexico City, the long jump and high jump events were changed for all time by two United States athletes. Bob Beamon's incredible 29-foot (8.9-m) long jump virtually destroyed the sport, and Dick Fosbury's laughable "Fosbury Flop" paved the road to what once seemed impossible—an eight-foot (2.4-m) high jump.

Bob Beamon, a 22-year-old New York native, entered the long jump as an uncertain favorite. No one doubted his potential—the gangly, 6-foot, 3-inch (190.5-centimeter), 160-pound (72.6-kg) Beamon could get tremendous spring from his long legs, and his thin body could float through the air. But unlike disciplined teammate Ralph Boston, a former gold-medal winner, Beamon was not consistent. More than other jumpers, he was prone to fouling and to taking off far behind the front edge of the takeoff board. Other jumpers had their steps and length of stride worked out precisely; Beamon did not.

After fouling on his first two jumps, Beamon needed a qualifying jump on his third and last attempt in order to get into the final round. Ralph Boston, remembering Luz Long's advice to Jesse Owens in a similar situation 32 years earlier, told Beamon to draw a line well before the edge of the board. Using the line as a target, Beamon made a fine jump and advanced to the finals.

During the final round, on October 18, the first three jumpers fouled, and Beamon, the fourth jumper, was concerned that he would also foul. After taking a few moments to focus his thoughts, Beamon charged down the runway. He did not feel he was running especially fast, but he hit the takeoff board perfectly. Pushed on by a gentle tail wind, he soared into the air.

The other long jumpers were amazed at the height he achieved. With his legs spread out and his arms flailing, Beamon appeared to be out of control. He landed far into the sand and bounced completely out of the pit.

Ralph Boston knew right away that his world record of 27 feet, 4¾ inches (8.35 m) had been broken. Some of the long jumpers thought that Beamon had even reached the unbelievable distance of 28 feet (8.53 m). When the judges tried to measure the jump, it became obvious that it had been a historic effort. The distance from the takeoff board to the mark made in the sand by Beamon's foot could not be measured by the sophisticated equipment. The astonished officials had to use an old-fashioned tape measure to measure the jump.

Minutes later, Beamon's mark of 8.9 meters was flashed on the stadium scoreboard. Unable to quickly convert metric numbers into feet and inches, Beamon still did not realize how far he had jumped. Boston finally told him that he had jumped more than 29 feet! When Beamon realized that he had jumped 29 feet, 2½ inches, he was so overwhelmed by his own accomplishment that his knees buckled, and he nearly passed out.

Beamon soars through the air on his way to setting an incredible world record in the long jump. His 8.9-meter jump has held up for more than two decades.

Beamon's competitors experienced a similar shock. Realizing that such a jump was far beyond their capabilities, they were almost embarrassed to continue trying. "Compared to that jump, we are all children," said one rival.

Knowing that he could never achieve any more than he already had, Beamon never jumped well again. About a year after the Olympics, he retired from competitive long jumping. His feat of breaking the existing world record in the long jump by almost two feet is generally regarded as the greatest single athletic achievement of all time.

While experts and spectators were still in shock over Beamon's jump, another United States athlete proceeded to throw the world of high jumping into chaos. Dick Fosbury, a 6-foot, 4-inch (193-cm) native of Medford, Oregon, outraged and embarrassed track coaches with his ridiculous style of high jumping.

Fosbury began high jumping when he was 11 years old. At the time, he was not coordinated enough to get over the bar using the traditional straddle method of jumping. In the straddle method, a high jumper jumps off his or her inside leg, lifts the other above the bar, and then rolls over it, facing the ground. Fosbury had better success with a "scissors" kick. He jumped off his outside leg, flung his inside leg over the bar and then brought the other one over.

Over the years Fosbury tried new ways of getting more height out of his scissors style. He began leaning farther back on

In 1968 most high jumpers, including the leading U.S. high jumper, Ed Caruthers, used a traditional straddle method of jumping over the bar.

his jump, and then he tried throwing his head and back over the bar before his legs. By his senior year of high school, Fosbury had cleared 6 feet, 5 inches (1.96 m) with his "Fosbury Flop," as a sportswriter had dubbed it.

Fosbury soon grew tired of being laughed at for his strange style. When his coach at Oregon State University offered to make a "real" high jumper out of him, Fosbury agreed to use the traditional style. As a result, he had trouble clearing 5 feet, 6 inches (1.68 m). Fosbury soon returned to his old method. Within a year, he was flopping over bars just a shade below 7 feet (2.13 m).

By 1968, the year of the Olympics, Fosbury had become one of the most consistent high jumpers in the country. But even after he had cleared 7 feet, 3

Using his "Fosbury Flop," Dick Fosbury set a new Olympic record in the high jump by clearing 7 feet, 4¼ inches (2.24 meters).

inches (2.21 m) to win a spot on the United States Olympic team, most coaches did not take him seriously. Ed Caruthers, who had beaten Fosbury at the trials with a traditional jump, was tabbed as the favorite. Fosbury was not expected to last long enough to claim a medal.

On October 20, the day of the Olympic finals, competition was keen. Thirteen jumpers had cleared 7 feet (2.13 m), but Fosbury was the one who delighted the crowd with his comical flight over the bar. As the bar inched higher, Fosbury kept sailing over it backwards. He succeeded on his first attempt at an Olympic record: 7 feet, 3¼ inches (2.22 m). Caruthers was the only other jumper able to clear that height.

The bar moved up to 7 feet, 4¼ inches (2.24 m). For the first time that day, Fosbury knocked down the crossbar. Caruthers also missed on his first attempt. Fosbury missed again. So did Caruthers.

As 80,000 spectators silently urged him on, Fosbury made his final attempt. He arched his back, brought up his hips, and snapped his legs over the barrier. He had made it! Another miss by Caruthers gave Fosbury the gold medal.

Rarely has any sport undergone as drastic a change as did high jumping following the victory by this unorthodox athlete. By the 1972 Olympics, 28 of the 40 high jumping contestants were using Fosbury's method. Within a few years straddle jumpers had become an oddity.

8

Turning Water into Gold

Mark Spitz

In 1968 an 18-year-old United States swimmer brashly predicted that he would win six gold medals in the Mexico City Olympics. Although Mark Spitz was regarded as one of the finest swimmers in the world, his prediction seemed outrageous. Don Schollander's four gold medals in 1964 were the most won by a single swimmer in the history of the Olympics.

Spitz's attitude did not win him many friends. Even some of his teammates were glad to see him fall on his face in Mexico City, where he won only two golds. Both of the victories came in relay events in which his team was strong enough to win just as easily without him. In his specialty, the 100-meter butterfly, Spitz lost to a U.S. teammate who had never beaten him before. The final indignity came in the finals of the 200-meter butterfly. He and another swimmer had tied for the fastest time in the qualifying heats. However, Spitz, the self-proclaimed wonder swimmer, finished dead last among the finalists.

The experience left the Sacramento, California, native a sadder but wiser person. He had been swimming ever since he had first splashed in the Hawaiian surf at the age of four, but Mark Spitz realized that there was still much to learn. He enrolled at Indiana University, where he competed for and learned from Doc Counsilman, one of the best coaches in the United States. After four more years of training, he traveled with the United States Olympic team to Munich, West Germany, for the 1972 games.

A stronger swimmer than ever, the 6-foot (183-cm), 170-pound (77.2-kg) star had qualified to swim in seven events. This time, though, Spitz did not announce

39

any bold predictions. Swimming fans, however, detected a sign that Spitz had lost none of his confidence: while many swimmers had shaved their heads to cut water resistance, Spitz swam with both a full head of hair and a mustache.

As luck would have it, Spitz's first event was the one at which he had failed so badly in Mexico City—the 200-meter butterfly. With the memory of this failure still on his mind, Spitz waited nervously

As a student at Indiana University, Mark Spitz, above, improved his technique with help from Coach Doc Counsilman.

for the start. Once the race started, however, Spitz swam strongly. He made the most of his second chance, splashing to victory in a world-record time of 2:00.70

Later that evening, Spitz swam the final leg of the 4 x 100-meter freestyle relay. His teammates gave him a comfortable lead, and Spitz increased it to finish more than three seconds ahead of the second-place Soviet team.

Spitz returned to the pool the next day for the 200-meter freestyle. There he overcame an amazing effort by teammate Steve Genter. Genter had been hospitalized with a collapsed lung until the day before the race. Yet after 150 meters, a determined Genter was still outswimming his favored teammate. Spitz finally caught and passed Genter, but it took a world record time of 1:52.78 to win the race.

After a day's rest, Spitz lined up for the finals of the 100-meter butterfly. Spitz was a heavy favorite to win, and he disappointed no one. He churned to victory in another world-record time, 54.27 seconds. An hour later, Spitz won his fifth gold medal of the games in the 4 x 200-meter relay. This was the easiest race of all, thanks to a brilliant third leg by Steve Genter. Spitz had a tremendous lead when he entered the water for the final leg. He touched the wall at the

While Vladimir Bure of the Soviet Union celebrates his own bronze medal performance, Mark Spitz checks the scoreboard after a narrow victory over teammate Jerry Heidenreich in the 100-meter freestyle.

7:35.78 mark, giving the United States team a winning margin of nearly 6 seconds over the West Germans and shattering the world record by 7½ seconds.

Teammate Jerry Heidenreich posed a serious challenge to Spitz's efforts in the 100-meter freestyle, held on September 3. Although he had secretly aimed for seven gold medals in the Olympics, Spitz considered scaling down his quest. He thought it would be better to drop out of the 100-meter freestyle and win all six of his other races, rather than racing in seven events and winning only six. After a time of indecision, Spitz decided to face the challenge. In the finals, he swam aggressively and held a sizable lead going into the turn. Heidenreich finished powerfully, though, and Spitz barely held him off, winning by less than a half of a second in a world-record time of 51.22.

There was little tension in the air the next day as Spitz set out to claim his seventh medal in the 4 x 100-meter medley relay (in which one person swims the backstroke, one the breaststroke, one the butterfly, and one freestyle). As in all the relays, the United States was clearly the best of the field. Spitz swam the third leg—the butterfly leg—of the relay. The United States team won the race easily, and Spitz had his historic seventh medal. As impressive as his seven gold medals is the way he won the races. By setting world records in all seven events, Spitz made all of those gold medals sparkle just a little more brightly.

Spitz takes off on his leg of the 4 x 100-meter medley relay as Tom Bruce finishes his portion of the race.

9

The Agony of Victory

Japanese Gymnastic Team

The grandeur of the Olympic games has occasionally inspired superhuman displays of courage. In 1912 middleweight Greco-Roman wrestlers Martin Klein of Estonia and Alfred Asikainen of Finland wrestled for 11 hours under a hot sun before Klein finally recorded a pin. In 1936 Konrad von Wangenheim finished his ride in the Equestrian Team Three-Day Event, despite breaking his collarbone in a fall from his horse early in the steeplechase course. Wangenheim then survived yet another fall in the show-jumping portion of the competition to help his team win a gold medal.

But for sheer courage, it would be difficult to top Shun Fujimoto of Japan. At the 1976 Montreal games, the gymnast helped his national team to victory despite a terrible injury. Few spectators were aware of the agonies he was enduring to bring Japan a gold medal.

The Japanese had dominated men's gymnastics for decades. Going into the 1976 games, the Japanese had won four consecutive Olympic team championships. However, the Soviets had placed a close second in each of those Olympic competitions. Led by superstar Nikolai Andrianov, the Soviets held high hopes of dethroning the Japanese in Montreal. It was expected to be a close competition, and each gymnast's performance would be important.

A year before the Olympics, no one would have expected Shun Fujimoto to play a key role for the Japanese team. It was not until September of 1975 that anyone thought he had even a chance to make the Japanese team. Although he was a steady and reliable performer, coaches did not think Fujimoto was as good as some of the more experienced Japanese athletes.

At a pre-Olympic meet later in the year, however, Fujimoto stunned observers with his performance in the preliminary round. Showing strength in all six gymnastic events, he eventually finished second to teammate Mitsuo Tsukahara in the all-around competition. That meet established him as a world-class gymnast. By the time of the Olympics, he was not only an important member of the Japanese team but was ranked among the top five gymnasts in the world.

In the opening round of the team competition, Fujimoto suffered a crippling injury. While finishing his floor exercise routine, he somehow broke his leg at the knee. Fujimoto, who did not know the leg was broken, decided to continue competing, in spite of the pain, for the good of the team. The competition with the Soviets was as fierce as had been expected, and the Japanese could scarcely afford to lose him. Without telling anyone of his injury, Fujimoto competed on the pommel horse, normally his weakest event. He withstood the pain well enough to earn a fine score of 9.5 (out of a possible 10).

The next event in the competition was the rings, one of Fujimoto's strongest events. Like the pommel horse, the rings rely mainly on arm and shoulder strength, and Fujimoto hoped to avoid further injury to his throbbing leg. A doctor who later examined him was shocked that Fujimoto was able to whirl through somersaults and twists on the rings without passing out from the pain.

While performing his rigorous routine, Fujimoto had to block out any thoughts of the terrible pain he would feel on his dismount. He would fly off the rings and soar high above the ground. After doing three somersaults and a twist, he would then land on his feet with horrendous force.

Fujimoto performed the routine and spun off into his dismount. Blinding pain shot through his body when the foot of his injured leg came down on the mat. The inability of his leg to support his full weight caused further damage to his knee. Yet somehow Fujimoto not only remained conscious, but performed the landing with scarcely a wobble. After holding his position for the required instant, he hobbled off in agony. The judges awarded him a splendid score of 9.7, the best of his career!

The pain was so bad that even Fujimoto could not hide it, and he finally agreed to have the leg examined. Upon discovering the mangled condition of the limb, the doctors immediately pulled him out of the competition. Since the scores of only five of the six gymnasts from each team are counted in each

Shun Fujimoto performs his routine on the pommel horse, right, and the parallel bars, below, during the 1976 Olympics at Montreal. After injuring himself in the floor exercise part of the competition, Fujimoto did his routines on the pommel horse and the rings before the pain forced him to forego the remaining events.

Shun Fujimoto, second from right, celebrates on the winners' stand with his teammates shortly before receiving his gold medal for the team gymnastics competition.

event, the Japanese team was able to continue through the last events without Fujimoto.

When Mitsuo Tsukahara came through with a brilliant 9.9 performance in the final exercise, the horizontal bar, Japan won its fifth straight Olympic gold medal in team gymnastics. The margin of victory was very small—576.85 to 576.45. Fujimoto's extraordinary self-sacrifice on the rings had provided the team with the fractions of a point it needed.

10

East German Juggernaut

Kornelia Ender

East Germany had very little tradition on which to build a swimming program in the 1970s. During the 1972 Olympic games held in Munich, West Germany, the East German women had failed to win even one gold medal in swimming.

Yet four years later, at the Montreal Olympics, the East German women won 11 of the 13 gold medals awarded in the sport. This was the first wave of what was to become a long-standing domination of Olympic sports by this small nation. Leading this incredible turnaround was Kornelia Ender.

Like many of the East German athletes, Ender was hand-picked for her task. At the age of eight, she drew the attention of coaches at a local swimming camp in Halle. She was immediately placed in one of East Germany's special sports schools, where her talent could be developed to the fullest.

Ender was only 13 when she competed in the Munich Olympics. Although regarded as one of her country's top swimmers, she did not expect to do well against international competition. Only after she qualified for the finals of the 200-meter individual medley (which combines the butterfly, backstroke, breaststroke, and freestyle) did she begin to think she might have a chance for a medal. In the finals, Ender pushed world-record holder Shane Gould of Australia to the limit and came within two strokes of beating her. She then added two more silver medals to her collection with East Germany's second-place teams in the 4 x 100-meter freestyle and 4 x 100-meter medley relays.

While the performance was astounding for one so young, few people realized that Ender was starting a new era. Within one year of the 1972 Olympics, the

East German women began dominating every phase of women's swimming. Not only did they break nearly every world record in existence, but they also caused a stir with their new, streamlined swimsuits and their powerful builds.

In their rush to the top, Ender and her teammates had to withstand grueling new training techniques. Their workouts called for far more weight lifting than swimmers previously had done. Most dreaded of all were the sessions in the "flume tank." The swimmers were placed in a tank and forced to swim against a controlled current of water. While they struggled against this exhausting, watery treadmill, technicians would measure their bodies' responses to the stress.

East Germany's rise in women's swimming came so suddenly that many fans thought it was a fluke. They expected that the traditionally strong United States women would regain their position as a swimming power. At the Olympics in Montreal, the East Germans ended that belief with the first event, the 4 x 100-meter medley relay. By the time Ender hit the water for the final leg, her teammates had given her a wide lead. She continued to build a lead and touched the wall at the 4:7.95 mark to break the world record by more than 5 seconds!

Ender captured her second gold medal just as easily. Exploding off the starting

Kornelia Ender

block, she instantly took control of the 100-meter freestyle race. Her world-record time of 55.65 seconds gave her a comfortable victory over teammate Petra Priemer.

A scheduling quirk, rather than another swimmer, gave Ender her toughest test of the games. The final round of the 200-meter freestyle was slated to begin within 25 minutes of the completion of the 100-meter butterfly finals, and Ender was entered in both events.

She decided it would be foolish to hold back any effort in the first race in order to keep fresh for the second. She would swim both events as hard as she could. Her decision turned out to be a wise one, because teammate Andrea Pollack was swimming the best butterfly race of her life. It took another world-record time, 1:00.13, for Ender to defeat Pollack—by less than a second.

Then, just five minutes after the ceremony in which she received her third gold medal, Ender returned to the pool to try for a fourth. There had only been enough time for her to change suits and loosen her muscles before the call came to line up for the 200-meter freestyle. In this event, a weary Ender

Ender swims the 100-meter butterfly to earn her third gold medal of the 1976 Olympics.

faced the United States' best swimmer, Shirley Babashoff, who had beaten her in the 1975 world championships.

In that defeat, Ender had relied on her usual strategy of charging out quickly, gaining a comfortable lead over her rivals, and then hanging on until she reached the finish line. This time, however, she held back and let Babashoff lead the first half of the race. At the halfway point, Ender made her move. She glided by Babashoff and launched a long, sustained finishing kick. It was no contest. Ender covered the distance nearly two seconds faster than the U.S. star, blazing to yet another world record of 1:59.26.

Ender nearly earned another gold medal in the final event of the swimming program. Her leadoff leg in the 4 x 100-meter freestyle relay gave her teammates a big lead over the rest of the field. Only a determined, world-record effort by the last three United States swimmers enabled them to inch past the East Germans for first place.

Even with that defeat, Ender earned a spot in the record books by being the first woman to win four gold medals in swimming during one Olympics. She blazed the trail that East Germany has since followed to win more Olympic medals per person than any other country in the world.

11

The Perfect 10

Nadia Comaneci

When computer programmers were preparing the electronic scoring equipment for the 1976 Olympics in Montreal, gymnastics consultants told them that a perfect score of 10 points was impossible. A Japanese gymnast, Haruhiro Yamashita, had once received a 10 from a single member of the judging panel. But in order to receive a final score of 10, all but one of the judges would have to award a 10, and for that to happen was unthinkable.

That was before Nadia Comaneci's first Olympic appearance. When the talented Romanian gymnast performed a heart-stopping routine on the uneven parallel bars at the Montreal Olympics, she was rewarded with what seemed to be an unbelievably low score. Several moments after Comaneci's routine, the scoreboard flashed "1.00."

The initial shock of the audience was

Nadia Comaneci looks at the scoreboard, which displays her perfect score as 1.00.

quickly replaced by cheers as the crowd realized what had happened. The programmers had not prepared for the impossible, so there was no way for the computer to display the number 10. But the impossible had happened, and the best the computer operators could do in this situation was to show 1.00.

Comaneci, the first gymnast to achieve a perfect 10 in Olympic gymnastic competition, was a tiny 14-year-old from the town of Onesti, near the Soviet border. When she was six, Comaneci's love of gymnastics caught the attention of coach Bela Karolyi. He tested her skills in sprinting, long jumping, and walking on a balance beam. He liked what he saw, and Comaneci was enrolled in a special school. There she practiced for four hours a day and ate a strict diet of fruit, milk, and cheese.

In 1970, at the age of nine, Comaneci won the Romanian National Junior Gymnastics Championship and was on her way to stardom. At the age of 13, she dominated the 1975 European championships, winning four of the five events.

Comaneci jumped so high, and was so steady and graceful that she occasionally received that unheard-of score of 10. Despite standing just under 5 feet (152 cm) tall, she had long legs that helped her perform difficult tricks. She was a serious girl who concentrated so hard that she rarely noticed other gymnasts' performances. But the key to her success was her fearlessness. She seemed unaffected by crowds or by the difficulty of her routines.

The ultimate test of her poise would be the Montreal Olympics. There Comaneci would be challenged by a trio of Soviet stars: the graceful, defending all-around champion Lyudmila Tourischeva; the tiny, crowd-pleasing Olga Korbut; and the athletic Nelli Kim. Although Comaneci was considered a slight favorite, observers wondered how the 14-year-old would perform under the pressure of the Olympics.

The crowd of 16,000 soon found out. On July 18, Comaneci hopped onto the uneven parallel bars and whirled into action. Spectators gasped as she completed a midair somersault on the bars. She floated so high and swung through her routine with such precision that the judges were left with a problem. Many were not convinced there was such a thing as a "perfect" gymnastics routine. Yet Comaneci had done her exercise better than those gymnasts who had received 9.9s in the past. The judges felt they had no choice but to award her a 10. The spectators, who had already cheered their approval of her routine, roared again with delight when they saw her score.

Although it had taken 24 years of Olympic competition to produce the first 10 in gymnastics, the second one was not long in coming. Later that same evening, Comaneci performed a thrilling routine on the balance beam. She finished her flawless effort with a

Comaneci performs in the floor exercise at the 1976 Olympics. While the floor exercise was one of her weaker events in 1976, when she earned a bronze medal, Comaneci returned to the Olympics in 1980 and won a gold medal in the event.

daring backwards somersault. Again, Comaneci's performance had been so brilliant that the judges awarded her a 10. Her efforts boosted the Romanian gymnastics team to the silver medal behind the more balanced Soviets.

Instantly Comaneci became the star of the Olympic games. She still was able to shrug off the pressure when the individual competition started. While competing in the same group as the veteran champion, Tourischeva, Comaneci earned several more perfect scores, including 10s in all of her uneven bar exercises. The crowd frequently called her back to the floor to acknowledge their cheers, which she did with a wave and a smile.

By the time the competition was over, Comaneci had won gold medals in the balance beam, the uneven parallel bars, and the all-around competition. She also earned a bronze medal in the floor exercise. The 14-year-old master technician had put her stamp on the 1976 Olympic games by not only achieving the "impossible" 10, but by doing it seven times in a single competition!

Comaneci acknowledges cheers from the fans after receiving another perfect score from the judges.

12

The Unknown Hero

Viktor Saneyev

The triple jump, also known as the hop, step, and jump, is a neglected event in Olympic track and field. Although the event has been held in every Olympic competition since 1896, triple jump champions rarely receive the recognition that follows championships in other events. To the casual observer, the triple jump seems to be a silly event—possibly a maneuver that a child dreamed up to make hopscotch more interesting.

Although it may appear odd, the triple jump actually requires a great deal of speed, strength, and coordination. While the other track and field events have received far more attention, the triple jump has offered spectators many thrilling moments. By far, the star of the triple jump has been Viktor Saneyev, the ageless wonder of the Soviet Union.

Saneyev, born in 1945, had studied the science of subtropical plants at an institute in the Soviet province of Georgia. His athletic skills eventually attracted the attention of Soviet sports officials, and Saneyev began training as a long jumper. But in 1967 he switched to the triple jump, for which his powerful legs seemed to be better suited.

Poland's Józef Schmidt had dominated the triple jump for most of the 1960s. He entered the 1968 Olympics in Mexico City as the world-record holder and two-time defending Olympic champion. Because of a serious injury to his Achilles tendon, however, Schmidt was not favored to win these Olympics. That role fell to the quick-learning newcomer, 23-year-old Viktor Saneyev.

Unfortunately, in the uproar over Bob Beamon's sensational long jump, the most remarkable triple jump competition in Olympic history was practically ignored.

Aided by the thin air in the high altitude of Mexico City, the triple jumpers took turns breaking world records, starting with Schmidt's. In the qualifying rounds, a bearded Italian named Giuseppe Gentile triple jumped 56 feet, 1¼ inches (17.1 m) to break Schmidt's world mark of 55 feet, 10½ inches (17.03 m). The effort was particularly astounding because Gentile had never jumped as far as 55 feet (16.76 m) before the Olympics.

Pumped up from his unexpected success, Gentile soared even farther in the finals. His first-round jump was measured at 56 feet, 6 inches (17.22 m). Saneyev responded to this challenge in the third round with a world-record jump of his own—56 feet, 6½ inches (17.23 m).

Saneyev's mark lasted until the fifth round, when Brazilian jumper Nelson Prudencio exploded for the jump of his life. Prudencio sailed more than three feet farther than his pre-Olympic best, and landed in the sand pit 56 feet, 8 inches (17.27 m) from the takeoff board!

Saneyev and Gentile were each left with only one more jump in which to claim victory. It was Saneyev who finally gained the victory with a monumental leap of 57 feet, ¾ inches (17.39 m). Saneyev claimed his first gold medal in a competition so fierce that Soviet leaper Nikolai Dudkin finished no better than fifth place, despite breaking the previous world record.

Four years later, Saneyev was hard-pressed to defend his title against East German challenger Jörg Drehmel, who had dethroned him in the 1971 world

Viktor Saneyev won three gold medals and one silver in the triple jump.

championships. But the festival atmosphere of the Olympics seemed to have the same effect on Saneyev as it did on Al Oerter. The Soviet made a leap of 56 feet, 11¼ inches (17.35 m) in the first round of the finals to put pressure on his rival. Shaken, Drehmel floundered through the first four rounds. When he finally managed a good leap, it was less than two inches short of Saneyev's mark. Saneyev was the only 1968 Olympic champion to repeat as a victor in 1972. Yet again, his accomplishments were swept away by more sensational news—this time the terrorist attack on the Israeli athletic compound that occurred the next morning, on September 5.

Four years later, Saneyev was back to try for a third gold medal. Few expected that he could do it. At the age of 30, he was already old for an event that favored fresh, springy legs. Furthermore, João Carlos de Oliveira of Brazil appeared unbeatable. One year earlier, Oliveira had put Saneyev's world record to shame with a leap of 58 feet, 8½ inches (17.89 m).

Oliveira seemed to be warming to the task as he got off the best leap of the qualifying rounds at 55 feet, 2 inches (16.81 m). But he struggled in the finals, and left the path to the gold clear for a variety of challengers. First, Pedro Perez of Cuba took the lead. In the third round, the veteran Saneyev vaulted ahead of

At Montreal's Olympic Park, Saneyev and others took turns capturing the lead. Saneyev finally prevailed for his third gold medal.

the competition with a jump of 55 feet, 11¾ inches (17.06 m).

James Butts of the United States topped that mark in the fourth round by soaring 56 feet, 4½ inches (17.18 m). Saneyev would once again have to come up with a great jump under pressure in order to win. As usual, Saneyev came through. On his second-to-last jump, he topped Butts' leap by more than four inches (10 cm) to claim his third straight Olympic triple jump championship.

Saneyev seemed to be winding down his career when the Olympics moved to Moscow in 1980. Out of respect for his previous successes, the old man of the Soviet track team was allowed to carry the Olympic torch into the stadium.

But at the age of 34, Saneyev showed he still had one more clutch triple jump left in him. In an event marred by questionable officiating, Jaak Uudmäe of the Soviet Union held the lead going into the final round. In the final jump of his Olympic career, Saneyev soared farther than he had in the past four years of competition. The jump was measured at 56 feet, 6¾ inches (17.24 m), four inches (10 cm) shy of Uudmäe's gold medal effort.

In claiming the silver medal when he was long past his prime, Saneyev showed the competitive spirit that made him one of the Olympics' most long-lived and inspirational champions.

13

The Pocket Hercules

Naim Suleymanoglu

Naim Suleymanoglu (pronounced na-EEM soo-lay-MAHN-oo-loo) stands no more than 5 feet (152 cm) tall and weighs only 132 pounds (59.9 kg). Pound for pound, he may be the world's strongest human being. During the 1988 Olympic

Suleymanoglu begins his winning lift at the 1988 Olympics.

games, he lifted over three times his own body weight.

In addition to his awesome strength, Suleymanoglu may be the only man to set world records under three different names. The changes in his last name illustrate the turmoil that the young man called the Pocket Hercules has experienced during his life.

He was born Naim Suleimanov to a family of poor miners and farmers in the village of Pticher, Bulgaria. He had little chance of growing to average size—his father stood only 5 feet (152 cm) tall and his mother was not quite 4 feet, 8 inches (142 cm).

But Suleimanov never let his short stature interfere with his dream of becoming a strong man. When he was very young, he would practice lifting rocks and branches. At the age of 10, the 3-foot, 9-inch (114-cm) boy began

59

After lifting the weights high over his head, Suleymanoglu holds his position for an instant, showing his gold-medal form.

working out at a weight-lifting facility. There he showed such promise that he was enrolled in a Bulgarian sports school.

At about this time, Bulgarian coaches developed a strenuous training program that helped their country become a world power in weight lifting. Lifting as often as five times a day, Suleimanov established himself as a world-class competitor while still a young teenager. In 1981, at the age of 14, he came within 5½ pounds (2.5 kg) of a world record for flyweights. Suleimanov so dominated his weight class over the next years, that he was an overwhelming favorite

to win a gold medal in the 1984 Olympics. Unfortunately, the East European boycott of the Los Angeles games denied him a chance at the gold medal.

Because of events that occurred in the next two years, Suleimanov very nearly missed the 1988 games as well. The Bulgarian government had insisted that all its citizens have Bulgarian last names. The Suleimanovs, who were part of Bulgaria's Turkish minority, were forced to change their last name to Shalamanov. For Naim, this was the final insult in a lifetime of persecution by the majority Bulgarians. Although he set many records under his new name, he seethed at the indignity.

In 1986, during the World Cup Weightlifting Championships in Australia, Naim quietly walked out of a banquet honoring the lifters and defected to Turkey. Protected by bodyguards, he proclaimed his new freedom by changing his name again, this time to its most Turkish form—Suleymanoglu.

Because of an international rule that declares athletes ineligible for one year after changing citizenship, Suleymanoglu had to sit out a year of competition. Bulgaria then threatened to prevent him from competing in the 1988 Olympics by exercising a rule that bans athletes from Olympic competition for three years after a change in citizenship.

Turkish officials reportedly paid Bulgaria $1 million to allow Suleymanoglu to compete in the 1988 Seoul Olympics.

When Suleymanoglu took the weight-lifting stage in Seoul, he went after the gold medal with a vengeance. As he prepared to lift each bar, he thought of his parents and two brothers, whom he had not seen since leaving Bulgaria.

Ironically, his closest competition was an old friend, his former teammate Stefan Topurov of Bulgaria. In the snatch competition (in which the bar is to be lifted over the head in one continuous motion), Topurov had set a new Olympic mark of 303 pounds (137.5 kg).

But Suleymanoglu followed that record with one of his own. In a sudden, easy motion, the 21-year-old Pocket Hercules broke his own world record by hoisting 330 pounds (150 kg), and smiling as he did so. A short time later, he increased his record to 336 pounds (152.5 kg).

In the clean and jerk competition (in which the bar is first lifted to the shoulders and then pushed overhead), Suleymanoglu further electrified the crowd. The tiny Turk lifted an incredible 415½ pounds (188.5 kg) to clinch the gold medal, and then topped it with a lift of 418¾ pounds (190 kg).

In one competition, the Pocket Hercules had shattered his own world records in the snatch, the clean and jerk, the combined lift (which includes the weights from both competitions), and then had broken all the records again! His combined lift beat silver medalist Topurov by 66 pounds (30 kg) and destroyed the old Olympic mark by more than 115 pounds (52 kg)! Suleymanoglu's total lift would have defeated 300-pound (136-kg) superheavyweight gold-medalist Paul Anderson in the 1956 Olympic games.

After his impressive victory, Suleymanoglu said that he had drawn strength from the 55 million Turks who believed in him. But while an entire nation celebrated its first weight-lifting medals, the Pocket Hercules was still thinking of his family. For him, the Olympics had merely been one satisfying moment in an emotional ordeal that still had no ending.

Suleymanoglu, nicknamed "The Pocket Hercules" because of his small size and great strength, celebrates after winning his gold medal.

14

The Champion's Last Dive

Greg Louganis

Greg Louganis was certainly the diver to beat in the men's two diving events at the 1988 Olympic games. The king of diving had reigned over his sport for a decade, and four years earlier in the Los Angeles Olympics he had easily won gold medals in both the springboard and platform events. The games in Seoul were to be the last Olympic competition of his long career, and Louganis would be primed to go out in style.

As Louganis stepped onto the springboard in Seoul, South Korea, for his ninth dive of the preliminary round, there was no hint of the near-disaster that would follow. By his own estimate, Louganis had performed roughly 200,000 springboard dives in his life. He had never even come close to hitting the diving board. Yet somehow Louganis misjudged his jump while attempting a reverse 2½ somersault. As he came out of his first somersault, the top of his head whacked the board. Louganis fell into the water with a heavy splash.

The spectators were in shock. Two-time Olympic gold-medalist Sammy Lee, who watched Louganis' dive, said that he had never, in 55 years of observing diving events, seen a top diver hit the board in competition like Louganis had. When Louganis came to the surface, his head was bleeding and his confidence was shaken.

His poor dive had dropped him from first to fifth place. He would have to perform two good dives with his 10th and 11th dives to remain among the top 12 divers and qualify for the final. Patched up with temporary stitches, Louganis stepped onto the diving board while the spectators gave him a tremendous round of applause. Summoning all his courage, he attempted one of his most difficult dives. The judges awarded him the highest score of the competition, and Louganis had qualified for the finals to revive his hope of a gold medal.

That night, however, Louganis could not sleep. The experience brought back images of a similar mishap nine years earlier. During a meet in Canada, a Soviet diver had struck the hard diving platform with his head. Louganis had seen them pull the unconscious Soviet diver from the water. That diver had died from his injuries.

Somehow Louganis would have to forget that tragedy and block out the memory of his own frightening mishap. The very next day, he would have to perform the same kind of dive as the one during which he had hit his head.

Louganis was unusually tense for the final round. After five rounds, he had forged a slender 7-point lead over Liangke Tan of China. He increased the lead over the next couple of rounds. But in the ninth round he would have to perform the reverse 2½ somersault that had turned out so badly the previous day. The waterproof patch on his head served as a constant reminder of that nightmare dive. Louganis stood on the board, trying to calm his nerves. As the crowd watched in silence, he leapt into the dive. Seconds later he pierced the water, and the crowd roared its approval

at his magnificent effort. Two rounds later, he had earned his gold medal.

With his confidence restored, Louganis shifted his focus to the last diving competition of his Olympic career—platform diving. As usual, he jumped out to an early lead off the high platform. But it soon became apparent that a brilliant 14-year-old Chinese diver, Ni Xiong, would give Louganis plenty of competition. To the amazement of observers, Xiong passed Louganis in the standings during the fifth round.

From that point, spectators witnessed a thrilling matchup—the grace and power of the muscular, 168-pound (76.3-kg) Louganis and the stunning acrobatics of the willowy Ni Xiong, who pierced the water with the smallest of splashes. Louganis regained the lead in the seventh round, but Xiong passed him again in the next round.

Going into the final round, Xiong held a narrow lead, and he seemed unaware of the pressure he should have been feeling. He finished his performance with a difficult inward 3½ somersault, and entered the water with the slightest ripple.

Louganis' Olympic career was ending in a mirror image of the way it had begun. Back in 1976, the veteran champion Klaus Dibiasi of Italy had been forced to hit a near-perfect last dive to

Louganis, above, was challenged in the platform diving event at the 1988 Olympics by 14-year-old Ni Xiong of China. Louganis won the gold medal in an extremely close competition.

fend off the 16-year-old Greg Louganis. Now the champion Louganis knew it would take a near-perfect dive to beat his own young challenger.

Louganis had felt as if he were on top of the world after conquering his fear on the springboard. But now he realized that despite all that he had accomplished, if he failed on this dive, many people would consider his final Olympic performance a failure.

As he did before every dive, Louganis reminded himself that no matter what happened, his mother would still love him. Then he launched himself into the most difficult dive of the competition, a reverse $3\frac{1}{2}$ somersault. When he climbed out of the pool, he was smiling, and the crowd was cheering. When the judges' scores were added up, Louganis broke into tears of joy and relief. He had survived incredible pressure to win his final gold medal over Ni Xiong by little more than 1 point!

APPENDIX

Medal-winning performances by the athletes featured in this book are listed on these pages.

WR = world record   OR = Olympic record   EWR = equals world record

Paavo Nurmi *(Finland)* long-distance runner

1920 Olympics

silver	5,000m	15:00.0	
gold	10,000m	31:45.8	
gold	cross-country (8,000m)	27:15.0	
gold	cross-country team		

Note: The cross-country and cross-country team races are actually one race; results from the race are used to determine individual and team winners.

1924 Olympics

gold	1,500m	3:53.6	OR
gold	5,000m	14:31.2	OR
gold	cross-country (10,000m)	32:54.8	
gold	cross-country team		
gold	3,000m team	8:32.0	

1928 Olympics

gold	10,000m	30:18.8	OR
silver	5,000m	14:40.0	
silver	3,000m steeplechase	9:31.2	

Jesse Owens *(United States)* sprinter, long jumper

1936 Olympics

gold	100m		10.3	
gold	long jump	26' 5½''	8.06m	OR
gold	200m		20.7	OR
gold	4 x 100m relay		39.8	WR

Fanny Blankers-Koen *(Netherlands)* sprinter, hurdler

1948 Olympics

gold	100m	11.9	
gold	80m hurdles	11.2	OR
gold	200m	24.4	
gold	4 x 100m relay	47.5	

Emil Zátopek *(Czechoslovakia)* long-distance runner

1948 Olympics
gold	10,000m	29:59.6	OR
silver	5,000m	14:17.8	

1952 Olympics
gold	10,000m	29:17.0	OR
gold	5,000m	14:06.6	OR
gold	marathon	2:23:03.2	OR

Dawn Fraser *(Australia)* swimmer

1956 Olympics
gold	100m freestyle	1:02.0	WR
gold	4 x 100m freestyle relay	4:17.1	WR
silver	400m freestyle	5:02.5	

1960 Olympics
gold	100m freestyle	1:01.2	OR
silver	4 x 100m medley relay	4:45.9	
silver	4 x 100m freestyle relay	4:11.3	

1964 Olympics
gold	100m freestyle	59.5	OR
silver	4 x 100m freestyle relay	4:06.9	

Al Oerter *(United States)* discus thrower

1956 Olympics
		ft.-in.	meters	
gold	discus	184-11	56.36	OR

1960 Olympics
gold	discus	194- 2	59.18	OR

1964 Olympics
gold	discus	200- 1	61.00	OR

1968 Olympics
gold	discus	212- 6	64.78	OR

Bob Beamon *(United States)* long jumper

1968 Olympics
gold	long jump	29′2½′′	8.90m	WR

Dick Fosbury *(United States)* high jumper

1968 Olympics
gold	high jump	7′7¼′′	2.34m	OR

Mark Spitz *(United States)* swimmer

1968 Olympics
gold	4 x 100m freestyle relay	3:31.7	WR
bronze	100m freestyle	53.0	
silver	100m butterfly	56.4	
gold	4 x 200m freestyle relay	7:52.33	

1972 Olympics
gold	200m butterfly	2:00.70	WR
gold	4 x 100m freestyle relay	3:26.42	WR
gold	200m freestyle	1:52.78	WR
gold	100m butterfly	54.27	WR
gold	4 x 200m freestyle relay	7:35.78	WR
gold	100m freestyle	51.22	WR
gold	4 x 100m medley relay	3:48.16	WR

Kornelia Ender *(East Germany)* swimmer

1972 Olympics
silver	200m individual medley	2:23.59	
silver	4 x 100m freestyle relay	3:55.55	
silver	4 x 100m medley relay	4:24.91	

1976 Olympics
gold	4 x 100m medley relay	4:07.95	WR
gold	100m freestyle	55.65	WR
gold	100m butterfly	1:00.13	EWR
gold	200m freestyle	1:59.26	WR
silver	4 x 100m freestyle relay	3:45.50	

Shun Fujimoto *(Japan)* gymnast

1976 Olympics

gold   team gymnastics   576.85   (84.55, 89th)

Note: In team gymnastics, the scores of the top five of the six gymnasts on each team are counted for each event. Before he was injured, Fujimoto managed to collect 84.55 points toward his team's total. With these points, he ranked 89th among all gymnasts in the competition.

Nadia Comaneci *(Romania)* gymnast

1976 Olympics

gold	all-around	79.275
silver	team gymnastics	462.350
gold	uneven bars	20.000
gold	balance beam	19.950
bronze	floor exercise	19.750

1980 Olympics

silver	team gymnastics	393.500
silver	all-around	79.075
gold	balance beam	19.800
gold	floor exercise	19.875

Viktor Saneyev *(Soviet Union)* triple jumper

		ft.-in.	meters	
1968 Olympics				
gold	triple jump	57-0¾	17.39	WR
1972 Olympics				
gold	triple jump	56-11¼	17.35	
1976 Olympics				
gold	triple jump	56-8¾	17.29	
1980 Olympics				
silver	triple jump	56-6¾	17.24	

Naim Suleymanoglu *(Turkey)* weightlifter

1988 Olympics

	60 kg snatch	152.5kg	WR
	60 kg clean and jerk	190 kg	WR
gold	combined total	342.5kg	WR

Greg Louganis *(United States)* diver

1976 Olympics
silver	platform diving	576.99

1984 Olympics
gold	springboard diving	754.41
gold	platform diving	710.91

1988 Olympics
gold	springboard diving	730.80
gold	platform diving	638.61

Read these other Sports Talk books by Nathan Aaseng:

Great WINTER OLYMPIC Moments
Football's INCREDIBLE BULKS
Football's MOST CONTROVERSIAL CALLS
Football's MOST SHOCKING UPSETS
Baseball's GREATEST TEAMS
Baseball's WORST TEAMS
College Football's HOTTEST RIVALRIES
Pro Sports' GREATEST RIVALRIES
RECORD BREAKERS of Pro Sports
ULTRAMARATHONS: The World's Most Punishing Races

ACKNOWLEDGMENTS: The photographs are reproduced by permission of: pp. 1, 2, 6, 8, 10, 17, 18, 21, 22, 25, 26, 30, 32, 36, 37, 38, 41, 42, 49, 51, 54, 56, 65, The Bettmann Archive; p. 12, Pressfoto; pp. 14, 16, Library of Congress; pp. 28, 40, 48, 64, International Swimming Hall of Fame; p. 34, Mexican National Tourist Council; pp. 45 (both), 46, Photo Kishimoto Corporation.; pp. 53, 57, Canadian Olympic Association Archives; pp. 59, 60, and 62, Theoman Güray.

Front cover photograph reproduced by permission of Duomo/Dan Helms. Back cover photograph reproduced by permission of Focus on Sports.

OTHER BOOKS BY ARTHUR KURZWEIL

Best Jewish Writing 2003, edited by Arthur Kurzweil

My Generations: A Course in Jewish Family History

Behold a Great Image: The Contemporary Jewish Experience in Photography, edited with Sharon Strassfeld

The Strife of the Spirit by Adin Steinsaltz, edited and with an introduction by Arthur Kurzweil

On Being Free by Adin Steinsaltz, edited and with an introduction by Arthur Kurzweil

FROM GENERATION
TO GENERATION

FROM GENERATION
TO GENERATION

*How to Trace Your Jewish Genealogy
and Family History*

Arthur Kurzweil

○

Foreword by
Elie Wiesel

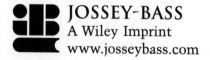

JOSSEY-BASS
A Wiley Imprint
www.josseybass.com

Published by Jossey-Bass
A Wiley Imprint
989 Market Street, San Francisco, CA 94103–1741   www.josseybass.com

Readers should be aware that Internet Web sites used within may have changed or disappeared between when the book was written and when it is read.

Jossey-Bass books and products are available through most bookstores. To contact Jossey-Bass directly call our Customer Care Department within the U.S. at 800-956-7739, outside the U.S. at 317-572-3986, or fax 317-572-4002.

Jossey-Bass also publishes its books in a variety of electronic formats. Some content that appears in print may not be available in electronic books.

Library of Congress Cataloging-in-Publication Data

Kurzweil, Arthur.
   From generation to generation: how to trace your Jewish genealogy and family history / Arthur Kurzweil; foreword by Elie Wiesel.—1st ed.
       p. cm.
   Includes bibliographical references and index.
   ISBN 0–7879–7051–4
   1. Jews—Genealogy—Handbooks, manuals, etc. 2. Kurzweil family. 3. Jews—Genealogy. I. Title.
CS21.K87 2004
929'.1'089924—dc22   2003021191

Printed in the United States of America
FIRST EDITION
HB Printing   10 9 8 7 6 5 4 3 2 1

CONTENTS

CHAPTER FOUR

How Is Jewish Genealogy Different
from All Other Genealogy?   81

CHAPTER FIVE
Avotaynu: The Premier Publisher in the World of Jewish Genealogy   162

CHAPTER SIX
JewishGen.org: Jewish Genealogy in Cyberspace   173

CHAPTER NINE
Holocaust Research: Changing Numbers into Names   243

CHAPTER TEN
Your Immigrant Ancestors   274

CHAPTER ELEVEN
Discovering the Old Country   306

CHAPTER TWELVE
Jewish Cemeteries:
Your History Chiseled in Stone   329

APPENDIX

Relationship Chart: How Are We Related?   349

For Miriam,

for Malya,

and for Moshe

———— o ————

*The process of the soul's connection with
the body—called the "descent of the soul into
matter"—is, from a certain perspective, the soul's
profound tragedy. But the soul undertakes this
terrible risk as a part of the need to descend in
order to make the desired ascent to hitherto
unknown heights. . . . Indeed Creation itself,
and the creation of man, is precisely such a risk,
a descent for the sake of ascension.*

RABBI ADIN STEINSALTZ,
THE THIRTEEN PETALLED ROSE

ACKNOWLEDGMENTS

DURING THE PAST TWENTY YEARS, while participating in the publishing of hundreds of books of Jewish interest, I have learned that an author brings only one part of what it takes to make a book. It also takes an author's parents, who raised their child to be fascinated by the world and to have the discipline to work hard; it takes friends and family who are supportive when you need them and even when you don't; it takes colleagues who have a generous spirit; it takes talented people on the publisher's staff who can take a raw manuscript and make it into a beautiful book. Whatever merit results from this book, I eagerly share it with all those who have helped me, knowingly and unknowingly. Any errors, misimpressions, or negativity that may come from my work is my own responsibility, and I will share it with no one.

Heartfelt gratitude goes to the following individuals:

Alan Rinzler, executive editor at Jossey-Bass. Thank you for your friendship, for recognizing the need for a new edition of this book, and for sharing your enthusiasm at all times.

Rob Kaplan, gifted editor, for your crucial impact on the life of this book and for your friendship.

Bob Bender, editor of the first edition of this book, for your talent, your integrity, and your friendship.

Julian Bach, for believing in my work twenty-five years ago and for doing something about it.

Sesil Lissberger, for your friendship and for the hundreds of speaking engagements that you have arranged for me for nearly a quarter of a century, in every corner of the United States, on the subject of Jewish genealogy.

Eric Goldman, Jewish media scholar and visionary and founder of Ergo Media, for your friendship and for producing a wonderful documentary video about my genealogy work.

Avery Corman, for helping me see, when I was a teenager, that I was a writer and for urging me to believe in myself.

Alan Kay, rabbi and friend, for writing the teacher's guide for the textbook I wrote, *My Generations*, and for all the years of mutual love and admiration.

Maris Engel, for your skills and talents and for good memories.

Robert Sobel, master teacher, brilliant professor, gifted writer, of blessed memory. You continue to be my teacher, and your inspiration will last me a lifetime.

David Christman, dean of New College at Hofstra University. You told me to stop writing short stories about teenage fantasies and to start writing about my Jewish family and other things about which I knew. Your lessons have stayed with me for thirty years.

Lucjan Dobroszycki, one of the great Jewish historians of the twentieth century, of blessed memory. I will always be so proud that I was your friend. Your kindness, support, and respect continue to nourish me.

Danny Siegel, master teacher, *baal tzedakah, talmid chacham,* and one of the great role models of my generation. You opened up the Talmud for me for the first time and thereby changed my life forever. You grabbed my soul and raised it up.

Alida Roochvarg, of blessed memory. You hired me to work in your bookstore, then urged me to leave and insisted that I pursue a master's degree in library science. Our mutual passion for books, new and old, was just one of our many shared interests. I still retell the stories and still repeat the wisdom that you shared with me thirty years ago.

Maurice Gottlieb, of blessed memory. You respected my quest when many did not, and you reached back to the memories in your soul and offered them to me with your blessings.

Hilda Kurzweil, who was thoughtful and generous to me when it mattered and helped launch my career as a public speaker.

Sam Kurzweil, of blessed memory, and Rose Kurzweil, who always fed me delicious food and memories at their table.

Michele Zoltan, who always said yes when I asked for help and who assisted in opening up a world to me that changed the course of my life.

Stanley Rothwax, of blessed memory, and my wonderful aunt, Ruth Rothwax. You have always been generous to me, in so many ways. I love you very much.

Zsuzsa Barta, my beautiful cousin originally from Budapest, now living in Australia, for your love and friendship and for traveling with me to the little towns in Hungary from whence our family comes.

Rabbi Malcolm Stern, of blessed memory, for the generosity you offered from the very beginning.

Gary Mokotoff and Sallyann Amdur Sack, founders of Avotaynu, for your generosity, kindness, friendship, and inspiration to me and countless others.

Tovia Frazer, for introducing me to the extraordinary Bobover Rebbe, of blessed memory, and for caring about my soul. You have made my life

much richer and helped me build what seemed like an impossible bridge and then aided me in crossing that bridge. For this, and much more, I am grateful.

Josef Schlaf, of blessed memory, my cousin from Warsaw, who took me into his home and was prepared to give me everything he had. I will never forget you.

Steven W. Siegel, who cofounded *Toledot: The Journal of Jewish Genealogy* with me. Your high standards and hard work have been an inspiration to so many of us. I knew you were my friend from the moment we met.

Dina Abramowicz, of blessed memory, surely one of the greatest Jewish librarians of all time, who treated all seekers with respect.

Zachary Baker, brilliant librarian, dedicated scholar, wonderful soul. Your work on behalf of Jewish genealogists everywhere has made a huge difference. Thank you for setting an example and for your friendship.

Irving Adelman and the reference department of the East Meadow Public Library. I grew up in your library and learned from you that the public library was the most exciting place in town.

Joseph K. Puglisi, inspirational and dedicated teacher. Your lessons have stayed with me for over forty years.

Harold Wise, of blessed memory, for your friendship and care. I came to your office for medical needs and always left with spiritual prescriptions.

Helen Hecht, friend, loving healer, and gentle, gifted physician. You inspire me with your knowledge of who the True Healer is, and you are such an extraordinary tool in the hands of the Holy One.

Rick Blum, lifelong *chevrusa*, fellow seeker, and loving friend.

Robin Bauer, devoted and loving friend.

Gary Eisenberg, coconspirator, true brother. Blessed are those who have someone like you in their lives.

Richard Carlow, loving, cherished friend, a true light in the world. You have stood by me through many incarnations. Fortunate are those who are given lifelong friendships such as ours.

Robin Minkoff, extraordinary person, faithful friend. I offer thanks to the Holy One for gracing me with your friendship and love.

Marc Felix, friend and confidant. The moment our paths crossed, it was clear who we were to each other.

Malya Kurzweil, precious daughter. You, Miriam, and Moshe are always eager to help me. I offer you special thanks for your flawless coordination of the interviews in this book.

Carolyn Starman Hessel, champion of the Jewish book, loyal friend. Your generosity to me over the years moves me deeply.

Ed Rothfarb, gifted artist, lifelong loving friend, special soul. We have shared our ideas, passions, and dreams with each other since we were little boys. I don't know anyone in our generation who has maintained as long and as close a friendship as we have.

Flash Rosenberg, gifted soul, good friend, profoundly funny seer. You always inspire me. I am your devoted student in the school of observing the world, in which you are the master teacher.

Rina Krevat, able assistant, lovely person. Your intelligence and ability have always served me well.

Saul and Evelyn Kurzweil, my parents. Thank you for taking such pride in my work and for encouraging my pursuit of our family history. You have given me the resources and the room to soar, and you have cheered me on without fail. If only all children would be as eager to speak with their parents as I am to speak with you each day. How blessed we are.

Ken Kurzweil, gifted teacher, generous spirit, wonderful brother. You get me out of every computer problem; you nourish me with music; you are always there when I need you.

Rea Kurzweil, lovely lady, beautiful and devoted co-parent. I hope I am as much a friend to you as you are to me.

Seth Schwartz, editorial assistant at Jossey-Bass. I feel uplifted every time we speak with each other. I'm grateful for your talents, your professionalism, and your gentle warmth.

Joanne Clapp Fullagar, editorial production manager at Jossey-Bass, gifted professional, delightful soul. Thank you for every conversation, every e-mail, every effort that you've made. I always feel in such capable hands when working with you.

Bruce Emmer, superb copyeditor, who gave my manuscript the fine-tuning it needed. Too few people know that it is the copyeditor who is the unsung hero of the publishing world.

Elie Wiesel, my generous, loving teacher. I knocked on your door when I was lost. You treated me like a welcomed guest and whispered secrets to me that helped me know my own soul.

Rabbi Adin Steinsaltz, my teacher, my Rebbe, Light of our generation.

Blessed are You, Lord our God, King of the universe, Who keeps us alive, sustains us, and has permitted us to reach this season.

A.K.

FOREWORD

הסכמה

WHAT IS A NAME? A mask for some, a vantage point, a reminder for others. Sometimes it signifies danger, often support.

For Paul Valery, nothing is as alien to a human as his or her own name. Understandably so. Imposed from without, the name dominates the person and invades him or her, ultimately taking the person's place. So then why not rid oneself of it along the way?

In the Jewish Tradition, a name evokes a deeper and more respectful attitude. We are Semites because we are the descendants of *Shem,* which signifies "name." We call God, who has no name, *Hashem,* "the Name." In other words, our relationship with the name is of a mystical nature; it suggests an imperceptible mysterious element. Its roots go deep into the unknown.

In the era of night, a name was a source of danger and death. But at the time of the first exile, in Egypt, it brought salvation. The Talmud affirms: Because our ancestors did not change their name, they knew deliverance.

In Jewish history, a name has its own history and its own memory. It connects beings with their origins. To retrace its path is thus to embark on an adventure in which the destiny of a single word becomes one with that of a community; it is to undertake a passionate and enriching quest for all those who may live in your name.

Note: This Foreword is actually a *Haskamah.* For centuries, it has been a Jewish custom for an author to seek, from a great scholar or rabbi, a *Haskamah* or approbation, which approves or recommends the work to its readers. I have asked my teacher, Elie Wiesel, may his light shine, to continue this Jewish tradition.—A.K.

Therein lies the value and the appeal of Arthur Kurzweil's beautiful and important book: it shows us that each name is a mysterious call transmitted from generation to generation in order to force themselves to question the meaning of their survival.

Let us listen to this call.

Elie Wiesel

INTRODUCTION

IN 1972, AT FLORIDA STATE UNIVERSITY in Tallahassee, I was studying for a master's degree in library science. One of my classes was called Resources in the Humanities. It was a course for future reference librarians who wanted expertise in areas like music, art, and literature. The final exam consisted of a single question, a reference question. Each of the twenty or so students in the class received the same question, we each had two days to answer it, we could work by ourselves or in groups, and although the professor told us that it would be nice if we could find the answer to the question, the real goal was so demonstrate our search strategy. The question was this: Can you find me a picture of *Will of the Wisp* by Harriet Hosmer?

The first two things the reference librarian needs to know, of course, are who is Harriet Hosmer and what is *Will of the Wisp*? Was it her dog, her boat, a painting? Well, it wasn't difficult to learn quickly (from standard biographical reference books) that Harriet Hosmer was a sculptor who lived in the United States in the 1800s. Slightly more difficult was learning that *Will of the Wisp* was a sculpture that she created. What was impossible for anyone in the class to locate, however, was a photograph of the piece, and that, after all, would be the reference librarian's true goal.

There we were, almost two dozen graduate students of library science, free to roam a huge university library, free to work in teams, free to use all the resources of a major American institution of higher learning, and yet we were unable to successfully answer the reference question given to us.

A few months ago, I was reminded of that final exam taken more than thirty years ago; I went to my computer and was able to locate a photograph of *Will of the Wisp* by Harriet Hosmer in about six seconds!

When I originally wrote this book in 1979, there was no Internet, of course. And when I wrote an updated edition in 1994, the major event that prompted the new edition was the breakup of the former Soviet Union and its implications for the growing number of Jews who were hoping that new sources and resources would be revealed. The Internet was already gaining momentum at the time, but I gave only brief reference to it. My major

preoccupation was the impact on Jewish genealogists of the political changes in the former Soviet Union and Eastern Europe. But today, nothing compares to the Internet in terms of its impact on the genealogical researcher. The phenomenal development of the Internet as a research tool is the main reason for this new edition. The possibilities, as you will see, are amazing.

Like many authors who have written a how-to-book, I originally wrote *From Generation to Generation: How to Trace Your Jewish Genealogy and Family History* because nobody else had written it. When it first occurred to me to go to the library to see if anyone had written a guidebook on the subject, I found that there was hardly a mention of Jewish genealogy in any book anywhere. How-to guides on genealogy were directed primarily at individuals who had Revolutionary War ancestors—or wished they had. However, no guidebook or advice was available for the Jewish person who was curious about his or her family history.

When I first began to trace my family history in the 1970s, I not only discovered sources that helped me but also began to see that there were in fact many sources that were of specific value to the Jewish family historian. I discovered, to my great surprise, that the average Jewish family can trace its background successfully. As I learned more and more about my own family, I also began to write articles for newspapers and magazines on my research in particular and the topic of Jewish genealogy in general. For two years I also wrote a weekly column for New York's *Jewish Week* called "Tracing Your Jewish Roots." In that column I shared my discoveries with my readers, telling them how they could track down information about their ancestors.

The writing I did on the subject also led to invitations from many Jewish organizations to speak on the subject. As I look back through my journals over the past years, I count over six hundred lectures that I have delivered to Jewish groups on how and why to do Jewish genealogical research. From college campuses to Jewish community centers, from synagogues to Jewish federations, invitations to speak on this subject have arrived in a steady flow ever since I first began to publicize my research successes.

When I wrote the first edition of *From Generation to Generation* in the late 1970s, I was as astonished as anyone by its success. But through my lecture engagements and the reputation of the book I came to understand that there is a deep thirst among American Jews to discover their Jewish roots. The successful hardcover edition of the book was followed by an equally successful softcover edition, and with it came a burst of growth in interest in the subject.

The first edition of *From Generation to Generation,* along with the enormous amount of traveling and lecturing I did, was but one part of the fantastic growth of the field over the past twenty-five years. When I began my own research, for example, there was no such thing as a Jewish genealogical society. Today there are dozens of them throughout the United States and the world, as well as the International Association of Jewish Genealogical Societies, which holds an annual conference (I am proud to say that I was given a lifetime achievement award by this organization several years ago). I'm also proud to say that some of the local Jewish genealogical societies began as a result of my lecture appearances, but the growth of popularity of Jewish genealogy and the progress that has been made in the field are the result of the efforts of many people. As anyone who has been involved in Jewish genealogical research in recent years knows, some extremely gifted people have made huge contributions to our knowledge and have helped considerably in the research of others. You will learn about many of them in this book.

The first edition of *From Generation to Generation* was published in 1980. It seems to have served many people well for many years, but it eventually suffered from simply not being able to keep up with the rapidly growing field. New sources and techniques were discovered; great changes were taking place in Eastern Europe and the former Soviet Union; addresses, fees, and procedures for many government institutions changed; and much more was happening. In 1994, a revised edition was published, reflecting many of the changes, new sources, and other developments in the world of Jewish genealogy.

One of the most significant changes over the past twenty-five years has been the attitude toward Jewish genealogy by many of the scholarly institutions that are most important to the Jewish researcher. When I first began my own genealogy research, most of the Jewish libraries and archives I visited didn't know how to help me. But I insisted that they had information that would be of great interest to laypersons tracing their family history (as opposed to scholars, who were the usual users of these institutions). In many cases I showed them resources in their own collections that at first did not seem to be of value but later proved to be extremely important to Jewish genealogists. Jewish genealogists have gained considerable respect over the past few decades. Librarians have come to see, I think, that genealogy is a serious pursuit and that its result is often life-changing. Librarians have seen how genealogical discoveries delight and transform the researcher, and they have discovered that the collections they maintain can make a difference in people's lives.

This volume now before you is a completely revised and updated edition of *From Generation to Generation*. Every address and source has been verified. Corrections and new information (such as fees and form numbers) have been thoroughly researched, and the most significant new sources in the field have been added. As every seasoned genealogical researcher knows, books in this field are out of date almost immediately upon publication. New discoveries are being made all the time, addresses and phone numbers keep changing, and whole new areas of research open up. This book is not an attempt to present the definitive guide to the field. No such guide is possible. Rather, *From Generation to Generation* is an attempt to help the reader get started on the path to making some successful genealogical discoveries.

As I mentioned, the most significant development for the Jewish family historian and genealogist is the Internet. Research that used to be impossible is now simple to do on the Internet, and research tasks that used to take weeks now take seconds! The most important Internet sources for Jewish genealogical research are identified throughout this volume.

Many people have said to me that they have read this book over and over and always find something new. This is not because they missed things the first time they read the book but because of the nature of the genealogical process. The very source that is of no use to you today becomes the missing link to information you will look for in the future. Like a big puzzle, it often happens that one little breakthrough opens up a whole new area. I have tried, in this new edition, to include all the useful sources that I think a researcher needs to get started. As you will see, there are many specialized books, journals, and other sources that provide far greater detail about many important Jewish genealogical resources. This book is intended to serve as a starting point.

I have included anecdotes and facts that came as a result of my own personal research throughout the book, particularly in the first chapter. Many readers have told me that my personal story serves the book well, so despite some temptation to exclude this personal aspect, I have left this material in. My own personal research has continued over the years in a few ways I'd like to mention.

One area of growth is the deepening relationship I have developed with some previously unknown relatives, particularly in Eastern Europe. Through my genealogy research I discovered close relatives in Hungary and Poland, and these relationships have become among my most important and cherished possessions.

Another significant area of growth has been my discovery of the more religious branches of my family. Before I began my research a quarter-cen-

tury ago, I saw myself as a fairly typical American Jew, far more involved in American culture and Western thought than in Jewish culture and religious thought. Perhaps the most surprising discovery I made in the early stages of my research was that my great-great-great-grandfather had been a Hasidic Rebbe in Europe and that there were still branches of my family that lived and breathed Jewish tradition each and every moment of their lives. I have spent much of my genealogical research time over the past two decades getting to know these branches of my family and what their lives are all about. The religious communities in Brooklyn and Jerusalem include many of my relatives. Getting to know them and their lives has had a profound effect on me.

I didn't know it when I began my research, but I see now that my own search for information about my family history was really, at its core, a yearning for a Jewish identity. Today, my family and I pursue a life filled with traditional Judaism. Study of Jewish texts is a regular activity for me and my household; Jewish celebrations and observances define the rhythm of my life; my three children, now teenagers, have been yeshiva students since they first entered school; and Jewish tradition transformed itself from a topic I wanted learn about to the foundation of my life.

When I am asked why I got interested in Jewish genealogy, I often joke and say that I discovered that I had more in common with my dead ancestors than I did with my living relatives . . . and they are also far easier to get along with. In some ways I am not joking. The fact is that at a certain point in my life, I was tired of hearing how my ancestors died as Jews; I wanted to know how they *lived* as Jews. As I discovered this, I also discovered that I belong there, with them. Slowly but surely, over the years, I have come to eat, pray, study, and generally live the way my relatives have lived for centuries. I am not tied to old customs for their own sake; rather I have learned that the eternal ideas that have sustained our people for generations still serve us well and contain profound wisdom.

Genealogy is more than names and dates on a chart. It is more than sentimental stories about the good old (or bad old) days. It is not an effort to gain status by discovering illustrious ancestors. Nor is it an effort to build walls between people. For me, genealogy is a spiritual pilgrimage. My generation comes after a terrible trauma for our people. A third of our family was murdered sixty years ago. Mass migration of Jews before and after the beginning of the twentieth century and the destruction of European Jewry during the Holocaust cut most of us off from our identities. I was once told by a hostile relative, "Why be Jewish? Just be human." The trouble is that by just being human, we become a part of the general culture that is far from "just human." My genealogical

research serves as a doorway for me. As I enter the world of Jewish culture, Jewish thought, Jewish life, I come to see that Jewish ideas are profound, Jewish sages are nourishing for my soul, and it is my obligation to fan the flame of Judaism by being an active part of it.

One specific mitzvah required of traditional Jews each day is to remember that we were slaves in Egypt. This mitzvah is not performed with a ritual object, nor is it an act that would cause someone to think you looked religious. Merely reflecting in your mind and heart and hearing that we were slaves is, in itself, considered a spiritual act of great significance. For me, this is the point of genealogy. The act of looking back on our heritage is a spiritual deed in itself. I am not saying that anyone who does Jewish genealogical research is going to become a traditional, religion-focused Jew. Nevertheless, I do maintain that each person who is doing Jewish genealogical research, whether or not he or she acknowledges it, is responding to an inner yearning for a connection to our heritage.

Much of my genealogical research over the past several years has not been centered on library or archival research, nor has it focused on obtaining more documentation from government agencies in the United States or in the "old country." Rather, I have spent much time and effort cultivating relationships with previously unknown relatives. I have also focused on understanding Jewish thought, especially Jewish theology. I have discovered that our sages were profound and original thinkers whose slant on life and whose approaches to the riddles of existence are the most nourishing that I have thus far encountered. My friend Gary Eisenberg, an expert on the Jewish involvement in religious cults, will tell you that there is a disproportionate number of Jews in these groups. I believe that this is because these individuals are thirsty for spiritual nourishment and have not been able to find it in their local Jewish community. Many genealogists have had the same thirst and have traveled centuries and continents, only to arrive home.

When I look at photographs of Jewish life in Eastern Europe before the Holocaust, I often see bookshelves in the backgrounds. This observation led me to wonder just what those books were about. They were volumes of the Talmud and other classical Jewish texts. It was owing to my genealogical interest that I pushed myself to learn what was inside those books. What I found was the most subtle, most profound, most uplifting, most nourishing wisdom I had ever encountered. Genealogy is not just names and dates on a chart: it is a search for meaning.

Genealogical research can be a painful activity. Family stories, like Jewish history, are often tragic. Recollections are often heartbreaking. But I firmly believe, based on my own experience and the experiences of count-

less others who have taken the time to pursue this research, that genealogy can be a life-changing activity. It is hard to explain from the outside, but when two genealogists meet, a silent bond connects them because they both know that somewhere in between all the family interviews and photographs and forms and documents, in between the books and journals, in between the last discovery and the next one is some intangible yet very real sense that this pursuit is in some way a mission.

My most sincere and heartfelt prayers include my hope that this book will serve its readers—and the Jewish people—well. In recent generations our loved ones have been torn from us, but like a plant that has been cut back, we are now in the midst of a burst of growth and creativity that is revitalizing the Jewish people. Those of us who are involved with Jewish family history research will surely be seen, in generations to come, as vital links between past and future.

——————— ○ ———————

I do not wish anything to happen in Jewish history without it happening to me.

—Elie Wiesel

Judaism is not just a matter of individual commitment. However personal one's involvement may be, Judaism always entails a linkup with past and future generations.

—Rabbi Adin Steinsaltz

——————— ○ ———————

CLIMBING UP MY FAMILY TREE

JEWISH GENEALOGY AS A SPIRITUAL PILGRIMAGE

IN THE SPRING OF 1970, I wandered into the Jewish Division of the New York Public Library for the first time in my life. The cross section of Jews who sat at the long tables in that room spread over many decades and many worlds. There were young Hasidic men leaning over rare rabbinic texts, and middle-aged Reform rabbis preparing for a future sermon. There were college women writing term papers on history and scholars writing books on obscure topics.

Standing near the doorway, I looked around at the faces of the readers and the books they were reading and wondered where I fit into this peculiar congregation of Jews. Some of them were reading Yiddish, a language barely known to me, and others were strict observers of the Law, a way of life I did not yet know. I was unlike them all, I concluded, and yet there I found myself, nonetheless, approaching the card catalogue, looking for my own way, my own Jewishness.

As I walked toward the drawer of the library card catalogue for a portion of the D titles and authors, I felt a twinge of suspicion that I was wasting my time. Why would this library—or any library—have information on the town of Dobromil, the town in which my father was born, the town I learned of as a child through the dozens of stories my father told me?

Ever since I was a child, my father had told me dozens of stories about the little shtetl in Galicia where he was born. I felt like there were dozens of stories, but there really were just a few, although these few had more power than any collection of wondrous tales that ever enchanted a child.

There was the story of the day my father was brought to the shul by his mother to change his name. He was gravely ill; his father was in America, saving up the money to send for his wife and three children. My father was possibly dying. His mother carried him to the shul and renamed her son. He was born Saul; now he was Chaim—for "life." Surely the Angel of Death would be fooled.

And of course the Angel was fooled, and I thought of this as my father told the story to me whenever I asked him to recite the tale again. Vividly I imagined my father being carried by his mother. Vividly I imagined the Angel of Death searching for a little sick boy named Saul who was nowhere to be found. I knew, as my father told me the story with pure seriousness, that I was born because many years before, the Angel of Death had been fooled.

Then there was the story of my grandmother's milk business in Dobromil. My grandfather was in New York, sending whatever money he could, but it was not enough. So my grandmother went into the milk business. She would go to the Christian peasants out in the fields and buy milk from them to bring back to the towns nearby and then resell it. My grandmother was a strong and healthy woman, but she could not carry all of the milk cans at once. So she would carry what she could as far as she could, and then she would return for the remaining cans. She would walk back to the point where she had left the first batch and then stop to rest. After this she would begin again, carrying what she could to the next point and then returning for the remaining milk jugs. All by herself, she sold milk to the people in the nearby village.

This story, too, I imagined in minute detail. I walked, in my dreams, with my grandmother as she struggled with the heavy cans of milk. I stood with her as she poured the milk from the larger containers into the small jars and bottles of the people to whom she sold the raw milk. I asked to hear the story over and over, visualizing the field that we walked across together.

I have dreamed about the shtetl of Dobromil a lot over the years, especially as a child, so although I grew up in a suburban town in New York, in some ways I've considered Dobromil home.

How can a young man, graduating from college, raised in the most modern country in the world, near the city of New York, having (at that time) never stepped outside the borders of the United States, consider a shtetl on the Russian-Polish border (which today hasn't a Jew in it) "home"? Every time I sat and daydreamed about the little town, I felt warm and at home. Throughout my childhood, my imagination ran wild with the few stories I was told, so that by the time I reached the card

catalogue at the library, I already had faces of townspeople, visions of dirt roads, corners of brittle shuls, and Shabbas candles on freshly laid table-cloths all crystal clear in my mind.

Expecting to find nothing as I flipped through the cards in the drawer in the library, I came across an item that startled me. The top of the card read "Dobromil," and the description of the item indicated a book.

A book on Dobromil? Impossible, I thought. As clear as my dreams of Dobromil were, as warm as my love was for the town that was my father's for the eight years before he came to America, I didn't think Dobromil deserved a book. By its importance in my life it deserved much more, but how could such a small town take up the pages of a book—in the New York Public Library, no less?

I filled out the form required for the librarian to retrieve the book and then sat at a table among the Hasidim and the scholars and the casual readers of the latest Jewish magazines. As I waited, I stared at the faces around me. Looking at the deep lines on the older faces, I wondered where these people were from, what they were reading, how they lived. Did they believe in God? Did they survive death camps? Who were they? What were their stories? As was a habit of mine, I began to create stories about the people around me. I invented histories for them. I gave men wives and women husbands. I gave them houses and apartments, pasts and tragedies.

And then the book arrived. I looked at the cover for a long moment, reading the words *Memorial Book—Dobromil* several times as I held the book and felt its weight of more than five hundred pages. Flipping through the book, I saw the Hebrew letters, English letters, and pho-tographs pass quickly before my eyes. Several times I flipped the pages rapidly, almost not wanting to stop to examine the detail, mostly because I was too excited to look at one page while I wondered impatiently what was on the next.

Turning to the first page, a full-page photograph, I read the caption: "Main Street in Dobromil." There is no way for me to know how many minutes I sat starting at the picture. The photograph showed an unpaved road, several small buildings with slanted roofs, and a few people on the street. No one will believe that the picture was familiar to me, but in fact I had imagined it just this way.

With this photograph my dreams of years were confirmed. There *was* a Dobromil, it *did* have dirt roads, and little houses, and people who stood at the shul while the Angel of Death was being plotted against. As I came out of the trance that had me reliving each of the stories in all of the detail that I had filled in over the years, I was able to begin to examine

Dobromil, Poland, about 1938, hometown of the author's father, grandparents, and great-grandparents.

the book more closely. I continued to have a sense of disbelief, not fully realizing that in my hands was a book on a subject as profoundly important to me as this. A book on the shtetl of Dobromil was for me what a walk on the moon would be for a boy who grew up wanting to be an astronaut.

The book was in three languages: Hebrew, Yiddish, and English. Turning to the English section, I read the titles of the chapters, including "Destruction of Dobromil," "Historic Dobromil," and "Personalities." One was called "Dobromiler Grandparents." My grandparents were Dobromiler grandparents, so I turned to the chapter to see what it said. It was a story written by a woman whose grandparents were from Dobromil. It was then that I looked at the front of the book to see when it was printed. The date was 1963. This confused me, because I could not understand how a book could be published so recently about a town that was such ancient history to me—regardless of the nature of my fantasies.

I decided to look through the book page by page in order to examine the photographs scattered in plentiful quantities throughout. As I turned the pages, I looked at the photos, glancing at the faces in each of the shots. It did not even cross my mind that I would see a face I would recognize. My father was just a boy when he left Dobromil, and his father was a simple tinsmith. My father's mother was in the milk business, and the only other person whom I could think of at the time was my great-grandfather, the man whom I was named after, who also was a tinsmith. The possibility that they would be in this book was too remote to even consider.

Organization of businessmen in Dobromil, Poland, about 1925. The author's great-grandfather is in the second row from the bottom, fifth from the left.

It was for this reason that I was absolutely stunned when I saw a picture of Avrahum Abusch, my great-grandfather, as I looked at a group photo that took up an entire page.

Had the man across from me not been engrossed in the Talmudic text in front of him, he would have seen me shake. I was overwhelmed by the just-discovered fact that my great-grandfather had his picture in a book in the New York Public Library! A picture of my great-grandfather! I could say it over and over and it would still sound unbelievable to me.

I could sit still no longer. I ran to the librarian at the desk in the front of the room to share my discovery. To the best of my recollection, she took the matter quite casually. What was at the time the most exciting thing that had ever happened to me was taken in stride by the woman at the desk before me. I didn't understand why she couldn't appreciate the importance of my discovery, because that discovery opened up the door to a search that has taken me many years and that, I am happy to say, offers no end in sight. The discovery of that photograph said one thing to me—one thing that changed my life: "You have a past," it said, "a past and a history, and you can discover it if you want."

The reason I recognized the photograph of my great-grandfather, Abusch, is because I had taken a great interest in him for years. Ever since I first heard the story of my father's name change from Saul to Chaim, I wondered about my name as well. I was told that I was named after my great-grandfather, so I have always asked questions about him and collected pictures of him and even became his imaginary friend. Actually, he became my imaginary conscience. For the longest time, I envisioned him in heaven, watching me. This didn't upset me, nor did it frighten me, but I have to admit that there have been many times when I would base choices on what my great-grandfather in heaven would think. Even during the periods of my life when I rejected anything supernatural, I still remained in a state of mind in which I would think about how my great-grandfather would feel if I did what I knew to be wrong. In those times, I did not believe that he was watching and judging but rather that because I was named after him, I had a responsibility to maintain his "good name." To this day I am convinced that this is a positive effect of learning about history and, in particular, family history. We have a responsibility to the past.

In the library, I took the book on Dobromil to the photocopy services and had a few pages duplicated. One was the picture of my great-grandfather. Another was the title page of the book. A third was a street map of the shtetl, Dobromil, complete with little squares representing houses and Yiddish captions on many of the houses that I would have to get translated. I took the photocopies and went to visit my parents.

My father was amazed at the discovery I had made and was most excited by the map of the shtetl. Glancing at the map for no more than a few seconds, he unhesitatingly pointed to a spot on the map and said, "We lived here."

The spot he pointed to had a number, and we looked at the number guide to the map where my father read the Yiddish caption. It said, "The Glazier Ennis." We looked at each other and smiled. Ennis was my grandmother's maiden name, and her family were glaziers. So not only did the book have a picture of my great-grandfather on my grandfather's side of the family, but it also had a map with the house of my grandmother's family.

How many times I had been in that house in my dreams! How many times I imagined eating at the table, playing outside, walking through the fields with my grandmother, helping her carry the milk cans back to the house! That house came to represent to me an entire world that I often longed for but knew I'd never find. It was a world that I knew had been destroyed; a world that only my dreams could capture. I would never know if I was nearly correct in the way I imagined it. But now I had it on

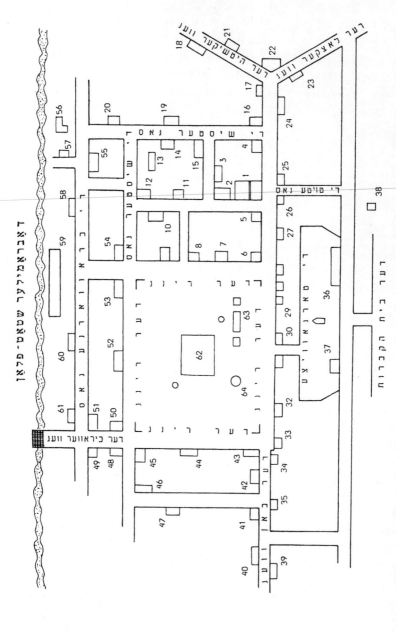

Street map of Dobromil, Poland, birthplace of the author's father, from the memorial book about the town.

Ruchel Ennis, the author's
paternal great-grandmother.

a map. Now I could place it at the exact point on earth where it still might
be standing.

Where it still might be standing. This was another part of my day-
dreams. Often I wondered what happened to the house where my father
grew up. Who lived there now? Who sat in the doorway that I have
wanted to sit in? Years later I spoke to a man who went back to Dobromil
shortly after the war. The town, which was once almost completely Jewish, was already occupied by the Ukrainians as if it had always been theirs.
They lived in our houses, ate at our tables, and slept in our beds.

As my father and I looked at the map, he remembered more stories
about his childhood and the town. I was delighted. I was also impressed
by my father's memory. He had left Dobromil as a child of eight, and he
had often been told by other family members that he could not remember much, probably because they themselves could not recall much,
though they were older. But as my father looked at the map of the town
where he spent the first eight years of his life, he proved them wrong time
and again. He began to identify many places on the map with ease and
finally turned to me and said, "See, I remember the place well."

I returned often to the New York Public Library Jewish Division to look at the Dobromil book. I was like a little child who asked for the same picture book time and again and sat with it, reliving the same fairy tale. It was not much different for me. I relived the fairy tale over and over again. Each time I returned to the book, I became more familiar with the faces in the photographs, and they became my neighbors. The only section of the book I avoided with each visit was "The Destruction of Dobromil." I would not read it or look at those pictures. Not yet: I was not ready. I was still building the town. There was no way that I would let it be destroyed so quickly.

One day I was able to use the photocopy of the title page that I had made the first day I discovered the book. It included the names of a few men who had apparently put the book together. They were identified as the Book Committee. The organization of which they were a committee was the Dobromiler Society, which was a landsmanshaft. At that time I had no idea what a landsmanshaft was.

Landsmanshaften are organizations consisting of people from the same town in Europe. In other words, people from Dobromil, and their families, joined together to form an organization when they arrived in America. (There are also landsmanshaften in Israel and other countries.) These organizations were homes away from home for new immigrants. People were able to associate with familiar faces, reminisce about the "old country," and provide emotional and financial support to each other. Often the first thing a landsmanshaft did was to raise money to buy burial plots for its members.

The title page of the Dobromil book indicated that the Dobromiler Society was located in New York, so I deduced that the men on the Book Committee were also New Yorkers. I decided to call them.

I searched through the several New York City area phone books for the names and finally came across one that matched. They were all uncommon names that made my search easier. The man whose phone number I found was Philip Frucht. I dialed his number, and a man answered.

"Is this Philip Frucht?" I asked.

"Yes."

"Are you the man who helped put the book on Dobromil together?"

"Yes. Who are you?"

"My name is Arthur Kurzweil," I answered. "You might have known my family. There was a picture of my great-grandfather in the book."

"What did you say your name was?" he asked.

"Kurzweil."

"I'm sorry," he said. "I knew most of the people in Dobromil, but this family I must not have known."

"But you must have known them. There was a picture in the book," I pleaded.

Again I repeated my name, but it did not help. It was then that an idea struck me. Though I knew my grandfather to be named Julius, his name in Yiddish—and therefore in Dobromil—was Yudl. I also knew that though my grandfather was a roofer in Brooklyn, he was a tinsmith in Dobromil. So I asked Mr. Frucht, "Did you know Yudl the tinsmith?"

Frucht's voice perked up. "Who are you to Yudl?" he demanded.

"I'm his grandson," I said.

The next thing I knew, Frucht was shouting into the next room to his wife, telling her that he was speaking to Yudl's grandson. He sounded as excited as I was.

"What did you say your name was?" he asked me again.

"Kurzweil," I said, pronouncing it the way I was always taught to say it, "Curz-wile."

"You mean 'Koo-utz-vile,'" Frucht pronounced it. "No wonder I didn't recognize it."

Inside myself, I was a bit ashamed. Though it was the way I was taught since childhood, it was not the way my grandparents said our name, or my great-grandparents, or their parents, or any of the people in Dobromil. I must have spoken my name "incorrectly" a hundred thousand times.

After Mr. Frucht gave me a lesson in pronouncing my own name, I asked him if he knew my family. He did, indeed, and quite well. I learned many things from the conversation that followed, including the fact that my grandfather Yudl had once been a president of the Dobromiler Society himself. Frucht proceeded to tell me many stories about Dobromil and his relationship to my family and finally suggested other people who would be able to fill me in on further details. After completing my talk with Mr. Frucht, I was elated and mystified. Perhaps it was the quality of Frucht's stories. He spoke about Dobromil as if it still existed as a shtetl. The affection he had for his town was inspiring, and it brought the town that much closer to me. But one of his comments made the biggest impact of all. After we spoke about Dobromil, the conversation turned to me. "What do you do?" he asked. I told him a little about myself, and Mr. Frucht replied, "That's wonderful. It's always nice to hear about the success of a Dobromiler."

It was all that he needed to say! Here was a man, born and raised in Dobromil, calling me a Dobromiler, calling me a member of the shtetl. He didn't know that I had walked the streets of the shtetl in my dreams, that I had imagined the town to be mine for years, or that I had longed so often to go there. He didn't know that I had relived the stories told to me

by my father so many times. Yet he called me a Dobromiler. My wish had been realized.

I have often wondered how many people would think all of this crazy. I still wonder. There is a touch of madness to this dreaming and feeling. Why in the early 1970s would a young man in his twenties, born and raised in the New York suburbs, be elated at being called a member of a shtetl? What was the point? What did it mean? Who really cares? I have no answer for it except to say that the more I learn about the shtetlach of my ancestors, the more at home I feel. It was in these places that my ancestors struggled to survive, and something within me drives my body and soul to visit the streets of my families' past. I visit them in photographs, in stories, in names, and in dreams. Mr. Frucht merely said out loud what I had been unable to say myself. I am a Dobromiler; I was born in New York but came out of a shtetl. In fact, as I reach farther and farther back in my past, I came out of Egypt as an Israelite. This is what the Passover Hagaddah says, and it is true. My experience with Dobromil teaches me this.

I am a child of America, but I am a Dobromiler.

Finding the Dobromil book and speaking to Philip Frucht launched my casual interest about family history into an obsession. I often wonder when it really began. For a while I thought it was with the discovery of the Dobromil book, but something had to have brought me to the library. Then I thought it was the stories my father told me, but something made me ask to have them told over and over again. I also recall an incident that occurred early in my childhood. I was in my parents' synagogue on Rosh Hashanah, and I can recall sitting next to my father listening to the rabbi's sermon—which I did not understand. I must have been eight years old or so. But at one point in the sermon, the rabbi said that at this time of year, God opens the book of life, a book with everyone's name in it, and decides who will live and who will die.

I remember wondering as the rabbi made that statement how God organized his book. Alphabetically or by family? I imagined it to be by family, and to this day I visualize it in that way. In fact, I hope someday to be God's librarian for those books.

Obviously, my interest in family relationships had an early beginning, and more obviously as time went on, I saw it become, as I said, an obsession.

I began to contact people in my family on a random basis, taking trains and buses (and making phone calls or writing letters to people too far away to visit) to gather information about the family. Each conversation led me to more people, and in very little time I had more than a hundred names of cousins and ancestors. I was particularly interested in talking to the oldest members of the family, asking them to reach back

Malya Kurzweil, paternal grandmother of the author (standing), with her three children and one of her sisters. The author's father, Saul Kurzweil, is at the far left.

in their memories to the earliest people and stories they could recall. The family tree grew with amazing speed, and I was admittedly surprised by the cooperation I had gotten. Everyone was interested in telling me what he or she knew. I even received letters from people who had heard of my interest and had decided not to wait for me to get around to them. I found I had gathered names, dates, towns, and stories about a large number of people. The family, which I never knew to be that large, became enormous. Of course, many of the names I had gathered were of people who were no longer living, but the family was still quite large. One factor became very helpful to my research: there is a Kurzweil Family Circle that has been in existence for more than sixty years. Although the organization did not have any historical information to hand me, it did have a membership list as well as a cemetery plot. I visited the cemetery and sent questionnaires to the members of the Family Circle.

The questionnaires asked for information about each person's immediate family and his or her own ancestors. I included return envelopes, and in no time my mailbox was overflowing with filled-in questionnaires. I spread them all out on the floor and began to build a sizable family tree

stretching back several generations. I also received more names and addresses of people who were not members of the Kurzweil Family Circle, and I wrote to them as well. Then I sent additional letters out to people asking for stories, and I received more history about the family. In the course of my research, I discovered a branch of the family that has lived in Israel for several generations, branches of the family in cities around the United States, and most surprising of all, the name of a cousin who was living in Poland. At that time he was just a name on a piece of paper, but he became an important relative and friend. I am saddened when I think that my cousin Joseph has died. I will always be grateful to have known him. He, along with his wife, Daniele, and his daughter, Anna, were among my greatest joyful discoveries as a Jewish genealogist. I visited them a few times at their home in Warsaw. Joseph was the only member of the Kurzweil family who survived the war and stayed in Poland. He was a writer of, among other things, Jewish history, which was surely a rare thing for anyone in Poland in the second half of the twentieth century. Until he died, we wrote to each other regularly. He also visited me once in New York!

In time I had accumulated a lot of information and was becoming quite familiar with the history of the family. My questions to older relatives surprised them. I asked them about things that they themselves hadn't thought about for decades. A crucial point came when I felt as if I was living in a different place at a different time. Again, my dreams at night took place far away in time and space. It was becoming unusual for me *not* to have a dream about some ancestor or other. I entered the world of my ancestors in my conscious and subconscious lives. At times I felt it unhealthy. Newspapers interested me less than historical accounts of Galicia that I borrowed from the library.

My picture collection grew as well, undoubtedly helping my dreams create vivid images of the shtetl and the past. Some people loaned me photographs, and others gave them to me outright. I also discovered a large box of pictures that my parents had filled with old photos of family members and street scenes. Eventually, I just about exhausted every possible lead that I had on people who could contribute information about the family.

The process of meeting these people was wonderful. In effect, I was doing two things at once: building a family history and making new friends and acquaintances. Both were rewarding and priceless. It was fascinating to learn what paths my cousins' lives had taken. We all descended from the same people, but because of the different kinds of choices our closer ancestors made, we went in various directions. Remarkable was the physical

resemblance between people who had never seen each other before. My cousin Joseph from Warsaw, for example, looked a lot like my father.

When I completed the stage of my research that dealt with people I had known or was referred to, I began searching through phone books. Since Kurzweil is an uncommon name, it was a rather easy task—at least compared with a name such as Schwartz or Cohen. The New York Public Library has a collection of just about every available phone book in the world, so I spent hours combing them, looking for Kurzweils to call or write to. Again I was met with remarkable success. I came up with people who were definitely related to me but who knew nothing about my family. Several generations back, their ancestors and mine went in different directions and sooner or later lost contact. Now, for the first time, cousins were getting to know one another. It was relatively easy for me to figure out if someone was a cousin. I had accumulated enough names and places to be able to discover the link in a rather short time. My family tree was organized well enough for me to have easy access to the material within it.

One phone call to an unknown Kurzweil met with an unusual series of circumstances. I called a man whose name was Arthur Kurzweil, just like mine. I identified myself on the phone and told him what I was doing. He voiced disinterest and told me that he'd call me back if he became interested. I was upset by this, having experienced nothing like it in the months that I was pursuing my family history. But I decided, some weeks later, to call again and try my luck. I asked him politely what his grandparents' names were, and when he told me I immediately knew who he was. His grandparents came to America long before most Kurzweils, and because of this they grew apart from the rest of the family, most of whom came to the United States rather late, historically. So it was obvious why we would not have known about him.

When he told me their names, I proceeded to tell him the names of some of his aunts and uncles.

"Your aunts and uncles must be Bessie, Morris, Pauline . . ."

"Who told you this?" he asked.

"And your parents must be Harry and . . ." I continued.

"Are we related?" he asked.

We certainly were, and I explained exactly what the relationship was. He still wasn't convinced. The phone conversation ended shortly after that, and there was still doubt in his voice. Later on, months later, he told me that he thought I was representing a business that does family tree research for a fee.

His disbelief troubled me, as did his unwillingness to cooperate, since he could have been the link between me and many other people in his

"missing" branch of the family. I wanted to make the family tree as complete as possible, and he was a source for quite a bit of information. Rather than give up, I decided to tackle the problem with even more energy than usual. It brought me to examining public records.

To this point, I had very little experience with the use of public records. Actually, the only time I ever used them for my family tree research was to get the death certificate of my great-grandfather, Abusch. Death certificates often provide the names of the deceased's parents, including the mother's maiden name. In this case, I was able to verify what I had been told by relatives as to my great-great-grandparents' first names, and I also learned the maiden name of Abusch's mother. This was important for two reasons. First, it added another major branch to my family tree. Second, it led me to the knowledge that my great-grandparents were first cousins.

So I began to do research into this unknown branch of the family. I used census records that gave me information about household members in 1900. I sent for immigration records that provided still more information, and I went to the surrogate's court and looked up the wills of several people. It all added up to a lot of facts, though it was the difficult way of doing what could probably have been done in a conversation. But it was a fortunate thing also because in the process of looking for the items I was after, I discovered things about other branches of the family. In the end, I had a thick file of data on my entire family, provided by public documents in the United States. This included the names of towns in Europe where people originated, dates of immigration, names of steamships taken to this country, and even copies of the passenger lists of the ships. I have in my possession the passenger list of the ship that took my father and his brother, sister, and mother to America in 1929. It is an important document to me, for obvious reasons.

Once a letter from a Kurzweil in Israel brought interesting results: one day I received a detailed piece of correspondence from a man named Dov Kurzweil. Although he was eager to exchange notes of the histories of our families, it was clear from his letter that we would not be able to establish any family links—at least not from what he knew. Although Kurzweil is not a common name, it is not altogether rare in Europe, so it is quite possible that many Kurzweils are not related (though I must add that I am beginning to doubt that since I continue to discover more originally unknown cousins all the time). I wrote Dov back, thanking him for his letter but adding that there appeared to be no relation.

Months later a letter arrived from a man in California, also a Kurzweil. He responded to one of my many inquiries to Kurzweils around the country and the world. Again, as I read his letter, it became clear that he was

not related. His letter, however, was quite enthusiastic, and he indicated that he would love to hear from me and share information regardless of whether or not we were cousins. He said this because I told him in my letter that I had collected a mass of material on Kurzweil families around the world. One comment in his letter was odd. Near the end he wrote, "My father was an atheist, but I always assumed that we were Protestant."

As I reread his letter, I had the feeling that some of the details he provided were familiar. Though it was obvious that his family and mine were unrelated—at least for the past several generations—I was sure I knew some of what he had written. Then I remembered: the information he gave and the information given by the Kurzweil in Israel matched! They were not related to me, but they were related to each other. I wrote him back, explaining this to him, and adding that it appeared that his family was originally Jewish.

After several years of research on one of the many branches of my father's family, I realized that I had made a mistake: I had neglected my mother's branches. In large part, it was the fact that my last name is Kurzweil, which subconsciously made me think that I was more a Kurzweil than a Gottlieb, which is my mother's maiden name. For that matter, I was equally an Ennis, which is my father's mother's maiden name. I am also just as much a Klein, a Loventhal, a Roth, a Grünberger, a Rosenwasser, and countless other names as well. The fact that we generally take the name of our father, added to the stronger family ties in my father's family, resulted in my becoming singularly obsessed with the Kurzweil family for, as I said, seven years.

There were some worthwhile results of this obsession, however. I would never have gotten as far as I did had I spread myself thinly over a few families. On the other hand, the worst enemy of the genealogist is time, and I am yet to learn, I am sure, of people in other branches who have recently died and who would have told me much had I begun earlier. The results of my Kurzweil research are dramatic: I have a nearly complete genealogy of my great-great-great-grandparents and all of their descendants—over six hundred of them! I have dozens of early photographs of the family, countless stories about individuals, and a wealth of information about the history of my ancestors. The one thing I did not forget to do is to obey a cardinal rule of family history research: *share your findings*.

I deeply wanted to let everyone know what I had found. I wanted children in the family to be able to look at our family tree and see who their ancestors were. The family tree included seven generations, and it would be important for family members to be able to glance at the tree and see their ancestors as well as to understand how large the family was and the

paths its various members had traveled. Another important part of my research, which I felt especially bound to share, was my Holocaust findings. More than one hundred members of the Kurzweil family were killed in the Holocaust. I collected their names, their relationships to the rest of the family, their ages, and in many cases their specific fates. There are no graves for these cousins of mine, no memorials. My family tree was their memorial. I wanted the family to know them and to remember them.

I decided to write a book. It would be a modest undertaking, privately printed as inexpensively as possible, which I would distribute to the family. It took me two years to finish the book, and it finally came to 140 pages, complete with all seven generations of the family, pages of photographs, history of the family, and an index so that anyone could easily find oneself (or others) on the tree. The book was a labor of love and a grand success. Kurzweils from all over the world asked for copies. More than one hundred copies are on bookshelves in the homes of Kurzweils that I know. While I was putting the book together, I became, once again, somewhat obsessed with it. I worked on it every spare moment at a frantic pace. I loved doing it, and the result is this: I now know that as long as those books exist, future generations of my family will know where they came from. They will know what tradition brought them to the point at which they are. They will know the names of the people who struggled to live and to bring up children. They will also know of those ancestors who were murdered by the Nazis. Most of all, they will know more about themselves.

After I printed the family books, I helped organize a party. To that party, which was a celebration of Hanukkah, I invited everyone whom I had contacted during the years of my research. On the day of the party, more than one hundred people came to celebrate. It was the largest gathering of Kurzweils—perhaps ever. Great-great-grandchildren of the same people saw each other for the first time. Friendships were made. Others were renewed (some people hadn't seen each other for forty years). It was everything that a family reunion should be. Most important, it provided us with the opportunity to understand firsthand what the Talmudic passage means when it says that if a human life is killed, it is as if a world has been killed, and if a human life is saved, it is as if a whole world has been saved. Each of us at that party were cousins, descended from the same two people. Had my great-great-great-grandparents not lived to marry and have children, none of us would have been there.

For several years, as I said, I neglected the history of my mother's family. My mother listened patiently to the unfolding story of my father's family, never expressing confusion over my apparent lack of interest in her history. In part, there was an obvious difference between families. My

father was born in Europe and remembered a significant amount for an immigrant who arrived here at age eight; however, my mother was born in New York and knew almost nothing about her European background. She had never met her father's parents and had met her mother's parents only briefly. She had very little to say when I asked her about the history of either side of her family.

In addition, her family was small. Whereas my father's family—both sides, in fact—had large family circles (family organizations with regular meetings, a cemetery plot, and a history), my mother hardly knew more than her immediate family. At a superficial glance, her family seemed not to have had much of a history that could be discovered. There were no older members of the family in America alive to speak about the family. Generally, my mother could understand quite well why I did not pursue her family and its history.

One final factor was that my mother's family was significantly different from my father's in terms of Jewishness. My mother's father arrived in the United States by himself as a teenager and adapted to the American way of life rather quickly. Although he retained an internal sense of himself as a Jew, he was mostly assimilated. My mother's mother also arrived in this country at a young age, with her sister, and she too assimilated quickly. My mother, however, grew up in a different kind of home from my father's. His was the home of Orthodox immigrants. Hers was the home of somewhat assimilated Jews.

Despite all of this, I had the desire to learn about my mother's family, and so I decided to begin. When I asked my mother who would be the best source, she instantly said that her cousin Maurice Gottlieb would be the person to see. Maurice, her first cousin (he has since died), was an intelligent, quick-witted, gentle man who was born in Europe and who my mother thought would remember some things. Although he lived in New York, I decided to write to him. Many people find it easier to talk than to write, but I knew that Maurice had once wanted to be a writer. I always try to get people to write about their history. Their letters become documents to save forever.

Maurice wrote back a lovely letter detailing what he knew about the family and its history. He named the towns in Europe where the family originated and the people who made up the family tree. He mentioned some occupations and a few other details. The most surprising item was that his grandfather—who was my great-grandfather—was a rabbi. I was shocked. Could it be that my grandfather, the assimilated American, was the son of a rabbi? On closer reading, I understood that although the man was a rabbi, he worked, at times, as a slaughterer (a *shochet*) and that he did not func-

Zalman Leib Gottlieb, the author's maternal grandfather.

tion in the way that I know American congregational rabbis to function. He had received *smichah* (was ordained) but did not have a congregation. It was fairly common for a man to have *smichah*. Nevertheless, it was startling to learn that this branch of my family was so religious.

I telephoned my mother and asked her if she knew that her own grandfather was a rabbi. She admitted that she recalled that her father told her this but that she never believed him. It just didn't seem likely.

Also in the letter from Maurice was the fact that the family name was not Gottlieb but had been changed from the original Rosenvasser. This interested my mother. Imagine spending your life thinking that your name is your own, only to find out that it was originally something entirely different—Rosenvasser!

Weeks passed and I did little more to pursue the history of my mother's father's family. The discovery that the family name was Rosenvasser and not Gottlieb became something of a family joke. My father began to call

Helen Klein, the author's maternal grandmother.

my mother Miss Rosenvasser, and I too made reference to the name on many occasions—perhaps to the point of being obnoxious. I checked the name Rosenvasser in several Jewish encyclopedias but found nothing. I looked through a few New York phone books and found the name spelled two different ways: Rosenvasser and Rosenwasser. Despite this, I did not call these people or write to them. What would I say: "My family name used to be Rosenvasser, and I wonder if we are related"? I did do this in my Kurzweil research, but at the time I did so, I had more information to offer. Usually when I call or get a call from someone named Kurzweil, I immediately know how the person is related after he tells me the name of his grandparents. But I had far too little to go on to begin to make telephone inquiries in this case. In addition, the news that our name was Rosenvasser was still too recent a discovery for me to fully believe it.

After a while it happened that my grandparents (my mother's parents) moved out of their apartment, which they had lived in for several decades,

and went to live with my parents. My grandparents were in their mid-eighties and had been held up at gunpoint; that signaled it was time to go. Their move was an opportunity for me to find things in their apartment that might give me additional leads concerning their family history. Both of my grandparents had denied for years that they had any photographs, letters, or anything that would help me in my search. They both told me their parents' names and that was all. They claimed that there was nothing else to know.

I was far from convinced. It is impossible to save *nothing* of family interest during a lifetime of more than eighty years. When my mother and I went to their apartment on Dyckman Street in upper Manhattan to put things in boxes and pack up the place, my belief was confirmed. Not only was it untrue that my grandparents had saved nothing, but the drawers, closets, and hidden compartments of their apartment were a virtual museum of family history. I found a box of photographs, some dating back to the early 1900s in Europe. I found a large bundle of letters received by both of my grandparents from their families in Europe who had stayed and were killed in the Holocaust. I found nearly every birthday card that my grandmother had ever received. I found scraps of paper with the names and birthdates of all of my grandmother's brothers and sisters, some of whom I would never have discovered had it not been for these papers. I found receipts for tickets on transatlantic steamships. I found copies of letters of inquiry regarding Holocaust victims in my family. I found old bills of European currency, now valueless save as souvenirs. And I found two framed pictures, each containing the images of married couples: one my grandmother's parents and the other my grandfather's parents.

I showed the photos to my mother immediately. "Of course," she said, "I haven't seen them for years. Those are my grandparents."

The contrast between the two couples was, as they say, like night and day. My grandmother's parents appeared to be a fairly modern, well-dressed, cosmopolitan couple. Her father was wearing a three-piece suit, cufflinks on the shirt, a ring on his finger, and pince-nez glasses. His wife wore a fancy dress, her hair appeared to be styled, and she wore a large brooch on her dress. They posed for the picture standing against each other, and the photo was taken indoors, a flowing curtain appearing in the background.

I am describing the picture in detail to stress the contrast between it and the photo of my grandfather's parents. His mother wore a peasant dress and a kerchief around her head. No hair was visible. His father wore a long black coat from neck to foot and a broad-brimmed hat. He had a long white beard and side-curls of a few inches. They posed for the

Morton Klein and Hannah Grünberger, the author's maternal great-grandparents, Presov, Slovakia.

picture outside, an old fence in the background. They were both sitting down, at least a foot apart.

I was fascinated by the contrast between these two couples whose children married each other several thousand miles away from where these photographs were taken, but my attention quickly was drawn to my grandfather's parents, who were obviously Hasidic. His father was the rabbi, the shochet! I could not take my eyes off the photograph. I stood staring into my great-grandfather's eyes, which stared back at me. I looked at his side-curls, his long coat, his hands folded gently on his lap, and I wondered who this man was. I was his great-grandson, and yet the dis-

Asher Yeshaya Gottlieb and Blima Roth, the author's maternal great-grandparents.

tance between us, not only in miles and years but also in ways of life, was startling. My own great-grandfather was a Hasid! If not for this photograph, I might have never known.

It was shocking that I had never been told about this. It was always my belief that my father's family was the religious side of the family, but here before me was the proof that just a few generations ago, my great-grandfather was a Hasidic man. The progression of history began to come clear. My grandfather, as a teenager, left Europe and his family and traveled to America, land of opportunity. He cut his side-curls, said goodbye to his rural Hasidic community, and went in search of a "better" life. Upon arrival in America, he discovered a different world and rapidly became a part of it. I have to admit that this used to trouble me. My Jewish involvement has over the years become more and more traditional, and it has been in many ways an uphill battle for me. I was not raised in a traditional home, and this was partly because of my family history: my mother's parents were not traditional, and this affected my upbringing. Had my grandparents been, I too might have had a different kind of life. But this feeling was dramatically resolved when I brought the newly

discovered photograph of my great-grandparents to their son—my grand-father. I also showed my grandfather another photograph I had found of him as a young man. In it, he was dressed in a modern suit with spats, sported a stylish hat, and was holding a cane!

The sight of both pictures excited my grandfather. He repeated over and over that those were his parents, and he also enjoyed seeing the picture of himself as a young man. He then told me that the picture of him was taken in Europe. I was confused because I knew that he had come to America as a teenager, and this was a later picture. He told me that he went back to visit his parents twenty years after he had left them. It was an incredible thing to imagine. Here was a picture of a fully American-ized man, the son of a Hasid, returning to see his parents and family. One could just imagine the scene when he arrived in town looking the way he did, compared to the way his father looked. And I was right! My grand-father told me that his own father was upset by how his son had changed. His father wanted him to stay there and not to return to America, the country that made him leave the old ways. My grandfather refused, of course, and returned to America. The rest of the story is obvious. Had my grandfather stayed and returned to the religious ways of his family, he would have shared their fate—the death camps. Yet he returned and con-tinued to assimilate, and I, his grandson, was born years later. *And today I connect once again with the tradition of my great-grandfather, through my family history research.*

I remembered that the letter from my mother's cousin, Maurice, who had originally written to me telling me about the family and what towns we had come from, also contained his regret that he could not find a pic-ture of his grandparents. Now that I had found one, I wanted to call him and share with him what I had found. I arranged to visit with him and show him the photograph. I also hoped to get more information from him. I suspected that he knew much more than he wrote in his letter. When I arrived at his home, it quickly became apparent that Maurice knew quite a bit about the family history. He identified many photographs for me, told me stories about members of the family, and taught me a lot. But one item, which he mentioned to me in passing, was the clue that became the key to centuries of family history. Maurice told me that as a child, he was scolded for playing a childhood prank. The way in which he was scolded was memorable, because he was told, "That's no way to behave, especially since you are an *ainicle* of the Stropkover Rebbe." At the time I did not know that the term *ainicle*, which generally means "grandson," actually means "descendant" in that context. In any case, my genealogical ears perked up, and I knew that I had hit upon a major find.

That night was somewhat sleepless for me. I couldn't wait to go to the library the next day and find out about "the Stropkover Rebbe." If my mother's first cousin was his descendant, then I was too, and it would be an important and meaningful discovery for me. The following morning I went to YIVO, the Institute for Jewish Research in Manhattan, and began to search for anything I could find about the Stropkover Rebbe.

YIVO, the finest archives and library of Eastern European Jewish material in the world, had a book with biographical material on Hasidic rebbes, indexed by town. It was just what I needed. I looked up Stropkov and found that there were several rebbes who were known to have been connected with the town at one time or another. I struggled with each entry written in Hebrew, and one by one I rejected each as possible ancestors. When I finally got to the last entry, I was startled to see the name of Chaim Joseph Gottlieb. My mother's name was Gottlieb. He must be my ancestor! I was terribly excited for about one minute until I remembered that Maurice wrote me that the name of our family was not originally Gottlieb but Rosenvasser. Suddenly I was afraid that this was not my ancestor at all but that we had simply taken his name because of his reputation as a rebbe. I knew that people named children after their teachers, and perhaps this was a similar case.

Still, there was something within me that said that he was my direct ancestor. I had a feeling about it and knew that eventually I would understand how the name Rosenvasser came into the picture. It seemed likely that Chaim Joseph Gottlieb was an ancestor because the names matched and because it also confirmed Maurice's story about being scolded as a child.

What I found myself doing from that point on was breaking just about every genealogical rule in the book, especially the following two: never make claims that you aren't sure of, and do research from the known to the unknown. You start with what you know and see how far back you can go, step by step. You should move backward, one generation at a time. This rule is to discourage people from picking out a famous individual from history and trying to make a connection. It has been shown often enough that people who set out to prove that they descend from an illustrious figure do it—regardless of how accurate their findings are. In other words, it is not respectable genealogy research to pick King David and then try to establish descent from him. Yet except for the fact that I had some good clues to go on, I was doing just that. It is not advisable methodology.

The other rule that I broke was telling everybody I knew that I was a descendant of the Stropkover Rebbe, Chaim Joseph Gottlieb. At the time

it was just circumstantial evidence, but it was such an exciting possibility to be a descendant of a Hasidic rebbe that I couldn't help it. The only good part about it was that it pressured me to get to work immediately and to find out the truth.

The short biography of the rebbe that I found included the fact that he wrote a book called *Teev Gitten v'Kiddushin*. YIVO did not have the book, but the New York Public Library Jewish Division did, so I went to examine it. I was amazed to see that the book contained a brief genealogy including the names of the rebbe's grandfather (which would take me back to the 1600s!) and the rebbe's sons, one of whom was named Usher. My great-grandfather was named Usher, and for a minute I thought I had solved the whole problem until I realized that the dates were wrong. There would have to be at least one generation between the rebbe's sons and my great-grandfather. I still hadn't established a link. It occurred to me that my great-grandfather, Usher, might have been named after the rebbe's son Usher, but it was still speculation.

After examining the rebbe's book in the library, I wondered if there were any disciples of his alive and in New York. I discussed the question with a librarian in the Jewish Division, and when she noticed that the "approbation" (seal of approval) for the book was written by Chaim Halberstamm, the Sanzer Rebbe, who was a contemporary of Chaim Joseph Gottlieb and whose descendants live in New York, she suggested that I contact them. I made a few phone calls, but no one seemed able to help me. A few days later, a Jewish newspaper in New York, *The Jewish Week*, called me for an interview. I was going to be interviewed on radio station WEVD the following week to talk about some of my genealogy research, and the newspaper wanted to make a feature story out of it. In the interview, I mentioned my belief that I was a descendant of the Stropkover Rebbe, well aware of the fact that it was still speculation. The newspaper ran the story, and it was the best thing that could have happened at the time.

In response to the article, I began to get phone calls from people who also claimed descent from the rebbe. The first call, in fact, was from someone whose name sounded familiar. I recalled that my mother's cousin, Maurice, had suggested I call him for more information about the family. I never did, although I did file his name and number away for future use. It is significant that I mention this because although it is true that my interview with the newspaper offered me an opportunity that few people get, it is equally true that had I followed the advice of my mother's cousin, I would have discovered the same thing. It is important to track down the most obscure leads because they might very well bring you to a pot of genealogical gold.

The man told me that he too was a descendant of the Stropkover Rebbe, and we proceeded to compare notes. Within a few minutes the man realized that he knew who I was and that we were definitely related. He knew my mother and her brother and her parents from years ago. When I asked him how we were related, he said, "We're cousins," but he knew little more than that. It was an answer I had learned to expect. So many times in my research I had encountered people who were sure we were related, but knew nothing more than that. Although he wasn't able to provide any more information about our relationship, just the fact that he felt we were related and that he also knew he was a descendant of the Stropkover Rebbe permitted me to be more at ease about my claim of descent. But of course, I was not satisfied and wouldn't be until I was able to document my relationship to Chaim Joseph Gottlieb with names and dates and carefully spell out each generation between us.

What the man on the phone was able to do, however, was give me the name of another man who might be able to help. His last name was also Gottlieb, and he was a cantor. I called him and was spared the need to make introductions, as he had heard me on the radio the night before. He asked me to hold the wire and came back a minute later with a copy of the rebbe's book, a more recent edition. It was a reprint of the original with an added preface that was a biography of the rebbe! On the phone I told the man everything I knew about my family, including all the names I knew, but he was unable to match me up with the genealogical information provided in the biography. I was disappointed but not discouraged. A final piece of information that he told me was that the man who wrote the biography lived in Brooklyn. He gave me the man's phone number.

The biographer's name was Rabbi Israel, and when I called him, he was nice enough to suggest that we meet to pursue the question. He also told me where I could get a copy of this book. The next morning I went to Williamsburg to purchase the book from the source suggested by Rabbi Israel.

It was the first time I had ever gone to Williamsburg. I have been a New Yorker all my life, however, I was always a bit afraid to go there. I had heard too many stories about the Hasidim in Williamsburg not liking outsiders. I felt hostile toward them, wondering why they thought they had the right to look down on other Jews who were not like them. But my experience that first time was just the opposite. I found the people on the street and in the shops to be quite friendly, and I realized that I had only heard the sensational stories. I liked everyone I met.

When I arrived at the address given to me by Rabbi Israel, a young girl answered the door and asked me to wait a minute. She returned soon

afterward and brought me down the street to a grocery store and a young man who appeared to be her brother. They spoke in Yiddish for a few seconds, after which she left. The young man, who appeared to be about my age, was dressed in traditional Hasidic street clothes with an apron for working. He brought me down the block to a storage room. It was there that the books were kept. He looked for a clear copy, brushed off the dust, and sold it to me. Together we walked back to his store. Before we said goodbye, I asked him why it was that he had these books to sell. He told me that his father printed them. I asked him why his father printed them. He answered me by saying that he was "an *ainicle* of the Stropkover Rebbe." He used the very same words that my mother's cousin Maurice had used when I first began this journey.

It then dawned on me that I was standing in Hasidic Williamsburg with a young man, a Satmar Hasid I later found out, who was a cousin of mine. He and I both were descendants of the same Hasidic Rebbe (assuming that my belief was correct). To be honest, I must admit that I did not tell him I was also a descendant of the rebbe. I was afraid that he would wonder why I was obviously not a Hasid. In some ways, I wondered myself—though I knew. Yet it was startling to see how strange fate is. There we were, both of us the same age, both of us stemming from the same family tree, and yet we were in two different worlds. His line took him to Williamsburg, and mine took me elsewhere. It was confusing and fascinating.

It was then that I remembered from one of the many conversations I had had, that there was a Gottlieb's restaurant in Brooklyn and that the owners of this restaurant were descendants of the same rebbe. I located the address and decided to go there for lunch. The owner of the restaurant wasn't there, but his son-in-law was, and we had a conversation, briefly, about the rebbe. Yes, he said, it was true that they were from that family, and the owner would be back the next day. I was disappointed, but I was also excited by my new possession—the book by the rebbe and the biography within it. I called Rabbi Israel, the biographer, and made an appointment for Sunday, just a few days away.

Those next few days were a blur to me. I was so preoccupied by the whole experience that I couldn't think about anything else. I simply counted the hours until I could see Rabbi Israel, who would surely be able to link my branch of the family with the rebbe. Finally, Sunday came, and I went to Rabbi Israel's home. The rabbi was a pleasant and kind gentleman who made me feel quite at home. He asked me if we could speak in Yiddish, and I was sorry to have to tell him that I could not. He took me down to his basement where his library was, and we discussed my family. Again I repeated everything I knew, but nothing

seemed to match. Again the name Usher was the same, but the dates were obviously wrong. I felt I had reached a dead end. It appeared that with all of the circumstantial evidence I had gathered, it was nothing more than that. If the rabbi who wrote the biography of the rebbe could not help me, then who could? I began to feel I was wrong from the beginning: I shouldn't have made any claims, even to myself, without knowing for sure. Now it seemed as if there was nothing more to do but go back to thinking that my mother's family was a small one, that they may have known the rebbe's family in Europe and may have even taken his name, but other than that there was no relationship. I would have to be satisfied with the truth and with a genealogy that went back no further than my great-grandfather.

I looked dejectedly at Rabbi Israel but continued a general conversation about my research. He too had the hobby of genealogy, and he showed me some of the material he had collected on Hasidic families. Since he was showing his collection, I decided to show him what I had brought with me. I gathered whatever I had concerning the Gottlieb family and showed him pictures and other documents. One piece of paper in particular interested him. It was a piece of stationery with a letterhead that read "Bistritz and Vicinity Aid Society." It also had my grandfather's name on it listed as financial secretary. I had found the stationery in my grandparents' apartment.

Rabbi Israel looked at it and told me that there was a man in the neighborhood who was from Bistritz. He was known as the Bistritzer Rebbe. Rabbi Israel suggested that he might be able to help me. Handing me his phone, Rabbi Israel looked up the rebbe's phone number and told me to call him. Thinking back on that morning, I'm glad I was forced into it. I doubt very much that I'd have had the courage to call a rebbe by myself. It's just not something that I'm accustomed to doing. When I dialed the number from Rabbi Israel's home, a man answered the phone. He asked me if I could speak Hungarian, and I said no. I asked him if he could speak English, and he said, "A little." I told him that I was a grandson of Zalman Lieb Gottlieb from Bistritz, and I asked him if he might have known him. He told me that he knew Pinchas Gottlieb. Pinchas was a brother of my grandfather, and I was excited to hear that I was speaking to a man, a rebbe, who knew a great-uncle of mine. I also knew that Pinchas had been killed in the Holocaust.

The rebbe asked me to come to his address, which was just a few blocks from where Rabbi Israel lived. I quickly left Rabbi Israel after thanking him for his help. I was disappointed by what had happened, but I was distracted by my imminent visit with a rebbe.

When I arrived at the address, I was surprised to be at a synagogue. I expected an apartment or a house, but there I was, standing at the steps of a synagogue with a sign in Yiddish announcing it to be the Bistritzer synagogue. The rebbe came to the door and asked me to come in.

At that moment, what I entered was not just another synagogue run by another rabbi but a different world from the one I had known. The shul was a room, a square room, crowded by benches and long tables with books spread on them. The room was dimly lit, *tallisim* hung in several spots around the place, and I stood there for a few moments taking it all in. It was unlike anything I had ever seen, except in photographs of shtiebels in Europe. And then I knew that I was in a shtiebel, just like the ones my ancestors prayed in, and the fact that this one was in Brooklyn and that my ancestors were in Europe made no difference once the door was closed. The rebbe was an elderly man, bearded, of course, and slightly bent from age. Yet he was very quick, and his eyes were bright. His countenance was serious, but friendliness came through. He asked me to sit down, and I did, at one of the long benches in front of one of the long tables. The rebbe said he would be back in a moment. I examined the room from every angle, imagining the activity that must occur each day at prayer times and each Shabbas. What was then a silent room must burst with religious energy, the same kind that my great-grandfather, with his long coat, wide-brimmed hat, and beard with side-curls must have had just three generations ago. I was truly in another world and was delighted by this opportunity.

The rebbe returned, and we spoke briefly about my family. He knew my grandfather's brother and also knew that he had been killed in a death camp. He told me they had studied together. After he had run out of things to tell me, in his broken English, about my family in Europe, I decided to tell him the story of my search for a connection with Chaim Joseph Gottlieb, the Stropkover Rebbe. I told him every detail, like a fool, as if he cared. But he listened with intense interest, asking questions along the way. I concluded by saying that Rabbi Israel had been unable to help me, and I wondered if he remembered whether my family descended from the rebbe.

One of the most intriguing aspects of this whole encounter was the seriousness with which he took what I was saying. He communicated to me, by his questions and his comments, that what I was doing was very important. He never explained why, but he continued to indicate this to me. I, on the other hand, wondered if I was taking up too much of his time by talking to him about what I thought must be dead ends. He never once seemed impatient, however; on the contrary, he seemed eager to spend as much time as I wanted in discussing the matter.

Handwritten genealogy found in the front cover of the Bible belonging to the author's grandfather.

One of the additional pieces of information I had discovered along the way was that my great-grandfather's father was named Shlomo. I knew this from the inside cover of my grandfather's Bible, where many years ago he wrote brief genealogies of his mother and father. Rabbi Israel was unable to use this additional name for my purposes, but the rebbe seemed interested. He looked through the biography of the Stropkover Rebbe that Rabbi Israel had written, and while flipping through the pages, he kept repeating "Usher ben Shlomo, Usher ben Shlomo, Usher ben Shlomo." The rebbe just repeated those names, the names of my great-grandfather and his father, over and over to himself as he looked through the biography. It was obvious that he was looking for the names, but I was sure he would not find them there. A few times while he was examining and reading the biography, a phone in a back room rang. The rebbe was so involved in the biography that it was not until the fifth or sixth ring that he stood up and walked to the back to answer it. Each time the phone rang, the rebbe took too much time to answer it, and it stopped before he got there. When he returned to look through the biography again, he seemed happy that he didn't have to talk on the phone so that he could get back to his reading.

In the meantime I just sat there, watching the rebbe continue to read the book and repeat the names, "Usher ben Shlomo, Usher ben Shlomo." I sat there staring and looking around the room. My imagination was active during those minutes, wondering what it was like when the room was filled with praying Hasidim. Suddenly, the rebbe spotted something on a page. He brought it to the window, since the light in the room was rather poor. He then came back and sat down and said, "Shlomo was the son of the rebbe."

I didn't know what to do. I knew that he was wrong; Rabbi Israel had told me each of the names of the rebbe's sons. But I was not comfortable telling this rebbe that he was incorrect. Somehow it just didn't seem right to contradict a rebbe. I decided to say "Really?" in a confused and somewhat doubting voice.

He looked again and said, "No, no, no, no, no." He shook his head in apparent disappointment in himself and sat in silence for a few minutes staring at the book. He then looked up and told me that where he was from it was a custom to take a mother's last name rather than a father's. In fact, he said, this was so in almost 50 percent of the cases in his community in Europe. Then he said, "The Rebbe Gottlieb had a daughter Gittel. Her husband was Shlomo Zalke." He paused and then said in a deep, confident tone, as if he were making a proclamation, "This is your Shlomo. You come from them and take her last name. This is my opinion."

His remarks sounded final, and he ushered me to the door. There was something unreal about the whole thing, especially the way it ended, but the rebbe seemed absolutely convinced that his opinion was right. When I left, I looked at the biography and reread where it said that the rebbe's son-in-law was named Shlomo Zalke, not just Shlomo. For some reason, the name Zalke sounded familiar. I rushed home and looked again at the genealogy written by my grandfather in his Bible. There it was. He did not just write the name Shlomo, but Shlomo Zalke! I had forgotten about this! It was now obvious. And it was obvious that I was, in fact, a descendant of the Stropkover Rebbe. Everything matched: the names, the dates, and even the story about the name not originally being Gottlieb. We had taken the name of the rebbe's daughter rather than his son-in-law. I had finally found the link.

The rebbe in Brooklyn was able to solve the entire issue for me. The fact that my great-great-grandfather, Shlomo Zalke Rosenwasser, took the name of his wife, Gittel Gottlieb, explains the fact that Maurice was told the name was not originally Gottlieb. I couldn't wait to call my mother and share the news with her. When I did she was delighted to hear all of my stories. My father, whose family I had researched for seven years, stood by with a smile on his face as I detailed the generations of my mother's family back farther than I was ever able to get with the Kurzweil family.

In response to the article in the newspaper, *The Jewish Week*, which ran the story about my research, I also received a letter from a delightful woman whose husband is a descendant of the Stropkover Rebbe. This makes us cousins, of course. Her name is Michele Zoltan, and we established a nice friendship based on our mutual interest in the history of this

family. Michele offered to translate the biography of the Stropkover Rebbe for me from the Hebrew. The first chapter was extraordinary.

The chapter speaks about the rebbe and his lineage and indicates that his mother was a descendant of Rabbi Isaiah Horowitz, a renowned rabbi of the 1500s and early 1600s. After doing a little bit of checking, I was able to trace Rabbi Horowitz's family back several generations to the 1400s. In other words, I am a descendant of Rabbi Isaiah Horowitz (known as "the Holy Shela'h"), and consequently I am a descendant of his ancestors as well.

My discovery that I am a member of this rabbinic family and a direct descendant of the Holy Shela'h was one of the most eye-opening moments in my entire search. The Shela'h, by the way, claimed to be a descendant of King David, thereby making me a direct descendant of King David as well. Whenever I think of this, my reaction is a mixture of pride as well as responsibility for me to try to live up to such a special past.

I also discovered that there is a yeshiva in Jerusalem named after Chaim Joseph Gottlieb, the Stropkover Rebbe, and that it is run by some of his other descendants. I was fortunate enough to schedule a trip to Israel in order to visit the yeshiva and its leaders. I cautiously walked into the yeshiva's modest building in the Mea Shearim section of Jerusalem, and as I crossed the threshold, I entered a new world—or perhaps I should say, an old world. There were lines of tables and benches with adult students sitting before open volumes studying the wisdom of sages. It looked like film footage from an era gone by, but I quickly learned that this scene is not unusual at all. It was just that I descended from a branch of my family that left the traditional Jewish way of life, so it is not surprising that it was foreign to me. I didn't know it at the time, but my discovery of being descended from the Stropkover Rebbe and my visit to this yeshiva was another step in my personal quest to find my place in the Jewish religious tradition.

I also discovered that a group in Borough Park, Brooklyn, also descendants of the Stropkover Rebbe, meet once a year on the occasion of the anniversary of the death of the Stropkover Rebbe. The gathering is both a fundraiser for the Jerusalem yeshiva as well as an opportunity for the descendants of the Stropkover Rebbe to come together to renew family ties. I have attended this event on occasion and have gotten to know a branch of my family that just a short time ago I didn't even know existed. These cousins, many of them Hasidim and many devoted to a *ric,* a traditional Jewish way of life, have opened their hearts and lives to me in a most generous way. At one of the annual gatherings, they even honored me. It was heartwarming to know that they recognized the long journey that I have been taking.

Recently, I have learned from a reliable source within the Hasidic community that my great-great-grandfather, Rabbi Shlomo Zalke Rosenwasser, is a direct descendant of Rabbi Moshe Isserles of Krakow, the illustrious rabbi whose Ashkenazic commentary on the Code of Jewish Law is the basis of Jewish practices throughout the world. All three of my children have learned about him in their yeshivas (he is known as "the Rema," an acronym of his name). His family descends from Rashi, the great commentator on the Bible and Talmud, who is in turn a descendant of Dovid HaMelech, King David! It is likely that I am, once again, a direct descendant of both Rashi and King David himself!

From the tiny, assimilated family of my mother, I am now able to document descent back through some of the most illustrious rabbis of the past several centuries to the 1500s and then back to approximately 1000, when Rashi was born. Rashi claimed descent from Hillel in the Talmud, and Hillel is said to descend from King David.

After having celebrated at some length the discoveries that I have made about my ancestors, I feel compelled to remind all of us that the Talmud warns: "A learned bastard takes precedence over an ignorant High Priest." In other words, illustrious ancestors are meaningless if we, ourselves, are not learned and worthy on our own. The crucial question that arises when genealogical discoveries are made is this: What do we do with the knowledge of who our ancestors were?

I find that learning about my family history draws me deeper and deeper into Jewish tradition. The more I learn about my ancestors, the more I learn about Jewish history and therefore Jewish learning. The more facts I have about the lives of my ancestors, the more I learn to respect them and feel grateful to them for their decisions. It matters little, on one level, whether they were religious or not. I respect them for surviving as Jews and for being able to live and raise children, who eventually raised me. I learn much about courage when I understand what it was like to make the decision to journey to America. I continue to learn about faith and belief as I discover the obstacles set before my ancestors in Jewish history.

A special kind of awe comes over me when I learn about an ancestor of mine such as Rabbi Isaiah Horowitz, who lived around 1600. Here was a man whose life and works are still admired today for their greatness. The energy and power that this man had can be described by comparing it to ripples in water: a small force pushed into a body of water will create small ripples that will last a few seconds. The more powerful the force, the greater the ripples and the longer the duration of the vibrations. Such a powerful force was this direct ancestor of mine. There is no question in

my mind that he was largely responsible for the religiosity of his descendants. As I examine those descendants, I can see how devoted they were to learning and Torah, and like strong ripples in water, he was one of the forces behind them. So powerful were the vibrations he sent that they began to reach me in the 1970s. His message traveled a great distance, not only in space but also in time. His influence has spread for nearly four hundred years.

I certainly do not claim to lead a life on a par with his, but I am influenced by him. Just the fact that I am able to document my descent from him indicates how powerful an influence he has been. As I make this kind of discovery about an ancestor, I am forced (delightedly so) to encounter his life and teachings and to learn from them. This is the purpose of family history within the Jewish tradition. It is not to make boastful claims about ancestors. It is not to take credit for the achievements of others, nor is it to take responsibility for the actions of others. But it is to continue to receive a message, first given at Mount Sinai and still transmitted today. The message of Sinai is handed down through generations, and as a famous Midrash says, the Torah is given at Sinai every moment if we will only listen for it and hear it. My family history helps me connect with that event and with the history of the Jewish people. In this way, I celebrate my ancestors and the lives they led.

2

GETTING STARTED

HOW TO BEGIN YOUR RESEARCH

HISTORY, IN MY OPINION, is usually taught backward. In grade school, I remember that each history class was structured the same way, whether it was world history, American history, or local history: we began as early as possible and worked our way to the present. I generally got lost, and bored, somewhere in the middle.

I think history should be taught from the present back. How did I get to where I am right now? What paths did my family take? World War II? My father fought in that war. World War I? My grandfather fought in that one. 1865? That was when the U.S. Civil War ended and when my great-grandfather (after whom I was named) was born.

The most current event in Jewish history is happening right this moment—with you and me. Surely there are some things happening now that will be remembered in the future, even though your life and mine may be forgotten. But in a real sense, you and I are a part of Jewish history. In the twenty-first century, Jews will look back and see our lives as Jewish history in much the same way that we look back on the lives of our grandparents and great-grandparents as fitting into special chapters of history.

It is in this spirit that I suggest Jewish genealogy be first approached: you are a part of Jewish history, and you must explore the rest of Jewish history by beginning at home with yourself. Jewish genealogy begins at home. Throughout this book, we will discuss the many libraries, Web sites, documents, books, photographs, and other materials that will help make your family history a rich one. Before we can go any further, however, we have to start now, with this very moment.

So we begin with a simple enough question, the answer to which is the key to the entire pursuit of genealogy. The question is this: How did you get to where you are at this very minute? By this I do not mean how did you travel to the spot on which you are sitting or standing but rather what were the circumstances under which you arrived where you are?

Another way to approach this question is by describing a game we often play. Have you ever thought to yourself, "If I never met you, I would never have met . . ." Or "If it weren't for my meeting you by chance, then this and that would not have happened to me?" For example, had I not skipped a grade in elementary school, many of my oldest and closest friends would not be my friends today, and my life in some ways would have been very different!

Every action we take sets off a chain reaction of events that affect the future. I am sure we can all think of dozens of things that would or would not have happened if it were not for something else.

So it is with genealogy and family history.

One of my grandmothers came to America with her older sister when they were fifteen and seventeen, respectively. In other words, two young girls, all by themselves, set off for America on a steamship early in the twentieth century. Had they not been on that ship, I would not exist.

This is a perfect illustration of our "game." Decisions made by our ancestors had significant (even vital) effects on our lives.

Mathematically speaking, each of us has had 1,024 direct ancestors in just the last ten generations. This is not aunts, uncles, or cousins. Just *direct* ancestors (parents, grandparents, great-grandparents, and so on). Again, in just ten generations, we've had 1,024 direct ancestors. We each have two parents, four grandparents, eight great-grandparents, sixteen great-great-grandparents, and so on. If we imagine *any one* of those people—let's say one of our several great-great-great-great-grandmothers— and imagine that she was killed as a child in a pogrom, we would not be here today. If any one of those 1,024 direct ancestors had been killed as a child before being able to marry and have children, we would not be here. Likewise, out of the 512 married couples in the last ten generations in our families, if one person had decided to marry someone else instead, we would not be here.

This illustrates how clearly the decisions and fate of our ancestors affected each of us. Even more dramatic perhaps is the fact that if any one of your ancestors had converted or married outside of Judaism, you might not be here as a Jew reading this book on Jewish genealogy.

Therefore, let's begin your journey into your family history with your-self and repeat the question: How did you get to where you are at this very minute?

To answer this question, you have to begin to explore the recent his-tory of your family. Actually, you have to ask the same question of your parents: How did *they* get to where they were in their lives? And of course, to answer that question, you must ask the question of *their* par-ents, and so on.

First Steps

Even though your research is unique and will therefore follow a different path from every other genealogist, I strongly suggest that you crawl before you walk. Too many beginners jump into a genealogy Web site, for exam-ple, look up their last name, don't find anything after a few minutes, and then conclude that there is nothing for them to find. Beginnings, especially when it comes to research, are important. Don't underestimate them.

1. *Where do I start? I've always wanted to trace my family but I don't know how to begin.*

Since everyone has a different family, there is no perfect system for every family historian. There is no chart for all families to use by filling in the blanks, since we each have different-sized families. There is no step-by-step order to your research, since each of us will find different prob-lems and successes when climbing our family trees.

The Kurzweil Family Circle, a cousins club in New York, ca. 1950.

There is a place where each of us can begin, however, and that is with ourselves. Get a big loose-leaf notebook to use exclusively for your family history. Eventually, you will probably be using your computer to record information, create charts, and organize your family history, but at the very beginning, I suggest you get used to using an old-fashioned loose-leaf notebook or ring binder. Begin by writing down everything you know. Your name. Your parents' names. Their parents (your grandparents). Aunts, uncles, cousins. Dates of birth, marriage, death. Places. In other words, take inventory of what you already know. If you know a lot— great! If not, that is why you are beginning your family history research.

2. *How do I keep track of what I write down? Is there a system or format that I should use?*

Some people use computer software specially designed for genealogy record keeping. Some people have devised elaborate coding and filing systems to keep track of their family history notes. Others have made simple and useful systems that serve the same purpose. Don't worry too much about your system at the beginning. Just make sure you *write down everything*. Don't rely on your memory for anything. If something is written down, you will find it. If not, you might lose it forever. Write clearly; the inability to read one's own handwriting is a common problem among researchers. At some point (which may be at the beginning of your research or sometime later), you will want to consider keeping all of your information on your computer (don't forget to back up everything!). But at the beginning, I believe all you need to do is write things down, get some old-fashioned paper notebooks, spread your notes out on a table, and start to piece things together.

Realize that when one does research, it often happens that two pieces of information that are at first unrelated "give birth" to new information. By spreading out your notes and looking at them, you can often see that happen before your eyes.

3. *After I write down everything I know, where do I go from there? Do I just trace one branch of my family, or do I trace all branches at once?*

When you are just beginning, your first priority is talking to relatives. Your first priority among the relatives is the oldest of them. Therefore, you ought to begin by phoning, visiting, or writing (via snail mail or e-mail) the oldest living relatives on *all* branches of your family. Otherwise, you might get very involved with one branch of your family while other branches, quite frankly, are dying off! I would bet that there is not one genealogist who has been able to avoid saying, "If only I had spoken to so-and-so a few years ago."

After you have spoken to your oldest relatives on all sides of the family, you can zero in on one branch.

Remember, the books, archives, and libraries will wait. The people will not. Please take this advice seriously. Mark my word: one day, as you do your Jewish genealogical research, you will regret not having made the opportunity to speak to someone with whom you could have spoken.

4. *Do you mean to say that I must research all branches of my family? What if I am just interested in one particular branch?*

Of course, you can do what you like. But consider two things. First, although you are interested in one branch today, your interest may broaden in the future. By then it may be too late to interview important family members. Second, keep in mind that if you don't become the family historian, chances are that nobody will. You have the opportunity to capture and save your family story. Don't let it disappear.

5. *What's next? After I have interviewed all or most of my relatives, where do I go from there? I'm anxious to trace back as far as I can, and most of my relatives don't remember too far back. Are there books or vital records that I can check to trace back through the generations?*

One of the two great misconceptions held by beginning family historians is that they can quickly go to a reference book and find out all about their family. Of course, the other great misconception is that no records exist and that tracing Jewish families is impossible. Both notions are wrong. There are plenty of excellent and effective sources (as you will learn by reading this book), but if you are just beginning, you are not ready for them *yet*. Be patient. You do not discover your family history overnight. Like any other hobby—stamp collecting, for example—you slowly build on your collection. Watching it grow and then suddenly, months later, seeing that you have really built something to be proud of is what it is all about. As my teacher, Rabbi Adin Steinsaltz, said to me in another context, "Remember, we are planting trees, not vegetables."

The same applies to family trees.

6. *That still doesn't answer the question. What's next?*

Again, there is no system for everyone. This book is not a simple step-by-step guide. Such a guide is not possible. I would suggest that you read through the book and see the *possibilities*. Learn what sources exist. This will give you a better idea of what information you *need*. Tracing your genealogy and family history is always a detective process. Your new discoveries will be based on information you already know. One fact will

lead to another and another. By reading through this book, you will get a good idea of what you need to know in order to discover new information. In fact, it would be a good idea to look over the entire book quickly even before talking to your oldest relatives. In this way you will learn what kinds of questions to ask and what kinds of information you ought to be looking for.

Two Web sites are of such importance that I will discuss them in detail elsewhere. But I do suggest that you begin to familiarize yourself with them. Although they are not part of my "first steps," they will serve to entice you and convince you that you will be successful in your research:

- Avotaynu: Publishers of Works on Jewish Genealogy, at http://www. avotaynu.com. (I would also strongly suggest that you subscribe to *Avotaynu: The International Review of Jewish Genealogy.* In fact, I believe that a subscription to *Avotaynu* is indispensable for every Jewish genealogist.)

- JewishGen: The Home of Jewish Genealogy, at http://www. jewishgen.org. (This site will blow your mind.)

7. *Do you mean to say that from this point on, I'm on my own? Isn't there a checklist of things to do? I feel lost.*

Research isn't easy, but don't be afraid of it. Just get involved. Decide what you'd like to know (with this book helping you to crystallize those ideas), and go after it.

If you really want a next step, I will at least share with you the mistake of *most* beginners: most of us *never* interview enough relatives! We are so eager to "begin the research and the discoveries" that we fail to understand that it is the *people* in your family who can offer you the most information.

So your next step, after contacting your oldest living relatives, is to contact other relatives. *The best leads, the best information, and the best stories I have gathered for my family history have come from relatives.* Although I have discovered a great deal on the Internet, in record books, and in libraries, none of that would have been possible without information provided by people.

I would also strongly suggest that you begin to make contact with the closest Jewish Genealogical Society in your area (see page 129), as well as with the International Association of Jewish Genealogical Societies (IAJGS) at http://www.jewishgen.org/ajgs.

By getting to know others who are also doing Jewish genealogical research, you will learn that there are endless possibilities.

8. *Isn't it true that Jews cannot trace their family histories because of name changes and the destruction of records?*

Not at all! In my own case, I've traced back to the 1500s on one side of my family and the late 1700s on another. In the latter case, I have traced five hundred descendants of my great-great-great-grandparents to places all over the world. On another branch of my family, I have located copies of my great-grandparents' marriage record in Hungary from the mid-1800s that includes information about my great-great-grandparents. I have also located information on 103 members of one branch of my family—all 103 of whom were killed in the Holocaust. I have met relatives from all over the world, I have discovered family connections with the most illustrious rabbinic families in Jewish history, and after more than a quarter of a century of research, there is no end in sight!

Jews *can* trace their genealogies and family histories, and that is what this book is all about. By the way, genealogy has been a part of our tradition ever since the first chapters of Genesis.

9. *Is there any special equipment needed for all of this?*

There will be more detailed discussions of this throughout the book, but I will mention briefly some standard items that will come in handy throughout your search.

○ *A cassette tape recorder, a camcorder, or both.* When you interview family members, record them. How I would love to have a recording of my great-grandfather—but I can't. What I *can* do is provide the same kind of thing for my descendants.

○ *File folders, paper, notebook, and writing implements.* Be generous with these items. The better your note keeping and record keeping are, the better off you'll be when you need to record or find something.

○ *Envelopes, stationery, and postage stamps.* Recognize that our oldest relatives are not always e-mailers. For some of us, e-mail is the easiest means of communication, but for others, the world of computers remains foreign. Family history has always depended heavily on writing letters. Keep a supply of these things at all times so that mailing letters and other requests for information does not get held up because you haven't had a chance to buy envelopes or go to the post office.

○ *Computer hardware and software.* When I began my own family history research, the Internet was but a concept, and the Jewish genealogical riches available online today did not exist. Good computer hardware and software are indispensable now. Please don't misunderstand: you can be a great Jewish family historian by doing nothing more than hearing stories from old relatives and retelling them to peers and younger rela-

tives. But if you want to get involved in serious Jewish genealogical research and join the thousands of Jews who have made extraordinary discoveries about their own family histories, a good computer to use for record keeping, as well as for Internet surfing, is essential. An excellent resource in this and all areas of Jewish genealogical research is the quarterly publication *Avotaynu* (see Chapter 5). This publication regularly reviews the software available for Jewish genealogists; obviously there are pros and cons to each, but the publication's editors and contributors are quite helpful in helping us navigate through what is out there. In particular, over the years, a number of articles written by Gary Mokotoff have been especially useful for beginners. Here are three of them:

> "Computers and Genealogy" (Spring 1990). Written eons ago in cyberspace time, this article contains great wisdom for those of us considering the purchase of hardware and software.
>
> "Internet for Greenhorns" (Fall 1996). An excellent introduction to the Internet for novices.
>
> "Software Review: Ilanot: Jewish Genealogy Software" (Summer 1998)

I also suggest that you read Question 19, "Computers and Genealogy," at JewishGen.org (http://www.jewishgen.org/infofiles/faq.html#Starting). It offers useful advice and recommendations.

10. *Should I aim for any specific goal in my family history? Should I try to go back as far as possible or to find as many living relatives as I can? Where does it end?*

Don't worry about it ending; you're just beginning. As far as your "goal" is concerned, that's up to you. You might want to specialize in one subject— say, what happened to your family during the Holocaust. Or you might want to go as far back as you can on one branch. Tracing your genealogy and family history is open-ended. People often ask me if I have finished my research. No, I haven't. I have been researching my family history for decades, and I have no intention of stopping. It hasn't been a full-time occupation. It's like any other hobby. Sometimes I work on the family history like a madman for a week or two. Other times I neglect it for months at a time. The only difference between it and other hobbies I have had is that this one has affected me in profound ways. I feel a great sense of connection with my family and with Jewish history. And I feel a responsibility to that history to continue as a link on an ancient chain of Jewish tradition.

On the other hand, I could have stopped at any point with the knowledge that I had gathered a lot of material about the history of my family

and that it was now saved from oblivion. It was now a part of the history of my family—a history that would not be forgotten.

As you enter your family history, you will find that it will take you in many directions. You will develop your own special interest within it as you proceed. If you want to trace back as far as you can, go in that direction. If you want to trace living members of your family, do that. If you have other interests within your family history, pursue them.

The most important advice is this: begin now. Don't wait until tomorrow.

Gathering Your History: Collecting Stories

Your family tree is only the bare framework of your family history. Without the stories, legends, and tales of your cousins and ancestors, all you will have is a dry collection of names and dates.

When you interview or correspond with relatives and others, encourage them to tell stories, and be sure to record these stories either by writing them down or by taping them. A cassette tape recorder and a camcorder are two of the finest tools a family historian can have. In future years, when your descendants listen to the family history you have recorded, they will have the priceless experience of seeing or at least hearing the voices you have heard, and they will be able to listen with their own ears to the tales you were told by the many people with whom you have spoken. Imagine what it would be like for you to be able to hear stories told by your great-grandparents. By recording stories yourself, you will be able to offer this precious gift to future generations of your family.

Cassette tape recorders are small enough and silent enough to be inconspicuous. They rarely inhibit the person whom you are recording. Even a camcorder is forgotten about when set on a tripod. A few years back, my oldest daughter, Malya, spent a week with her grandparents and recorded hours of tapes of my father recalling his World War II memories as a member of the 82nd Airborne Division. He parachuted behind enemy lines just before D-Day. The silent camcorder on its stationary legs was the tool that created a priceless family document.

Nonetheless, for ethical reasons, it is important that you tell people when you are recording them. In addition, you can purchase, for a few dollars, an attachment for your telephone so that you can record phone conversations. But again, you must tell people what you are doing.

The camcorder is also a wonderful tool for the family historian. If your interview subjects are willing, consider using a camcorder to preserve the

Saul Kurzweil, the author's father, on the occasion of his bar mitzvah.

interview. And the ease with which camcorder data can be transferred to your computer only adds to the potential value of the camcorder.

○

The stories I most like to tell are the ones I heard from my grandfather.

—Elie Wiesel, *A Jew Today*

○

Family Legends: Are They True?

In one of the many conversations I have had with Elie Wiesel about my family history research, he said to me, "Are you getting stories?"

I told him I was.

"Are you writing them down?" he asked.

"Yes, I'm writing them all down."

"Very good," Wiesel said. "This is very important. You should collect as many stories as you can. Write them down. Save them. You should have a file. Label the folders by name and save the stories. This is very important."

I was well aware of Elie Wiesel's interest in stories, but I was also taken by the personal concern that he expressed and the detail with which he explained a file system for me to use. In fact, I had been maintaining just the kind of file system he had suggested.

After a pause, I said, "Of course, I don't think that all of the stories I've been told are true."

"What does it matter if they are true?" Wiesel replied, a glimmer in his eyes. "They're stories!"

I mention this conversation with Elie Wiesel because a discussion regarding the "truth" behind family legends is an important one. Genealogists who are serious about their work have tried to be strict for a long time in accepting only facts that can be documented and verified. This is a reaction to the many people who have made false claims about who their ancestors were and what they did. I, too, want to underline the notion that claiming things that are false is the worst family history "sin" possible. On the other hand, there is something to say for recording and even investigating family tales that have dubious origins.

The rule of thumb I use is this: I record everything. Even the wildest stories (and I've heard some good ones!) are saved. The stories become an important part of the family history—not as fact, but as legend. I am careful to record not only the tale but also its source. Even if it's not true that my great-great-grandfather once offered a plate of food to a hungry man who happened to be Emperor Franz Josef, who in turn made my great-great-grandfather his personal guard, I still think it's important that the story has survived and has come down to me.

Don't perpetuate a fraud, but don't rob your family history of its richness by being "scientific." A tale that is not true in fact can be quite true in its message. In the case of my great-great-grandfather, the story says that he offered food to a stranger and did not know he was the emperor. He also did not think he would be rewarded for his act of charity. It's a good lesson.

Rabbi Joshua ben Levi said: He who teaches his grandson Torah, the Writ regards him as though he had received it direct from Mount Sinai.

—Talmud, *Kiddushin* 30a

Ten Common Family Myths—or Truths!

Over the past twenty-five years, I have had the great opportunity to speak on the subjects of Jewish family history and genealogy to hundreds of groups. In addition, I have received letters from hundreds of readers of my books and articles on the same subject. I am constantly hearing family stories from people who have heard the same tales from their relatives. These people are often quite eager to share their stories with me and believe wholeheartedly that their stories are true.

After hearing scores of stories by so many different people, I began to realize that many of the same legends kept popping up. Over and over again, I would hear variations of the same stories. Here are the bare outlines of ten tales I have heard most often.

1. *"We are descended from the Baal Shem Tov."*

The Baal Shem Tov, founder of Hasidism, is the subject of a great number of legends, including family legends. He is claimed as an ancestor by large numbers of people and is in competition with the next two individuals as "the most often-claimed Jewish ancestor of all time."

2. *"We are descended from the Vilna Gaon."*

The Vilna Gaon, one of history's great Talmudists, was an eighteenth-century Lithuanian luminary. A fascinating article on the subject appeared in *Avotaynu* (Fall 1997), titled "Verifying Oral Traditions: A Case Study: The Gaon of Vilna," by Chaim Freedman. Freedman is also the author of a remarkable genealogical study of the Vilna Gaon called *Eliyahu's Branches: The Descendants of the Vilna Gaon and His Family,* published by Avotaynu. There are other publications as well that treat the genealogy of the Vilna Gaon.

3. *"We are descended from King David."*

Jewish tradition states that the Messiah will spring from the House of David, so to descend from King David is to open the possibility that the Messiah will come from your family. In fact, a genealogy in the New Testament attempts to document the connection between King David and Jesus.

One way to trace back to King David is to trace back to Rashi, the great biblical and Talmudic commentator who lived in the eleventh century in France. Many families (including a few branches of my mother's family) can trace descent from Rashi. In the 1920s in New York City there was in fact an organization called the Association of Descendants of Rashi. Well, Rashi claimed descent from Hillel, a great sage quoted in the Mishnah (there is no complete documentation of this; just oral tradition). And Hillel claimed descent from King David (this is also tradition, not

documented). So to get back to King David, one needs to connect with Rashi. (There are others ways too.)

4. *"We are related to the Rothschild family."*

I do not know whether it is to claim rights to the fortune or simply to say that once they brushed shoulders with one of the richest Jewish families in modern history, but a large number of people seem to claim this relationship.

5. *"My ancestors were rabbis."*

It is very possible that this is true for most Jewish families, but sometimes I have the sense that someone remembers an old man with a long beard and therefore assumes he must have been a rabbi. The world of "rabbinic genealogical research" is quite significant. Of particular note has been the work of Dr. Neil Rosenstein, both a pioneer and a major contributor to our knowledge of the genealogy of the rabbinic families of the past and present. I have interviewed Dr. Rosenstein for this book (see Chapter 7).

Also, I'd recommend exploring the Rabbinic Genealogy Special Interest Group (SIG) connected to JewishGen.org (http://www.jewishgen.org/Rabbinic), discussed in greater detail on page 198.

6. *"There is a fortune of money buried under our house in Eastern Europe."*

If I were to add up the amount of money each of the tellers of this tale has claimed is hidden in a box below his or her old home in Eastern Europe, it would be greater than the contents of Fort Knox.

7. *"My family left Spain during the Inquisition."*

Certainly many of us do indeed descend from Jews who left Spain centuries ago. But there is little documentation of individual families who left or were expelled. This means that either many families are adopting these stories as their own or that the story has in fact been handed down from generation to generation since that time. Of course, either reason could be true for different people!

8. *"My ancestors were horse thieves."*

Frequently this is said as a joke. Often people will speculate and say, "If I trace my family, I'm sure we'll find horse thieves," as if to say, "The truth will finally come out!" The fascinating thing is that so many people also make this claim in all seriousness.

9. *"Everything in our town was destroyed in the Holocaust. Not a house or person was left. Nothing was saved."*

I am moved when people say this, not because it is true, but because they believe it. I am certainly not disputing the fact that people have these

kind of awful events in their memories. But I have visited many towns in Eastern Europe that were at one time Jewish towns. The vast majority of the Jewish populations of these towns, along with many of the buildings, were destroyed, but the towns were not—in many cases—as completely obliterated as people say. I have found Jewish cemeteries in places where people report they were leveled. I have found surviving Jews in places where people say every last Jew was killed.

My point is not to denigrate the damage done or to belittle the person who tells this but rather to point out the psychological as well as physical effect of the Holocaust. I also mention this to encourage the researcher not to give up his or her research simply because something like this is reported.

10. *"My family knew Emperor Franz Josef personally."*
Franz Josef I of Hapsburg lived from 1830 to 1916 and became emperor in 1848. Friendly to the Jews of his empire, he became a popular figure among the Jewish population, something of a folk hero. Often Jews would speak of him as "the emperor, may his majesty be exalted." It was not uncommon to find a picture of Franz Josef on the wall in the homes of Jewish families. He was kinder to the Jews than most other European leaders in history, and it is probably for this reason that so many Jewish families claim they knew him personally. My family, too, has a Franz Josef story as part of its history.

Each of these ten stories has got to be true in some cases. Some of us *do* descend from King David, the Baal Shem Tov, or the Vilna Gaon. Some of us *do* come from Spain originally. Some of us *are* related to the Rothschilds. Many of us *do* have rabbis in our past. Some of us *must* have been horse thieves.

It is striking how often these claims are made, however. The purpose of discussing these stories is not to say that if you have a similar story in your family, you should automatically dismiss it. On the contrary, record the story, remember it, and even pass it along to the next generation. It is my belief that there is a germ of truth in every story. It is our job to learn the stories, enjoy them, check them out if we can, and perhaps speculate as to how or why the story originated.

○

The study of history will never become obsolete, and a knowledge of one's grandfathers is an excellent introduction to history.

—Maurice Samuel

○

What Questions Should You Ask?

When you interview a relative or any other individual for your family history research, it is important that you prepare yourself in advance for the meeting. Effective oral history cannot occur if you just ask questions off the top of your head with little or no thought about what you want to know, what is important to ask, and what are the best ways of asking.

You will want to be thorough, but it is my own personal opinion that you should strike a balance between your own specific interests and more general topics. In other words, try to cover a broad range of areas, but don't avoid focusing on the areas of greatest interest to you. In my own case, I have little interest in politics but a large interest in religion. I try to ask questions concerning politics when it is relevant, but my interviews with relatives have a decided slant toward the religious. I am most interested in the religious thoughts, activities, and evolution of my family.

The following questions should serve as a guide to your oral history interviews. Do not simply go down the lists of questions and ask them one by one. Rather, pick the questions that interest you, and use them to begin a conversation. Rely on the questions and on your notes to get started, but know when to put them aside in order to engage in a free-flowing dialogue. If you simply go down the lists asking questions, the oral history will be dull and stiff. Each of these questions has the potential to begin a long, in-depth discussion about the topic at hand.

Feel free to adapt the questions to fit your needs. For example, far fewer of us have living relatives who were immigrants to America than I did when I began my Jewish family history research more than thirty years ago. At that time, I was able to interview dozens of relatives who came to America by steamship. Today, I am sad to say, very few of those people are still alive.

ORAL HISTORY QUESTIONS AND TOPICS

EUROPEAN ROOTS

1. What towns did your family come from in Europe? Where were those towns located?

2. Who were the immigrants to America? Did you come here, or was it your parents, grandparents, great-grandparents? Did the immigrants who came to America have any siblings who also came here?

3. Do you know the specific reasons for your family's coming to America? Did your direct ancestors who came to America have relatives who were already here?

4. If you came to America, who came with you?

5. Describe the trip.

6. Did you experience anti-Semitism in Europe?

7. In what port did your ship dock? Do you know the name of the ship or the date it arrived?

8. What was life in Europe (or wherever else you lived) like? What are some of your early childhood memories?

9. Did your family live all in one town in Europe, or did various branches of the family live in different places? Did your own family move from one place to another?

10. Who was the first person in the entire family to come to America?

11. What contact continued with the old country? Did you receive letters from relatives who remained in Europe? Were those letters saved?

PERSONAL AND FAMILY LIFE

1. What were your parents' names? What was your mother's maiden name?

2. Where were your parents from?

3. How many brothers and sisters do you have? What are their names? What was the order of their birth?

4. Did they marry? Have children? What are their names?

5. What are their occupations? What was your father's occupation?

6. Did your mother work?

7. What do you remember about your grandparents? Do you know their names, including maiden names? Where were they from? What were their occupations?

8. Do you remember your great-grandparents? Their names? Anything else about them?

9. Where were they from?

10. Whom were you named after? What do you know about that person or those people?

11. What is your spouse's name? What are your children's names?

12. Where did your family live in the United States? Did they live in more than one place? Do you know where?

13. What memories are especially vivid from your childhood?

14. Do you remember your first job and how old you were?
15. What were the living conditions in your home as a child?

RELIGIOUS LIFE

1. Was your family religious? What memories prompt you to draw that conclusion?
2. In Europe, were they Orthodox? Hasidic?
3. If they were Hasidic, did they follow any particular rebbe?
4. Did the religious life in your family change when you came to America or over the years after arriving in America?
5. Was there any resistance to coming to America on the part of anyone in your family for religious reasons?
6. Did your family belong to a synagogue in America?
7. Is there a family cemetery plot? Where is it? Who bought or organized it?
8. Do you remember your childhood during holidays such as Passover or the High Holidays? Others?
9. Is there a family Bible?
10. Did you have a bar or bat mitzvah?
11. Do you remember the shul in Europe? What was it like?

ARTIFACTS

1. Do you have your *ketubah* (marriage document) or the *ketubah* of your parents or grandparents?
2. Is there a family photo album?
3. Do you have old photographs?
4. Are there any family heirlooms that have been passed down from generation to generation? Do you know through whom they have been passed down?
5. Do you have any old candlesticks, kiddush cups, or tefillin? Would it be possible for me to see them or see photos of them?
6. Do you have your passport? Your parents' or grandparents' passports?
7. Do you have your or their citizenship papers? Your or their "first papers"?
8. Do you have your birth certificate or the birth certificate of your parents?

9. Do you have any old letters written by family members?

10. Are there any recipes that have been in the family for a long time?

11. Are there any other old family history items, such as diaries, Bibles, or books?

12. Is there a written genealogy or family tree in the family?

13. Do you know anyone else in the family who would have old family documents?

---○---

Tell ye your children of it, and let your children tell their children, and their children another generation.

—Joel 1:3

---○---

Tips on Interviewing Relatives

1. Try to interview people twice, on consecutive days if at all possible. The reason for this is simple: after the first interview, the person being interviewed will go to bed and dream about things that he or she had not thought of in years. The interview the next day will be great!

2. Don't ask yes or no questions. Phrase your questions so that they will inspire stories and anecdotes.

3. Sometimes relatives don't want to be interviewed. One way to inspire them is to have them present while you are interviewing someone else. The "silent" one will often add his or her two cents. Another effective idea is to show your interview subject a document or photograph of himself or herself. This will often open up an otherwise shy or uncooperative relative.

4. Old photographs inspire great conversations. Sit with relatives and ask them to tell you about the people and places in your old photographs.

5. Tell the people whom you are interviewing that you will report your genealogical discoveries to them. This promise (be sure to keep it!) is usually an effective incentive.

6. Prepare your interview. Don't think that you can ad-lib a good interview. Quality interviews come as the result of careful thought and planning.

7. Record all of your interviews on audio or video. Even telephone conversations can be taped.

8. If you don't tape your interviews, type your notes as soon as you can. Too many genealogists have scribbled so fast that they can't read their own notes when they get around to transcribing them.

9. Interviewing relatives, especially those you don't know, takes courage. Be proud of yourself for pursuing your genealogy. Remember that your research has the potential for changing a person's life. When a young person in your family needs to know about his or her place in the world, his or her ancestors, your research will be beneficial.

Grandparents, ever a source of family lore, may also be living examples to be emulated. If one's grandparents are no longer accessible, it may still be possible to trace one's Jewish roots back to earlier generations. Such a search amounts to an acceptance, not merely a reluctant acknowledgment, of the pluralism and diversity in Jewish tradition. Even in Ezekiel's messianic vision, there are separate gates to the Temple for each of the twelve tribes.

—Rabbi Adin Steinsaltz,
Teshuvah: A Guide for the Newly Observant Jew

Observations on People Who Don't Appreciate Genealogy

Some people think genealogy is a waste of time. They have a right to their opinion. It is noteworthy that many of the biggest skeptics undergo a change of heart once you share your research discoveries with them. Sometimes people say that they are not interested because they are afraid you will ask questions they don't know how to answer. They are afraid of appearing foolish or ignorant.

Don't get discouraged by people who tell you you have your head in the past or you're wasting your time. When people say such things to me, I try to use it to remind myself not to be judgmental of others.

Many people have a misconception about genealogy. They think that it is names and dates on a chart. It's our responsibility to show people that genealogy is far more. Don't bore people with long stories about the family; instead, infect them with your enthusiasm.

Following Leads like a Detective

Family history is not a simple matter. You will not be able to find out everything you want to know from any one book, relative, library, archive, or photograph. Like a detective, you will have to listen carefully for leads that will help you discover more and more. When you interview a second cousin of your mother's who suggests that "Aunt Bertha could tell you more," you must get in touch with Aunt Bertha. If someone mentions, in passing, that a branch of the family once lived in Omaha, Nebraska, you should check it out. If a family legend says that an ancestor of yours was in the Civil War, do the research to find out if it's true.

In my own particular case, one tiny clue, mentioned once, was able to send me on the road to trace my family back to the 1500s! In another case, a small lead helped me discover a cousin and his family who survived the Holocaust and still live in Warsaw. I can tell countless stories of dramatic family history discoveries that I have made due simply to the fact that I investigated the most obscure clues I heard. In almost every case, the effort paid off.

○

Our past is not behind us, it is in our very being.

David Ben-Gurion, *Call of the Spirit*

○

Taking Notes

An important part of your family history research will be taking notes. If you are in a library checking out a book source, in an archive examining public records, or visiting a relative for oral history, note taking will be vital. Many amateur researchers make the dangerous mistake of thinking that they will remember what they have been told during an interview or what they have seen in a book. Caution: *you absolutely will forget!* If you are like the vast majority of people, you will, very shortly into your research, begin to get sources and places confused.

It is much like a fabulous vacation you have taken. After a while, you begin to forget where you saw or did what. When you return home and tell your friends about your trip, you are unsure if it was Rome or Florence where you ate at that fantastic restaurant or saw that wonderful work of art.

Take notes. Good note taking is a skill that develops over a time, so it is generally best to write down as much as possible. It is also advisable to

type your notes after a session of note taking. Type your notes as soon as possible to avoid being unable to read your own handwriting (which happens maddeningly often!). Also, if you type your notes the same day you have taken them, they will be fresh in your mind, and so your transcription will be accurate.

Some people feel that note taking is a waste of time, but if you plan to do a good job on your family history, it is essential—a fact you will discover yourself after very little time as a researcher.

As noted earlier in this chapter, for the serious family historian, note-related questions soon arise: "How do I keep track of my information? Should I set up a file system? What software should I buy and use? How do I make sense out of all my little notes and papers?" These are difficult questions to answer. I can make two suggestions. The first is to devise a system that works for you. Don't worry about whether it's the "right" system or the "best" system. If it works for you, it is the system you should use. My second suggestion is to begin to explore the software options available. I recommend exploring the JewishGen Discussion Group (see FAQ 18 at http://www.jewishgen.org/infofiles/faq.html#Starting). You might also ask other people what software they use, to help you discover what might work for you.

_____ o _____

I, Ahimaaz, the son of Paltiel ben Samuel ben Hananel ben Amittai, sought God's aid and guidance in order to find the lineage of my family and He bountifully granted my request. I concentrated my mind and soul upon this work; I put the family documents and traditions in order, and I narrated the story in rhymed form. I began with the earliest tradition during the time of the destruction of Jerusalem and of the Temple by the Romans; then I traced it through the settlement of the exiles in the city of Oria in Italy (where I am now living) and the arrival of my ancestors in Capua; and finally, I have concluded with my own generation. I have written it all in this book for the use of future generations.

—Ahimaaz ben Paltiel, Jewish poet born in 1017

_____ o _____

Visiting Relatives and Others

One of the most rewarding yet time-consuming aspects of family history research is visiting people. Yet regardless of how much time is required, the investment invariably pays off.

Do not expect or even hope that all your information will come to you. Often people do not write letters or e-mails or do not write them well. In addition, a story told by a relative will almost always be better in person than on a page. Think of yourself: If you had to write a story on paper, you would probably not embellish it the way you would if you had the opportunity to tell it aloud.

Also, family history is not simply the collection of names, dates, and stories. The process of meeting new people, sharing discoveries and experiences, and making new friends is a fringe benefit of your family history project, if not a reason in itself.

Another fascinating phenomenon has happened to me many times. I will establish a correspondence with a relative and will acquire a lot of new information. On occasion I will call the person and will receive even more family history over the phone. Then the information source will "run dry," but I will visit the same person who had no more to tell me and discover that there is much more to hear and see. Photographs will be found, old passports and documents will appear, additional stories will be remembered, and I will regret not having visited sooner.

It is a mitzvah to visit an elderly person. So often I have been given the opportunity to bring a little bit of joy into someone's life by visiting with a person who was delighted to share information with me. One strong suggestion concerning the visiting of older relatives in particular: don't just visit once and forget about them. An occasional phone call, a note, or even additional visits are important. Otherwise you have just "used" them. After you have made an acquaintance or have reestablished a family relationship, it is incumbent upon you to take responsibility for it. It takes very little effort to call and say hello or to write a short letter to someone who has shared a part of his or her life with you.

○

A people's memory is history; and as a man without a memory, so a people without a history cannot grow wiser, better.

—I. L. Peretz

○

Family Photographs

You must ask of each person whom you interview for your family history to show you his or her old photographs. Family photographs are an important and exciting part of your family history pursuit, and it is a special experience to be able to see pictures of your ancestors, of

your ancestors' siblings, and of Holocaust victims whose photographs may exist.

As I visit people and see their photographs, I know that I want to have copies of many of them. Yet I am hesitant to ask for them (old photographs are among people's most precious possessions). I even hesitate to borrow them. I do not want to risk losing them.

But copying photographs is easier than ever, now that we have scanners attached to our computers. If you can borrow the photographs, you can scan them and return them quickly. If you don't want to borrow photographs, you can find out where the closest copy center is located and scan them on the same day that you visit and interview someone. You can also copy photographs using a digital camera or a camcorder.

---
o

> Jews who get a certain spiritual tonic from the reflection that they are somehow related to the creators of the Bible and to its ethical values forget that the relationship was passed on to them by the men who begot their fathers. Who were these men? Under what circumstances did they nurture the relationship for transmission? What tone and color had their lives? What purpose did they conceive themselves to be serving in their obstinate fidelity to the relationship? What hopes had they for themselves—and for their grandchildren?
>
> —Maurice Samuel, *The World of Sholem Aleichem*

---
o

Writing Letters

Although it is almost always better to visit relatives when searching for family history, distance forces us to write letters at times. Sometimes you must use snail mail, while at other times e-mail works great. Family historians use the mail to make inquiries to strangers who might be related or who might be of help. (Of special interest in this regard, see the JewishGen Family Finder section of JewishGen.org at http://www.jewishgen.org/infofiles/faq.html#JGFF.)

There are several guidelines to consider following when writing for family history information:

1. Try to avoid using a form letter, even if you are writing to many people for the same kind of information. You will get better results with personal letters.

2. Explain clearly at the beginning of your letter what you are doing and why. Many people are suspicious when it comes to talking about

"family matters," especially since there are some companies that try to make money by offering to research your family tree. I have never had a problem with people suspecting my motives, but I think this is the result of my making them clear from the beginning.

3. Identify yourself in the letters. The more you say about yourself, the more other people will offer about themselves. Tell them about your family history, both to inspire them to do the same and to help them trust you.

4. Promise that you'll write them again and that you'll share your discoveries with them—and then keep your promise!

5. Do not ask too many questions in one letter. A letter filled with questions is not apt to get a response.

6. You might want to try a questionnaire, but keep it simple and short. It is more effective to ask a little with each letter than to try to "get everything" at once. Also, you do not want to "use" people. You want to establish friendships. The longer the relationship, the more rewarding it will be—both personally and informationally.

7. Always enclose a self-addressed stamped envelope with letters sent by conventional mail. This is for the convenience of your respondent. Although you should not expect everyone to answer every letter, a self-addressed stamped envelope will increase your rate of return. You cannot send such an envelope outside the United States, but you may want to send an addressed envelope and postpaid International Reply Coupons, which can be purchased at your local post office. These coupons can be redeemed for return postage in other countries.

8. Finally, be warm, friendly, and polite in your letters. Do not insist that people send you information. Writing letters is an opportunity to be pleasant, to share your enthusiasm, and to brighten someone's day. Take that opportunity and use it!

Final Tips on How to Begin

Start now, not tomorrow. Every family historian has, at one time or another, wished that he or she began earlier.

Write down what you know. Anywhere. It doesn't have to be input into a fancy database or inscribed with elegant calligraphy in a fancy book. Just scribble down what you know: names, dates, and towns. Genealogists go, as they say, "from the known to the unknown." Writing down what you know about your family history makes what you need to find out much clearer.

Get your tape recorder or camcorder in order, and make sure the batteries work. A cassette tape recorder is inexpensive and is an essential tool for the family historian.

Identify your oldest relatives. That means make phone calls, write letters, and do whatever else you can to locate the oldest relatives. It may be a second cousin whom nobody has been in touch with for years. Be the one to get in touch. The oldest relatives need to be interviewed, visited, coaxed. They have old photographs, old letters, old documents. Make your oldest relatives your best friends.

Don't let anyone discourage you. There will be people who will think you are wasting your time by doing genealogy; there are people who will think you are nosy; there are people who will not be willing to talk with you; there are people who will not answer your letter; there are librarians who will not want to be "bothered"; there are archivists who will try to make you think they own the material in the archives that pay their salaries; there are librarians who will not think that genealogy is important enough for them; there are siblings who will be puzzled by you; there are cousins who will think you are a fanatic. Don't let anything discourage you. Genealogy is a holy pursuit. For those who believe, no explanation is necessary; for those who don't believe, no explanation is possible.

3

ARE YOU READY TO CHECK THE RECORDS?

PLEASE MAKE SURE that you are ready to take the next step in your research, the obtaining of public records, before you begin your serious investigation of this chapter and its resources. Too many eager family historians rush to the records before they do adequate interviewing of relatives and searching for family resources (like citizenship papers or wills or photo albums).

The libraries and archives and Web sites will most likely still be there when you want them. But the people in your family get older by the moment, and one day you will no longer have an opportunity to speak with them. Please understand: I don't mean to sound morbid. The cycle of life and death is part of human existence. It is surely a key part of genealogy. And to ensure that the future generations know about the past, our older relatives must be the first priority for the family historian. Just about everyone who has ever done genealogical research realizes that if they had begun just a short time earlier, they would have had additional relatives with whom to speak.

It is also a great mitzvah to visit the older relatives in our families. They are almost always grateful for the visit or phone call or letter. We need them for our research—and they need us to need them!

In addition, the preliminary homework you do will undoubtedly make your record searches more fruitful. The more information you know, the more you can find out.

Prepare Yourself

It is now time to prepare yourself to enter the world of libraries, archives, governmental agencies, Web sites, and databases. Keep in mind that your journey can be an endless one. This is good news and bad news. The good

news is that the resources available are substantial and growing all the time. You can *never* investigate all the possibilities in one lifetime. The bad news is that libraries, archives, and governmental agencies are not always easy to work with. It is clear, however, as more and more organizations and agencies establish and develop their Web sites, that the situation is better than ever.

Sometimes a library is well staffed, well funded, and well organized, a dream come true.

Sometimes an archivist is also a sensitive person who not only cares about "the collection" but also about people.

Sometimes the human being who opens up your letter at some bureaucracy you had to be in touch with is interested in helping and perhaps even has a supervisor who cares about such things.

Sometimes the opposite is true.

Nevertheless, prepare yourself for some astounding discoveries, amazing breakthroughs, and lots of information about your family and its history. There will be forms to fill out, directions to follow, fees to pay, and patience required, but the results will be worthwhile.

People often say to me, "There's nobody left to talk with about the family history." I have two responses. My first response is that I don't believe it. I don't believe you have tracked down every possible living source. There is some distant cousin somewhere to be found. My second response is that libraries, archives, and governmental agencies throughout the world have information about my family. And yours.

Prepare yourself.

―――――――○―――――――

Blessed is he that remembers what is forgotten!

—S. Y. Agnon

―――――――○―――――――

Telephone Books

Contemporary telephone books can be of help when searching for missing or new relatives. Although it is almost impossible to use a telephone book when looking for relatives named Cohen or Levine, you might find it productive if your name is less common.

I have looked up the name Kurzweil in hundreds of phone books and have contacted many of the people whose names I have found. In a great number of cases, I have discovered relatives who did not know we were related—nor did I know about them until I made the contact. Often it was

just a matter of asking a few questions to determine where on the family tree a newly discovered branch belonged. Over the past several years, I have discovered "lost" branches of my family in Israel, across the United States, and in Poland.

Many large public libraries have good collections of telephone books. The New York Public Library Research Library, for example, has nearly every available telephone book in the world! Also, many foreign telephone books have English editions.

When contacting a stranger, either by phone or through the mail, it is important that you identify yourself and explain what you are doing. You want to inspire trust. Tell the person about yourself and something of what you have already researched, and promise to share your results (and do it!). I have sometimes found it difficult to call a stranger and to begin a conversation about family history, but it has almost always been rewarding.

You should surely check the Israeli phone books if you have an uncommon last name. There is even an English-language edition, and you might discover a branch of your family that settled there either before the Holocaust or afterward.

I never thought that I had relatives living in Israel until I looked up the name Kurzweil in the Israeli phone books. I wrote to several people, and when they wrote back, the information about their parents, grandparents, and towns in Europe where they came from matched with my family tree.

Several years ago I was eager to locate a cousin of my father's who survived the Holocaust and was reported to have remained in Poland. I did not know his address, nor did I know where he had been for the past thirty years. But I went to the Warsaw phone book of 1974 and found his name, address, and telephone number. I wrote to him, and a few weeks later I received a letter in return. It was indeed my cousin, whom nobody had been in touch with for years! We have since written to each other every few weeks, and we have become quite close. I have visited him in Poland, and I helped sponsor a trip for him to visit my family in New York. His daughter also visited us in New York; as one can imagine, the trip to America, for her, was extraordinary. I have no doubt that it changed her life. All because I looked up his name in the Warsaw phone book. (See Chapter Nine for information on pre-Holocaust telephone books.)

There are many Web sites that offer to search white pages, yellow pages, and other directories for a fee (or free). The problem with these sites is that they are designed to help you search for specific people in specific places. In other words, you can't simply search for "everyone named Kurzweil." It is always best to do the searches yourself with the real books so that your search can be more effective.

Do a search for "Find People" using Google or your favorite search engine and you will find lots of Web sites with services that do searches for individuals.

Vital Records

Birth, death, marriage, and divorce records in the United States can be quite helpful, but it would be impossible to generalize as to what information each provides. This varies both from place to place as well as from year to year. Costs for these documents also vary.

The National Center for Health Statistics' Web site makes it easy to obtain information on how to locate the documents you want. Visit the agency's state-by-state listing at http://www.cdc.gov/nchs/howto/w2w/w2welcom.htm.

You can also obtain a guide to these records from the U.S. Department of Health and Human Services in a booklet called *Where to Write for Vital Records,* available from the U.S. Government Printing Office, Washington, DC 20402–9325, or from HHS branch offices around the country (check locally). This booklet currently costs $3.50 and provides information on each state regarding the procedure required to obtain copies of birth, death, marriage, and divorce documents.

As I mentioned, the information on these documents is not standard and therefore will vary from place to place as well as from year to year in the same location, but a few interesting examples of what I have found would be useful in illustrating the value of these American sources.

Often a person will say to me, "My great-grandmother came to the United States many years ago. She is no longer alive, nor is anyone else in her generation who can answer some questions. I cannot even find out the names of her parents." My immediate response is, "Have you obtained her death certificate?" More often than not, a U.S. death certificate asked (and still asks) the name of the parents of the deceased. Although there might be no one alive today who knows the answer to that question, chances are someone *did* know at the time of her death.

One of my great-grandfathers came to America and died here. I wanted to know his parents' names, so I sent for his death certificate. When it arrived, I learned his father's name and his mother's name. Most important, I learned the maiden name of his mother! When death certificates ask for the names of the parents of the deceased, they will usually include a request for the maiden name of the mother. So when my great-grandfather's death certificate arrived, another branch of my family began to appear.

Interestingly, his mother's maiden name was the same as his wife's maiden name. So my first thought was that there must have been a mistake: How can his wife and his mother have had the same last name? Unless, of course, they were related! I asked around in the family and was told that my great-grandparents were first cousins. (If your great-grandparents are first cousins, that makes you your own fourth cousin!)

Marriage records are also of great value, since these records will ask the names of the bride's parents and the groom's parents.

There is one additional thing to keep in mind when searching for these records. Often you will send to the appropriate agency for copies of these records and they will reply that they do not have them. A number of possibilities exist. It may be an error on the part of the clerk who made the search. Or it may be your error—perhaps your grandmother died somewhere other than where you think. Or possibly the record was lost. In any of these cases, do not give up. Try other alternatives. For example, if you cannot locate your grandmother's death certificate but are anxious to find her parents' names, try to locate the death certificate of one of her brothers or sisters. The same thing goes for marriage records: try to find records of siblings. In other words, you must be a detective. You must think of every possibility and every alternative. It isn't always easy, but it's almost always worthwhile.

Another Web site of great interest provides information from the Social Security Death Index, which indexes the millions of U.S. residents who had Social Security numbers and whose deaths were known to the Social Security Administration from 1962 to the present. Available on a number of Web sites, I recommend http://ssdi.genealogy.rootsweb.com.

―――――○―――――

Be fruitful and multiply, and replenish the earth.

Genesis 1:28

―――――○―――――

Federal Census Records

The federal government has taken a census of the country's population every ten years since 1790. Census records can all be consulted for family history research, although some have restrictions on them. The only census that is not available is the 1890 federal census, which was destroyed (except for small portions) in a fire.

The census records can be of enormous assistance to you when you are researching your family history. The information will be valuable on its

own, and it will give you clues to seek additional facts. You will also be able to search the census records for people with your last name in an effort to locate new or unknown relatives. By reviewing the kinds of information to be found in the records, you can see how helpful they can be.

There are many differences among these census records from decade to decade. For example, the records of 1790–1840 list only the head of the household by name, whereas the later records list the names of each member of the household. You will have no choice, obviously, but to accept the differences among the records.

Each federal census from 1790 through 1930 is available on an unrestricted basis to researchers. Although you can do your own research from the census records up to 1930, someone will have to do it for you for the records compiled since then. The address is as follows:

Bureau of the Census
Personal Census Service Branch
P.O. Box 1545
Jeffersonville, IN 47130
phone: (812) 288-3300

The United States Census Bureau has a Web site that provides a good explanation of what is available, along with other information. Of particular value is the Genealogy FAQ part of the site. The site might make the novice think that census records are not available. This is not true. Read this site carefully. Go to http://www.census.gov/genealogy/www.

Great efforts have been made to index census records, and while most of these records have been indexed, not all have. Here is a summary of what has been indexed:

1790–1880	Most states have indexes that were privately created. There is a partial index for all states, but it includes only households with children age ten and under. There is a soundex index (organized by sound, not by letter, often making searches easier) for every state.
1890	Almost the entire 1890 census was destroyed in a fire.
1900	There is a complete soundex index for each state.
1910	There is a soundex index for only twenty-one states: Alabama, Arkansas, California, Florida, Georgia, Illinois, Kansas, Kentucky, Louisiana, Michigan, Mississippi, Missouri, North Carolina, Ohio, Oklahoma, Pennsylvania, South Carolina, Tennessee, Texas, Virginia, and West Virginia.

1920	There is a complete soundex index for each state.
1930	There is currently a soundex index for only twelve southern states: Alabama, Arkansas, Florida, Georgia, Kentucky, Louisiana, Mississippi, North Carolina, South Carolina, Tennessee, Virginia, and West Virginia.

As you can see, if your research takes you back before 1850 in the United States, most of the censuses from 1790 to 1850 have been indexed, and these indexes are in book form. The 1850 index in particular will be very useful for German-Jewish families that arrived at the beginning of the major German-Jewish wave of immigration to America. Many of the National Archives branches have these indexes, as do major genealogical libraries.

The National Archives in Washington, D.C., and the regional branches of the National Archives have all of the federal census records from 1790 to 1930 on microfilm.

It is always best to do the research by yourself, because you cannot be sure that anyone else has been thorough. Once I searched a federal census for a few hours until I found a part of my family in the records. I was sure they were listed (at least I believed they were), and it wasn't until I checked several alternate spellings of the name that I found it. Someone else probably would have given up after a few minutes—and appropriately so.

Many local libraries have different parts of the federal census, and it would be worthwhile to check the nearest large public library to see what it might have. In addition, as I mentioned before, there are branches of the National Archives around the country. The following is a list of those branches.

REGIONAL ARCHIVES OF THE NATIONAL ARCHIVES
AND AREAS SERVED

New England Region
380 Trapelo Road
Waltham, MA 02154
phone: (617) 647-8100
    Serves Connecticut, Maine, Massachusetts, New Hampshire, Rhode Island, and Vermont.

Northeast Region
201 Varick Street
New York, NY 10014
phone: (212) 337-1300
    Serves New Jersey, New York, Puerto Rico, and the Virgin Islands.

Mid-Atlantic Region
Ninth and Market Streets, Room 1350
Philadelphia, PA 19107
phone: (215) 597-3000
    Serves Delaware, Pennsylvania, Maryland, Virginia, and
West Virginia.

Southeast Region
1557 St. Joseph Avenue
East Point, GA 30344
phone: (404) 763-7477
    Serves Alabama, Georgia, Florida, Kentucky, Mississippi,
North Carolina, South Carolina, and Tennessee.

Great Lakes Region
7358 South Pulaski Road
Chicago, IL 60629
phone: (312) 581-7816
    Serves Illinois, Indiana, Michigan, Minnesota, Ohio, and
Wisconsin.

Central Plains Region
2312 East Bannister Road
Kansas City, MO 64131
phone: (816) 926-6272
    Serves Iowa, Kansas, Missouri, and Nebraska.

Southwest Region
501 West Felix Street
P.O. Box 6216
Fort Worth, TX 76115
phone: (817) 334-5525
    Serves Arkansas, Louisiana, New Mexico, Oklahoma,
and Texas.

Rocky Mountain Region
Building 48
Denver Federal Court
P.O. Box 25307
Denver, CO 80225
phone: (303) 236-0817
    Serves Colorado, Montana, North Dakota, South Dakota,
Utah, and Wyoming.

Pacific Southwest Region
24000 Avila Road
P.O. Box 6719
Laguna Niguel, CA 92607
phone: (714) 643-4241

Serves Arizona; the Southern California counties of Imperial, Inyo, Kern, Los Angeles, Orange, Riverside, San Bernardino, San Diego, San Luis Obispo, Santa Barbara, and Ventura; and Nevada's Clark County.

Pacific Sierra Region
1000 Commodore Drive
San Bruno, CA 94066
phone: (415) 876-9009

Serves Northern California, Hawaii, Nevada except Clark County, and the Pacific Ocean area.

Pacific Northwest Region
6125 Sand Point Way, N.E.
Seattle, WA 98115
phone: (206) 526-6507

Serves Idaho, Oregon, and Washington.

Alaska Region
654 West Third Avenue
Anchorage, AK 99501
phone: (907) 271-2441

Serves Alaska.

A useful booklet called *Aids for Genealogical Research* is available free from the National Archives:

National Archives and Records Administration
Product Sales Staff (NWPS)
Room G-7
700 Pennsylvania Avenue, N.W.
Washington, DC 20408
phone: (800) 234-8861; fax: (301) 713-6169

A warning must be sounded regarding the accuracy of the census records, as well as all other public records: you cannot be sure that anything is 100 percent accurate. There is always room for human error, and if you find two conflicting pieces of information, you must use your own judgment—or independent corroboration—to determine what is true.

State Census Records

In addition to the federal census, states have also taken censuses, often during years when the federal government did not. Check to see whether the states you are interested in have census records. You might inquire at your public library, state libraries, and genealogy libraries of local historical societies for this information.

To give one example, there was a 1905, 1915, and 1925 census for New York. The ones for 1915 and 1925 are available at the State Archives in Albany, and all three are available from the county clerks throughout New York State. Also see the New York State Library Web site (http://www.nysl.nysed.gov/genealogy/nyscens.htm) for more information on these documents for New York State.

—————— o ——————

A clan and a family resemble a heap of stones: one stone taken out of it and the whole totters.

Genesis Rabbah

—————— o ——————

Tips on Dealing with Government Agencies

Some people might think that the government will find their genealogical questions inappropriate. This is not true. Genealogy is a business for many government agencies. If they have information you want and they can provide you with it, they will. And they'll charge a fee for it. So don't hesitate.

In most cases, you have every right to the information you are requesting. Although there are certainly a lot of restrictions on access to information, there is also a lot of information available. The Freedom of Information Act is only one of many pieces of legislation that protects the "right to know" in the United States.

Don't take no for an answer (but always be polite). When you ask for a document from a government agency, it is often by filling out a form and mailing or e-mailing it in. You wait days, weeks, or months, and then you get a reply. Sometimes you hit pay dirt; sometimes you are told, "We can't find it." Don't believe it. I have heard many stories and have had my own experiences to back this up: what one clerk cannot find, the next clerk will. (Does this mean that when you get a no answer, you should repeat your efforts? It's up to you.)

Don't be intimidated by the forms you have to fill out. Do the best you can. If you didn't do it right, you'll be so informed (usually via another

form letter). Some of the forms are pretty scary. Just go line by line and you'll probably get it right.

City Directories

A city directory looks like a phone book and serves much the same purpose—which is to identify people by name and address. City directories have been published in hundreds of cities and towns, large and small, since the 1800s. Some cities still publish these directories, although New York City stopped in the 1930s. If a city of interest to you has ever published city directories, a collection of them is probably in the public library of that city.

City directories for communities throughout the United States have been put on microfilm and are available for purchase. I suggest that you do a Web search for them if you are interested. There are many places where you can see comprehensive lists. One place is called "Cyndi's List of Genealogical Sites on the Internet" (http://www.cyndislist.com/citydir.htm). Cyndi's List is a well-known Web site among genealogists. I suggest that you check it out.

There is also a list (in Appendix D) in *Genealogical Sources in New York,* revised and edited by Estelle M. Guzik, published by the Jewish Genealogical Society in New York.

Of what use is a directory? Suppose you know that your great-great-grandfather came to New York City in the 1880s but you know little more about him. If you check the directories of New York City for that time period, you might find him listed. The listing might include his occupation (it usually does), and sometimes the directories even include a wife's name in parentheses next to the listed name. You will also learn his address. If you begin to check the directories by year for this period, you can determine what year he is first listed and what year he stops being listed. These are clues to the year he arrived in the city (and perhaps the country) as well as when he died (or moved away).

A city directory can also be useful in connection with census research. For most census records, you must know the address of the person. Since phone books are relatively recent publications, a city directory is an excellent source of old addresses.

○

No father should give his son the name of a wicked man.

Rashi

○

Synagogue Records

There is no systematic way of searching out synagogue records, nor is there any guarantee that they exist for the particular location or time period that you want. Nevertheless, you should keep in mind that synagogues have generally kept records of different kinds, and it might be worth your while, if you know which U.S. synagogues your ancestors joined, to investigate the possibility that the synagogue still exists or that the records do.

Synagogues have each kept their own kind of records; they vary from place to place. Often birth, marriage, and death records were kept in addition to membership records. Inquire whether or not the synagogue still exists. If it does not, a local investigation might turn up the location of the synagogue's records.

According to the late Rabbi Malcolm H. Stern, who was genealogist for the American Jewish Archives, synagogues have been known to keep four types of records:

○ Minute books of congregational meetings (which Rabbi Stern says have often been lost)

○ Account books that contained lists of membership (many of which have also been lost)

○ Congregational histories and communal histories, which are often privately published and are available from the synagogues themselves as well as from large Jewish libraries

○ Vital records, which include birth and circumcision records, bar mitzvah records, marriage records, and death records

Availability of all of these records varies from synagogue to synagogue, and at this point there is no general accounting of these records.

Both the American Jewish Archives and the American Jewish Historical Society have collections of synagogue records. It would be worthwhile to write or visit these organizations in an attempt to locate old U.S. synagogue records.

The Web address for the "Genealogy" page of the American Jewish Archives is http://www.americanjewisharchives.org/aja/genealogy/index.html. As you will see, the AJA welcomes inquiries from Jewish genealogists.

The American Jewish Historical Society also has a "Genealogical Research Service" at http://www.ajhs.org/reference/GeneoInst.cfm.

If an old synagogue to which your family belonged is still functioning, writing or visiting might prove worthwhile. Be aware, however, that the

average synagogue is not staffed to search through records. The staff might be very hesitant to do a search for you—or even to let you search the records. There is no rule of thumb or formula for success here.

○

Every man has three names: one his father and mother gave him, one others call him, and one he acquires himself.

Ecclesiastes 7:1–3

○

The National Archives

Although we have already mentioned the National Archives in connection with census records and will mention it again in various parts of this book, it would be useful to mention it here in a general context. The National Archives, located at Eighth Street and Pennsylvania Avenue, N.W., Washington, DC 20408, (202) 501-5400, has millions of records in its collections. Among those of particular genealogical interest are the following:

Census schedules 1790 to 1930

Passenger arrival lists

U.S. military records (Revolutionary War, War of 1812, Indian wars and related wars, Mexican War, Civil War, Spanish-American War, Philippine Insurrection)

Burial records of soldiers

Veterans' benefits records

Pension records

Land records

Passport applications

A complete description of these and other records can be found in the third edition of the *Guide to Genealogical Research in the National Archives,* available from the U.S. Government Printing Office, Washington, DC 20402, or from National Archives local offices. The current price is $25 for the softcover edition.

The records of the National Archives can prove incredibly valuable, particularly if your family has been in the United States for several generations.

The National Archives' Web site (http://www.archives.gov) is in itself a fascinating place to explore. It has a special section for genealogists

(http://www.archives.gov/research_room/genealogy/index.html) that is quite helpful in guiding you through the various collections and procedures.

What if You Were Adopted?

The subject of an adopted child's search for his or her natural parents is, for some people, a controversial one. Complex feelings exist on the part of all concerned: the adopted child, the adoptive parents, the natural parents, and the people who keep the records.

A full discussion of the issue would not be possible or appropriate here. However, the subject of an adopted child's search for natural parents and the subject of genealogy have an obvious relationship. It is certainly an issue that must be continuously explored rather than avoided or feared. An observation based on experiences of mine may be appropriate here: *each and every time* I have lectured on the subject of Jewish genealogy to children or teenagers, a question is raised by someone in the audience regarding this issue. The question is usually a simple one: "How can someone who is adopted trace his or her family?" I have lectured to dozens of young groups, and the question never fails to be raised, sometimes in front of the whole group and sometimes privately afterward, by a young person who is struggling with this problem.

My response is always the same. I begin by noting that it is an important and deeply personal issue. I then add that the decision to search for one's natural parents is a serious one and that much thought must go into the decision in order to be considerate to everyone involved. I then mention that there are organizations that help in the process of searching for one's natural parents (as well as aid in the emotional issues that spring from this). My concluding comment directed at the young questioner, who most probably is an adopted child considering such a search, is this: Jewish genealogy and family history offer a special and unique opportunity for someone who is adopted. If you were adopted, I would strongly suggest that you research the family history of your adoptive parents. Just as they adopted you as their child, you can adopt their history as your own history. This is one powerful way for you to tie the link even more strongly between you and your parents—people who have loved you very much.

If you are an adopted child, there is an organization that can help you in your research for your natural parents—if you decide to make that search. It is the Adoptee's Liberty Movement Association (ALMA):

ALMA
P.O. Box 727
Radio City Station
New York, NY 10101–0727

ALMA publishes a newsletter and a handbook for members called *Handbook for the Search*.

An excellent book exploring the entire subject of adopted children searching for their natural parents is *Lost and Found: The Adoption Experience* by Betty Jean Lifton (New York: HarperCollins, 1988). This book is worthwhile reading for all individuals involved in the "adoption experience." Also included in the book is a long list of adoptee search groups around the country. This is the best and most moving book on this difficult subject that I have seen.

There is a Web site that deals with this subject: http://www.birthfamily.com.

○

To honor parents is more important even than to honor God.

Simeon B. Yohai, Talmud J, *Peah* 1.1

○

Canadian Research

The first step in beginning research on Canadian genealogy and family history is to go to the section of the Web site for the National Library of Canada and the National Archives of Canada that helps genealogists: http://www.archives.ca/02/020202_e.html.

The National Archives of Canada (395 Wellington Street, Ottawa, Ontario K1A 0N3) also publishes a free booklet, *Tracing your Ancestors in Canada*, which describes the major genealogical sources available at the National Archives and makes reference to sources in other Canadian repositories. You can send for it or download it. See http://www.archives.ca/04/0420_e.html.

Canada has census records; birth, marriage and death records; land records; military records; immigration records (including some passenger lists); and naturalization (citizenship) records.

In many cases there are sources in Canada equivalent to those in the United States, particularly passenger arrival records. There are three types of landing records maintained by the Canadian government: records of arrival in Canada prior to 1900, records of arrival from 1900 to 1921, and records from 1921 to the present.

Prior to 1900   Records of ship arrivals at Quebec City from 1865 and Halifax from 1881 are kept by the archives branch in Ottawa. You must know the name of the passenger, year and month of arrival, and the port into which the immigrant came.

1900 to 1921   Passenger lists (manifests) have been maintained for this period but are on microfilm in chronological order. There is no index, which means that you must have fairly precise information concerning any individual in order to locate his or her records. Complete information on contacting the National Archives of Canada can be obtained at http://www.archives.ca/09/09_e.html.

Arrivals from 1921   These records are the easiest of the three to obtain since they are filed alphabetically. If you have the correct spelling as it was upon arrival, the records can usually be located. Of course, if you can provide additional information, it will be that much easier for the archives staff to be of help. Again, the archives branch should be contacted for more information.

A Few Important Canadian Resources

Lawrence Tapper has made remarkable contributions to Jewish genealogical research in Canada. An archivist at the National Archives of Canada and founding president of the Jewish Genealogical Society of Ottawa, he is the author of a few important publications:

> *Archival Sources for the Study of Canadian Jewry* (1987), published by National Archives of Canada

> Two excellent articles in *Avotaynu:* "Jewish Genealogical Research in Canada" (Summer 1988) and "Jewish Genealogical Research in Canada" (Winter 1998)

> *A Biographical Dictionary of Canadian Jewry: From the Canadian Jewish Times, 1909–1914,* published by Avotaynu in 1992. This book includes listings of births, bar mitzvahs, marriages, and deaths, as well as information concerning communal and synagogue activities of Canadian Jewry taken from the pages of *The Canadian Jewish Times.*

An audiotape by Lawrence Tapper titled *Jewish Genealogical Research in Canada,* recorded on July 12, 1998, at the Eighteenth Annual Seminar on Jewish Genealogy, is available for $8.50 (Canadian). One source for this tape is http://www.audiotapes.com/product.asp?ProductCode='ASJGCA34'.

You can reach Lawrence Tapper at the following address:

Lawrence Tapper, Archivist, Manuscript Division
National Archives of Canada
395 Wellington Street
Ottawa, Ontario K1A 0N3
e-mail: ltapper@archives.ca

───────○───────

Why did God create one man, Adam, rather than creating the whole human race together? It was to show that if anyone causes a single soul to perish, it is as though he caused a whole world to perish, and if anyone saves a single soul, it is as if he had saved a whole world.

Mishnah, *Sanhedrin* 4:5

───────○───────

Cardinal Rules When Dealing with Libraries, Archives, and Other Institutions

Throughout this book you will learn about libraries, archives, and other institutions that will be of interest when pursuing your Jewish family history. The following are some basic principles to keep in mind when making contact with them.

1. Many historical institutions are understaffed, and the employees are overworked and underpaid. Be friendly and polite when making your inquiry, and be appreciative when receiving your answer.

2. *Do not* expect the staff members of historical institutions to do research for you (unless they have a system whereby they charge by the hour for such a service). Librarians and archivists can and should help you locate material, but just so that *you* can then do the research. They can be of general assistance in helping you find material on your subject, but they cannot read the material with you or for you.

3. Much of the material of use to you in Jewish research is *not* in English. Staff members of Jewish historical institutions *cannot* translate for you. Translation is very time-consuming. Bring someone along who

can translate for you, or be prepared to photocopy material and get it translated.

4. The questions you are about to ask a librarian might be brand-new for you but have probably been asked a thousand times by a thousand others. Be patient with the librarian who is not patient with you. On the other hand, keep in mind that the staff of the library is there for you. Don't monopolize their time, but use their skills. Most of all, appreciate their help.

5. When you write to an institution for information, always include a self-addressed stamped envelope. Not only is it the correct thing to do, but also, since most people do not do this, the receiver will appreciate you.

6. Most important, be prepared with an intelligent question. Of course, there is no such thing as a stupid question; it is stupid only if you do not ask it. But librarians are always being confronted by people who have not done their own homework and think that the librarian should do it for them. For example, *do not* enter a Jewish library with an interest in researching your family history if you have yet to interview your family for basic information. The more information you can bring with you, the better the librarian will be able to assist you.

7. Specifically relating to family history and genealogy, avoid questions such as "I'm doing research on my family from Russia named Schwartz. Can you help me?" If all you know is that your family is from Russia and their name was Schwartz, you have not done your homework.

8. Finally, most Jewish institutions offer their resources free of charge, but that does not mean that you are without a responsibility toward that institution. Consider joining the organization if membership is offered. If not, a donation would be appreciated.

Tips on Dealing with Librarians

As the holder of a master's degree in library science and as a member of Beta Phi Mu, the national librarian's honor society, I feel entitled to offer the following observations:

1. Most librarians are human. Some are saints. Others are impossible. I've met some librarians who are creative, enthusiastic, and wonderful. I've met others who should switch careers. Again, most librarians are human, just like you and me.

2. I've said this before, but I'll say it again: don't ask a librarian a question without doing your homework. If you give the impression that you

know what you are doing, the librarian is far more likely to be responsive. If you haven't even done the smallest amount of preparation, the librarian will have less respect for you or will take you less seriously. Some people don't even formulate their questions until they walk up to a librarian. Don't do this. Be prepared.

3. Most libraries have several librarians. Try to figure out who is who. If you find one you like, try to go back to that same person before settling on another one. Some librarians like genealogists; others don't. Stay alert to this.

4. Don't tell the librarian your whole family history. As fascinating as your family is to you, others often could not care less. Just get to the point with your questions.

5. If you don't think a librarian is serving you well, I suggest that you complain to the administration of the library. Just make sure you have a good case.

Publishing Your Family History

There will probably come a time when you will want to publish your research findings for the benefit of other members of your family who want a copy of what you have discovered. Hundreds of Jewish family histories have been privately printed and range from several typed pages that have been photocopied and stapled to professionally printed hardcover books running to the several hundreds of pages.

There are many things to consider when thinking about printing your family history. All considerations must include the price of production, of course. If you have only a few pages of information, you can easily type them and print them on your computer's printer. The more ambitious you are, the more it will cost. If you want to have a small book printed, the cost could be considerable. A conversation with a good printer can answer most of your questions.

I would suggest that you go to a large public library or any of the major Jewish libraries I discuss in this book (especially YIVO and the Leo Baeck Institute). They will have many samples of Jewish family histories for you to examine, from inexpensive products to fancy volumes. Not only can you get an idea of what to aim for with your own project, but you can also see the various formats designed to record the information you have gathered. Don't decide against publishing a family history just because you cannot produce a fancy one. Even the most modest family history will become a cherished heirloom for your family members.

An excellent source (one of many) that deals with the subject of writing and publishing family histories, available from Avotaynu, is *Producing a Quality Family History*, by Patricia Law Hatcher. The book explains the necessary steps is assembling and publishing a family history book. The author provides all the information needed for production decisions such as selecting type styles, grammar and punctuation, bibliography format, organization, and incorporating photos and illustrations.

———— o ————

Rav Judah has said in the name of Rav: Ezra did not leave Babylon to go up to Eretz Yisrael until he had written his own genealogy.

—Baba Bathra 15a

———— o ————

4

HOW IS JEWISH GENEALOGY DIFFERENT FROM ALL OTHER GENEALOGY?

ALEX HALEY, THE AUTHOR OF *Roots,* the groundbreaking book (and TV miniseries) that celebrated black family history, had an interesting impact on the image of genealogy in the United States. Before Alex Haley, the word *genealogy* conjured up images of the Daughters of the American Revolution and direct descendants of the passengers on the *Mayflower.* But with the enormous success of *Roots* came an equally enormous surge in interest in genealogy among such ethnic groups as Italian Americans, African Americans, and Jewish Americans.

The reference librarians who work in the Local History and Genealogy Division of the New York Public Library are quick to point out that not only has interest in genealogy grown over the past twenty-five years, but it has actually shifted. Genealogy used to be a preoccupation with Americans who wanted to prove "illustrious" descent. Today, genealogy is a tool used by members of ethnic groups for rebuilding a sense of ethnic identity. America used to be called a "melting pot." We have come to learn that it's more like a tossed salad; it is important for ethnic groups to maintain their identities while at the same time uniting as one people.

Genealogy has always been an important topic within Jewish tradition. We find genealogy in the very first chapters in the Bible itself, and genealogy can be seen as playing a part in the lives of Jews from ancient times to the present.

In the Torah we see many references to genealogy. One of the Torah portions read in the synagogue is even called *Toledot,* the Hebrew word for *genealogy.*

In Chapter 10 of Genesis, one can find the "Table of Nations," which purports to constitute the foundation of the human family tree. This comes directly after the story of the Flood. The chapter lists, in detail, generation after generation, the descendants of the three sons of Noah. Each of the descendants represents not only an individual but also the founder of a future nation, hence the name "Table of Nations." As the many books of the Bible unfold and nations, tribes, and individuals appear, most of them find their source back in Chapter 10 of Genesis.

As you can see from the genealogical chart, the following list of names appears as descendants of the three sons of Noah. Based on early beliefs as well as recent biblical scholarship, the list indicates which groups and nations each name represents:

Gomer: People of Asia Minor known as Cimmerians

Ashkenaz: From Armenia and the upper Euphrates (not to be confused with Ashkenazim, Jews from Germanic countries)

Tubal: Tibareni

Meshech: From Asia Minor, identified with Assyrian sources

Madai: People of Indo-Iranian origin known as the Medes

Javan: From Greece

Elishah: From Cyprus

Kittim: From Cyprus

Tarshish: Tartessians

Dodanim: From Rhodes

Magog: The Scythians, located on the border of the Caucasus

Tivas: Etruscans

Joktan: South Arabian tribes

Elam: Elamites, identified with Iran

Assur: Assyrians

Aram: Aramaeans

Cush: Ancient kingdom of Northeast Africa

Mizraim: Egypt

Casluhim: Philistines

Caphtorim: Crete

Phut: Region of Libya

Canaan: Canaanites and various other groups

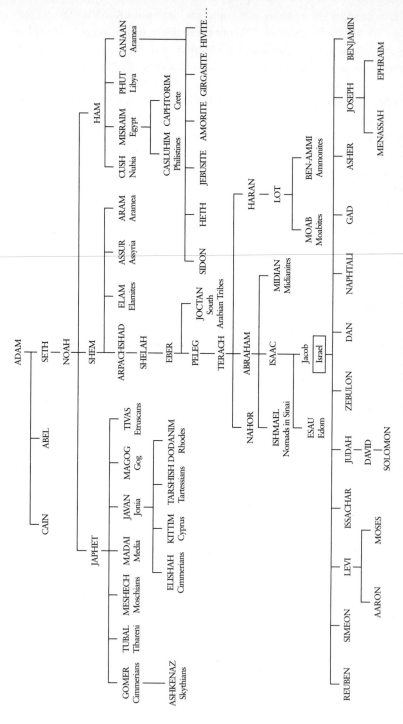

Biblical genealogy including the Table of Nations.

The Table of Nations is not complete, nor does it claim to be. Genesis 10:5 states, for example, "From these the maritime nations branched out." This implies that although the narrative is explaining the origins of many nations of the world, it is not supplying a complete inventory. Again, however, most of the known ancient world is represented.

There are also many places in the Jewish tradition where interest in the subject of genealogy can be found. For example, the three groups of Jews, known individually as Kohen, Levi, and Yisroel, are ancient designations that we continue to identify with to this day. But remember that the Talmudic sages teach, "A learned bastard takes precedence over an ignorant high priest" (Horayot 3:8).

There are several characteristics of Jewish genealogical records that make them recognizable and set them apart from records of other types; for example:

- Jewish names are traditionally two-generation names connected by *ben* ("son of"). My Hebrew name is Avraham Abba ben Chaim Shaul. My son's name is Moshe Yosef ben Avraham Abba.

- In Europe, Jewish records were often kept separately from others.

- Many Jewish last names are distinctively or commonly known to be Jewish.

- Because the Holocaust, only sixty years ago, profoundly affected most Jewish families in the world, extensive Nazi and Holocaust records are also, ironically, mostly of Jewish families.

- There are unique Jewish documents, such as *ketubot* (marriage contracts), *mohel* books, memorial (Yizkor) books, and *haskamot* (approbations), that can be helpful to the Jewish genealogist.

- Rabbis from rabbinic families often maintained extensive family trees.

---
o

The search for roots, even in the simplest genealogical sense, is likely to be a meaningful experience on both the personal and religious levels.

—Rabbi Adin Steinsaltz,
Teshuvah: A Guide for the Newly Observant Jew

If a man's relative is rich, he claims kinship; if poor, he disowns him.

—D'varim Rabbah 2

---
o

Memorial Books (Yizkor Books)

One of the best sources for learning about Jewish communities is memorial books. I never dreamed, when I walked into the New York Public Library more than thirty years ago, that I would find a book of several hundred pages devoted entirely to the tiny town in Poland from which my father's family came—*and* that the book would contain photos of my great-grandfather and my grandmother and a street map of the town, with an indication of where my family lived! The book was a Yizkor or memorial book.

Memorial books tell the story of the Jewish community of a single town (or a town and the surrounding villages). They have been published and from time to time continue to be published by landsmanshaften or individuals. A wonderful example of a recent Yizkor book, in this case written and compiled by one individual, is *Between Galicia and Hungary: The Jews of Stropkov,* by Melody Amsel, published by Avotaynu. I am particularly interested in this book because a branch of my mother's family comes from Stropkov. As I indicated earlier, I am a direct descendant of the Hasidic rebbe of Stropkov, Rabbi Chaim Yosef Gottlieb. He was my great-great-great-grandfather. Melody Amsel, who worked on the book for years, did a superb job. The book is both beautiful and filled with information.

Members of landsmanshaften, because of their affection for their old community as well as their admirable historical sense, have published memorial books as a tribute to their old homes and the people who were murdered during the Holocaust.

Several hundred memorial books, corresponding to the same number of villages, shtetlach, and cities, have been published. Often the tiniest village will have a large book devoted to its history, reflecting the devotion of the survivors. Most of the memorial books have been published since the Holocaust, though many books of a similar nature were published before then. Books were often written and published to describe tragic events in the lives of communities and to memorialize the victims of those events. Many books can be found in response to pogroms, for example.

Post–World War II memorial books usually have a similar format. There are historical articles about the location, photographs, maps, illustrations, and names of Holocaust victims. Many of these books also contain advertisements; ordinarily, space was sold to survivors in order to raise publication money. These advertisements are in themselves good sources of information about individuals. The ads often contain photographs as well.

Memorial books have usually been written by many people, not just one author. The landsmanshaften gather articles on different aspects of life in the location, and these are collected for the book. Although the major emphasis of most memorial books is the fate of the town during the Holocaust, the books also contain some of the finest historical material about the towns. It is for this reason that these books are a good general source, regardless of when a family left a town. Even if your family left the town of Skala in 1901, the Skala memorial book published after World War II would be of interest.

Although the Jewish communities of Eastern Europe have been the largest producers of memorial books, Jewish communities in Western Europe, especially in Germany, have produced many as well. However, a general difference between most of the German works and the Eastern European ones is that the German books are usually the effort of one person, whereas the Eastern European books are collective works.

One of the drawbacks to the use of memorial books for many people is that they are often written in Hebrew and Yiddish, although many books have English sections containing translations of some of the Yiddish or Hebrew, in most cases. However, this should not stop you from examining these books. Certainly, people can be found who can translate the material.

Of special note is the effort on the part of JewishGen.com (http://www.jewishgen.org/Yizkor/translations.html) to gather translations of memorial books. Progress on this project has been amazing. (See "The Yizkor Book Project" later in this chapter for details on the translation effort.)

In addition to the factual information, the photographs contained in the books are wonderful to experience, although the photographs themselves are hardly "wonderful" in that they document Holocaust atrocities that took place in the localities discussed in the books.

Another feature of a majority of these books is a name index that is of great assistance when doing family history. The indexes are never complete, though, and should not be relied on as the only thing to check for family history.

Memorial books can be used in a variety of ways. The most obvious is to read them to find material on members of your family. Your prospects for success are quite good, particularly since in the case of smaller communities, the chances of your being related to many people in the town, through marriage if nothing else, are great. But in addition to personal family research, memorial books can provide other information. I have already mentioned the value of the photographs, which are often the greatest source of information on particular towns that

exists. Memorial books also often discuss religious life in the towns and frequently focus on the rabbis or masters who taught in the towns. The influence of a rabbi on his following was often (and continues to be for many) the most profound in a person's life. There is little question but that knowledge about an ancestor's rabbi or rebbe is knowledge about an ancestor.

Many of the memorial books have street maps of the towns as well. These maps range from the most general of views to house-to-house details. Often you can, with the aid of a relative who was from the town, locate the exact place where your family's home stood. These maps can also give you a vivid idea of the size of the town of your ancestral home.

In the same way that you can "enter" the life of a historical figure by reading his or her biography, you can enter the towns of your ancestors by reading the biographies of the towns themselves. Memorial books are exactly that: biographies of towns that no longer exist but that at one time were known as home to your ancestors.

One day I was showing a student of mine the wonderful book collection in the New York Public Library Jewish Division, which is where I originally found my great-grandfather's picture. When we entered the room, I asked my student to tell me the names of the towns where her ancestors were from. She looked at me knowingly, and said, "It's not going to happen to me. Don't be funny."

I insisted that we look anyway, and we found several photographs of members of her family, as well as an essay written by her grandfather!

I could tell many other true stories just like this one. The moral: look for memorial books of your towns!

Are There Memorial Books for Your Towns?

Zachary Baker, former librarian at YIVO and currently Reinhard Family Curator of Judaica and Hebraica Collections at the Stanford University Libraries, was for a number of years the man who was keeping track of which memorial books exist. I included his excellent bibliography of memorial books, compiled in 1993, in the 1994 edition of *From Generation to Generation*.

On the next few pages is a list of the names of the towns included in Zachary Baker's bibliography, with a few additions. My main motive in providing this list is to interest you in going further in your research. If you find towns of interest on this list, track down the book (I'll tell you how soon). If you *don't* find a town, there still might be a memorial book— perhaps on the book itself, the name of the town is spelled differently.

If you come from a particularly small town, you need to look on a map or consult the book *Where Once We Walked* (see page 166) to find out what the nearby towns were. Often a memorial book will focus on one town but also include information about nearby shtetlach.

Sometimes the towns on this list appear more than once with different spellings. Although Zachary Baker didn't give every alternative, he gave a lot of the more common ones. For example, my great-grandfather's town of Przemysl also appears on this list as Premisle.

○

Towns That Have Memorial Books

Akkerman	Belz	Bobruisk
Aleksandria	Bendery	Boiberik
Aleksandrow	Bendin	Bolechow
Alt Lesle	Beresteczko	Bolimow
Amdur	Bereza-Kartuska	Boremel
Amshinov	Berezno	Borsa
Andrychow	Berezo	Borszczow
Annopol	Bershad	Boryslaw
Antopol	Berzhan	Bransk
Apt	Beszterce	Braslaw
Augustow	Betlen	Bratislava
Auschwitz	Biala Podlaska	Braynsk
Babi Yar	Biala Rawska	Brest Litovsk
Bacau	Bialobrzegi	Breziv
Baia Mare	Bialystok	Brezova nad Bradlom
Baklerove	Biecz	Briceni
Baligrod	Bielica	Brichany
Balin	Bielitz-Biala	Brichevo
Balmazujvaros	Bielsko-Biala	Briegel
Banffy-Hunyad	Bielsk-Podlaski	Brisk
Baranovka	Biezun	Brisk Kuyavsk
Baranow	Bikovsk	Brody
Baranowicze	Bilgoraj	Broslev
Barylow	Bisk	Broszniow
Baytsh	Bistrita	Brzesc Kujawski
Beclean	Bitolj	Brzesc nad Bugiem
Bedzin	Bitshutsh	Brzesko
Belchatow	Bivolari	Brzezany
Belgorod-Dnestrovski	Bledow	Brzeziny
Beligrod	Bobrka	Brzeznica

Brzozow
Buchach
Buczacz
Budapest
Budzanow
Bukaczowce
Bukowsko
Bursztyn
Busk
Byalovzig
Bychawa
Byten
Cakovec
Calarasi
Capresti
Cernauti
Cetatea-Alba
Charsznica
Chelm
Chernovtsy
Chervonoarmeisk
Chmielnik
Chodecz
Cholojow
Chorostkow
Chorzele
Chrzanow
Ciechanow
Ciechanowiec
Ciechocinek
Cieszanow
Cluj
Cmielow
Cracow
Csaktornya
Csenger
Czarny Dunajec
Czerbin
Czernowitz
Czestochowa
Czortkow
Czyzewo
Dabrowa Gornicza
Dabrowica
Daugavpils

Daugieliszki
David Horodok
Dawidgrodek
Debica
Deblin
Debrecen
Dej
Delatycze
Dembits
Demblin
Derecske
Dereczyn
Derewno
Des
Devenishki
Dibetsk
Dieveniskes
Dinov
Disna
Divenishok
Dmytrow
Dnepropetrovsk
Dobromil
Dobryn
Dobrzyn
Dokszyce
Dolhinow
Dombrava Gornitsha
Dombrovitsa
Drodzyn
Drohiczyn nad Bugiem
Drohiczyn Poleski
Drohobycz
Droshkopol
Druja
Drujsk
Druzkopol
Dubene
Dubiecko
Dubno
Dubossary
Dubrovitsa
Dukszty
Dumbraveny
Dunajska Streda

Dunaszerdahely
Dunilowicze
Dusetos
Dvart
Dvinsk
Dyatlovo
Dynow
Dzerzhinsk
Dzialoszyce
Dziewieniszki
Dzikow
Dzisna
Edineti
Eger
Ejszyski
Ejszyszki
Ekaterinoslav
Erlau
Falenica
Fehergyarmat
Felshtin
Filipow
Frampol
Gabin
Gargzdai
Garwolin
Ger
Gherla
Glebokie
Glina
Gliniany
Glinojeck
Glubok
Glusk
Gniewaszow
Golub
Gombin
Gomel
Goniadz
Gora Kalwaria
Gorlice
Gorodnitsa
Gorzd
Gostynin
Goworowo

Grabowiec
Grajewo
Greiding
Gritsa
Grodek
Grodek Jagiellonski
Grodno
Grojec
Gross Magendorf
Grosswardein
Grozovo
Gusiatyn
Gwozdziec
Gyor
Hajdunanas
Hajdusamson
Halmi
Harlau
Haydutsishok
Hivniv
Hlusk
Hoduciszki
Holojow
Holszany
Holynka
Homel
Horochow
Horodec
Horodenka
Horodlo
Horodno
Horodok
Horyngrod
Hoszcza
Hotin
Hrubieszow
Huedin
Husiatyn
Iampol
Ignatowka
Iklad
Ileanda
Ilja
Indura
Istrik
Ivano-Frankovsk

Ivanovo
Iwacewicze
Iwie
Iwieniec
Jablonka
Jadow
Jaisi
Janova
Janow
Jaroslaw
Jaryczow Nowy
Jaslo
Jaworow
Jedrzejow
Jedwabne
Jeremicze
Jezierna
Jezierzany
Jeznas
Jod
Jonava
Jordanow
Jozefow
Jurbarkas
Kadzidlo
Kalarash
Kalisz
Kalov
Kalusz
Kaluszyn
Kalwaria
Kamenets-Litovsk
Kamenets-Podolskiy
Kamien
Kamien Koszyrski
Kamieniec Litewski
Kamiensk
Kammeny Brod
Kapreshty
Kapsukas
Kapulye
Karcag
Karczew
Kartuz-Bereze
Kaszony
Kazimierz

Kedainiai
Kelts
Keydan
Khmelnitskii
Kholm
Khotin
Khozhel
Kibart
Kielce
Kiemieliszki
Kiernozia
Kikol
Kislowszczyzna
Kisvarda
Kitai-Gorod
Kitev
Klausenburg
Kleck
Kleinwardein
Klobucko
Klosowa
Knenitsh
Knihynicze
Kobryn
Kobylnik
Kock
Koidanovo
Kolarovgrad
Kolbuszowa
Kolki
Kolno
Kolo
Kolomyja
Kolonia Synajska
Kolozsborsa
Kolozsvar
Koltyniany
Komarno
Konin
Konyar
Kopin
Koprzywnica
Kopyczynce
Kopyl
Korczyna
Korelicze

Korets
Koriv
Korzec
Kosice
Kosow
Kosow Lacki
Kostopol
Kosyno
Kotsk
Kowal
Kowel
Kozangrodek
Koziany
Kozieniec
Krakinovo
Krakow
Krakowiec
Krasnik
Krasnobrod
Krasnystaw
Krekenava
Krememits
Kripa
Krivitsh
Kroscienko
Kroshnik
Krosniewiec
Krynki
Krzemienica
Krzemieniec
Krzywicze
Kshoynzh
Ksiaz Wielki
Kunow
Kurow
Kurzeniec
Kutno
Kuty
Kuzmir
Kybartai
Lachowicze
Lachwa
Lancut
Lanovits
Lanowce
Lapichi

Lashwa
Lask
Laskarzew
Leczyca
Lemberg
Lenin
Leonpol
Lesko
Levertev
Lezajsk
Libovne
Lida
Likeva
Linshits
Linsk
Lipkany
Lipniszki
Lipno
Litevisk
Lizhensk
Lodz
Lokacze
Lomza
Lopatyn
Losice
Lowicz
Lozisht
Lubartow
Lubcza
Lubenichi
Lubicz
Lublin
Luboml
Lubraniec
Luck
Ludmir
Ludwipol
Lukow
Luniniec
Lutowiska
Lutsk
Lvov
Lwow
Lyngmiany
Lynki
Lyntupy

Lyskow
Lyszkowice
Lyuban
Mad
Magyarlapos
Makow-Mazowiecki
Makow Podhalanski
Malecz
Margareten
Margita
Marijampole
Markuleshty
Markuszow
Marosvasarhely
Marvits
Medenice
Melits
Meretsh
Merkine
Meytshet
Mezhirechye
Mezritsh
Miava
Michalovce
Michow
Miechow
Miedzyrzec
Miedzyrzec-Wolyn
Mielec
Mielnica
Mikepercs
Mikolajow
Mikulince
Mikulov
Milosna
Minkovtsy
Minsk
Minsk-Mazowiecki
Miory
Mir
Miskolc
Mizocz
Mlawa
Mlynow
Modrzyc
Mogielnica

Molczadz
Monasterzyska
Monastir
Mosty
Mosty-Wielkie
Motele
Motol
Mszczonow
Mukacevo
Munkacs
Murawica
Myjava
Mysleniec
Myszyniec
Nadarzyn
Nadworna
Nadzin
Nagybanya
Nagyilonda
Nagykallo
Nagymagyar
Nagymihaly
Nagyszollos
Nagytapolcsany
Nagyvarad
Naliboki
Narajow
Navaredok
Naymark
Nemirov
Nestilye
Neumarkt
Nevel
Nieswiez
Nieszawa
Nikolsburg
Novograd-Volynskiy
Novo Minsk
Novyi Vitkov
Novyi Yarichev
Nowe Miasto
Nowogrod
Nowogrodek
Nowo-Swieciany
Nowy Dwor
Nowy Sacz

Nowy Targ
Nowy Zagorz
Odessa
Okmieniec
Okuniew
Olkeniki
Olkusz
Olshan
Olyka
Opatow
Opoczno
Opole
Opsa
Oradea
Orgeyev
Orhei
Orlowa
Oshmena
Oshpitsin
Osiek
Osipovichi
Ostra
Ostrog
Ostroleka
Ostrowiec
Ostrow-Lubelski
Ostrow-Mazowiecka
Ostryna
Oswiecim
Oszmaiana
Otvotsk
Otwock
Ozarow
Ozieran
Ozorkow
Pabianice
Paks
Papa
Parafianowo
Parczew
Parichi
Parysow
Perehinsko
Petrikov
Piaski
Piatnica

Piesk
Piestany
Pilev
Pinczow
Pinsk
Piotrkow Trybunalski
Pitshayev
Plantsh
Plawno
Plintsk
Plock
Plonsk
Plotsk
Plusy
Poczajow
Podbrodzie
Podhajce
Podwoloczyska
Pogost
Pohost
Pokshivnitsa
Polaniec
Poligon
Polonnoye
Porcsalma
Porisov
Porozow
Postawy
Postyen
Pozsony
Praga
Premisle
Pressburg
Proshnits
Proskurov
Pruszkow
Pruzana
Przasnysz
Przeclaw
Przedborz
Przedecz
Przemysl
Przytyk
Pshaytsh
Pshedbozh
Pshemishl

Pshetslav
Pshitik
Pulawy
Pultusk
Punsk
Raab
Rabka
Rachev
Rachov
Raciaz
Raczki
Radikhov
Radom
Radomsko
Radomysl Wielki
Radoszkowice
Radzanow
Radziechow
Radzin
Radziwillow
Radzymin
Rakhov
Rakishok
Rakospalota
Rakow
Ratno
Rawa Ruska
Raysha
Rayvits
Rejowiec
Rembertow
Retteg
Rietavas
Rimszan
Riskeva
Rohatyn
Rokiskis
Rokitno
Romanova
Rotin
Rovno
Rowne
Rozan
Rozana
Rozanka
Rozhan

Rozhinoy
Rozniatow
Rozprza
Rozwadow
Rozyszcze
Rubeshov
Rubiel
Rubiezewicze
Rudki
Ruscova
Ryki
Rypin
Rytwiany
Rzeszow
Saloniki
Sambor
Sammerein
Samorin
Sanok
Sants
Sarkeystsene
Sarnaki
Sarny
Sasow
Satmar
Satorujhely
Satu Mare
Schodnica
Schutt
    Szerdahely
Secureni
Sedziszow
Sekiryani
Selib
Selish
Selts
Semyatichi
Sendishev
Serock
Sevlus
Shchedrin
Shebreshin
Shedlets
Shelib
Sherpts
Shidlovtse

Shimsk
Shkud
Shpola
Shransk
Shtruvits
Shumen
Shumla
Siedlce
Siedliszcze
Sielec
Siemiatycze
Sienkow
Sierpc
Siniawka
Sislevitsh
Skala
Skalat
Skarzysko-
    Kamienna
Skepe
Skierniewice
Sknilow
Skole
Skuodas
Slobodka
Slonim
Slupia
Slutsk
Sluzewo
Smorgonie
Smotrich
Soblas
Sobolew
Sobota
Sochaczew
Sofyovka
Sokal
Sokolka
Sokolovka
Sokolow
Sokoly
Sombor
Somorja
Sompolno
Sonik
Sopockinie

Sopotkin
Sosnovoye
Sosnowiec
Stanislawczyk
Stanislawow
Starachowice
Starobin
Starye Dorogi
Stary Sambor
Staszow
Stavische
Stawiski
Stefanesti
Stepan
Steybts
Stiyanev
Stoczek-Wegrowski
Stojaciszki
Stojanow
Stok
Stolin
Stolpce
Stramtura
Stremiltsh
Strimtera
Strusow
Stryj
Strzegowo
Strzemilcze
Strzyzow
Stutshin
Sucha
Suchocin
Suchowola
Suprasl
Suwalki
Swaryczow
Swieciany
Swierzen
Swir
Swislocz
Szamosujvar
Szarkowszczyzna
Szatmarnemeti
Szczawnica
Szczebrzeszyn

Szczekociny
Szczuczyn
Szczurowice
Szereszow
Szikszo
Szkudy
Szransk
Szumsk
Szurdok
Szydlow
Szydlowiec
Targowica
Targu-Lapus
Targu-Mures
Tarnobrzeg
Tarnogrod
Tarnopol
Tarnow
Tartakow
Tasnad
Teglas
Telechany
Telenesti-Targ
Telsiai
Telz
Teplik
Terebovlya
Ternovka
Thessaloniki Tighina
Tiktin
Timkovichi
Tishevits
Tlumacz
Tluste
Tluszcz
Tolmitsh
Tolstoye
Tomaszow-Lubelski
Tomaszow
    Mazowiecki
Topolcany
Toporow
Torczyn
Torna
Torun
Trembowla

Trisk
Trokhenbrod
Troki
Trovits
Trzebinia
Tshebin
Tshekhanov
Tshekhanovets
Tshenstokhov
Tsheshanov
Tshizheva
Tshmelev
Tuczyn
Turbin
Turcz
Turek
Turets
Turka
Turna
Turobin
Turzec
Turzysk
Tykocin
Tysmienica
Tyszowce
Ubinie
Uhnow
Ujhely
Ujpest
Ungvar
Urechye
Uscilug
Ustila
Ustrzyki Dolne
Utena
Utyan
Uzhorod
Uzlovoye
Vamospercs
Vas
Vashilkov
Vashniev
Vasilishok
Vayslits
Velky Mager
Vengrov

Venice
Verbo
Verzhbnik
Vidz
Vilna
Vilnius
Vinogradov
Vishneva
Vishnevets
Vishogrod
Viskit
Visooroszi
Visotsk
Vitebsk
Vitkov
Vizna
Vladimirets
Vladimir Volynskiy
Vloyn
Voislavitsa
Volozhin
Voltshin
Voronovo
Voydislav
Vrbove
Vurka
Vysokoye
Wadowice
Warez
Warka
Warsaw
Warta
Wasiliszki
Wasilkow
Wasniow
Wegrow
Werenow
Widze
Wieliczka
Wielun
Wieruszow
Wierzbnik
Wilejka
Wilno

Wiskitki
Wislica
Wisniowiec Nowy
Wiszniew
Witkow Nowy
Wloclawek
Wlodawa
Wlodzimierz
Wlodzimierzec
Wodzislaw
Wojslawice
Wolborz
Wolbrom
Wolczyn
Wolica-Wygoda
Wolkowysk
Wolma
Wolomin
Wolozyn
Wolpa
Wsielub
Wysock
Wysokie-
    Litewskie
Wysokie-
    Mazowieckie
Wyszkow
Wyszogrod
Wyzgrodek
Yagistov
Yampol
Yanova
Yanovichi
Yartshev
Yavoriv
Yedintsy
Yedvabne
Yekaterinoslav
Yendrikhov
Yendzheva
Yurburg
Yustingrad
Zablotow
Zabludow

Zagaipol
Zakopane
Zaloshits
Zambrow
Zamekhov
Zamosc
Zamosze
Zaracze
Zareby Kowcielne
Zarki
Zaromb
Zarszyn
Zassow
Zastawie
Zawidcze
Zawiercie
Zbaraz
Zborow
Zdunska Wola
Zdzieciol
Zelechow
Zelow
Zelwa
Zemplen
Zeplenmegye
Zetel
Zgierz
Zhelekhov
Zhetl
Zholkva
Zinkov
Zloczew
Zloczow
Zofiowka
Zolkiew
Zolochev
Zoludek
Zoludzk
Zombor
Zvihil
Zwiahel
Zwolen
Zychlin
Zyrardow

The Yizkor Book Project

The Yizkor Book Project (http://www.jewishgen.org/Yizkor), hosted by JewishGen.org, was begun in 1994 by a group of JewishGen volunteers. The effort was led by Leonard Markowitz and Martin Kessel, according to the JewishGen Web site. Their translation project was developed by Susannah Juni and implemented by Joyce Field. The Web site states, "It is our purpose to unlock the valuable information contained in Yizkor Books so that genealogists and others can learn more about their heritage." They certainly are living up to their goals.

A main feature of this part of JewishGen.org's Web site is the Yizkor Book Database. It is divided into parts:

○ The *Yizkor Book Catalog* lists all Yizkor books known to exist, as well as many other books written about particular towns. The database currently contains the titles of more than one thousand books.

○ The *Yizkor Book Contacts* database tries to match up people who own copies of the same memorial book or who are interested in the same memorial book "to help defray the cost of the translation of portions or the complete book." To date, the database contains more than fourteen hundred contact entries.

○ *Library Holdings:* The Yizkor Book Project is doing a wonderful job of collecting Yizkor book call numbers from libraries and archives with significant Yizkor book collections. If you learn of a Yizkor book of interest, chances are good that one of these libraries will have it.

Here are a list of the libraries that are currently included:

California	Los Angeles: Hebrew Union College
	Los Angeles: Simon Wiesenthal Center/Yeshiva University Library
	Los Angeles: UCLA Research Library
	Los Angeles: University of Judaism
	San Francisco: Holocaust Center of Northern California
Florida	Gainesville: Price Library of Judaica, University of Florida
Maryland	Baltimore: Joseph Meyerhoff Library
Massachusetts	Boston: Boston Public Library
	Brookline: Hebrew College

	Cambridge: Harvard University Library
	Waltham: Brandeis University Library
Michigan	Ann Arbor: Harlan Hatcher Graduate Library, University of Michigan
New York	New York: American Jewish Historical Society
	New York: Bund Archives (collection at YIVO)
	New York: Hebrew Union College-Jewish Institute of Religion Library
	New York: Jewish Theological Seminary Library
	New York: New York Public Library Jewish Division
	New York: Yeshiva University Library
	New York: YIVO Institute for Jewish Research Library
Oregon	Portland: Congregation Neveh Shalom
Great Britain	Cambridge: Cambridge University Library
	Finchley: JGS of Great Britain, Finchley Synagogue
	London: University of London, School of Oriental and African Studies
	London: Weinser Library
Israel	Ramat-Gan: Bar-Ilan University
	Tel Aviv: Ahad Haam Library
	Tel Aviv: Hitachdut Yotzei Polin
	Tel Aviv: Moadon Ha'Bund
	Tel Aviv: Rambam Library

Other Places to Look for Yizkor Books

JewishGen.org's Yizkor Book Project also offers an impressive list of libraries that collect Yizkor books organized by state and by country. Go to http://www.jewishgen.org/Yizkor/yizlibs.html. This list of libraries includes information about all libraries and archives that have substantial collections of Yizkor books (defined as "more than twenty-five").

Genealogical Resources in New York, edited by Estelle M. Guzik, was revised and reissued in 2003. It is published by the Jewish Genealogical Society of New York. Included is the "Bibliography of Eastern European Memorial (Yizkor) Books with Call Numbers for Five Judaica Libraries in New York." The five libraries are the YIVO Institute for Jewish Research, the New York Public Library Jewish Division, the Jewish Theological Seminary Library, the Mendel Gottesman Library at Yeshiva University, and the Hebrew Union College–Jewish Institute of Religion.

If you do a Google search for the terms "memorial book or Yizkor book," you will find lots of Web sites, including those of specific libraries and institutions that have Yizkor book collections. But JewishGen.org's Yizkor Book Project is probably comprehensive enough to help you to locate the Yizkor books you want to see.

How to Obtain Copies for Yourself

Once you have located a relevant memorial book, you will undoubtedly want to own a copy. A memorial book is not the kind of publication you would find in a local bookshop, nor can a local store order a copy for you. In almost all cases, memorial books have been privately published and are distributed by the people who have the book printed—usually a landsmanshaft. In some cases, you may be able to either track down the individuals or organization that had the book published or find someone who will track them down for you. Keep in mind that you might have to resort to doing some extensive photocopying if you cannot obtain the memorial book in which you are interested. But if you put effort into your search, a copy of the book you want may turn up.

For example, when I found a memorial book for my father's town of Dobromil, I examined the book and found that the editors lived in New York. I looked through the New York City phone books and tracked them down—finally locating a copy of the memorial book. Remember that many memorial books were published in Israel, so when you travel to Israel, you will want to do the same kind of searching for editors—and it will of course be rewarding just to meet these landsmen. (By the way, if you do locate a memorial book of interest, see if you can buy more than one copy; someone else in the family might want one.)

Another way of locating memorial books, and one that is both the most rewarding and the most difficult, is to track down the people or landsmanshaft that published the book in which you are interested. In this way

you will also have personal contact with interesting people—and that is what genealogical research is all about. (See "Locating Landsmanshaften" in Chapter Eleven.)

There are also some booksellers who handle memorial books. Part of the Yizkor Book Project Web site is devoted to "Retail Establishments with Yizkor Book Holdings." The Web page for this is http://www.jewishgen.org/yizkor/yizret.html.

The Yizkor Book Special Interest Group (SIG)

The Yizkor Book SIG has its own e-mail list to permit participants to learn more about Yizkor books. Go to http://www.jewishgen.org/yizkor/list.html.

○

A scattered nation that remembers its past and connects it with the present will undoubtedly have a future as a people and probably even a more glorious life than the one in the past.

—Lev Levanda

○

Two Traditional Sources: Mohel Books and *Ketubot*

The mohel book is a Jewish phenomenon that helps us view Jewish history through individuals. A mohel book is a record book kept by the mohel, or circumciser, listing each boy whom he circumcised. These books, many of which still exist from old communities, are an intriguing and unique record of Jewish male births in communities.

Finding a mohel book for a particular community and then finding a reference in it to someone in your family is a long shot, but it would be worth checking by more ambitious family researchers. The Leo Baeck Institute (see page 111) has a collection of mohel books of German origin. The Central Archives for the History of the Jewish People in Jerusalem (see page 120) also has mohel books for scattered communities around the world.

The *ketubah,* or marriage certificate, reflects another custom in Jewish history that puts the focus on the individuals who are a part of it. Very often *ketubot* will be handed down from generation to generation within a family. *Ketubot* record the names of the individuals being married and often include other family names as well. In the seventeenth and

eighteenth centuries, illuminated *ketubot* were popular, making the documents attractive as works of art.

Archives, Libraries, and Organizations

If I were to quantify all of the results of my genealogical research over the years, I would say that the majority of what I learned was not found in archives, libraries, or government offices but gleaned from interviews with my relatives. The stories, the photos, and the flavor of my family history come from the human contact I have had with the relatives I've discovered around the world.

But although the heart and soul of my family history comes from living sources, the basic structure of my family history is made up of the names and dates and bits of information stored in institutions or on documents.

Many of these institutions and documents provide information for individuals in the United States regardless of family background. The other government agencies that we discussed in Chapter Three pertain to all Americans.

But some of the most important sources for Jewish genealogists can be found in uniquely Jewish archives and libraries or in collections that are specific to Jews. The following are the most important and will be of the greatest value to you.

American Jewish Archives

The American Jewish Archives (AJA), founded in 1947, is devoted to collecting historical documents relating to American Jewry. Of special interest to the family history researcher is the AJA's collection of family trees and family histories. The organization also has a large collection of synagogue records (mostly Reform, because of their affiliation with the Reform movement, but others as well) that would be quite valuable if your family belonged to one of the synagogues whose records are deposited there.

The American Jewish Archives Web site at http://www.huc.edu/aja/intro.html has a section on the AJA's genealogical interests (http://www.americanjewisharchives.org/aja/genealogy/index.html). The Web site states: "Jewish genealogy is a highly developed field of study. There are numerous resources for the beginning and advanced genealogist that are available on the Internet and in most bookstores and libraries. A basic knowledge of genealogy procedures will allow researchers to make better use of their time and improve their chances of success. As part of our service, the AJA staff will be happy to provide you with a listing

of some of these most popular resources." It goes on to say: "The American Jewish Archives welcomes genealogy inquiries. All inquiries should be in writing by either fax, e-mail, or regular mail. Each inquiry will receive a personal response."

Explore the American Jewish Archives Web site. As noted, the AJA answers inquiries and will often photocopy relevant material. You cannot expect the organization to do much research for you, but it is willing to make initial searches to determine whether it has something of interest. The AJA also has a great deal of valuable material useful for doing research regarding a town or city in the United States.

If you have published a family history, written a town history, or simply drawn a family tree, send a copy to the AJA. Your work will then become a part of its holdings; you can never tell when a person might check the AJA for a certain surname and it will be yours. Depositing your research at the AJA is also serving the cause of American Jewish history. The address is as follows:

American Jewish Archives
3101 Clifton Avenue
Cincinnati, OH 45220

The Center for Jewish History

The Center for Jewish History is among the most important new institutions on the American Jewish landscape. The idea itself is brilliant: the major Jewish historical institutions in the United States should occupy one building, share resources (save money), and thereby improve their services to the public. This surely has happened. The American Jewish Historical Society, the American Sephardi Federation, the Leo Baeck Institute, the Yeshiva University Museum, and the YIVO Institute for Jewish Research are all under one roof in a beautiful building near the heart of Greenwich Village—15 West 16th Street, New York, NY 10011; (212) 294-8301; fax (212) 294-8302.

The building is modern, there is a clean kosher cafeteria, access to materials is better than ever, and in addition to these five institutions, the Center for Jewish History also maintains the Center for Jewish History Genealogy Institute, surely the most important new development for Jewish genealogists in regard to three of the five organizations: YIVO, the Leo Baeck Institute, and the American Jewish Historical Society.

With combined holdings of approximately 100 million archival documents, a half million books, and thousands of photographs, artifacts,

paintings, and textiles, the Center for Jewish History is the largest repository documenting the Jewish experience outside of Israel.

When I first discovered the existence of the YIVO Institute about twenty-five years ago, I felt that I had stumbled on a treasure trove, an amazing and priceless inheritance. I made some of my most important discoveries at YIVO, including one discovery that took my family tree back centuries. But at that time, YIVO was unprepared to handle the increasing number of people who were looking for information about their Jewish roots—in part due to my own writing and frequent lecturing about how and why to do Jewish genealogy research. One day, years ago, I was standing in the lobby of YIVO when one of the senior staff approached me and said that I was the one "making all the trouble." What this person meant, of course, was that I was one of the loudest spokespersons for Jewish genealogy, and I was telling everyone what they could find at YIVO!

In those days, there were also some extraordinarily helpful and supportive people at YIVO, including the late Dina Abramowicz and the late Lucjan Dobroszycki. Both of these individuals were amazingly knowledgeable and always encouraging; they were wonderful souls. I will forever be indebted to them for their help and friendship. Another shining light at YIVO was Zachary Baker, who was the former head librarian there. He too was always a great supporter of genealogists who wanted to discover YIVO's many amazing collections, including, as noted earlier, its superb collection of memorial books and its profoundly moving collection of Holocaust survivor lists. Zachary Baker is a role model for professional librarians: he knows his field, he is always growing, and he treats library users as important guests.

But as I said, YIVO was largely unprepared for the onslaught of Jewish genealogists. It was used to helping students and scholars, not laypeople who did not speak or read Yiddish, Russian, Polish, Hebrew, or other languages in its files and who did not even know how to use a library properly. In addition, most Jewish genealogists don't really know what they are looking for when they enter YIVO. I had no idea that I would discover books at YIVO containing lists of Holocaust survivors. I had no idea that I would find a book of Hasidic rebbes indexed by town, ultimately leading me to discover my great-great-great-grandfather, Rabbi Chaim Yosef Gottlieb, the Stropkover Rebbe. I had no idea that I would find photographs of tiny towns that didn't even appear on most maps but that my family had lived in a century ago.

YIVO didn't really know either. It was clear that most of YIVO's staff, twenty-five years ago, did not themselves appreciate what materials they

had that would be life-changing for future users of their collections. Since then, thousands of people have used the YIVO collection in search of their family's history and come away enriched.

The situation at the Leo Baeck Institute and the American Jewish Historical Society was different. The librarians and archivists at these institutions seemed somewhat better able to handle genealogical researchers, at least in my experience. But there always seemed to be far more people using YIVO's collection, and YIVO just didn't have the manpower to handle the growing numbers of library and archives users.

The Center for Jewish History Genealogy Institute has changed all that. Now located within the Center for Jewish History, it is an institute that helps people to do Jewish genealogy research and helps researchers use the collections housed at the Center for Jewish History. The staff is friendly and inviting, their enthusiasm for Jewish genealogy is high, and their mandate is to be as helpful as they can be!

The institute's Web site (http://www.cjh.org/family) states: "The Genealogy Institute helps new and experienced family history researchers learn about the world of their ancestors. We help you learn about your ancestors by providing reference and educational services, and creating programming on family history and its connections to the broader sweep of Jewish history. The Institute also leads researchers to the primary sources at the Center: Yizkor books and landsmanshaft records at YIVO, family and community histories at the Leo Baeck Institute, and military records at the American Jewish Historical Society are just a few of the rich primary sources open to researchers."

The Frequently Asked Questions part of the Web site is excellent—go to http://www.cjh.org/family/faq.cfm.

○

A Conversation with Robert Friedman

Robert Friedman is director of the Genealogy Institute at the Center for Jewish History in New York City. After many years in the public health field, he turned his passion for genealogy into a new career. He began his family history research in 1994, focusing on Hungary, Transylvania, eastern Slovakia, and the former Suwalki province in Russian Poland. An active H-SIG (Hungarian Special Interest Group) correspondent, he has also participated in the ROM-SIG (Romania Special Interest Group), the IAJGS (International Associate of Jewish Genealogical Societies) Cemetery Project, and the JewishGen Yizkor Book Project. He has served on the

executive council of Jewish Genealogical Society of New York, volunteered at the Museum of Jewish Heritage library and the Center for Jewish History Genealogy Institute, and recently obtained a degree in library and information science from Long Island University. As a YIVO archives intern, he arranged and described the personal papers of William O. McCagg Jr., a historian of Austro-Hungarian Jewry.

Q. How would you describe the Genealogy Institute to someone who has never heard of it?

A. The Center for Jewish History Genealogy Institute is a place for beginning genealogists to receive guidance on general methods, strategies, and resources and for more advanced researchers to receive assistance in accessing the various collections at the center. We provide information through our Web site, fact sheets, and in-house reference collection of print and electronic resources. People can come in at any time, without an appointment, and get reference assistance from a staff member or volunteer. We also respond to inquiries by e-mail, letter, fax, or telephone and offer several educational programs.

Q. Who is Rachel Fisher? What is her relationship to the institute?

A. Rachel Fisher is the founding director of Center for Jewish History Genealogy Institute. She holds a Ph.D. in religious studies and wrote her dissertation on genealogy and its effect on Jewish identity. As the institute's first director, she planned and implemented all aspects of its operations. Currently she heads the Samberg Family History Program, a summer activity for high school students under the aegis of the Genealogy Institute. She will continue to work with the institute to develop other educational offerings.

Q. How did you get involved with Jewish genealogy?

A. When I was a teenager, I became very close with my father's parents, who came to the United States from Transylvania in 1921. My grandfather told many tales of his life in the countryside and his World War I experiences in the Austro-Hungarian army—getting shot, losing toes to frostbite, and eventually escaping his imprisonment in a Russian hospital—and my grandmother taught me a few special Hungarian recipes. Although my primary interest had been my father's family, and I had always dreamed of going back to the old country and digging into the family past, I was actually inspired to get started by the efforts of a cousin on my mother's side. Jerry Delson, an active member of the San Francisco Bay Area Jewish

Genealogical Society, began researching the Reinschreiber family of Vishtinetz (Vistytis, Lithuania) and distributed an impressive family tree in 1987. After a few more years went by, I finally got around to reading Dan Rottenberg's *Finding Our Fathers* and your own *From Generation to Generation* and began following JewishGen, paying special attention to Warren Blatt's FAQ. Eventually I became involved with a number of volunteer projects, which ultimately led me to a career change so that I could "practice" Jewish genealogy full time.

Q. Why do you think there has been such a growing interest in Jewish genealogical research over the past few decades?

A. From a practical standpoint, the opening of Eastern European archives since the fall of communism and the explosion of data and communications on the Internet have facilitated a tremendous growth in Jewish genealogical activity. However, these developments by themselves do not account for the current level of interest. I think we are part of a grassroots movement involving many ethnic groups and nationalities, with some aspects that are unique to the Jewish experience. Since the landmark television broadcast of Alex Haley's *Roots* in the 1970s, ethnic pride has motivated millions of Americans to search for their personal heritage. But most genealogists also want to know how their family history fits into the fabric of social history and world history.

Earlier generations arriving in the United States often rejected contact with the societies whose harsh conditions they had fled. Particularly for Jews, restricted immigration after World War I, the Holocaust, and the Iron Curtain created immense barriers that further separated Americans from their overseas relatives. These trends have reversed during the past few decades. The generation that immigrated prior to World War I has largely died out, and as the second and third generations grow older, we are looking back at the events of the past century and trying to make sense of our collective experience.

Many Jewish genealogists are also trying to document the fate of relatives who perished during the Holocaust, so that their names and lives can be commemorated. Finally, the recent exodus of Jews from the former Soviet Union and other Eastern European countries has led many of the new immigrants to seek connections with the descendants of family members who emigrated more than seventy-five years ago.

Q. Twenty years ago, organizations like YIVO, the American Jewish Historical Society, and to a lesser degree the Leo Baeck Institute were not only unprepared for the genealogist but, rumor has it, even a bit hostile at times. What has changed—and why do you think this change has occurred?

A. Since the pursuit of genealogy has become an extremely widespread and popular phenomenon, libraries and archives—and the people who staff them—have had to adapt accordingly. Not only the Center for Jewish History partner organizations but most comparable institutions as well found that they could benefit by forming cooperative relationships with genealogical societies. Genealogists support libraries and archives by volunteering, making financial contributions, and mobilizing political support for public funding, among other activities. Librarians and archivists create guides, finding aids, Web sites, and other educational tools that help genealogists help themselves. Although academics and professionals were historically viewed as the most important users of research libraries and archives, genealogists now enjoy recognition and respect.

Q. To make the best use of your institute and the organizations associated with it, what kind of homework should a person do before visiting?

A. To get the most out of a visit to the Center for Jewish History, a genealogical researcher should understand what kinds of resources we have and what kinds of resources are found elsewhere. Our Web site (http://www.cjh.org) has extensive information that a researcher should review in advance. First, read the summary descriptions of the various archives and library and museum collections, and then visit the individual partner Web sites for more detailed descriptions. Next, review the genealogy pages, starting from http://www.cjh.org/family, and read all the fact sheets relevant to your research. Finally, use the online catalogue, finding aids, and searchable indexes to identify specific items of interest. I also recommend consulting Estelle Guzik's *Genealogical Resources in New York* (New York: Jewish Genealogical Society, 2003) for its extremely detailed listing of genealogical materials available at the Center for Jewish History, as well as Fruma Mohrer and Marek Web's *Guide to the YIVO Archives* (New York: YIVO, 1998).

○

YIVO Institute for Jewish Research

The YIVO Institute for Jewish Research is a gold mine for the student of Eastern European Jewry. The YIVO library and archives collections are filled with material on seemingly every aspect of the history of Eastern European Jews. Equal to these superb collections are the helpful staff, who are aware of the fact that many of us cannot read the material in all the languages represented there and do everything they can to help researchers. But do not expect them to translate for you! This would be an unreasonable request.

YIVO (whose initials stand for Yidisher Visnshaftlekher Institut, or Jewish Scientific Institute) was founded in Vilna (Vilnius), Lithuania, in 1925. Its history is a story in itself, particularly in light of the fact that the Germans seized YIVO's collection in 1940. Much of it was recovered. YIVO must be visited by anyone interested in the Jews of Eastern Europe.

You can get acquainted with YIVO and its collections and services by visiting its Web site at http://www.yivoinstitute.org. YIVO's genealogical resources are described athttp://www.yivoinstitute.org/archlib/archlib_fr.htm.

Although YIVO cannot always be of help when you are doing research on individual family members, there is no finer place to find background material on locations in Eastern Europe. References to various parts of YIVO's collection are made throughout this book. Of particular note are the several photography collections there, consisting of thousands of photographs, indexed by town. In other words, there is a good possibility that you can find photographs of the smallest towns at YIVO.

It would take months to discover all of the resources at YIVO, and it would be time well spent. I myself discovered the first reference to my great-great-grandfather, the Stropkover Rebbe, at YIVO.

In 1977, Schocken published a beautiful book drawn from YIVO's Polish photograph collection. Titled *Image Before My Eyes: A Photographic History of Jewish Life in Poland, 1864–1939*, the book is the result of the skillful and scholarly efforts of Lucjan Dobroszycki and Barbara Kirshenblatt-Gimblett. A historian and a folklorist at YIVO, respectively, the authors produced a book that should be in the home library of anyone with the slightest interest in Jewish history in general and Polish Jewish history in particular. One of the most remarkable results of the book's publication has been the large number of people who have recognized people in the old photographs in the book.

o

A Conversation with Zachary Baker

Zachary M. Baker has been the Reinhard Family Curator of Judaica and Hebraica Collections at the Stanford University Libraries since September 1999. Before that he was head librarian of the YIVO Institute for Jewish Research in New York (1987–1999), head of technical services at the Jewish Public Library in Montreal (1981–1987), and chief Yiddish cataloguer and genealogical reference librarian at YIVO (1976–1981). He has written numerous articles on genealogy, and these have been published in *Toledot*, *Avotaynu*, and various genealogical newsletters. Baker is also the compiler of the *Bibliography of Eastern European Jewish Memorial (Yizkor) Books*, which was first published in *Toledot* in 1980, and most recently in the second edition of *From a Ruined Garden: The Memorial Books of Polish Jewry* (1998). He has lectured before numerous genealogical audiences, including several national and international seminars on Jewish genealogy (starting in 1984). He was also involved in the early planning for the Center for Jewish Genealogy, at the Center for Jewish History in New York. Baker is past president of the Association of Jewish Libraries and also of the Council of Archives and Research Libraries in Jewish Studies. He claims descent, on his father's side, from a long line of Lithuanian bakers.

Q. You were librarian at YIVO for a number of years. Did genealogical activity at YIVO change over the years?

A. My first contact with genealogists dates back to late 1977 or early 1978. That's when I attended one of the first meetings of the Jewish Genealogical Society (JGS). Actually, I was sent there by the late Dina Abramowicz, who was then YIVO's head librarian and was already fielding many phone calls and answering letters from people in search of their roots. Sending me to the JGS meeting was her way of delegating work, because the following day I was thrust into the unofficial position of genealogical reference librarian. That's how I got to know people like you, Steve Siegel, and the late Malcolm Stern. The reference tools that these and other experts produced made it a lot easier for genealogists to get at the collections they needed at YIVO. But many genealogists were naturally frustrated by the fact that so much of YIVO's material is not in English. Also, especially while the Cold War was still going on, YIVO

was being described in how-to books as *the* place to go for genealogical resources relating to Eastern European Jews. But YIVO did not have vital records, passenger lists, and many of the other building blocks of genealogical research. Rather, it was and still is the place to go for studying the historical, cultural, and literary background of the civilization of "Yiddishland." YIVO also has one of the most important libraries and archives relating to the Holocaust.

Looking back, the most striking (and even surprising) fact to me is that genealogical activity did not abate but continued at a constant pace. Genealogy was not a passing fad.

Q. Did attitudes about genealogy on the part of the YIVO administration and staff change as time went on? Twenty years ago, YIVO didn't seem prepared for the onslaught of amateur genealogists. Is this true?

A. There's no question but that YIVO's administration and much of its staff were bewildered and caught unaware by the flood of genealogical inquiries in the early days. Dealing with the genealogical clientele requires a fair degree of self-education by librarians and archivists, about the sorts of materials that may be of interest to researchers. Working with genealogists—so many of whom came to YIVO on vaguely defined fishing expeditions—also required a lot of patience, and we were not always successful in our attempts to communicate to visitors (and telephone callers and letter writers) on what we could or could not provide for them. As the years passed, though, service to genealogists became a more regular part of our work, and I ought to mention that YIVO served as copublisher of Miriam Weiner's archival guides to research in Poland and in Ukraine and Moldova. That constituted recognition by YIVO's board of directors—as official as it gets—of the importance of reaching out to this constituency. I might add that as planning for the Center for Jewish History got under way in earnest, the very first working group that librarians and archivists from the partner organizations (including YIVO) established was the Genealogical Task Force, which also included a representative from the Jewish Genealogical Society.

Q. What advice would you give to the family historian considering using a collection like YIVO's?

A. It's been four years since I worked at YIVO, and a lot has changed since then, so what I have to say may be outdated. Now there is a Center for Jewish History Genealogy Institute, and that didn't exist four years ago. For the individual researcher, a visit to

15 West 16th Street is not a visit to YIVO but to the CJH as a whole. Genealogical researchers have access to the CJH partners' archives and libraries from a single reading room, and the Genealogy Institute provides a formal vehicle—an infrastructure—for guiding them. Because I haven't worked there since 1999, I can't really speak to the overall experience of doing genealogical research "at YIVO" (or rather, at the CJH). I can say this: YIVO's incomparable resources remain what they were, but its library catalogues and archival finding aids are in a much better state than ever before. Now, for example, an important segment of its photo collections is accessible on the Web, and other resources will go online in the future. But to any family historian I would still say, Be prepared. Much of what you will be looking at is in Yiddish, Hebrew, Polish, Russian, German, French, and other languages. Some of the books and documents are very rare, and others are extremely fragile. They need to be handled with care, and please be patient and understanding if conservation requirements prevent something from getting photocopied or scanned.

Q. Are there any typical errors made by the family history researchers who came to YIVO?

A. Rather than answer this question directly, I'd recommend that family history researchers carefully consult the fact sheets and FAQs that are available on the CJH Genealogy Institute's Web site. These provide helpful guidance on what researchers can and cannot expect to find in YIVO's and its partners' libraries and archives. As I've mentioned, it's been a few years since I had direct contact with YIVO's genealogical clientele, and most of the specific questions are no longer fresh in my memory.

Q. Why do you think there has been such growing interest in genealogy among Jews? And what do you think is the core reason people search for their roots?

A. On the one hand, I don't think that Jews' interest in genealogy can be viewed in isolation from the widespread popularity of the subject among American society at large. In addition, I think that genealogy is only one piece of a much larger puzzle as far as the American Jewish community is concerned. Think about what's been going on in this country since the mid-1970s. The growth of interest in genealogy and family history coincides—almost to the minute—with the klezmer revival, for example. During the 1970s, awareness of the Holocaust also spread, and the first Holocaust centers opened their doors then. My own search for roots took me in a somewhat different direction. I became fascinated with Yiddish, and that led me to learn how to speak

and read the language, and I worked in Yiddish settings (YIVO and the Jewish Public Library of Montreal) for over two decades. I was not alone. The National Yiddish Book Center was founded in 1980 and developed its grassroots constituency totally from scratch. Genealogy, Holocaust commemoration, the klezmer revival, and neo-Yiddishism— individuals' motivations for getting involved in these causes may be very different, but it is really striking that they all emerged in the last quarter of the twentieth century, as living memory of the immigrant era was ending and as Jewish community life was losing so much of its intimacy and immediacy. People like to point to the publication of Alex Haley's book, *Roots,* as the pivotal event that turned geneal-ogy into a popular pastime. For American Jews there is another best-selling book to be reckoned with, Irving Howe's *World of Our Fathers,* which, like *Roots,* came out in 1976. The search for roots has many dimensions. We construct our identities; we pick and choose who and what we want to be and how we want others to regard us. We've entered what I like to call the "postethnic" phase of Ameri-can Judaism. For many people, genealogy has become the primary vehicle for Jewish "memory work"—for the recovery of what, ulti-mately, can never truly be recovered. That does not by any means diminish the importance of the endeavor. F. Scott Fitzgerald said it best, in the closing line of *The Great Gatsby:* "So we beat on, boats against the current, borne back ceaselessly into the past."

○

○

Yesterday did not vanish, but lives.

—Elisheba, Hebrew poet

○

The Leo Baeck Institute

If any of your ancestors came from Germany or were primarily German speakers, the Leo Baeck Institute should be of significant interest. The insti-tute includes a library containing more than fifty thousand volumes, archives, and an academic center and publishes books on German Jewry.

Although the entire collection of the Leo Baeck Institute is fascinating and important, a few items in particular should be noted. The institute has a large collection of family trees of German Jewish families, many of

which are a few centuries old. German Jews have been known to have a keen interest in genealogy, and this is reflected in the outstanding collection of material of this kind at the Leo Baeck Institute.

In addition, the institute has a collection of family histories and community histories pertaining to German Jewry, as well as a large number of unpublished memoirs.

You can learn more about the Leo Baeck Institute at http://www.lbi.org. The Web site also has a special section for "family research": go to http://www.lbi.org/familyservices.html.

Although the Leo Baeck Institute specializes in German Jewry, its collection also contains material related to other countries where German-speaking Jews lived before the Holocaust.

If you have located the town or region in Germany where your ancestors came from, you should check the institute for background information. A review of its family tree collection might also be worthwhile. Do not assume, however, that finding a family tree with a familiar surname means that it is your family, however tempting this might be. Many unrelated German Jewish families had the same last name.

See *Toledot: The Journal of Jewish Genealogy,* Volume 2, Number 4 (Spring 1979), for an excellent article on the genealogical resources of the Leo Baeck Institute, written by Sybil Milton, a former chief archivist at the institute.

Although I highly recommend visiting the Leo Baeck Institute, its Web site states, "Genealogical researchers who are unable to visit the Institute are welcome to send inquiries by e-mail to kfranklin@lbi.cjh.org or regular mail."

If you are interested in German Jewish genealogy, find out about *Stammbaum: The Journal of German-Jewish Genealogical Research,* published twice yearly by the Leo Baeck Institute. Its Web site is http://www.jewishgen.org/stammbaum. Established in 1993, *Stammbaum* is dedicated to furthering German Jewish genealogy. It is an English-language publication that supports research and publication of reliable family histories, and it "facilitates the exchange of helpful and sound information, techniques, sources, and archival material."

---------- ○ ----------

Man lives not only in the circle of his years but also, by virtue of the subconscious, in the provinces of the generations from which he is descended, and Jewish life, to a very great extent, is based here.

Leo Baeck, *The Jew*

---------- ○ ----------

American Jewish Historical Society

The American Jewish Historical Society (AJHS) functions as a library, an archive, an organization, and a publisher.

As a library and archive, the AJHS can be most helpful in your family history research when it comes to synagogue records, family histories that have been published, genealogies, Jewish organization records, and the histories of towns in the United States. The library staff is quite helpful. I have made several inquiries through the mail over the years and have always received a prompt and thorough reply. However, it would be best to visit the society if you can, particularly if a reply through the mail indicates the availability of material of interest; you cannot expect the librarians to do too much research for you.

The AJHS Web site is http://www.ajhs.org; the section known as "Genealogical Reference Services" is at http://www.ajhs.org/reference/GeneoInst.cfm.

The American Jewish Historical Society also runs the Genealogical Research Service, directed by Nancy Arbeiter, a professional genealogist certified by the Board for Certification of Genealogists. The AJHS will help you determine your need for a professional researcher and will provide a qualified person for you at an hourly fee. See details on the Web site.

It would be appropriate to mention the AJHS as a good depository of Jewish records—if you have records of your own. Too often people discard records of synagogues, charitable organizations, landsmanshaften, and the like, throwing away gems of history. If you know of any Jewish records or other items of Jewish historical interest, contact the American Jewish Historical Society or the American Jewish Archives.

―――――――― ○ ――――――――

The future of Judaism belongs to that school which can best understand the past.

Leopold Lowe, Hungarian rabbi

Research into the past, as an aim in itself, without the present, is not worth a bean.

Chaim Nachman Bialik, Hebrew poet

―――――――― ○ ――――――――

Jewish Historical Societies Around the World

Many Jewish historical societies can be found throughout the United States and around the world and would be worth contacting for information concerning the regions of which they are a part. Most of these societies hold regular meetings, and some publish historical material on a regular basis. If you live in the vicinity of any of these societies, you may want to join. Historical societies are always looking for new members.

OUTSIDE THE UNITED STATES

AUSTRALIA
Australian Jewish Historical
   Society
Level 2, Mandelbaum House
385 Abercrombie Street
Darlington, NSW 2008

CANADA
Association for Canadian Jewish
   Studies
Department of Religion
Concordia University
1455 De Maisonneuve
   Boulevard, W.
Montreal, Quebec H3G 1M8
e-mail: robinso@
   vax2.concordia.ca
phone: (514) 848-2066
fax: (514) 848-4541

Jewish History Society of
   Western Canada
C116–123 Doncaster Street
Winnipeg, Manitoba
   R3N 2B2
e-mail: heritage@jhcwc.org
phone: (204) 477-7460
fax: (204) 477-7465

Jewish Historical Society of
   British Columbia
950 West 41st Avenue
Vancouver, British Columbia
   V5Z 2N7
e-mail: jhsofbc@direct.ca
phone: (604) 257-5199

Ottawa Jewish Historical Society
   Archives
151 Chapel Street
Ottawa, Ontario K1N 7Y2
phone: (613) 798-4696 ext. 260

ENGLAND
Jewish Historical Society of
   England
33 Seymour Place
London W1H 5AP
e-mail: jhse@dircon.co.uk
phone: (020) 7723-5852

ISRAEL
History Society of Israel
P.O. Box 4179
91041 Jerusalem

WITHIN THE UNITED STATES

ARIZONA
Arizona Jewish Historical
    Society
4710 North 16th Street #201
Phoenix, AZ 85016
e-mail: AZJHS@aol.com
phone: (520) 621-6423

Leona G. and David A. Bloom
Southwest Jewish Archives
1052 North Highland Avenue
Tucson, AZ 85721
phone: (520) 621-5774

Jewish Historical Society of
    Southern Arizona
P.O. Box 57482
Tucson, AZ 85732
e-mail: ajfmaz@mindspring.com
phone: (520) 882-6648

CALIFORNIA
Jewish Historical Society of
    Southern California
5700 Wilshire Boulevard,
    Suite 2512
Los Angeles, CA 90036
e-mail: jhsociety@juno.com
phone: (323) 761-8950

Jewish Historical Society of
    San Diego
1934 Pentuckett Avenue
San Diego, CA 92104
e-mail: schwartz@cts.com
phone: (619) 232-5888

San Francisco Bay Area Jewish
    Historical Society
c/o Robert Weiss
3916 Louis Road
Palo Alto, CA 94303
phone: (650) 424-1622

Western Jewish History Center and
    Judah L. Magnes Museum
2911 Russell Street
Berkeley, CA 94705
e-mail: wjhc@magnesmuseum.org
phone: (510) 549-6932

COLORADO
Rocky Mountain Jewish
    Historical Society
Center for Judaic Studies
2000 East Asbury Street
Denver, CO 80208
phone: (303) 871-3020

CONNECTICUT
Jewish Historical Society of
    Greater Bridgeport
3135 Park Avenue
Fairfield, CT 06432
phone: (203) 335-3638

Jewish Historical Society of
    Greater Hartford
335 Bloomfield Avenue
West Hartford, CT 06117
phone: (860) 236-4571

Jewish Historical Society of
    Greater New Haven
P.O. Box 3251
New Haven, CT 06515
e-mail: whirsch@snet.net
phone: (203) 392-5860

Jewish Historical Society of
    Greater Stamford
P.O. Box 3326
Stamford, CT 06905
e-mail: imvm@aol.com
phone: (203) 321-1373
    ext. 150
fax: (203) 322-6081

Jewish Historical Society of
    Waterbury
P.O. Box F
Waterbury, CT 06798

DELAWARE
Jewish Historical Society of
    Delaware
505 Market Street
Wilmington, DE 19801
e-mail: jhsdel@hotmail.com
phone: (302) 655-7161

DISTRICT OF COLUMBIA
Jewish Historical Society of
    Greater Washington
701 Third Street N.W.
Washington, DC 20001
phone: (202) 789-0900
fax: (202) 789-0485

FLORIDA
Jewish Historical Society of
    South Florida
4200 Biscayne Boulevard
Miami, FL 33137

GEORGIA
Southern Jewish Historical Society
P.O. Box 5024
Atlanta, GA 30302
e-mail: info@jewishsouth.org

ILLINOIS
Chicago Jewish Archives, Spertus
    Institute of Jewish Studies
618 South Michigan Avenue
Chicago, IL 60605
e-mail: archives@spertus.edu
phone: (312) 922-9012

Chicago Jewish Historical Society
618 South Michigan Avenue
Chicago, IL 60605
phone: (312) 663-5634

INDIANA
Indiana Jewish Historical Society
203 West Wayne Street, #310
Fort Wayne, IN 46802

IOWA
Iowa Jewish Historical Society
910 Polk Boulevard
Des Moines, IA 50312
e-mail: jcrc@jon.cjfny.org
phone: (515) 277-6321

KANSAS
Heart of America Jewish
    Historical Society
9648 Walmer Lane
Overland Park, KS 66212

LOUISIANA
Louisiana Jewish Historical
    Society
Temple Sinai
6227 Saint Charles Avenue
New Orleans, LA 70118

MARYLAND
Jewish Museum of Maryland
Jewish Heritage Center
15 Lloyd Street
Baltimore, MD 21202

e-mail: info@jhsm.org
e-mail: info@
  jewishmuseummd.org
phone: (410) 732-6400

Jewish Historical Society of
  Annapolis
5 Sampson Place
Annapolis, MD 21401
phone: (410) 268-4887

MASSACHUSETTS
Berkshire Jewish Archives
  Council
75 Mountain Drive
Pittsfield, MA 01201

Jewish Historical Society of the
  North Shore
One Community Road
Marblehead, MA 01945–2704
e-mail: jhsns1@aol.com
phone: (781) 631-0831

MICHIGAN
Jewish Historical Society of
  Michigan
6600 West Maple Road
West Bloomfield, MI 48322
phone: (248) 661-1000

MINNESOTA
Jewish Historical Society of the
  Upper Midwest
1554 Midway Parkway
Saint Paul, MN 55108
e-mail: history@jhsum.org
phone: (651) 637-0202
  ext. 202

MISSISSIPPI
Museum of the Southern
  Jewish Experience
P.O. Box 16528
Jackson, MS 39236
e-mail: information@msje.org
phone: (601) 362-6357

MISSOURI
Saint Louis Jewish Archives
Saul Brodsky Jewish Community
  Library
12 Millstone Campus Drive
Saint Louis, MO 63146
phone: (314) 432-0020

NEBRASKA
Nebraska Jewish Historical
  Society
333 South 132nd Street
Omaha, NE 68154
e-mail: njhs@jewishomaha.org
phone: (402) 334-6442

NEW JERSEY
Jewish Historical Society of
  Central Jersey
c/o Rachel Weintraub
228 Livingston Avenue
New Brunswick, NJ 08901
e-mail: jhscj@cs.com
phone: (732) 249-4894

Jewish Historical Society of
  MetroWest
901 Route 10 East
Whippany, NJ 07981
e-mail: jsettanni@ujfmetrowest.org
phone: (973) 884-4800 ext. 565

Jewish Historical Society of
    North Jersey
P.O. Box 708
West Paterson, NJ 07424
phone: (973) 785-9119

Trenton Jewish Historical Society
c/o Selma Litowitz
282 Glenn Avenue
Lawrenceville, NJ 08648
phone: (609) 883-0251

NEW MEXICO
New Mexico Jewish Historical
    Society
5520 Wyoming Boulevard, N.E.
Albuquerque, NM 87109
e-mail:scholder@earthlink.net
phone: (505) 348-4471

NEW YORK
Orthodox Jewish Archives of
    Agudath Israel
84 William Street
New York, NY 10038
phone: (212) 797-9000

NORTH CAROLINA
Charlotte Jewish Historical
    Society
c/o Sam Eneman
P.O. Box 13574
Charlotte, NC 28270
e-mail: enemansj@charweb.org
phone: (704) 366-5007
fax: (704) 365-4507

NORTH DAKOTA
North Dakota Jewish Historical
    Project
P.O. Box 2431
Fargo, ND 58102

OHIO
American Jewish Archives
Dorothy Smith, Archivist
Hebrew Union College
3101 Clifton Avenue
Cincinnati, OH 45220
e-mail: AJA@huc.edu
phone: (513) 221-1875
    ext. 311
fax: (513) 221-7812

Cleveland Jewish Archives of
    the Western Reserve
    Historical Society
10825 East Boulevard
Cleveland, OH 44106
phone: (216) 721-5722

Columbus Jewish Historical
    Society
1175 College Avenue
Columbus, OH 43209
phone: (614) 238-6977

OREGON
Oregon Jewish Genealogical
    and Historical Society
Mittleman Jewish Community
    Center
6651 Southwest Capitol
    Highway
Portland, OR 97219
phone: (503) 245-5196

PENNSYLVANIA
National Museum of
    American Jewish
    History
55 North Fifth Street
Philadelphia, PA 19106
phone: (215) 923-3811

Western Pennsylvania
Jewish Archives,
Historical Society
of Western
Pennsylvania
Judith Ross, Archivist
4338 Bigelow Boulevard
Pittsburgh, PA 15213
phone: (412) 681-5533

RHODE ISLAND
Rhode Island Jewish
Historical Association
130 Sessions Street
Providence, RI 02906
email: rjhist@aol.com
phone: (401) 331-1360

Society of Friends of Touro
Synagogue
85 Touro Street
Newport, RI 02840
phone: (401) 847-4794

SOUTH CAROLINA
Jewish Historical Society of
South Carolina
Jewish Studies
College of Charleston
Charleston, SC 29424
e-mail: jswt@cofc.edu
phone: (843) 953-5682

TENNESSEE
Archives of the Jewish
Federation of Nashville
and Middle Tennessee
801 Percy Warner Boulevard
Nashville, TN 37205
phone: (615) 356-7170

Jewish Historical Society of
Memphis and the Mid-South
P.O. Box 17304
Memphis, TN 38187

TEXAS
Dallas Jewish Historical
Society
7900 Northaven Road
Dallas, TX 75230
phone: (214) 739-2737 ext. 261

Galveston County Jewish
Historical Association
2613 Oak Street
Galveston, TX 77551

Texas Jewish Historical
Society
P.O. Box 10193
Austin, TX 78766
e-mail: txjhs@yahoo.com
phone: (817) 927-8765

VIRGINIA
Peninsula Jewish Historical
Society
25 Stratford Road
Newport News, VA 23601

WASHINGTON
Washington State Jewish
Historical Society
2917 N.E. Blakely Street
Seattle, WA 98105
phone: (206) 443-1903

WISCONSIN
Wisconsin Jewish Archives
State Historical Society of
Wisconsin
816 State Street
Madison, WI 53706
phone: (608) 264-6460

○

We cannot rid ourselves of the past without destroying our present and ruining our future.

Harry A. Wolfson, "Escaping Judaism"

One of the early rabbis, Ben Azzai, translated the words of Genesis 5:1, "This is the book of the generations of man," and declared them to be "a great fundamental teaching of the Torah." As all human beings are traced back to one parent, he taught, they must necessarily be brothers.

J. H. Hertz, Soncino Pentateuch

○

The Central Archives for the History of the Jewish People

In 1969, the Central Archives for the History of the Jewish People was established by the Israeli government, the Jewish Agency for Israel, the Historical Society of Israel, the Israel Academy of Sciences and Humanities, the Hebrew University of Jerusalem, Tel Aviv University, and Bar-Ilan University. Their Web site (http://sites.huji.ac.il/archives) states that "the Central Archives are rich in genealogical material from various communities." This site has a special "Genealogy" section (http://sites.huji.ac.il/archives/page7.htm) that explains what they can and cannot do for the individual researcher. The archives are in possession of "the most extensive collection of documents, *pinkassim* (registers), and records concerning Jewish history in the Diaspora from the Middle Ages to the present day." Although the archives staff attempt to collect original documents, they are also involved in the microfilming of historical records around the world. A unique aspect of the archives is the fact that whereas other Jewish archives specialize in one region or period of Jewish history, the Central Archives collects material from every Jewish community in the world.

The collection at the Central Archives is arranged by country and town. If you want to know what they have of interest to you, it would be best to send them a letter asking for an inventory of their holdings for a specific town or region. In their reply, they will tell you what they have. It might be a marriage register from the 1840s or a mohel book from 1909 or a record book from the community, or they might not have anything for your community. However, if they do have something, you can arrange to purchase microfilm or other copies of the material. The address is as follows:

Central Archives for the History of the Jewish People
46 Jabotinsky Street
P.O.B 1149
91010 Jerusalem, Israel
phone: (972) 2-5635716
fax: (972) 2-5667686

o

A Conversation with Sallyann Amdur Sack

Sallyann Amdur Sack, Ph.D., is the founder and first president of the Jewish Genealogical Society of Greater Washington, recipient of the Lifetime Achievement Award of the International Association of Jewish Genealogical Societies (IAJGS), past president of the IAJGS, and co-owner and editor of *Avotaynu: The International Review of Jewish Genealogy*. A genealogist for more than twenty-five years, Sack has chaired or cochaired seven annual Jewish genealogy conferences, initiated and organized the project to microfilm, and computerized the confiscated Russian consular records held at the U.S. National Archives and the project to create a Holocaust-era asset database and locate living heirs. She is the author or coauthor of several Jewish genealogy books, including *Jewish Genealogical Research in Israel* (with the Israel Genealogical Society); *Russian Consular Records Index and Catalog; Jewish Vital Records, Revision Lists, and Other Holdings in the Lithuanian Archives* (with Harold Rhode); *Some Archival Sources for Ukrainian Jewish Genealogy* (with Alexander Kronick); and the prizewinning *Where Once We Walked* (with Gary Mokotoff). Most recently she has been compiler and editor of *The Avotaynu Guide to Jewish Genealogy*. Sack is currently collaborating with two schoolteachers on a curriculum for teaching genealogical research to schoolchildren of all ages in Jewish day schools and congregational schools. A speaker and consultant on Jewish genealogy, Sack has served as a member of several genealogical advisory boards and is listed in *Jewish Women in America*. She lives in Bethesda, Maryland, and is a clinical psychologist in full-time private practice.

Q. What's a psychologist doing with genealogy? How did you get involved with genealogy?

A. Let me answer the second question first. I got into genealogy through Kathy, the youngest of our three children. One day in the fall

of 1997, Kathy came home and announced, "I bought you a present," and handed me Dan Rottenberg's *Finding Our Fathers*, saying, "I want to learn all about my ancestors." She had been hanging out in Crown Books, had come across Rottenberg, and found my maiden name, Amdur, in its index of several hundred typically Jewish family names. Kathy had spent the summer at a debate camp in Vermont learning how to do research and now wanted to test her skills.

I was so thrilled to have this fifteen-year-old talk to me, let alone want to do anything with me, that I responded with alacrity. We live in suburban Washington, D.C., a wonderful place to do genealogical research. In short order we were writing letters to relatives, known and unknown, haunting the Hebraic section of the Library of Congress, and nearly going blind peering at microfilms at the National Archives.

Then the inevitable happened. Kathy discovered that at fifteen there are pursuits—like boys—that are far more interesting than answering letters from relatives you have never even met. She lost interest, and it was left to me to answer the mail. Somewhere along the way, a remarkable thing happened. I simply got hooked—and nothing has been the same since.

So you see, on the surface at least, the fact that I am a practicing clinical psychologist in full-time private practice has nothing directly to do with my interest in genealogy. On the other hand, it is rather clear that both fields have much in common. In both cases we are trying to understand the forces that have shaped either a specific individual or, in the case of genealogy, a group of related individuals, a family. Moreover, as we look back and understand the generations that came before us, we come to understand how and why they were as they were, how and why they acted as they did, and the effect this had on us. As we understand them better, we come to understand more about ourselves.

Q. Can you share some psychological insights as to why you think some people are captivated by genealogy and others couldn't care less? Have you thought much about the psychology of genealogy? What conclusions have you drawn? Do you have any advice for the genealogy "widow" or "widower," the spouse who doesn't understand why his or her partner would rather sit in front of a microfilm machine than go out to dinner?

A. It is difficult to say why some people are so captivated by genealogy while others couldn't care less. I know that in my case it is my curiosity about people, my interest in history, my passion for

puzzles and love of being Jewish. For others, it may be something else, but at the bottom I think that genealogy is all about belonging. How issues of belonging (or not belonging) play out in each individual's life varies, of course. I suspect, however, that if I could interview everyone passionate about genealogy, I would fairly soon discover what it is that hooks them. I also think that some factors are at play with Jewish genealogists that may not be operating in genealogists who are not Jewish. The fact of our Jewishness and our feelings about our Jewishness clearly seem to be important.

As for "genealogy widowhood"—is that really very different from any other passion that is not shared by a spouse? It could be archeology, collecting chintzware all over the country, or any other hobby that fascinates and absorbs someone. The National Institutes of Health is here in Bethesda where I live. It is filled with scientists who are completely absorbed in the study of this or that microbe, illness, whatever. They work huge numbers of hours, tend their experiments in the middle of the night, and have many "widows" at home. Each couple that stays together finds the balance that works for them. I remember discussing this with Louise Stern, widow of the late Rabbi Malcolm Stern, the father of Jewish genealogy. Louise told me that once when they were on a Caribbean cruise, Malcolm went looking for old Jewish cemeteries on every island they visited. Louise did not share Malcolm's passion, and after she had had enough, she announced that if he tramped off looking for "one more dead Jew," she was going to file for a divorce the minute they arrived home! She then laughed and said that fortunately for their marriage, there were no Jewish cemeteries on the remaining islands of that trip. That had happened several years before our conversation, and Malcolm's involvement had only intensified since then, so I asked Louise if she really minded all the time Malcolm devoted to Jewish genealogy. Louise answered immediately, "Oh, no! He enjoys it so much; it's a wonderful thing to be that interested in something. I would never interfere with it." My husband has almost no interest in pursuing genealogy himself, although he certainly has enjoyed many of the people we have met through genealogical travel and conferences. On the other hand, he is enormously involved in social and political issues related to his profession (psychiatry). I don't share his level of passion about that—but I am thrilled that there is something so meaningful to him—and I have been enriched by the people I've met through him.

In sum, I suppose that if each is able to find something enjoyable in the other's passion, if each has interests of his or her own, and if the amount they share in common suits their individual needs, then the balance works. Otherwise, no. Genealogy, because it touches us so personally, tends to become incredibly absorbing, at least initially. Except for that, I don't think it is essentially different from any other pursuit.

Q. One of your areas of expertise is Israel. Other than buying your book on the topic, what would the best piece of advice be for the researcher regarding Israel? And if there were just three places that I had to visit for genealogical research in Israel, what might they be?

A. I love to talk about Israel. I hope I can find the right words to express my feelings. I remember particularly noticing something that Rottenberg wrote about Israel. I don't know if I can quote exactly, but it was something like "When you visit Israel—and you will . . ." At that point in 1977, I had never been to Israel. Though I had wanted to go for years, it wasn't as high on my husband's list, the children were young, money for travel was in short supply— all the usual excuses. I read those words, and they "clicked." I knew that I had to go. For our twenty-fifth wedding anniversary in 1981, I told my husband that there was only one gift I wanted—a trip to Israel. That was my first trip. I've been back almost every year since. A few of the times my husband has come with me, but since I mostly want to pursue genealogical interests (and the genealogy friends I've made there), he usually doesn't come. And of course, I've organized and cochaired two Jewish genealogy conferences there.

First, there is the fact that there is no place on earth that feels so special to me as Israel—especially Jerusalem. I have a feeling of belongingness that is stronger there than anywhere else. It's like coming home. So now when people ask why I have continued to go every year despite the intifada, I say that I have to go; Israel calls me. After about six months, I begin to long to be there again, and I start to plan another trip. It's as if I simply must go and touch and pat it.

For Jewish genealogy, though, there is no place better. You ask about three places to go for genealogy research, where would they be. The first "place" is not a place at all. It is the people. I maintain that if you define family (as I do) to include second, third, and maybe even fourth cousins, then there is not a Jew anywhere in the world who does not have cousins in Israel. Find those cousins, and

they will be able to tell you much about your family that you can never learn anywhere else. Remember, when the practical Eastern European Jews, in search of a better life, were emigrating to the United States and other Western destinations at the turn of the twentieth century, one out of about every ten was an idealistic Jew who emigrated to Eretz Yisrael to rebuild Zion. So you will find the descendants of those relatives. Most Israelis, however, came after the end of World War II—the remnant of those Hitler had not managed to murder. Initially, most Jewish survivors went to Palestine/Israel. Some later migrated onward to the United States, Australia, and elsewhere, but most didn't. Find those families, and they will be able to tell you directly about life in the old country, about how your family lived, and so on. Many times you don't need to find relatives but simply landsmen—people (and their children and grandchildren) who lived in the same town as your relatives. How do you find these people? Through the landsmanshaft organizations, many of which are listed in Israeli telephone directories. Yad Vashem [the Holocaust memorial in Jerusalem] has a list of others (and I do too at the end of my book). Of course, with the big Russian *aliyah* of the 1990s, there is another chance to find descendants of relatives who never emigrated—and you will find that almost always they are delighted to have you find them!

Clearly, Yad Vashem is an essential resource for Jewish genealogists. It has material found nowhere else—most especially the Pages of Testimony in its Hall of Names. Not only do these testimonies tell you about family members who were murdered (and we all had family murdered if you define family beyond your immediate relatives), but if you look for the person who submitted the testimony (or the children of the person, who may now be deceased), you very often find new relatives or people who were close friends of your relatives.

I am having trouble finding a third choice because there are so many candidates for that spot! I think I must decline to pick just one and instead say that since you will be in Jerusalem already to go to Yad Vashem, also go to the Israel State Archives to look for naturalizations—written in English—during the British mandate period, to the Central Archives for the History of the Jewish People for all sorts of unexpected finds, and to the Central Zionist Archives, which hold the valuable records of the (now unfortunately closed) Jewish Agency Search Bureau for Missing Relatives. I also can't leave out the Jewish National and University Library.

Q. Tell us a little about *Avotaynu*. How did it start? What is your involvement? What are its activities?

A. *Avotaynu* began as an idea the week before the 1984 genealogy conference in Jerusalem, which was sponsored by my "home" society, the Jewish Genealogy Society of Greater Washington, and chaired by Naomi Gershan and myself. We were sitting in Naomi's kitchen getting ready to travel to Jerusalem. I believe that most things don't happen by chance, so I started to think about what I wanted to come out of the conference. (This was going to be our first international conference.) Naomi and I agreed that we wanted to make sure that there was another overseas (that is, non-U.S.) conference in the future. Two men were coming from London, so we agreed that somehow we would persuade them to "volunteer" to host another. (They did.) I also wanted to be able to stay in touch with the people who were coming from the far corners of the world. This was before Internet and e-mail, of course. Naomi responded that that meant we needed a publication. We decided that we'd keep our eyes open during the week to try to identify people whom we thought had potential leadership ability. Then on the last day, which was Shabbat, we invited a group of about ten or twelve people to sit around a conference room table with coffee and cake and brainstorm about the future of Jewish genealogy. I proposed the idea of a publication. We went around the table in turn, everyone offering an opinion or idea. When it got to Gary Mokotoff, whom I didn't even know at that point, Gary announced that he ran a computer company and offered that if someone would give him camera-ready copy, he'd produce the publication. We kept going around the room until it came back to me. No one had volunteered to write or edit the still unnamed publication, and my "baby" was about to die stillborn. To keep that from happening, I offered to "do it for now." We are in our nineteenth year and I am still doing it "for now." My children jokingly call *Avotaynu* my fourth child.

After we got back home, Gary and I met. We agreed to be fifty-fifty partners, and we divided up responsibilities and titles. Since I am responsible for content, we decided that I would be "editor." Since Gary is responsible for production, we agreed that he would be "publisher."

We formed Avotaynu, Inc., specifically to publish *Avotaynu: The International Review of Jewish Genealogy,* but we have branched beyond that and now have published several books of direct use to Jewish genealogists, three of which have received the Best Research

Book of the Year award from the Association of Jewish Libraries. Since most commercial publishers are not interested in Jewish genealogy books, we decided that we'd be the "publisher of last resort"—that is, if a book was worth publishing and we didn't think we'd lose money on it, we published it. Later we formed Avotaynu Foundation, a nonprofit, 501(c)(3) corporation whose purpose is to publish meritorious works related to Jewish genealogy that would not otherwise be published because they are not commercially feasible.

Q. What is the most pressing issue in the world of Jewish genealogy today? Is there one?

A. The most pressing issue in the world of Jewish genealogy is probably the same issue for genealogists generally. That is the growing tendency for governmental bodies to restrict access to personal information. Some countries, like Canada and Australia, have moved to destroy their censuses—actions that appear to have been halted (at least for now) by concerted action from organized genealogical groups. In various states around the United States, access to vital records once available to the public is increasingly being restricted. In the Jewish world, however, the biggest problem is the continuing refusal of the International Tracing Service (ITS) of the International Committee for the Red Cross to open its archival collection to researchers. ITS has the world's largest archival collection of information about individuals who were caught up in the Holocaust. Its continued closure is nothing short of a scandal.

Q. If you had to give one piece of advice to the beginner, what would it be?

A. My one piece of advice to a beginner would be to remember that this is a hobby, not a matter of life and death, to keep a sense of humor and perspective—and always to record where you obtained every piece of information! When we start, we are sure that we will always remember every single item. Alas, memory fades, and after twenty-five years, we often don't recall where we obtained those fascinating bits of information.

○

Jewish Genealogical Societies Around the World

When I first began my own personal search for my family history, there were no genealogical societies. For that matter, there were no books on the subject, no publications being issued, no organizations to give guidance.

Most librarians and archivists I contacted knew little, if anything, about how a Jewish person could do successful genealogical research. The picture has changed considerably, in particular in regard to Jewish Genealogical Societies.

It is moving to note that before the Holocaust, there were groups that got together to share their enthusiasm for Jewish genealogy. Publications were produced, meetings were held, and the pursuit of Jewish genealogy had been of keen interest to many. With the destruction of European Jewry came the end of all these activities. Yet today, throughout the world, a network of Jewish genealogical societies exists. The first one after the war was founded in 1977 at the suggestion of Dr. Neil Rosenstein. He invited several people to his home in the hope of launching a successful organization. This first meeting gave birth to the Jewish Genealogical Society of New York. Quite rapidly, other JGSs came into being. Some meet every month, others less frequently. Some publish newsletters (of varying quality). The New York JGS has also published a book, offers classes and beginners' seminars, and is involved in additional related efforts.

Genealogists learn from each other, and the meetings of these groups have become particularly valuable for the swapping of new sources, mutual encouragement and support, and the sharing of materials. Many groups invite guest speakers to their meetings, some maintain lending or research libraries, and all participate in the rebirth of Jewish genealogical research as an important pastime.

On the next few pages is a list of the JGSs that exist as I write this. New groups seem to spring up all the time. If there is no JGS in your area, you may want to start one. I'd suggest that you contact the International Association of Jewish Genealogical Societies for guidance and for advice on how to start your own JGS. The IAJGS Web site, http://www.jewishgen.org/ajgs, hosted by JewishGen.org, has information on how to start a JGS group.

The IAJGS describes itself as a nonprofit umbrella organization coordinating the activities of more than seventy-five national and local Jewish Genealogical Societies around the world. It holds an annual conference that generally attracts one thousand or more participants.

I urge you to get involved in the Jewish Genealogical Society near you. I'd also like to suggest that you subscribe to the newsletters of some of the JGSs. Even though some of the newsletters are quite sophisticated and others are pretty primitive, they are all filled with specialized bits of information that can come in very handy.

The best source for current information about Jewish Genealogical Societies around the world, organized by country and city, is the *Jewish Genealogy Yearbook* at http://www.jewishgen.org. The Web address for the most current yearbook (2003) is http://www.jewishgen.org/ajgs/year-book-2003.html.

The following list of Jewish Genealogical Societies is provided by the Douglas E. Goldman Jewish Genealogy Center Web site and is based on information from the International Association of Jewish Genealogical Societies and other sources. Be aware, however, that the specifics of this kind of information, especially the names of people, change over time. If you compare this list with the information at the *Jewish Genealogy Yearbook* Web pages, you will see some discrepancies. My hunch is that the information provided at the *Jewish Genealogy Yearbook* is more up to date.

EUROPE

BELGIUM
Jewish Genealogical Society of
    Belgium
Daniel Dratwa
avenue Stalingrad, 74
B-1000 Bruxelles
e-mail: d.dratwa@mjb-jmb.org
Web site: http://www.mjb-jmb.org
phone: (32-2) 512.19.63
fax: (32-2) 513.48.59

FRANCE
Cercle de Généalogie Juive
Claudie Blamont
14, rue Saint Lazare
F-75009 Paris
e-mail: cgjgenefr@aol.com
Web site: http://www.genealoj.org
phone and fax: (33-1)
    40.23.04.90

Association de Généalogie Juive
    Internationale (GenAmi)
Micheline Gutmann
76, rue de Passy
F-75016 Paris
e-mail: michelinegutmann@free.fr
Web site: http://asso.genami.
    free.fr/v2/index.html
phone: (33-1) 45.24.35.40

GERMANY
Hamburger Gesellschaft für
    jüdische Genealogie e. V.
c/o Jürgen Sielemann
Staatsarchiv Hamburg
Kattunbleiche 19
D-22041 Hamburg
e-mail: juergen.sielemann@
    staatsarchiv.hamburg.de
phone: (49-40) 428.31.31.38

GREAT BRITAIN
Jewish Genealogical Society of
  Great Britain
George Anticoni
P.O. Box 13288
London N3 3WD
e-mail: jgsgb@ort.org
Web site: http://www.jgsgb.org.uk
phone: (44) 1923-825-197
fax: (44) 1923-820-323

NETHERLANDS
Nederlandse Kring voor Joodse
  Genealogie
Erna Houtkooper
Abbingstraat 1
NL-1447 PA Purmerend
e-mail: info@nljewgen.org
Web site: http://www.nljewgen.org
phone: (31) 299-644498

RUSSIA
Jewish Genealogical Society of
  the Former Soviet Union
  in Moscow
c/o Jewish University in Moscow
9, Mokhovaya Street #329
  Moscow
e-mail: paley@jum.ru
Web site: http://geocities.com/
  Heartland/Estates/6121
phone: (7-095) 203-3441

SWEDEN
Jewish Genealogical Society
  of Sweden
Carl H. Carlsson,
  c/o Gerber
P.O. Box 7427
SE-10391 Stockholm
e-mail: Maynard.gerber@
  mbox200.swipnet.se
e-mail: Carl-henrik.carlsson@
  hist.uu.se
Web site: http://www.
  ijk-s.se/genealogi
phone: (46-8) 5878-5817

SWITZERLAND
Schweizerische Vereinigung
  für Jüdische Genealogie/
  Association Suisse de
  Généalogie Juive/Swiss
  Society for Jewish
  Genealogy
c/o Albert Sobol
Steinbuhlallee 15
CH-4027 Basel
phone and fax:
  (41-1) 361.71.54

CANADA

ALBERTA
Jewish Genealogical Society of
  Alberta
Florence Elman
1607 90th Avenue S.W.

Calgary, Alberta T2V 4V7
e-mail: haflo@cadvision.com
Web site: http://www.jewishgen.
  org/jgssa

BRITISH COLUMBIA
Jewish Genealogical Institute of
    British Columbia
Cissie Eppel
950 West 41st Avenue
Vancouver, British Columbia
    V5Z 2N7
e-mail: hgoldman@
    interchange.ubc.ca
Web site: http://www.geocities.com/
    Heartland/Hills/4441
phone: (604) 321-9870

MANITOBA
Jewish Heritage Centre of
    Western Canada
Bev Rayburn
Genealogical Institute
C116–113 Doncaster Street
Winnipeg, Manitoba R3N 2B2
e-mail: bjrayburn@aol.com
Web site: http://www.jhcwc.org/
    geninst.htm
phone: (204) 477-7460
fax: (204) 477-7465

ONTARIO
Jewish Genealogical Society of
    Canada (Toronto)
Gert Solnik Rogers
P.O. Box 446
Station "A"
Willowdale, Ontario M2N 5T1
e-mail: Gert.Rogers@sympatico.ca

Jewish Genealogical Society
    of Ottawa
Charles B. Lapkoff
1780 Kerr Avenue
Ottawa, Ontario K2A 1R9
e-mail: lapkoff@netrover.com
phone: (613) 995-9227

QUEBEC
Jewish Genealogical Society of
    Montreal
Stanley M. Diamond
5599 Edgemore Avenue
Montreal, Quebec H4W 1V4
e-mail: SMSDiamond@aol.com
Web site: http://www.
    jgs-montreal.org
phone: (514) 484-0100
fax: (514) 484-7306

UNITED STATES

ARIZONA
Greater Phoenix Jewish
    Genealogical Society
Sam Arutt
P.O. Box 4063
Scottsdale, AZ 85261
e-mail: sarutt1@
    mindspring.com

Jewish Historical Society of
    Southern Arizona
Genealogy Group
Alfred E. Lipsey
4181 East Pontatoc Canyon Drive
Tucson, AZ 85718
e-mail: lipseya@prodigy.net
phone: (520) 299-4486

CALIFORNIA
Jewish Genealogical Society of
    Los Angeles
Sonia Hoffman
P.O. Box 55443
Sherman Oaks, CA 91413
e-mail: Sonia@jgsla.org
Web site: http://www.jgsla.org
phone: (818) 771-5554

Jewish Genealogical Society of
    Orange County
Rob Weisskirch and
    Jim Huggins
e-mail: rweisskirch@
    fullerton.edu
e-mail: jhuggs@mailbug.com
Web site: http://www.jewishgen.
    org/jgsoc
phone: (714) 278-2896

Jewish Genealogical Society of
    Palm Springs
Gay Lynne Kegan
40111 Portulaca Court
Palm Desert, CA 92260
phone: (760) 340-6554

Jewish Genealogical Society of
    Sacramento
Art Yates
2351 Wyda Way
Sacramento, CA 95825
e-mail: jgs_sacramento@
    hotmail.com
Web site:
    http://www.jewishgen.org/
    jgs-sacramento
phone: (916) 486-0906
    ext. 361

San Diego Jewish Genealogical
    Society
Roberta Berman
P.O. Box 927089
San Diego, CA 92191
e-mail: danber@cts.com
Web site: http://www.homestead.
    com/sdjgs
phone: (858) 459-2074

San Francisco Bay Area Jewish
    Genealogical Society
Rodger Rosenberg
P.O. Box 471616
San Francisco, CA 94147
e-mail: eandr@ix.netcom.com
Web site: http://www.jewishgen.
    org/sfbajgs
phone: (415) 666-0188

COLORADO
Jewish Genealogical Society of
    Colorado
Myndel Cohen
6965 East Girard Avenue
Denver, CO 80224
e-mail: Hermyn@aol.com
Web site: http://www.jewishgen.
    org/jgs-colorado
phone: (303) 756-6028

CONNECTICUT
Jewish Genealogical Society of
    Connecticut
Jonathan Smith
P.O. Box 524
Middletown, CT 06457
e-mail: DeborahRachel@
    hotmail.com
Web site: http://www.geocities.
    com/jgsct
phone: (202) 268-2923

DISTRICT OF COLUMBIA
Jewish Genealogical
Society of Greater
Washington
Ellen Shindelman
P.O. Box 31122
Bethesda, MD 20824
e-mail: grapevyn@
erols.com
Web site: http://www.jewishgen.
org/jgsgw
phone: (202) 546-5239

FLORIDA
Jewish Genealogical
Society of Broward
County
P.O. Box 17251
Fort Lauderdale, FL 33318
e-mail: bobkolt@aol.com
Web site: http://jgsbroward.org

Jewish Genealogical Society of
Greater Miami
Ron Ravikoff
P.O. Box 560432
Miami, FL 33156
e-mail: JGSMiami@aol.com
phone: (305) 358-5000
fax: (305) 579-9749

Jewish Genealogical Society of
Greater Orlando
Sim Seckbach
P.O. Box 941332
Maitland, FL 32794
e-mail: sseckbach@aol.com
Web site: http://www.rootsweb.
com/~fljgscf
phone: (407) 644-3566

Jewish Genealogical Society of
Palm Beach County
Sylvia Furshman Nusinov
P.O. Box 7796
Delray Beach, FL 33482
e-mail: curiously@aol.com
phone: (561) 483-1060

Jewish Genealogical
Society of Southwest
Florida
Kim Sheintal
4462 Violet Avenue
Sarasota, FL 34233
e-mail: klapshein@aol.com
Web site: http://www.
jewish-sarasota.org/jgs/j
gsofswfl.htm
phone: (941) 921-1433

Jewish Genealogical Society
of Tampa Bay
Mark Baron
P.O. Box 3252
Holiday, FL 34690
e-mail: mark_baron@
yahoo.com
phone: (727) 539-4521

GEORGIA
Jewish Genealogical Society
of Georgia
Hilary Henkin
P.O. Box 681022
Marietta, GA 30068
e-mail: jewishgenofga@
ixpres.com
Web site: http://www.jewishgen.
org/jgsg
phone: (404) 352-8700

HAWAII
Jewish Genealogical Society
    of Hawaii
Marlene Hertz
237 Kuumele Place
Kailua, HI 96734
e-mail: marhertz@hgea.org
phone: (808) 262-0030

ILLINOIS
Champaign-Urbana Jewish
    Genealogical Society
Dr. Sheila Goldberg
808 La Sell Drive
Champaign, IL 61820
e-mail: Sheila@prairienet.org
phone: (217) 359-3102

Illiana Jewish Genealogical
    Society
Trudy Barch
P.O. Box 384
Flossmoor, IL 60422
e-mail: ijgs@lincolnnet.net
Web site: http://www.lincolnnet.
    net/ijgs
phone: (708) 957-9457

Jewish Genealogical Society of
    Illinois
Judith R. Frazin
P.O. Box 515
Northbrook, IL 60065
e-mail: jrfraz@corecom.net
Web site: http://www.jewishgen.
    org/jgsi
phone: (847) 509-0201

INDIANA
Jewish Genealogical Society
    of Indiana
Barry Levitt
P.O. Box 68280
Indianapolis, IN 46268
e-mail: balcpa@iquest.net
phone: (317) 388-0632

LOUISIANA
Jewish Genealogical Society of
    New Orleans
Jacob and Vicki Karno
25 Waverly Place
Metarie, LA 70003
e-mail: jkarno@karnovsky.com
phone: (504) 888-3817

MARYLAND
Jewish Genealogical Society
    of Maryland
c/o Jewish Community
    Center
3506 Gwynbrook Avenue
Owings Mills, MD 21117
e-mail: JGSMaryland@aol.com
phone: (443) 255-8228

MASSACHUSETTS
Jewish Genealogical Society of
    Greater Boston
Jay and Daphnah Sage
P.O. Box 610366
Newton Highlands, MA 02461
e-mail: info@jgsgb.org
Web site:
    http://www.jewishgen.org/
    boston
phone: (617) 796-8522

MICHIGAN
Jewish Genealogical Society of
 Michigan
Marc D. Manson
30141 High Valley Road
Farmington Hills, MI 48331
e-mail: jgsmi@usa.net
Web site: http://www.jgsmi.org
phone: (248) 661-8515
fax: (248) 661-2306

MISSOURI
Jewish Genealogical Society of
 Kansas City
Steven B. Chernoff
14905 West 82nd Terrace
Lenexa, KS 66215
e-mail: schernoff@
 chernoff.com
phone: (913) 894-4222

Jewish Genealogical Society of
 Saint Louis
Jerry Goldberg
13039 Musket Court
Saint Louis, MO 63146
e-mail: jerfransl@cs.com
Web site:
 http://uahc.org/congs/mo/
 mo005/jgsstl
phone: (314) 434-2566

NEVADA
Jewish Genealogical Society of
 Southern Nevada—West
Carole Montello
P.O. Box 29342
Las Vegas, NV 89126
e-mail: carmont7@juno.com
phone: (702) 871-9773

NEW HAMPSHIRE
Jewish Genealogical Society of
 New Hampshire
Gary Wallin
P.O. Box 1019
Manchester, NH 03105
e-mail: gary@wallin.com
phone: (603) 623-1212

NEW JERSEY
Jewish Genealogical Society of
 Bergen County
Edward Rosenbaum
135 Chesnut Ridge Road
Montvale, NJ 07645
e-mail: erosenbaum@yahoo.com
Web site: http://erosenbaum.
 netfirms.com/jgsbc
phone: (201) 384-8851

Jewish Genealogical Society of
 Central Jersey
Nathan M. Reiss
228 Livingstone Avenue
New Brunswick, NJ 08901
e-mail: reiss@rci.rutgers.edu
Web site: http://www.jewishgen.
 org/jhscj
phone: (732) 249-4894

Jewish Genealogical Society of
 North Jersey
Evan Stolbach
Charles & Bessie Goldman
 Library
One Pike Drive
Wayne, NJ 07470
e-mail: Estolb7395@aol.com
Web site: http://community.
 nj.com/cc/jgsnorthjersey
phone: (973) 595-0100 ext. 36

Morris Area Jewish Genealogical
    Society
Gary R. Platt
21 Rolling Hill Drive
Morristown, NJ 07960
e-mail: grplatt@hotmail.com
phone: (973) 993-1744

NEW YORK
Jewish Genealogical Society of the
    Capital District
Norman Tillman
P.O. Box 5002
Albany, NY 12205
e-mail: Ntill10123@aol.com
phone: (518) 482-5295

Jewish Genealogical Society
    of Buffalo
Dr. Renata Lefcourt
3700 Main Street
Amherst, NY 14226
e-mail: lefcourt@localnet.com
phone: (716) 833-0743

Jewish Genealogical Society of
    Long Island
Norman Berman
37 Westcliff Drive
Dix Hills, NY 11746
e-mail: nberman@worldnet.att.net
Web site: http://www.jewishgen.
    org/jgsli
phone: (631) 549-9532

Jewish Genealogical Society of
    New York
Estelle Guzik
P.O. Box 6398
New York, NY 10128
e-mail: JGSNY@aol.com
Web site: http://www.jgsny.org
phone: (212) 294-8326

Jewish Genealogical Society of
    Rochester
Bruce Kahn
265 Viennawood Drive
Rochester, NY 14618
e-mail: bkahn@
    servtech.com
Web site: http://www.rit.edu/
    ~bekpph/jgsr
phone: (716) 271-2118

OHIO
Jewish Genealogical Group
Joe Cohen
2673 Florabunda
Columbus, OH 42209
e-mail: joeacohen@aol.com
Web site: http://www.gcis.net/
    cjhs
phone: (614) 231-7006

Jewish Genealogical Society
    of Cleveland
Arlene Blank Rich
966 Eastlawn Drive
Highland Heights, OH 44143
e-mail: BR1595@aol.com
phone: (440) 449-2326
fax: (216) 621-7560

Jewish Genealogical Society
    of Dayton
Leonard Spialter
P.O. Box 60338
Dayton, OH 45406
phone: (937) 277-3995
e-mail: spialterr@about.com

OREGON

Jewish Genealogical Society of
Oregon
Ronald D. Doctor
6651 Capitol Highway
Portland, OR 97219
e-mail: rondoctor@qwest.net
Web site: http://www.rootsweb
.com/~orjgs
phone: (505) 244-0111

Oregon Jewish Genealogical Study
Group
Reeva Kimble
2352 Van Ness
Eugene, OR 97403
e-mail: rkimble@oregon.
uoregon.edu
Web site:
http://www.users.qwest.net/~c
fleishman/eugenegen.html
phone: (541) 345-8129

PENNSYLVANIA

Jewish Genealogical Society of
Greater Philadelphia
Joel. L. Spector
109 Society Hill
Cherry Hill, NJ 08003
e-mail: jlspector@aol.com
Web site: http://www.jewishgen.
org/jgsp
phone: (856) 424-6860

Jewish Genealogical Society of
Pittsburgh
Julian Falk
2131 Fifth Avenue
Pittsburgh, PA 15219
e-mail: JulFalk@aol.com
phone: (412) 471-0772

TEXAS

Dallas Jewish Historical
Society, Genealogy
Division
George L. Smith
7900 Northaven Road
Dallas, TX 75230
e-mail: geode16@aol.com
Web site: http://www.dvjc.org/
history/genealogy.shtml
phone: (214) 739-2737

Greater Houston Jewish
Genealogical Society
Jeff Olderman
7115 Belle Park Drive
Houston, TX 77072
e-mail: jeffel55@aol.com
phone: (281) 495-9211

Jewish Genealogical Society of
San Antonio
Edwin Henkin
12500 N.W. Military
Highway
San Antonio, TX 78231
e-mail: sajgs@jcc-sa.org
phone: (210) 302-6860

VIRGINIA

Jewish Genealogical Society of
Tidewater
Kenneth R. Cohen
7300 Newport Avenue
Norfolk, VA 23505
e-mail: kcohen4@juno.com
phone: (757) 351-2190

WASHINGTON
Jewish Genealogical Society of
    Washington State
Sheryl Stern
3633 86th Street S.E.
Mercer Island, WA 98040
e-mail: jgsws@hotmail.com
Web site: http://members.
    tripod.com/~JGSWS
phone: (206) 232-2666

WISCONSIN
Wisconsin Jewish Genealogical
    Society
Penny Deshur
9280 North Fairway Drive
Milwaukee, WI 53217
e-mail: pdeshur@wi.rr.com
phone: (414) 351-2190

SOUTH AMERICA

ARGENTINA
Sociedad Argentina de Genealogia
    Judia
Paul Armony
Juana Azurduy 2223, P. 8 (1429)
Buenos Aires
e-mail: genarg@infovia.com.ar
Web site: http://www.agja.org.ar

BRAZIL
Sociedade Genealogica Judaica do
    Brasil
Dr. Guilherme Faiguenboim
Caixa Postal 1025
13001–970 Campinas SP
e-mail: faiguen@attglobal.net

OTHER PARTS OF THE WORLD

AUSTRALIA
Australian Jewish Genealogical
    Society, Adelaide
Marjorie Luno
c/o Beit Shalom Synagogue
P.O. Box 47
Stepney, SA 5069
e-mail: chatsworth@
    picknowl.com.au
Web site: http://www.ajgs.
    org.au

Australian Jewish Genealogical
    Society, Brisbane
Morris Ochert
3/23 Lucinda Street
Taringa, QLD 4068
e-mail: stirk@uq.net.au
Web site: http://www.ajgs.org.au

Australian Jewish Genealogical
    Society, Canberra
Sylvia Deutsch
c/o ACT Jewish Community
P.O. Box 3105
Manuka, ACT 2603
e-mail: deutand@ozemail.com.au
Web site: http://www.ajgs.org.au

Australian Jewish Genealogical
  Society, Melbourne
Les Oberman
P.O. Box 189
Glenhuntly, VIC 3163
e-mail: ajgs@exist.com.au
Web site: http://www.ajgs.exist.
  com.au

Australian Jewish Genealogical
  Society, Perth
Michelle Urban
P.O. Box 225
Claremont, WA 6912
e-mail: urban1@iinet.net.au
Web site: http://www.ajgs.org.au

Australian Jewish Genealogical
  Society, Sydney
Rieke Nash
P.O. Box 42
Lane Cove, NSW 1595
e-mail: society@ajgs.org.au
Web site: http://www.ajgs.org.au

ISRAEL
Galilee Genealogical Society
Louis ZetlerHoshaya
M.P.O.
17915 Hamovil
e-mail: zetler@kinneret.co.il
Web site: http://www.geocities.
  com/Heartland/Hills/9698
phone and fax: (972-4) 646-8180

Israel Genealogical Society
Abraham Lebowitz
P.O. Box 4270
91041 Jerusalem
e-mail: aileb@actcom.co.il
Web site: http://www.isragen.org.il
phone: (972-3) 652-5466

Israel Genealogical Society,
  Netanya,
Branch of Israel Genealogical
  Society
Joe Isaacs
e-mail: isaacsj@netvision.net.il
Web site: http://www.isragen.org.il
phone: (972-9) 882-8402

Israel Genealogical Society of
  the Negev
Branch of Israel Genealogical
  Society
Martha Lev-Zion
e-mail: Martha@bgumail.bgu.ac.il
Web site: http://www.isragen.org.il
phone: (972-8) 646-0494

Israel Genealogical Society, Tel Aviv
Branch of Israel Genealogical
  Society
Eitan Shilo
e-mail: eitanshilo@attglobal.net
Web site: http://www.isragen.org.il

Jewish Family Research
  Association (JFRA Israel)
Schelly Dardashti
11/57 Grinberg Street
69379 Tel Aviv
e-mail: dardasht@barak-online.net
phone: (972-3) 699-1693

Jewish Family Research
  Association, Petah Tikva
Branch of Jewish Family Research
  Association
Susan Edel
e-mail: susan@deldent.com
Gilda Kurtzman
e-mail: gildak@zahav.net.il

Jewish Family Research
   Association, Raanana
Branch of Jewish Family Research
   Association
Ingrid Rockberger
e-mail: ingrid_100@hotmail.com

JAMAICA
Jamaica Jewish Genealogical
   Society
Ainsley Cohen Henriques
58 Paddington Terrace
Kingston 6
e-mail: ainsley@cwjamaica.com
phone: (876) 927-9777
fax: (876) 927-4369

SOUTH AFRICA
Jewish Family History Society of
   Cape Town
Paul Cheifitz
P.O. Box 51985
Waterfront 8002
e-mail: jewfamct@global.co.za
phone: (21) 434-4825 or (21)
   423-0223

Jewish Genealogical Society of
   Johannesburg
Colin Plenn
P.O. Box 1388
Parkland 2121
e-mail: evancol@africa.com

○

The Douglas E. Goldman Jewish Genealogy Center

Located in the Nachum Goldmann Museum of the Diaspora in Israel, the Douglas E. Goldman Jewish Genealogy Center, on the third floor of the Permanent Exhibition, describes itself as "the only Jewish Genealogy Center of its kind in the world. In the Center, visitors can search a computerized database containing thousands of genealogies of Jewish families from all over the world and can also register their own family trees."

More than 1.5 million names have been entered into the constantly expanding database. Visitors can "explore their ancestry, record and preserve their own family trees for future generations, thus adding their own 'branch' to the family tree of the Jewish People."

You can also ask the center, by e-mail, to search for you at $5 per search. For details, go to http://www.bh.org.il/Genealogy/index.aspx.

The Goldman Center has also developed and is marketing Jewish genealogical software called Ilanot. Features of the software include the following:

> Hebrew-to-English date converter
> Special fields for bar and bat mitzvah dates and information
> Drop-down listing for all Torah portions
> Submission of your family's genealogical records for listing at the center, where they will be preserved for future generations

The Ilanot Web site is at http://www.bh.org.il/Shop/ilanot.aspx.

There are many other features at the Douglas E. Goldman Jewish Genealogy Center. I suggest that you explore its Web site thoroughly: http://www.bh.org.il.

LDS Family History Library

The Church of Jesus Christ of Latter-Day Saints (the Mormon Church, often abbreviated LDS) administers what are undoubtedly the most ambitious genealogy archives and library in the world. The Family History Library, which is the genealogical arm of the Mormon Church, is located in Salt Lake City, Utah, in a granite mountain that has been hollowed out and has the capacity to house 6 million reels of microfilm. The archive in the mountain is carefully controlled for temperature and other climate variations and is also supposed to be able to withstand nearly every possible disaster, natural or human-made.

To understand the Mormons' interest in genealogy, one must know something about their religious beliefs. The Mormons believe that people can be baptized even after death and that genealogy research leads them to candidates for this rite. Because the religion is dependent on and interested in converts, the Mormon Church is interested in *all* genealogical records.

Of particular interest to Jewish researchers is the fact that the Mormons have been able to gain access to Eastern European records and in this way have acquired Jewish records, including census materials, synagogue and Jewish communal records, and other documents. Their collection already contains significant Polish, German, and Hungarian records of Jewish interest, and they continue to gather more documents all the time.

Here's a description of the Mormons' genealogical resources:

o The collection includes over 2.2 million rolls of microfilmed genealogical records; 742,000 microfiches; 300,000 books, serials, and other formats; and 4,500 periodicals.

o The Ancestral File database contains approximately 35.6 million names that are linked into families.

o The International Genealogical Index database contains approximately 600 million individual names. An addendum to the International Genealogical Index contains an additional 125 million names.

o The Pedigree Resource File database contains 36 million names that are linked into families.

- Records from the United States, Canada, the British Isles, Europe, Latin America, Asia, and Africa are available.
- In 2000, the collection increased monthly by an average of 4,100 rolls of film and 700 books.
- A majority of the records contain information about persons who lived before 1920.
- Approximately 242 cameras are currently microfilming records in over forty countries. Records have been filmed in more than 110 countries, territories, and possessions.

To gain access to the material gathered by the Mormons, you need not travel to Salt Lake City. Rather, you must locate a branch library of the church (there are many throughout the country), where you will find a microfilm copy of the index to the Mormons' holdings. When you find what you want in the index, you can send for the material through the branch library at a nominal price per reel of microfilm. The index is arranged by country. If you are interested, for example, in seeing what Polish records they have, you must look up "Poland—Jews." I have also found material under the heading "Poland—Minorities—Jews." You might also seek material of a general nature. For example, a census taken in Hungary might have included Jews and non-Jews. Again, find what you want by location—first by country and then by county or city.

The Jewish Genealogy Institute, located at the Center for Jewish History, has negotiated a loan agreement with the LDS Family History Library so that researchers can order microfilmed international vital records through the Institute and study the films at the Center for Jewish History. I strongly recommend that if you want to use the Mormon records, you should seek guidance from the Jewish Genealogy Institute.

There is an article of great importance for Jews about using the Mormon material. You can read "Using the LDS Family History Library Catalog on the Internet for Jewish Genealogy" by Gary Mokotoff at http://www.jewishgen.org/jgsi/fhlc.htm.

The JewishGen.org Web site has a lot of important information and some tools to help gain access to and use the incredible Jewish material in its collection. Take special note of http://www.jewishgen.org/databases/FHLC. There you will find "Jewish Records in the Family History Library Catalog Prepared by the Family History Library for the IAJGS," described as "an inventory of the microfilms, microfiche and books in the LDS Family History Library Catalog (FHLC) which are specifically Jewish genealogical sources. It is a valuable finding aid for persons researching their Jewish

1892   Születési

Folyó szám	A születés hava és napja	A gyermek neve	Neme férfi	nő	Álla-pota törvényes	törvénytlen	Az atya neve állása v. foglalkozása és születés helye	Az anya neve és születés helye	A szülők lakása és a gyermek születésének helye
111	1892 ápril. 22	Margit	/	/			Gülöp Berta lan, mészáros Moralka	Keimovics Be la, nagy Ka ló	Moralka
112	1892 ápril 24	György *pp. 201*	/	/			ifj. Schwarcz Jakab, vasáru Moralka	Weinberger Ro za, Kis Helmec	Moralka
113	1892 ápril 26	Majer! Menyhért	/	/			Schwarcz Áb rahám, szücs Moralka	Weisz Jani Ó-Paly	Moralka
114	1892 ápril 28	Relli	/	/			Weinberger Sámuel, gazdá Kos Barapenya	Braun Lina Kisvárda	Parapenya
115	1892 máj. 2 *201*	Heléna	/	/			Klein Márton üveszfös Karász	Grünberger Háni Moralka	N. Bátor, Moralka
116	1892 máj. 11	Eszter	/	/			Friedländer József, kereske dő Gerebakács	Löwi Relli Gebe	Gebe
117	1892 máj. 15 posthuma	Jolán	/	/			Czuckerman Mózes, fuvaros Gebe	Grünstein Má ria, N. Bátor	Gebe
118	1892 máj. 15	Dezső	/	/			Zafir Jakab gazdálkodó Gebe	Czuckerman Cili, Jehertő	Gebe
—	72	*illegible*		/	/		Winkler Ábra hám, csizpez	Wagner Záli	

Birth record of Helen Klein, the author's maternal grandmother (item 115). This record was located among the Jewish material accumulated by the Mormon Church.

ancestry but is not intended to be a replacement for the FHLC. The complete FHLC can be consulted at http://www.familysearch.org."

Note that I have used the Mormon library for years and have never been approached to join the church or to read a pamphlet. The Mormons seem to separate their religious work from their genealogical work. I would recommend using their library, but I would also suggest that you protest firmly if someone approaches you on a religious matter.

There is legitimate concern among many Jews that the Mormons should not use information about Jews, especially those killed in the Holocaust, in their baptism-related activities. I urge you to stay informed on the subject as you consider using and supporting the Mormon genealogical efforts. The JewishGen.org site contains important information regarding this issue; go to http://www.jewishgen.org/infofiles/ldsagree.html.

The address is LDS Family History Library, 35 North West Temple Street, Salt Lake City, UT 84150, and its Web site is http://www.familysearch.org. Be forewarned that the Web site contains material about the Mormon religion. Do not forget that the Mormons are a proselytizing denomination.

Other Valuable Jewish Sources

A variety of publications are of great assistance to genealogical researchers. Here are a few more of particular interest and value.

Toledot: The Journal of Jewish Genealogy

In the winter of 1977, Steven W. Siegel and I got together to found *Toledot: The Journal of Jewish Genealogy*. I remember the first time I met Steve. Here was a person who was obviously very articulate and extremely capable, an absolute mensch. Over the years I have come to appreciate Steve's skills and talents even more. When others talk, Steve works. He's a doer; he makes things happen. And he is impeccably ethical. Every Jewish organization with which Steve has been affiliated knows how special he is. After discovering that we both had a passion for Jewish genealogy, we also discovered that we both saw the need for a publication devoted to the subject. We were coming across new sources, new information, and new search strategies all the time, and we wanted to share them with others. *Toledot* became a forum for everyone who wanted to build a network of Jewish family historians for the purpose of helping one another.

We published *Toledot* as a quarterly for several years, sometimes missing a quarter, sometimes offering a double issue, but always pleasing its readers. We included how-to articles, bibliographies, articles about sur-

names, and much more. One very popular and useful series was our catalogue of the towns in Poland, Hungary, and Germany for which the
Mormons have Jewish records.

After we stopped publishing in 1982, we continued to make back issues
available; but now much of the content of the back issues of *Toledot* is out
of date. Nevertheless, it would be worthwhile to find a library that owns
the back issues. Or contact *Avotaynu,* which offers the back issues on
microfiche. You never know what you might find. And while we're on the
subject of *Avotaynu,* I'd once again strongly urge you to subscribe. It is
truly an essential publication for Jewish genealogists.

Looking back on the time we spent publishing *Toledot* makes me
proud. Steve Siegel and I were publishing what was at the time the only
periodical in the world specializing in Jewish genealogy.

The Encyclopedia of Jewish Genealogy

If the book you are now reading is "Jewish Genealogy 101," *The Encyclopedia of Jewish Genealogy* was meant to be "Jewish Genealogy 102."
Edited by Miriam Weiner and me, the *Encyclopedia* was our attempt to
bring all sorts of useful information to the serious researcher.

One highlight of the *Encyclopedia* is its catalogue of towns whose Jewish
records have been microfilmed by the Mormon Church, along with information on how the church can be useful in Jewish genealogical research.
Another extremely useful section is its state-by-state presentations of the
Jewish genealogical resources that are available in the United States.

The Encyclopedia of Jewish Genealogy was published in 1997, so
much of it is out of date. But it still has much of value.

Encyclopedia Judaica

I can recall the moment, more than three decades ago, when I first discovered the remarkable *Encyclopedia Judaica* (known among Jewish
librarians and others as the "EJ"). Sixteen volumes in length, with a beautiful binding, attractive endpapers, and articles on just about every topic
you can imagine, the EJ is a gold mine of information. One volume is the
index for the other fifteen volumes and the key to using this magnificent
set of books.

Most synagogues have an EJ, as do most public libraries with at least
medium-sized collections. It is also available for purchase, and I highly
recommend it. It will provide your home with a lifelong repository of Jewish knowledge. It is now available on CD.

These are just some of the things you can find in the EJ:

- *Towns.* Do you know the names of the towns in your family history? You'll be pleased at how many of these towns have brief histories in the EJ.

- *Your last name.* It might not be as remote as you think to locate someone with your last name through the EJ. If your name is unusual, give it a try.

- *Background information.* The EJ provides material on just about every Jewish topic. As you learn details about your family history, the EJ will answer lots of questions.

- *Hasidic dynasties.* The EJ has many family trees in it, especially of Hasidic families.

- *Maps.* There are lots of useful maps in the EJ. Look up countries of interest as well as obsolete geographical areas (like Galicia).

- *Fascination.* I often just take a volume of the EJ and browse. Dipping into it anywhere provides a rich Jewish education for its readers.

First American Jewish Families

I have yet to meet a man as generous as the late Rabbi Malcolm H. Stern. I was proud that Rabbi Stern called me a friend. It was Rabbi Stern to whom I first turned for help when I began my Jewish genealogical research.

It was in the early 1970s, and when I went to the card catalogue of a large university library seeking information on Jewish genealogy, the only work on the subject was a book, called *Americans of Jewish Descent*, written by Rabbi Malcolm H. Stern. I arranged to see the book through interlibrary loan, and when it arrived, I was impressed and also disappointed. I was impressed because Rabbi Stern's book was an attempt to document the family tree of every Jew in the United States before the year 1840. In 1840, there were about ten thousand Jews in the country, and Rabbi Stern (with the support and talents of his wife) wanted to trace each of their families and their descendants. The book was huge and, as I said, most impressive.

I was disappointed because I knew that the contents of the book had little to do with my ancestors, who arrived in America in the next century. Nevertheless, I wrote to Rabbi Stern, asking for advice, and he promptly wrote back with suggestions and encouragement. I have since learned that over the years, countless Jewish family historians have received support— in many ways—from the remarkable Rabbi Stern.

When Steve Siegel and I launched *Toledot: The Journal of Jewish Genealogy,* we began our efforts at the dining room table in Rabbi Stern's home. He allowed us to search through all of his correspondence (I think he saved everything) to compile a mailing list of potential subscribers. The result was quite beneficial to us.

Over the years Rabbi Stern became an important force in the world of genealogy, Jewish and general. He assumed leadership positions in national organizations, he was highly regarded by genealogists and archivists worldwide, and his contributions to the development of the field of Jewish genealogy are incalculable.

Unfortunately, the last update of Rabbi Stern's work, titled *First American Jewish Families,* is currently out of print. You will have to consult this masterpiece at a library that has it or consider searching for an out-of-print copy. For example, it is available secondhand through the Amazon.com Web site.

My Generations: *A Jewish Genealogical Textbook*

For the past fifteen years, I have lectured to hundreds of Jewish groups around the United States on the subject of Jewish genealogy. Slowly but surely, the message that genealogy can be an effective teaching tool has been heard by Jewish educators. This is reflected in the fact that more and more children attending Jewish afternoon, Sunday, and day schools are coming home with homework assignments having to do with family history. Teachers know that genealogy can be exciting and informative—and fun! I can think of no better way to influence a young person's sense of responsibility for the future of the Jewish people than to show the child that he or she is the result of many past generations. When a young person sees himself or herself as a link in the chain of history, that chain grows longer and stronger.

My Generations: A Course in Jewish Family History has been used in hundreds of synagogue schools as part of the religious school curriculum since 1984. The book is essentially a "fill-in-the-blanks" book in which I show the young reader how I was able to gather lots of information from my family by simply talking to relatives. I then provide spaces for the young person to record the results of his or her own family history information gathering.

My Generations: A Course in Jewish Family History also has a teacher's guide available, written by my friend, the gifted writer and Jewish educator Rabbi Alan A. Kay. Ideal for classroom use, Dr. Kay's guide provides teachers with project ideas, lesson plans, duplicating

The wedding photo of Avraham Abusch Kurzweil and Hinda Ruchel Lowenthal, paternal great-grandparents of the author.

machine masters, and lots of tips on how to use Jewish genealogy in the classroom.

I am pleased—and not just because I am its author—that teachers find *My Generations* a lively topic. It's not "just another subject"; it can change lives. I have also heard that some synagogues use the book for intergenerational projects. One synagogue on Long Island has an annual "Grandparents' Shabbat" when grandparents and grandchildren come together in the synagogue for activities. One of those activities is using *My Generations*.

My Generations: A Course in Jewish Family History and its teacher's guide are published by Behrman House and can be ordered at http://behrmanhouse.com/cat/tbgs/68mgac.shtml.

Other Jewish Genealogical Publications

Although *Avotaynu* is the finest periodical of its kind, there are other newsletters and publications that deal specifically with Jewish genealogy. No list would be definitive, as new developments are happening all the time. Many of the local Jewish Genealogical Societies publish newsletters. Check out the listing for local Jewish Genealogical Societies on the International Association of Jewish Genealogical Societies (IAJGS) Web site: http://www.jewishgen.org/ajgs/yearbook-2002.html.

The Belarus Special Interest Group (SIG) has an online newsletter: http://www.jewishgen.org/Belarus/newsletter/bnl_index.htm.

Gesher Galicia (also a SIG) has a newsletter, *The Galitzianer:* http://www.jewishgen.org/Galicia/newsletter.html.

The Kielce-Radom SIG journal is *K-R SIG Journal:* http://www.jewishgen.org/krsig/YearOne.html.

The Latvia SIG has a newsletter, *Latvia SIG:* http://www.jewishgen.org/Latvia/SIG_Newsletter.html.

The Litvak SIG has an online newsletter, *LitvakSIG Online Journal:* http://www.jewishgen.org/Litvak/journal.htm.

The Southern Africa SIG has a newsletter, *The SA-SIG Newsletter:* http://www.jewishgen.org/SAfrica/newsletter/index.htm.

Stammbaum: The Newsletter of German-Jewish Genealogical Research is published twice a year by The Leo Baeck Institute, 15 West 16th Street, New York, NY 10011; e-mail: kfranklin@lbi.cjh.org. Back issues are also available: http://www.jewishgen.org/stammbaum.

The Suwalk-Lomza Interest Group has a quarterly journal called *Landsmen*: http://www.jewishgen.org/SuwalkLomza/Contents.html.

Keep in mind that in a sense all the Special Interest Groups (SIGs) hosted by JewishGen.org are "publications." Their Web sites should be examined

closely, and you should subscribe to those of interest: http://www.jewishgen.
org/JewishGen/sigs.htm.

Professional Genealogical Assistance

There are many extremely talented researchers who have made themselves
available for freelance assignments. Although I would surely urge you to
do as much research yourself as you can, I wouldn't want to rule out the
possibility that a professional researcher can help.

Research is an art. This became clear to me when I was studying for my
degree in library science. When a librarian is given a research question, a
search strategy must be developed. Some people have minds that work like
a flowchart. They can easily figure out how to put things together to get
results in their research. Where one librarian will be stumped by a question, another will know what research tools are available, what questions
to ask, what leaps of faith to take, and how to make progress.

The same is true for professional genealogists. Some are better,
some worse. Some are quick, others slow. Since they usually charge by
the hour, the costs can add up. But if you locate a top-notch researcher
and can clearly define the assignment and the parameters, hiring
a researcher can be quite useful. I'd especially urge you to consider a
researcher for very specific tasks, such as obtaining particular documents
from government agencies.

I strongly recommend that you read the section of JewishGen.org
Web site called "Hiring a Professional Genealogist"—go to http://www.
jewishgen.org/infofiles/profgen.txt. You will also see ads placed by freelance professional researchers in the pages of *Avotaynu*. When you speak
with a researcher, don't be bashful. Ask for references. *Avotaynu* usually
includes ads from researchers in Eastern Europe.

Eileen Polakoff is one of the leading professional genealogists in the
Jewish world. I also have personal experience as one of her clients. For
example, I once wanted to give someone a gift of some documents about
her family and ancestors. I hired Eileen, discussing with her just the kinds
of things I was imagining she might find. She tracked down exactly the
documents I was hoping for.

Eileen is also the author of a regular column in *Avotaynu* called "Ask
the Experts."

I asked Eileen to help me to understand the role of the professional
researcher. She said, "Genealogy is a wonderful hobby, but to many, it is
also a career. Individuals, from hobbyists to attorneys to courts, may look

to engage the services of a professional genealogist for a variety of reasons. Expertise, experience, deadlines, or location can all be factors in making a decision to hire a professional. People with little time for genealogical pursuits or for whom speed in gathering information is important may find hiring a professional a worthwhile expenditure.

"Consumers should be aware of organizations that issue credentials for professional genealogists, such as the Board for Certification of Genealogists, and professional organizations with codes of ethics, such as the Association of Professional Genealogists."

I recommend that you consider contacting Eileen Polakoff if you think you want to hire a researcher. If Eileen can help you, she will. If she cannot, she can refer you to someone who can. Contact her at 240 West End Avenue, Apt. 15-A, New York, NY 10023; e-mail: eileenpolakoff@avotaynu. com; phone: (212) 787-4371 or (201) 387-3818; fax: (201) 387-2855.

○

A Conversation with Ladislau Gyémánt

Ladislau Gyémánt was born in Oradea, Romania, in 1947. He received his Ph.D. from the University of Cluj in 1982. The author of nineteen books and ninety studies, he is a professor of Jewish history and European history at Babes-Bolyai University in Romania. Professor Gyémánt is a senior fellow researcher at the Institute of History of the Romanian Academy in Cluj, the director of the Dr. Moshe Carmilly Institute for Hebrew and Jewish History in Cluj, and deputy dean of the Faculty of European Studies of Babes-Bolyai University.

Q. Please tell us a little about your interest in Jewish genealogy.

A. Beyond my professional interests in European and Jewish history, I have been involved in Jewish genealogical research since 1990, when such studies became possible and available in my country after the fall of the Communist regime. I am a member of the Jewish Genealogical Society of New York and of the Association of Professional Genealogists and editor for Romania of *Avotaynu*.

Q. How do you describe your research services?

A. I offer family history research services in Romania and Hungary. Starting with a list of basic information and research targets, I obtain copies of birth, marriage, and death registrations kept in the registers of vital records stored in the archives of those two countries.

I send copies of these records together with their English translations. My services cover only the present territory of the two countries and do not include Ukraine, Slovakia, or Moldova, which historically were provinces of those countries.

Q. Do you have any advice for people who are considering the services of a researcher? How does one evaluate a researcher, his fees, client expectations, and so on?

A. I like to establish a relationship between researcher and customer based on reciprocal trust. So, for instance, I never ask for an advance deposit; I do the research first and send my bill with the results of the work done. It is important too to settle the terms of cooperation and the targets of the research at the outset. I bill based on the results of the research (a flat fee per relevant record found) and not on a research time basis. If the results are much beyond what the customer is expecting, I first send a list of the findings and offer the client the opportunity to choose the records he wants to have copied and translated.

Q. Let's offer readers of this book an example of your services. My grandmother, Helen Klein, was born in Nyirbator or Mateszalka, Hungary, as were her siblings and parents. What do you suppose you could find about her and her family and ancestors for me? What would it cost me? Did I provide enough information to have some expectation that your services would be useful? How much time would your research take?

A. The registers of vital records for Nyirbator and Mateszalka are stored in the Hungarian National Archives for Budapest for the period 1850–1895. These are rabbinical registers of births, marriages, and deaths. I can research the requested names and obtain copies of the relevant records for the family history. For the period before 1850, census records are available—for instance, for the year 1848. For the period after 1895, there are state registers stored in the town halls of the towns you mentioned. For these state registers, photocopying is not permitted, but I could obtain official transcriptions of the registrations. As far as cost is concerned, my fee is U.S. $20 per record found, copied, and translated into English. So the costs are dependent on the results of the research. To this would be added the cost of the travel and accommodation expenses—around $100 to $150 altogether.

Q. Can you give us some examples of some of your research successes? Also, do you ever find nothing for a client?

A. I have conducted successful research projects in Maramures, Moldavia (Iasi, Botosani, Bacau, Suceava areas), Oradea, Arad,

Budapest, Bucuresti, and many other towns. But I am proudest of a research project in Cluj when I found, in a little house spared by the demolitions of the Communist era, a family who had been living there since the 1950s without any contact with the father, who had gone to California after the war and died there. The happy family inherited a small fortune due to my efforts to find them.

Of course, there is no guarantee that the research will be successful. The basic information could be wrong or the registers could be in a poor state of preservation—this is especially the case in northern Transylvania, where the Jewish community archives were destroyed during the Holocaust. In such cases, the loss is mine. I do not require payment for unsuccessful research work.

Q. Do you think there is a core reason why those interested in genealogy are involved with it?

A. Family history research is a fascinating field, and it could be the start of long-lasting friendships. One of my customers who was very satisfied with the results of my research work declared me an honorary cousin of the family, and I am very proud of this!

○

○

A Conversation with Miriam Weiner

Miriam Weiner, the first Jewish genealogist to be certified by the Board for Certification of Genealogists in Washington, D.C., is an expert in Jewish genealogy and Holocaust research. She is president of Routes to Roots (http://www.routestoroots.com), a firm offering in-depth archive research, town visits, and customized tours to ancestral towns of the former Soviet Union and Poland. She is also president of the Routes to Roots Foundation (http://www.rtrfoundation.org), a nonprofit foundation that has published, in collaboration with the YIVO Institute for Jewish Research, a town-by-town inventory of Jewish and civil records in Eastern European archives. The first volume in the series, *Jewish Roots in Poland*, appeared in 1997 and the second, *Jewish Roots in Ukraine and Moldova*, in 1999. Weiner is currently preparing an online database of archive inventories with updated inventories from those two volumes (Poland, Ukraine, and Moldova) plus new material from archives in Belarus and Lithuania. Miriam Weiner can be contacted at 136 Sandpiper Key, Secaucus, NJ 07094; e-mail: mweiner@ routestoroots.com; phone: (201) 866-4075; fax: (201) 864-9222.

Q. What is Routes to Roots? How long have you been in business?

A. My company, Routes to Roots, offers archive research services, "town visits," and customized tours of ancestral towns in Poland and the former Soviet Union. This company was formed after my first trip to Poland in 1989. We are specialists in Jewish genealogy and Holocaust research, with the main emphasis on archival research in Poland, Belarus, Ukraine, and Moldova. The town visits include interviews, photos, and video. Customized private tours can also be arranged for individuals or families to ancestral towns in the countries I mentioned. The euphoria and emotional impact of walking the street of one's ancestral town in the old country cannot be measured. I have owned my own apartment-office in Ukraine for about ten years and also maintain a small office in Warsaw.

Q. Would people have as much success if they traveled and did the research themselves? Why or why not?

A. Of course, it depends somewhat on the country, but in general, most individuals are not fluent in the Russian, Polish, Ukrainian, Romanian, or other languages they may encounter. Also, finding someone to serve as a translator who is also familiar with archival procedures and document formats as well as Jewish naming patterns is not easy. Archive research takes a lot of patience and much longer than one expects. Some people have had success in trying to do this themselves but often grow frustrated with the bureaucratic delays often encountered in accessing the archives and the material. Travel conditions and security are serious issues not familiar to most people on a first-time visit to the old country.

Q. How do you determine fees for your services?

A. All of my assignments are customized for the individual inquirer. Costs are determined by a number of factors, including how many surnames, how common they are, the number of surviving documents to be searched, how many archives hold relevant material, and how many different towns and countries must be visited for the research project.

For example, researching documents for the city of Ivano-Frankovsk (formerly Stanislawow) in Ukraine would involve travel to seven different archives in three different cities in two countries. Researching documents for Volkovysk would involve research in five archives in four cities in three different countries.

Q. Tell us about your books.

A. Both books, *Jewish Roots in Poland* and *Jewish Roots in Ukraine and Moldova,* include a town-by-town inventory of archive documents, including document type, years available, which archive has the documents, file numbers for the documents, and contact information for the archives. Both books took ten years to research and publish. Most important, the archival material was verified by the archivists in multiple reviews, and the books were published in official cooperation with the archivists in each country, according to written agreement.

In addition, both books include hundreds of color images (more than three hundred in the Poland book and more than one thousand in the Ukraine-Moldova book). The books also include articles by archivists and Jewish community leaders, numerous maps, and a great many document examples.

The Poland book can be purchased directly from the Routes to Roots Foundation by going to the foundation Web site at http://www.rtrfoundation.org, clicking on "Publications," and then downloading the order form. The Ukraine book is out of print and will not be reprinted.

Q. Tell us about the Web site hosted by the Routes to Roots Foundation.

A. The Web site includes a searchable database accessible by town or district name, consisting of document information from archives in Belarus, Lithuania, Poland, Ukraine, Moldova, and some Holocaust-related entries from archives in Russia.

The Web site is actually a book (350 pages), published online, with a searchable database. The menu includes "Introduction," "Archive Acknowledgments," "Archive Chapters," "Archive Database," "Maps," "Foundation Data," "Publications," "Related Web Sites," and "Supporters." Many of the Web site pages are excerpted chapters from *Jewish Roots in Poland* and *Jewish Roots in Ukraine and Moldova,* supplemented by similar new chapters from archivists in Belarus and Lithuania (all in PDF format in order to preserve the format in the books). There are numerous links to other sites throughout this Web site, which will save the user extensive time. For example, there is a link to a Web site in Poland where one can find addresses of *Urzad Stanu Cywilnego* offices (civil registration offices, usually in the local town halls) throughout Poland. There are links to Web sites where one can find

archives and libraries by country throughout the world, as well as numerous links for map resources.

A database search for the town of "Bialystok" produces nineteen record groups consisting of thirteen different record types located in six different archives in three countries. From this list, one can select which record type to view, click on that link (census lists, for example), and then see that the census records cover the periods 1853, 1858, 1860–1865, 1869, 1874, and 1883–1896 and that the documents are located in the National Historical Archives of Belarus in Grodno; the specific archive file numbers are also listed. By clicking on "Archive Name," the inquirer will find the contact information for the archives along with other important resources for researching ancestral towns in Poland.

A town or locality search may be done in three ways: by the exact current spelling of the town name, by the Daitch-Mokotoff soundex search, or by "begins with." The results produce a list of document types in archives throughout the five countries. To search for specific family names, it is then necessary to initiate a search of the relevant archive (methods of archive access are described on the Web site).

The Web site is updated regularly, including the archival database, new chapters and articles written by archivists and historians, and additional relevant links to other Web sites.

The "News Alert" feature provides updates on new information.

Q. What advice can you give to the person who is considering hiring a researcher? Do you have any tips?

A. The foundation Web site (http://www.rtrfoundation.org) provides an excellent answer:

It is recommended that one obtain:

An agreement in writing as to exactly what is to be researched, signed by both parties

The time period of the assignment

The costs involved (research time, travel costs, copy costs, etc.)

Method and terms of payment

What you are to receive: a report that includes:

1. List of documents searched

2. Years searched

3. Archive numbers (fond/opis/delo [file] in former Soviet Union and zespol/sygnatura in Poland)

4. Location and name of archive where search was done

5. Translation of documents

6. Document copies (if requested)

According to Gary Mokotoff, publisher of *Avotaynu,* a genealogist should work with an individual or company with offices near the genealogist's home so as to have convenient recourse if the genealogist should become unhappy with the results or a lack of responsiveness.

Q. Can you give a few examples of some discoveries you've made for your clients?

Also, do you ever find nothing for a client?

A. Before I undertake an assignment, we spend significant time discussing the client's sources for ancestral names and town names. If the client does not have sufficient documentation, I help obtain documents in the United States that provide that type of information. Therefore, by the time I prepare the letter of agreement or contract for the research project, the client is virtually certain of these two vital pieces of information.

I have never had a situation where I did not find the requested surnames in the specific town. During more than a dozen years of doing this research, I can recall a couple of instances when it was difficult to connect the client's family with the archive data, even though it was the same name and same town. Usually, additional research (either in the United States or in the European archives) produced the connection.

It is quite common to find hundreds of documents for clients and to trace their families back several previously unknown generations to the early or mid-1700s.

Furthermore, in doing "town visits" on behalf of clients, I have frequently found relatives of my clients, unknown to them beforehand. As a result, they have traveled to the ancestral town, met the relatives, and in several instances invited the family members to visit them in the United States.

One of my clients is a neurosurgeon in Pennsylvania. My first assignment for him was an archival research project in the Vinnitsa area of Ukraine, where I not only found archive documents but was also able to locate his father's first cousin. He and his father

subsequently visited the cousin in Vinnitsa and since then my client has made several trips back to Vinnitsa to see this cousin. She went with him to their ancestral town of Novaya Priluki, where the cousin was able to describe in graphic detail the Nazi occupation and the murder of forty-one of their family members. During the last two trips, his daughter accompanied him to Ukraine. Next year, his daughter will be married, and the Ukraine relatives have been invited to attend the wedding in the United States.

In another situation, we discovered my clients' second cousins living in Rovno during an archive research and "town visit" assignment. As a result, my clients made multiple trips to Rovno to meet the new cousins and have continued the relationship.

Q. If you had to give one piece of advice to the beginner, what would it be?

A. My advice is to interview family members (on videotape, if possible) about what they remember and to identify the old family photos before it is too late.

Q. Why do you think so many people are becoming interested in their family history, and what has contributed to this growing interest?

A. Several factors have contributed to the rapid increase in interest in researching family history. Certainly Alex Haley's *Roots* awakened an interest throughout the world. The Bicentennial celebration in 1976 contributed further to the focus on family heritage. The continuing focus on the restoration of Ellis Island and the Statue of Liberty played a significant role in drawing attention to the immigration experience. On a personal level, two factors combine to motivate many of us to action now—the immigrant generation is dwindling rapidly, and Holocaust survivors—the last group of people to actually witness life in our ancestral towns—are getting older and are dying at the rate of 10 percent per year. Finally, the Internet is making it easier for people to post queries and discover resources and relatives. With the recent access to the Ellis Island database, millions of people worldwide are now able to find information about their ancestors and relatives.

Q. Does Jewish genealogy differ from general genealogy, and if so, how?

A. Researching Jewish roots presents special problems, beginning with the name changes at Ellis Island. Additional barriers to connections in the old country occur because many documents were destroyed during the Holocaust and many of the localities where our

ancestors once lived have little or no trace of Jewish life or Jewish historical sites. The frequent border changes also complicate research because it makes it difficult to know where to look for the town's documents. Also, until about ten years ago, it was not possible to access documents or visit former Communist countries and particularly the former Soviet Union.

Q. Why do some genealogists have more success than others?

A. Many factors come into play here. For instance, researching an unusual name from a small (but not tiny) locality is easier than researching the Cohens from Warsaw. Coming from a rabbinic line increases the possibility of tracing back further because there is significant documentation of rabbinic families. Practical considerations are also a factor, such as how much time and money a family historian is willing to invest. Country of origin also makes a difference. Although some material has become accessible in the former USSR, the lack of indexes and inventories, coupled with difficult travel conditions, makes it very difficult for the average traveler to successfully research this material. Finally, luck does play a part. Being in the right place when a family name is mentioned, such as a social gathering, can have great significance.

Q. What has been your most rewarding experience so far?

A. That is a difficult question to answer because several things come to mind. The first rewarding experience was reuniting a father with his adopted daughter after a forty-year separation. The second highlight was discovering dozens of new relatives in the USSR by tracing them through Soviet telephone books at the Library of Congress in Washington, D.C. This discovery was the subject of one of my newspaper columns, which I called "Researching Russian Roots with 'Ma Bell' in Moscow." Next, I can still remember the euphoria of obtaining seventeen birth records from a small archive in Ukraine for my grandmother, three of her first cousins, and other family members. In 1990, I led a group of twenty-one Jewish family historians to Poland, where they had access to on-site research (not normally available to foreigners) at the Polish State Archives in Warsaw, Lublin, and Krakow. Moreover, access to the archives at Auschwitz was allowed (first-time access for a group), and many tour participants found records for family members among the more than one million cards on file. Many tour participants visited their ancestral towns, where they found vital records for family members. In 1996, clients of mine traveled to Ukraine to meet a previously unknown first cousin I found for them in a

research trip a few months earlier. Of course, working in the archives of the former USSR fulfills a dream that I never thought would be possible. Many books I work with have pages stuck together. Since this material was closed to foreigners for generations, I know that I was the first person to open these books in perhaps seventy years.

Q. How has genealogy changed and enhanced your life?

A. I began researching my family history more than thirty years ago, and for some time it continued as a hobby, as it is for thousands of other amateur family historians. In the mid-1980s, while employed as executive director of the American Gathering of Jewish Holocaust Survivors, I realized that a full-time job would never permit me to spend the kind of time I preferred in the field of Jewish genealogy. In 1986, I left my position with the American Gathering to begin my column "Roots and Branches," which has since been published in more than one hundred Jewish newspapers and journals worldwide. I began lecturing on Jewish genealogy and Holocaust research under the auspices of the B'nai B'rith Lecture Bureau. I am coeditor (with Arthur Kurzweil) of *The Encyclopedia of Jewish Genealogy,* published in 1990. Since 1989, I have been working in Poland and the former Soviet Union to identify, compile, and publish a town-by-town inventory of archive documents. This is the material that was published in *Jewish Roots in Poland* and *Jewish Roots in Ukraine and Moldova.* Most recently, I have posted a new Web site on the Internet that features the archive database from those two books, with updated and new information from the archivists plus the addition of archival information from Belarus and Lithuania.

The whole focus of my life has changed with this career change. I have experienced a renewed commitment to my Jewish heritage and a strengthening of my Jewish identity. I feel very strongly about the importance of documenting family history and hope that others will also explore their roots.

○

Ten Commandments for Jewish Genealogists

Another important contribution made by Rabbi Malcolm Stern was that of a role model. Anyone who ever met him knows that he was an exceptional soul. His way with people was compassionate and sensitive. The following "Ten Commandments for Genealogists," written by Rabbi Stern, should be taken seriously. A master genealogist created them.

    I. I am a genealogist dedicated to true knowledge about the families I am researching.

    II. Thou shalt use family traditions with caution and only as clues.

    III. Thou shalt not accept as gospel every written record or printed word.

    IV. Thou shalt not hang nobility or royalty on your family tree without verifying with experts.

    V. Thou shalt clearly label the questionable and the fairy tale.

    VI. Thou shalt handle all records in such a way that the next users will find them in the same condition you did.

    VII. Thou shalt credit those who help you and ask permission of those whose work you use.

    VIII. Thou shalt not query any source of information without supplying postage.

    IX. Thou shalt respect the sensitivities of the living in whatever you record but tell the truth about the dead.

    X. Thou shalt not become a genealogical teacher or authority without appropriate training and certification.

5

AVOTAYNU

THE PREMIER PUBLISHER IN THE
WORLD OF JEWISH GENEALOGY

TO SAY THAT THE FIELD of Jewish genealogy has advanced significantly due to the creative output of Avotaynu (http://www.avotaynu.com) would be an understatement. When the first edition of this book was published, Avotaynu did not even exist. Today, I devote an entire chapter to it.

Avotaynu is the name of both a quarterly publication (*Avotaynu: The International Review of Jewish Genealogy*) and a publisher and distributor of books, monographs, and microforms. As its Web site states, "Avotaynu, Inc., is the leading publisher of products and information of interest to persons who are researching Jewish genealogy and Jewish family trees." Its founders, Gary Mokotoff and Sallyann Amdur Sack, are important trailblazers and highly regarded Jewish leaders; their extraordinary work has had a huge impact on all of us who are involved with Jewish genealogy.

Avotaynu: The International Review of Jewish Genealogy

Avotaynu (it means "our ancestors" or "our forefathers"), the publication, is essential for all Jewish genealogists. *You must subscribe to it.* Back issues are also available.

Gary Mokotoff recalls the origins of the name *Avotaynu:*

> When Sallyann and I decided to publish a magazine of Jewish genealogy, we both concluded the name should be a Hebrew word that symbolized genealogy. I went to my Hebrew dictionary and looked up the

word for genealogy and found out it was *Toledot*. Nope, that name was taken. What about *Generations*? Nope, *Dorot* was taken. *Families*? No, *Mishpocha* was in use. I pondered the problem for a number of weeks.

One Shabbos morning, while in synagogue, we came to the Amidah portion. Its opening words are, of course, "*Eloheynu, v'elohey Avotaynu*," and I said to myself, "That's it! *Avotaynu*. Our forefathers."

I knew I would be criticized as being sexist by choosing such a name (I actually received such letters), so when I designed the *Avotaynu* logo, I created a globe with the symbols of the twelve tribes inside (stolen from a box of Hanukkah candles) and across the top, in Hebrew, *Avotaynu*, "our fathers," and across the bottom *Imoteynu*, "our mothers."

You can subscribe online at http://www.avotaynu.com/journal.htm. You can also write to Avotaynu, Inc., 155 North Washington Avenue, Bergenfield, NJ 07621. The order phone number is (800) AVOTAYNU (286–8296).

What Will You Find in *Avotaynu: The International Review of Jewish Genealogy*?

Each time a new issue of *Avotaynu* arrives, I read it from cover to cover. It is really quite a remarkable journal. As a writer and editor, I admire it greatly. Let me review a number of *Avotaynu*'s important features:

○ **Timeliness** Breaking news does not only happen in the national and international world. It also happens in the world of Jewish genealogy. When something important is occurring that has significance to the serious Jewish family historian, I can always depend on *Avotaynu* to bring me the latest information. When new documents are found, when new sources have been discovered, when important archives lift restrictions, Avotaynu is on top of the story and brings the details to its readers.

○ **Book Reviews** King Solomon was right, of course, when he wrote, "Of the making of books there is no end." Publishers are bringing out new and often important volumes continuously, and I can always depend on *Avotaynu* to alert me to what's new. I happen to dislike book reviews intensely! I'd much rather read a simple or even lengthy description of a book, and then I'd be happy to go to a bookstore and make my own decision. Too often book reviews display the petty biases that people have, and these biases seem more transparent than ever. But I must commend *Avotaynu*'s book reviews. They are usually far more informational than

opinionated. I am grateful to the editors for simply letting me know when new books of interest to genealogists appear.

○ **Articles** In the last edition of *From Generation to Generation*, I included the entire index to the back issues of *Avotaynu* because I wanted readers to see for themselves exactly what a goldmine *Avotaynu* really is. I want you to do the same! The index is now available on-line. Take a look at the index to the first eighteen volumes of this amazing publication. It can be found on the web at: http://www.avotaynu.com/journal.htm. *Avotaynu*'s back issues contain hundreds of articles on every aspect of Jewish genealogical research. To give you a quick sense of how comprehensive *Avotaynu* is, here is a list of the subjects that are included, both geographically and topically:

GEOGRAPHICAL LISTINGS

Algeria	Egypt	Morocco
Argentina	England	New Zealand
Australia	Estonia	North Africa
Austria	Ethiopia	Poland
Austro-Hungary	Europe—General	Portugal
Belarus	Finland	Romania
Belgium	France	Russia
Bermuda	Galicia	Scotland
Brazil	Germany	Serbia
Bulgaria	Greece	Slovakia
Canada	Holland	Slovenia
Canary Islands	Hungary	South Africa
Caribbean	India	South America
China	Iraq	Spain
Costa Rica	Ireland	Switzerland
Croatia	Israel	Syria
Cyprus	Italy	Tunisia
Czech Republic	Latvia	Turkey
Denmark	Libya	Ukraine
East Europe—	Lithuania	United States
General	Moldova	USSR

TOPICAL LISTINGS

Book Review	LDS (Mormon)	Rabbinic
Computers	Family History	Seminars
DNA	Library	Sephardic
Holocaust	Methodology	

This list does not even begin to do *Avotaynu* justice. The articles in each and every issue of *Avotaynu* are extraordinary. In each case, these general subjects reflect dozens of articles, written by experts or by people with first hand experience.

○ Contributing Editors In every issue of *Avotaynu* there is a section called "From Our Contributing Editors." These are brief articles from people who are indeed experts in their countries of interest. I have no doubt that in addition to their excellent articles, these contributing editors are also advising many researchers like you and me.

○ As I See it In this column, *Avotaynu* editor Sallyann Amdur Sack writes consistently insightful and inspiring articles about some aspect of Jewish genealogy that is on her mind. I find that I usually read her column first because I am always grateful for what she has written. Dr. Sack is one of the great leaders in the field of Jewish family history research.

○ Ask the Experts Each issue of *Avotaynu* includes an "Ask the Experts" column written by Randy Daitch and Eileen Polakoff. This extremely important column, written by two of the true experts in the field, is a great illustration of how much one can learn about genealogy research even when the question is about someone else's family. Readers like me enjoy watching how these experts' minds work, how they approach a question and analyze exactly what the question is asking, how they use source material in creative ways. Experienced and talented researchers such as Daitch and Polakoff show us how one can often put two sources together in order to discover a third source.

○ Advertisements I subscribe to a few dozen periodicals. Most of them include pages of ads that I ignore. This is not case with *Avotaynu's* ads. Where else will you find an ad from someone who lives in Romania and will do research for you? Or an ad from a researcher who specializes in New England research? Or someone who lives in the Ukraine and will be your guide and translator when you travel there? Or a Yiddish translator? Or a writer who will create a family history for you? *Avotaynu* has become, in its ads and its articles, an indispensable tool for the Jewish genealogist.

Avotaynu Back Issues on CD-ROM (1985–2002)

Since its founding in 1985, *Avotaynu* has developed a reputation for being a *must-read* publication for persons doing Jewish genealogical research. The sixty-nine issues published between 1985 and 2002 include more than 2,600 articles—2.6 million words.

All back issues of *Avotaynu* from 1985 to 2002 are available on a CD-ROM that can be ordered at http://www.avotaynu.com/cds.htm.

Books from Avotaynu

Avotaynu's book publishing program is superb. The company has published the most important books in the field, many of which are unique, groundbreaking, and essential reading for all Jewish family historians. Look carefully at all of the resources available from Avotaynu, and keep your eye on them in the future. Avotaynu is on the cutting edge of the Jewish genealogy world.

Most of the books published by Avotaynu are research "tools." Each needs to be understood as a tool, and each tool can be used in a number of ways. The following are the most important books published by Avotaynu:

Avotaynu Guide to Jewish Genealogy, edited by Sallyann Amdur Sack and Gary Mokotoff. Written by more than sixty authors, each an expert in his or her own field, this essential book contains more than one hundred chapters covering all aspects of the rich body of information available for doing Jewish genealogical research. The publishers describe the contributors as "a veritable 'Who's Who in Jewish Genealogy.' I wrote the foreword!

Sephardic Genealogy, by Jeffrey S. Malka. This book was awarded the 2002 Best Judaica Reference Book award by the Association of Jewish Libraries. A comprehensive guide to researching Sephardic ancestry, its 384 pages are crammed with Sephardic history, genealogical methodology, and research resources from twenty countries. It includes Internet sites and surname lists. The book is useful for beginners as well as advanced researchers.

Where Once We Walked (revised edition), by Gary Mokotoff and Sallyann Amdur Sack with Alexander Sharon. *Where Once We Walked* (WOWW) is recognized by librarians, archivists, and researchers around the world as a major contribution to Jewish scholarship. Since its initial publication in 1991, it has been completely revised and updated to reflect the changes in the political geography of Central and Eastern Europe. The new edition identifies more than 23,500 towns in Central and Eastern Europe where Jews lived before the Holocaust and includes 17,500 alternate names. WOWW also gives the latitude and longitude of each town, the Jewish population before the Holocaust, and the names of as many as fifty books that reference each town. The book includes a soundex index and a "nearby town" index.

Getting Started in Jewish Genealogy, by Gary Mokotoff and Warren Blatt. Written by the cofounder of *Avotaynu* (Mokotoff) and the editor of

JewishGen.org (Blatt), both experts in Jewish genealogy, this book exposes the reader to many techniques and resources for doing Jewish genealogical research and points to more advanced areas to continue research.

Documents of Our Ancestors, by Michael Meshenberg. The publisher writes, "This reference book can save you countless hours of searching for the documents you need. It includes the actual forms needed to request documents from various archives and organizations and record the results." Forms included in this clever and useful book pertain to U.S. government census records, passenger records (1883–1920), World War I draft registrations, naturalization petitions and declarations of intention (1906–1941), alien registrations, requests for veterans' records, and Social Security forms. It also contains, for New York State, forms to request and record census and vital records; for New York City, vital record request and recording forms are provided for pre-1900 through the present. The final chapter covers forms for the International Red Cross, International Tracing Service, Hamburg Emigration Lists, Polish Vital Records, the Family History Library, Pages of Testimony from Yad Vashem's Hall of Names, Hebrew Immigrant Aid Society, and the Jewish Agency's Search Bureau for Missing Relatives.

Following the Paper Trail: A Multilingual Translation Guide, by Jonathan Shea and William Hoffman. This book is a guide to translating vital statistic records in thirteen languages: Czech, French, German, Hungarian, Italian, Latin, Lithuanian, Polish, Portuguese, Romanian, Russian, Spanish, and Swedish. The authors show the alphabet of the language, sample vital statistic records and their translations, and a list of words commonly encountered. This is truly an indispensable reference source for anyone whose research involves European languages.

How to Document Victims and Locate Survivors of the Holocaust, by Gary Mokotoff. This is a superb guidebook for finding documentation for Holocaust victims and survivors. The book identifies the principal sources of information about Holocaust victims and survivors, identifies the major repositories in the world that have this information, and tells how to contact them. The author takes you step by step through the process for locating information about the fate of people caught up in the Holocaust and includes a list of more than four thousand towns for which there is documentation at Yad Vashem in Jerusalem, the principal repository of Holocaust information.

Finding Your Jewish Roots in Galicia: A Resource Guide, by Suzan F. Wynne. This book organizes what is known about record searching and

other resources to assist genealogists in tracing their Jewish Galician roots. Resources include archival collections of Jewish vital and other records; geographical, visual, and language aids; books; documents related to the Holocaust; and articles about travel and research in specific towns by members of Gesher Galicia, the special interest group for Jewish genealogy. The book directs you to the addresses of archives, researchers and translators, organizations that hold important resource information, and travel agencies that can assist with organizing individual and group travel to Poland and Ukraine. The book includes the Galician Gazetteer, a compilation of more than one thousand communities where Jews lived in the 1870s and the administrative districts of each community.

Guide to Jewish Genealogical Resources in Israel, by Sallyann Amdur Sack and the Israel Genealogical Society. This 256-page hardcover book contains information about more than twenty-five repositories in Israel, with in-depth descriptions of their holdings and how to reach them by mail or phone. Eighteen appendixes provide details of key collections at Yad Vashem, the Central Archives for the History of the Jewish People, the Jewish National and University Library, and elsewhere. It is the definitive work on genealogical resources in Israel.

Biographical Dictionary of Canadian Jewry, 1909–1914, by Lawrence Tapper. Tapper, the leading expert on Canadian Jewish genealogy, has gathered the listings of births, bar mitzvahs, marriages, and deaths, along with information concerning communal and synagogue activities of Canadian Jewry, all taken from the pages of *The Canadian Jewish Times.*

Jewish Vital Records: Revision Lists in the Lithuanian Archives, by Harold Rhode and Sallyann Amdur Sack. This volume is an index to all Jewish vital records in the Lithuanian archives, some as early as 1808, and all revision lists (censuses), some as early as 1795. There are twelve thousand entries for more than 220 towns. Each entry includes the exact file where the records are located, making it easy to order searches through the Lithuanian Archives or independent search services.

Library Resources for German-Jewish Genealogy, by Angelika G. Ellmann-Krüger. This monograph is a directory to German-Jewish library and archival resources and a guide on how to use these sources efficiently. The publisher states that the monograph contains "information that readers will find in monographs, periodical articles or collective works, such as family histories, genealogies, autobiographies and biographies, details on Jewish cemeteries and name adoptions, lists of victims of the Holocaust, etc., and lists of members of Jewish communities. The book gives details of

German libraries, among them, scientific and university libraries, as well as specialized libraries, all holding literature relevant to Jewish family research as well as how to access access to the most important Online Public Access Catalogues and to the online ordering services." The publication also provides addresses, phone and fax numbers, and e-mail addresses for about fifty of the most important German libraries in the field, as well as Internet addresses (URLs) of the German Online Public Access Catalogues and virtual catalogues.

Sourcebook for Jewish Genealogies and Family Histories, by David Zubatsky and Irwin Berent. The publisher asks, "Did you know that there are Jewish genealogies and family histories, both published and unpublished, for over 10,000 family names?" Compiled from books, newspaper and journal articles, Jewish encyclopedia entries, family papers, and family trees, this bibliography tries to include all Jewish collections in the United States and other countries. The book includes the contents of volumes 1 and 2 of the highly acclaimed *Jewish Genealogy: A Sourcebook for Family Histories and Genealogies* plus thousands of additional entries compiled by David Zubatsky—three books in one. More than 22,000 sources are identified.

Eliyahu's Branches, by Chaim Freedman. This book documents some twenty thousand descendants of Rabbi Eliyahu ben Shlomo Zalmen, known as the Gaon of Vilna. Written and complied by the noted Israeli genealogist Chaim Freedman, it solves many of the mysteries as to how various families are descended from the Gaon and his siblings. The publisher states, "The author does not merely identify individuals but provides documentation and analyses to the links between them. Each descendant is assigned a unique code which exactly identifies the relationship between the individual and the Vilna Gaon."

A Dictionary of Ashkenazic Given Names: Their Origins, Structure, Pronunciation, and Migrations, by Alexander Beider. The publisher describes this book as "The most comprehensive compilation and analysis of Ashkenazic given (first) names ever," and that is surely correct. This 728-page book identifies more than fifteen thousand given names derived from just 735 root names. Each root name includes a detailed description of the origin (etymology) of the name, a list of the variant and derivative names displayed in a scheme that reveals how the variants evolved, and references to variations of the root names throughout the centuries—some as far back as the eleventh century. An index to the fifteen thousand variations guides you to the proper root name. Also included in this book is

a 300-page thesis on the origins, structure, pronunciation, and migrations of Ashkenazic given names.

A Dictionary of Jewish Surnames from the Russian Empire, by Alexander Beider. This book is a compilation of fifty thousand Jewish surnames from the Russian Pale of Settlement (excluding the Kingdom of Poland). It provides the etymology, along with variants and indications of where in the Russian Empire the name appeared. The ninety-page introduction defines the origin and evolution of Jewish surnames from this area.

Library Resources for German-Jewish Genealogy, by Angelika G. Ellmann-Krüger with Edward David Luft. This directory of important library sources also describes information that readers will find in selected monographs, periodical articles, and collective works such as family histories, genealogies, autobiographies, and biographies. It also provides details on Jewish cemeteries, name adoptions, and lists of victims of the Holocaust. It is a valuable resource for German Jewish research.

A Dictionary of Jewish Surnames from the Kingdom of Poland, by Alexander Beider. The author has created a compilation of more than 32,000 Jewish surnames with their origins. The book provides information on where in the Kingdom of Poland the name was prevalent at the turn of the twentieth century, all likely etymologies of the name, and spelling variants and derivatives. A soundex index makes it simple to locate a given surname with its proper Polish spelling. The introductory portion of the book describes the origins and evolution of Polish Jewish surnames.

Avotaynu publishes other books for the Jewish genealogist in addition to those just described; I've selected the volumes that I think are the most important. It also distributes important resources for Jewish genealogists that are published by other publishers. The Avotaynu Web site (http://www.avotaynu.com/allbooks.htm) offers a remarkable selection.

Avotaynu also offers maps, microfiche, videos, and other resources for the Jewish family historian. Explore the entire Web site, subscribe to the quarterly journal, and purchase a few books. That is the easiest way to build a Jewish genealogy resource library in your home.

o

A Conversation with Gary Mokotoff

Gary Mokotoff is the first person to receive the Lifetime Achievement Award from the International Association of Jewish Genealogical Soci-

eties. He is an author, lecturer, and teacher of Jewish genealogy and co-owner of Avotaynu, Inc.

Q. How did you first get involved, professionally, with the world of Jewish genealogy?

A. In 1984, at the conclusion of the First International Seminar on Jewish Genealogy, which was held in Jerusalem, a group of leaders in Jewish genealogy met to decide what to do next to promote Jewish genealogy worldwide. It was decided that there was a need for a magazine devoted to Jewish genealogy. Sallyann Amdur Sack of Bethesda, Maryland, volunteered to be editor of the publication, and I agreed to be the publisher. This was the start of *Avotaynu: The International Review of Jewish Genealogy.*

Q. How has Jewish genealogical research changed since you first got involved with it?

A. In one word: Internet. What used to take months or years has now been reduced to hours with the access of information on the Internet primarily through JewishGen.org and its associates.

Q. You've published many books in the field. Is there one of which you are most proud? Is there one in particular that you think is of especially great long-term value?

A. Actually two. *A Dictionary of Ashkenazic Given Names* by Dr. Alexander Beider may become one of the most important books for an understanding of Jewish history. Its title is deceptive. The 300-page introductory portion includes many important breakthroughs in an understanding of medieval Jewish history—a time period from which records are rare.

Where Once We Walked, which I coauthored, has made it possible for hundreds of Jews to identify their towns of ancestry when previously they could not locate them. This was made possible primarily through the use of the Daitch-Mokotoff soundex system.

Q. What is on the horizon for Jewish genealogy? Can you predict any aspect of its future?

A. The Internet is going to create even greater access to records through digitizing of images and making them available on the Internet. The brick wall of the seeming lack of records and the lack of surnames in eighteenth-century Central and Eastern Europe is going to fall or at least have large chunks removed.

Q. If you had to give one piece of advice to the beginner, what would it be?

A. Network with other Jewish genealogists though JewishGen.org, *Avotaynu,* local Jewish Genealogical Societies, and special

interest groups. You are not alone. Take advantage of the trailblazing efforts of your predecessors.

Q. Do you think there is a core reason why people interested in genealogy are involved with it?

A. It is fun, it is challenging, and you are researching the history of the most important person in the world: yourself.

○

6

JEWISHGEN.ORG

JEWISH GENEALOGY IN CYBERSPACE

IN THE FALL OF 1997, *Avotaynu* published an impressive and important essay by Dr. Sallyann Amdur Sack titled "Jewish Genealogy on the Eve of the 21st Century." In it, the author wrote, "With JewishGen, we have gained the ability to reach Jewish genealogists worldwide easily and instantly." The Web site JewishGen.org: The Home of Jewish Genealogy describes itself as "the primary Internet source connecting researchers of Jewish genealogy worldwide."

Susan E. King founded JewishGen in 1987. It began as a bulletin board with only 150 users; today it is a major grassroots effort that brings together hundreds of thousands of individuals worldwide in a virtual community centered on discovering Jewish ancestral roots and history. On January 1, 2003, JewishGen became a division of the Museum of Jewish Heritage: A Living Memorial to the Holocaust, in New York City (http://www.mjhnyc.org). Susan King remains its managing director.

In my view, JewishGen.org is the single most important development for Jewish genealogists *ever.*

When you arrive at the Web site (http://www.jewishgen.org), you are apt to be overwhelmed. You will ask yourself questions like "Where do I begin? What should I be looking for? Help!" I am going to walk you through the site, step by step, helping you become familiar with what this extraordinary tool for the Jewish genealogist can do for you.

A Few Basics

If you are a beginner, you are probably not yet ready to explore JewishGen. org. But go there anyway. Wander around like it's a new neighborhood to explore or a great museum to discover. You can't do it all at once, and

sometimes it's much better the second time around, after you have a basic familiarity. Your initial peek into JewishGen will surely make an impression that there are a lot of possibilities out there for the researcher. When I began my own family history research in the early 1970s, the most frequent remark made to me, both by laypeople and professional historians, was that all the records were destroyed and that Jews cannot trace their family trees. JewishGen disproves that once and for all.

The first time you visit the site, give yourself lots of time. Don't rush. Sit back, explore, and marvel at the incredible amount of information and possibilities offered to the Jewish family historian. Don't get discouraged if you don't find something immediately. JewishGen is a huge toolbox containing lots of great tools. Respect the tools; learn how to use them; understand their potential. All of this takes time.

The keys to Jewish genealogical research, as mentioned many times in this book, are surnames and names of towns. When you visit relatives and interview them, you are looking for stories, surnames, and names of towns. It would be useful for you to make a list of surnames you are looking for. My own list looks like this (note that after each surname, I list names of the towns):

> Kurzweil (Przemysl, Dobromil, Sambor, Lemberg, Jaraslaw)
>
> Gottlieb (Stropkov, Borgo Prund, Bistritz)
>
> Ennis (Dobromil, Stary Sambor)
>
> Klein (Matezsalka, Nyirbator, Presov)
>
> Rosenwasser (Stropkov)
>
> Grünberger (Matezsalka)
>
> Loventhal (Przemysl)
>
> Roth (Stropkov, Borgo Prund)

By keeping this list in front of me when I do searches, I make sure I have all the key names and towns for my research at the ready. These names and towns are essential when you want to use the resources of JewishGen.

A Guide to the Site

On its home page, JewishGen.org divides its site into various sections. We will explore most of the sections. Here is a list of all of them:

> Learn
>
> Research

Discussion Groups

Projects and Activities

Contributions and Fundraising

Special Interest Groups

Hosted Organizations

JewishGen-eral Information

Let's explore the most important sections in my perceived order of importance.

Learn

"Learn" has three sections: JewishGen FAQ (Frequently Asked Questions), JewishGen Info Files, and JewishGen Tools.

JEWISHGEN FAQ (http://www.jewishgen.org/InfoFiles/faq.html). This section might also intimidate the beginner; there is just so much information! But I would suggest that like the whole Web site, this FAQ section should be looked over because it will give you a lot to think about as you gather facts, photos, dates, letters, anecdotes, and documents. A basic principle of research is that the researcher can often put two seemingly unrelated pieces of information together to achieve a productive result. I am honored by the fact that the answer to FAQ #1 is the book you are now reading! Here are the topics covered in the FAQ:

Getting Started

Publications

JewishGen Family Finder (JGFF)

Books

Vendors

Jewish Genealogical Societies (JGSs)

Seminars on Jewish Genealogy

National Archives

U.S. Vital Records (Births, Marriages, and Deaths)

Passenger Lists

Finding Your Ancestral Town

Naturalization Records

LDS (Mormon) Family History Centers

Other Archives

Holocaust Research

Family Tree of the Jewish People (FTJP)

Jewish Names

JewishGen Discussion Group

Computers and Genealogy

Glossary, Abbreviations

JEWISHGEN INFO FILES (http://www.jewishgen.org/InfoFiles). This section of JewishGen connects you with lots of great information on a wide variety of topics and on a long list of countries. I don't mean to be repetitious, but this section on the Web site is also overwhelming in its quantity of information. Speaking of being repetitious, this section of JewishGen repeats information in different places and also refers you to many places on its site that you will get to in other ways. It's similar to a book in a library having a multiplicity of subject cards in the card catalogue. A book can be about more than one main topic. It might appear on lots of catalogue cards, but it's just one book. First, look over the topics covered:

Basics

Books and Periodicals

Cemeteries

Genealogical Techniques

Genealogists

Genetics

Holocaust

Immigration

Internet Sources

JewishGen Resources

LDS (Mormon) Resources

Libraries and Archives

Military

Miscellaneous

Names

Postal Matters

Preservation

Rabbinic

Seminars

Sephardim

Social Security

Special Interest Groups

Translation

Travel

Vital Records

The more experience you acquire in this research, the more meaningful many of these categories will become, but each of them provides you with wonderful sources and resources. You might not be ready yet to explore Holocaust sources, for example, but once you have surnames, names of towns, names of countries, and other information, you will be amazed at what the "Holocaust" section will provide.

Here is a list of the countries that each has its own section of sources and resources on the JewishGen site:

Argentina	France	Poland
Austria	Germany	Romania
Australia	Hungary	Russian Empire
Belarus	Ireland	South Africa
Belgium	Israel	Sweden
Brazil	Italy	Switzerland
Canada	Latin America	Ukraine
Croatia	Latvia	United Kingdom
Czech Republic	Lithuania	United States
Denmark	Netherlands	
Finland	Norway	

For each of these countries, JewishGen provides important information. If you see a country on this list that you know will be a focal point of your genealogy research, take extra time to explore that section.

The JewishGen Info Files also provide access to other parts of the JewishGen site. They are called "JewishGen Operational Files," and I will describe them for you elsewhere in this chapter. The Operational Files are just another doorway into them.

JEWISHGEN TOOLS (http://www.jewishgen.org/jos). JewishGen provides visitors with four great tools that will come in handy at some point or other in your research:

Soundex. The Daitch-Mokotoff and National Archives soundex codes can be quite helpful for researchers. For example, federal census records are not indexed alphabetically but rather by sound, using the soundex code system. This first tool calculates the codes for you. The Daitch-Mokotoff system has become the standard for all indexing projects done by Jewish genealogical organizations. It has been accepted by the Hebrew Immigrant Aid Society (HIAS) and is the standard at the U.S. Holocaust Memorial Museum in Washington, D.C., and elsewhere.

JOS Calendar Converter. The JOS Calendar Converter can convert a civil (Gregorian calendar) date into the equivalent date on the Hebrew calendar, and vice versa. It can also display Yahrzeit dates for consecutive years.

JOS Jewish Festival Dates. The JOS Jewish Holiday Calendar will provide you with a list of all Jewish holidays for any year using the civil year (Gregorian calendar) or the Jewish year (Hebrew calendar).

JOS Distance Calculator. When you enter two locations by latitude and longitude, this tool will calculate the distance and direction from the first to the second one.

Research

"Research" has three sections: JewishGen Family Finder, JewishGen Databases, and the Family Tree of the Jewish People.

JEWISHGEN FAMILY FINDER (JGFF) (http://www.jewishgen.org/jgff). The Web site states "The JewishGen Family Finder is a compilation of surnames and towns currently being researched by over 60,000 Jewish genealogists worldwide. It contains over 300,000 entries, 80,000 ancestral surnames and 20,000 town names, and is indexed and cross-referenced by both surname and town name. The JGFF was created in 1982 by Gary Mokotoff, and is now maintained by JewishGen, Inc."

The concept of the family finder was used in the 1970s by *Toledot: The Journal of Jewish Genealogy* and was a very popular part of that journal. *Toledot* had borrowed it from another genealogical publication. Today, the JewishGen Family Finder is simply the most effective way for individuals doing Jewish family history research to find one another.

In the FAQ part of JewishGen, the JGFF is described as "a database of surnames and towns currently being researched by Jewish genealogists worldwide. It contains ancestral surnames and town names, and is indexed and cross-referenced by both surname and town name." It goes on to say, "The JGFF contains names of ancestral towns and ancestral surnames

submitted by people around the world who are researching their Jewish family roots." The JGFF is available to be researched online, in printed form, and on microfiche.

Every day, new individuals record their interests on the JGFF. As the Web site boasts, "The online JGFF at the JewishGen web site is updated instantaneously, as new entries are added on-line by users all over the world, via the Internet. An average of new 30 users and 150 new surname/town entries are added every day."

The JGFF makes it clear what it is by also describing what it is not: "The JGFF is *not* a database of individuals. The JGFF is *not* a database of families. It does *not* contain any information about people, places or times. The JGFF is *not* a missing persons service. It does *not* contain data collected from any historical sources."

Do not underestimate the power of the JewishGen Family Finder. When I type in every surname and every town of interest to me, the database sends me contact information about dozens of individuals around the world who are also researching the towns or surnames that I am researching!

JEWISHGEN DATABASES (http://www.jewishgen.org/databases). The database section of JewishGen would have been part of a genealogical science fiction story when I began my research in the 1970s. Today, of course, when "search engine" is part of the common vocabulary and just about everyone I know uses Google on the Web, the databases available to be searched at the JewishGen Web site are not science fiction but something of a dream come true. Each database is an education in itself. What an extraordinary collection of Jewish genealogical material is now at our fingertips thanks to the efforts of JewishGen!

Look at the list of databases and their descriptions as they appear on the site:

GENERAL

The JewishGen Family Finder (JGFF). Surnames and ancestral towns being researched by 60,000 Jewish genealogists worldwide. Over 300,000 entries.

The Family Tree of the Jewish People (FTJP). Data on over 2 million people, from family trees submitted by 1,800 Jewish genealogists worldwide.

The JewishGen Discussion Group Message Archives, 1993–2003. Search over 100,000 previous JewishGen postings.

The JewishGen SIG Lists Message Archives, 1998–2003. Search messages posted to the JewishGen SIG mailing lists.

Jewish Records at the Family History Library. An inventory of the Jewish-specific resources at the LDS (Mormon) Family History Library in Salt Lake City.

The JewishGen Holocaust Database. Over 320,000 entries regarding Holocaust victims and survivors, from many sources.

Ellis Island Foundation Database One-Step Search Tools. Enhanced search capabilities for easier access to data at http://www.ellisisland.org.

EASTERN EUROPE

The JewishGen ShtetlSeeker. Locate towns in Eastern or Central Europe, by name or location. U.S. Board on Geographic Names databases for twenty-four countries.

The Yizkor Book Project Database. Eastern European memorial books—bibliographic database.

The Yizkor Book Necrology Database. Over 150,000 entries from lists of Holocaust martyrs, published in Yizkor books.

Vsia Rossia Database. Over 34,000 entries from Russian Empire business directories, 1895–1911.

Jewish Religious Personnel in Russia, 1853–1854. Over four thousand synagogue employees from nine hundred towns throughout the Pale of Settlement.

Jewish Given Names Database. Given names (first names) used in Europe, 1795–1925.

BELARUS

The "All Belarus" Database. Over 200,000 records from many different sources: vital records, voter lists, business directories, ghetto records.

LATVIA

The "All Latvia" Database. Over 60,000 records for Courland, Livland, and Vitebsk provinces, from a variety of sources, including voter lists, tax records, census records, newspaper articles, police and military records, memorial books, and extracts from the Extraordinary Commission lists.

LITHUANIA

LitvakSIG "All Lithuania" Database. More than 300,000 records from many different sources, including complete revision lists (censuses) as well as vital records, tax, voter, and cemetery lists.

HaMagid Lithuanian Donors, 1871–1872. Names of five thousand donors to Persian famine relief, listed in this Hebrew periodical.

HaMelitz Lithuanian and Latvian Donors. Names of almost twenty thousand Lithuanian and Latvian charity donors, listed in this Hebrew periodical, 1893 to 1903.

Lithuanian Medical Personnel. Information about 874 Jewish medical personnel, found in two Lithuanian medical directories, 1923 and 1925.

Sugihara Database. Names and visa dates of 2,139 Lithuanian, Polish, German, and Russian Jews, all of whom were saved by passports from the Japanese diplomat Chiune Sugihara in 1940.

Kelme Database. Indexes to various archival and published records about the town of Kelme, 1816–1944.

Keidan Cemeteries Database. Tombstone inscriptions from seven Keidaner cemeteries in Lithuania, New York, and Chicago.

Kovno Ghetto Cemetery, 1941–1943. Transcripts of nearly nine hundred burials from the register of the *Chevra Kadisha* of Viliampole Slobodka.

Vilna Gubernia Conscripts Photographs. Names and photographs of 1,222 Jewish conscripts from Vilna province into the Russian army, 1900–1914.

1897 Census for Lithuania. Names of 13,465 Jews residing in Kovna and Vilna provinces, extracted from the 1897 census of the Russian Empire.

POLAND

Jewish Records Indexing—Poland. An index to over 1.5 million nineteenth-century Jewish birth, marriage, and death records from over 250 Polish towns.

1929 Polish Business Directory—Town Index. An index to more than 34,000 locations in interwar Poland, with links to directory pages for each city, town, and village.

LDS Microfilm Master: Poland. Lets you locate LDS microfilms of records from Poland, based on geographical coordinates.

The 1891 Galicia Business Directory. Over twenty thousand names from more than one thousand towns throughout Galicia.

Lvov Ghetto Database. Names of more than ten thousand Jews in the Ghetto of Lwów, 1942–1945.

Kraków Ghetto Database. Names of over nineteen thousand Jews in the Ghetto of Kraków in 1940.

1890–1891 New York Immigrants from Poland, Austria, and Galicia. An index to over 96,000 passenger arrivals.

Oshpitsin Yizkor Database. Information on more than five thousand residents of the town of Oshpitsin (Oswiecim).

Warszawa Death Notices from *Nasz Przeglad*. Over 2,700 death notices from this Warsaw newspaper, 1923 and 1937–1938.

Warszawa Homeowners Lists. Data on more than nine thousand homeowners in Warsaw and Praga in 1852, 1869, and 1870.

Warszawa Gubernia Duma Voters Lists, 1907. Names of more than ten thousand Jewish men living in Warsaw province, eligible to vote for the czarist State Duma.

GERMANY

Aufbau Survivors Lists. Names of more than 33,000 Holocaust survivors, published in the German-language newspaper *Aufbau,* New York, 1944–1946.

Germans, Swiss, and Austrians Deported from France. Information about 825 Holocaust victims, 1942–1944.

Jewish Families of Northern Germany. List of three thousand families from Lower Saxony, North-Rhine-Westphalia, Hamburg, Bremen, and Hessen.

Westphalian Jews and the Holocaust. The fate of more than eight thousand Westphalian Jews.

German Jews at Stutthof Concentration Camp. Names of 2,750 German Jews at this concentration camp near Gdansk (Danzig).

West Prussia 1812 Citizenship. Names of 2,400 Jews in fifty towns in West Prussia who were granted Prussian citizenship in 1812.

Jews in Würzburg, 1900–1945. Biographical dictionary of more than thirteen thousand Jews living in Würzburg, Lower Franconia, in the early twentieth century.

CZECH REPUBLIC

Nikolsburg Graveyard Register. Names of more than 4,500 persons buried in the Jewish cemetery of Nikolsburg (now Mikulov).

HUNGARY

All Hungary Database. Over 45,000 records from many different sources: vital records, census records, property tax records, and so on.

ROMANIA

U.S. Consular Post, Bucharest, Romania. Emergency passport applications and other item—nearly one thousand records from the U.S. State Department, 1860–1941.

Bessarabia Duma Voters Lists, 1906–1907. Names of more than five thousand men of Bessarabia province (today, Moldova), eligible to vote in the Russian parliamentary elections of 1906 and 1907.

1942 Census of Jewish Males Born Between 1881 and 1892. Census of 3,200 "older Jewish males" in 1942.

GREAT BRITAIN

The Jews of London (pre-1850). Names and addresses of nine thousand Jews in London in the first half of the nineteenth century, compiled principally from London trade directories of the period.

Bristol Cemetery Database. Index and tombstone photographs of three cemeteries in Bristol, England. 815 entries.

Welsh Census Returns—1851, 1891. Entries on eighteen hundred Jewish residents listed in the 1851 and 1891 census returns of South Wales.

ISRAEL

U.S. Department of State Consular Post Records. Index to more than nine thousand records of U.S. consulates in Jerusalem, Jaffa, and Haifa, 1857–1935.

SOUTH AFRICA

South African Jewish Year Book Database. Index to more than one thousand biographies of Jews in South Africa, from publications in 1929 and 1945.

UNITED STATES

American Jewish Historical Society Manuscript Catalogue. Full descriptions of over eleven hundred manuscript collections held by the AJHS.

The Boston *Jewish Advocate* Obituary Database. Index to more than 23,000 obituary notices from this Massachusetts newspaper, 1905–2002.

The *Cleveland Jewish News* Obituary Database. Index to 24,500 obituary notices from this Ohio newspaper, 1964–2002.

The Chicago Obituary Database. Index to over 8,800 obituary notices from an Illinois newspaper, 1994–1998.

Chicago Marriages—Sinai Congregation. Index to more than five hundred marriages performed by Rabbi Bernhard Felsenthal in Chicago from 1861 to 1905.

The Boston *Jewish Advocate* Wedding Announcements Database. Index to more than 27,000 wedding announcements from this Massachusetts newspaper, 1905–2002.

Boston Marriages—Rabbi Aaron Gorovitz. Index to nearly one thousand marriages performed by Rabbi Aaron Gorovitz of Boston, 1910 to 1956.

Jewish-American Civil War Veterans. Names of more than seven thousand Jewish American U.S. Civil War Veterans, both Union and Confederate.

American Jewish Year Book Obituary Index. Index to more than three thousand obituaries of prominent Jews, 1948–1998.

The Rabbi Samuel Langer Database. Over five thousand entries from personal notebooks—births, bar and bat mitzvahs, marriages, funerals, unveilings, and so on, in the eastern United States, 1930s–1960s.

The *Connecticut Jewish Ledger* Obituary Database. Index to five thousand obituary notices from this New Haven newspaper, 1975–2002.

Jewish Names in Selected U.S. State Department Files, 1910–1929. Nearly ten thousand entries from the Central Decimal Files of the U.S. Department of State, Record Group 59.

One of the goals of JewishGen is to continue to add new databases to its already amazing gathering of sources. As I worked through each of

these databases, I found information on family members, towns, and lots of leads for more research. Do not underestimate these databases. If you are from a Jewish family, a great many things in these databases will be of direct interest to you.

THE FAMILY TREE OF THE JEWISH PEOPLE (FTJP) (http://www.jewishgen.org/gedcom). The JewishGen Web site describes the ambitious Family Tree of the Jewish People as "a cooperative project among JewishGen, Inc., the International Association of Jewish Genealogical Societies (IAJGS), and the Nahum Goldmann Museum of the Jewish Diaspora (Beit Hatefutsot). The central purpose of the FTJP is to enhance Jews' ability to connect and reconnect their families and to increase interest in Jewish genealogy. The three agencies will disseminate the information in differing ways: IAJGS will provide the data on a CD-ROM, Beit Hatefutsot at its facility in Tel Aviv, and JewishGen as a freely searchable database on this internet Web site."

In 1985, the Dorot Center at Beit Hatefutsot (Museum of the Diaspora) in Tel Aviv began to collect family trees in GEDCOM format. GEDDOM stands for "genealogical data communication." It is a computer file format developed by the Family History Department of the Church of Jesus Christ of Latter-Day Saints (the Mormon Church). It provides a flexible uniform format for exchanging computerized genealogical data. By 1990, the Dorot Center had collected 100,000 entries. Then, in 1991, Gary Mokotoff, who was president of the Association of Jewish Genealogical Societies (AJGS) at the time, announced plans for a Jewish Genealogical People Finder (JGPF). He published its first edition in July 1992, a second edition in 1993, and a third edition in 1995 which contained over 310,000 individuals, submitted by over two hundred Jewish genealogists.

In 1997, the Association of Jewish Genealogical Societies announced plans for a Family Tree of the Jewish People (FTJP), to be issued on CD, and in August 1999, the International Association of Jewish Genealogical Societies issued the first FTJP on CD-ROM. It contained 800,000 names from seven hundred contributors. Two months later, a three-way agreement among JewishGen, IAJGS, and Beit Hatefutsot was made. Within weeks the JewishGen FTJP had surpassed 1 million names, and by December 2001 it contained more than 2 million names submitted by 1,850 contributors.

The success of the FTJP is based on the participation of people who are willing and able to submit information. You will need to read the instructions on the site carefully to submit information.

To search this part of the JewishGen site, you need to have a researcher code and a password, both of which you obtain free of charge by going

to the JewishGen Family Finder, registering there, and submitting at least one surname and town name of interest to you. You are then part of the system and can freely participate. This is still one more remarkable way to search for Jewish genealogical information at the JewishGen site.

Discussion Groups

"Discussion Groups" has two sections: JewishGen Discussion Group and JewishGen Special Interest Group (SIG) Mailing Lists.

JEWISHGEN DISCUSSION GROUP (http://www.jewishgen.org/gedcom). The JewishGen Web site describes its discussion group as "an Internet forum which fulfills the vision to unite Jewish genealogical researchers worldwide as they read and discuss each day's messages. They share information, ideas, methods, tips, techniques, case studies and resources. Their dedication is to Jewish family history with particulars from their own family lore and reminiscences. Not only do they want to know more, [but] most JewishGenners are very willing to help others along the way. This continual sharing is the very essence of JewishGen."

If you are familiar with the phenomenon of the discussion group on the Web, the JewishGen Discussion Group will be familiar to you. If you are new to such things, I suggest that you explore the whole idea of the discussion group. Essentially, a discussion group allows you to read the e-mail sent by participants to the discussion group moderator. The moderator decides if a message written by a participant is relevant and follows the guidelines of the discussion group (for example, most moderated discussion groups do not tolerate personal attacks).

There are thousands of discussion groups on the Web, reflecting narrow and specific interests. I happen to belong to several discussion groups reflecting interests of mine, including magic (I perform as a magician), Jewish law, and several other topics. Each day I read thoughtful e-mails from other people around the world who share my interests. Sometimes I will write an e-mail for others (if you belong to a discussion group but never participate, you are known as a "lurker").

Since September 1993, all of the e-mails that have been a part of the JewishGen Discussion Group have been saved and are available for searching and reading at http://data.jewishgen.org/wconnect/wc.dll? jg~jgsys~archpop.

Have fun searching this database, reading what other people are doing in their genealogical research, and take the opportunity to connect with people who share your interests.

JEWISHGEN SPECIAL INTEREST GROUP (SIG) MAILING LISTS (http://www.jewishgen.org/listserv/sigs.htm). The JewishGen site describes its special interest group (SIG) as follows: "JewishGen provides Special Interest Group (SIG) mailing lists (a.k.a. discussion groups) for the exchange of information, ideas, methods, tips, techniques, case studies and resources. The intent is to augment discussions and resource gathering for all JewishGen participants."

In other word, in addition to the JewishGen Discussion Group, there are many specialized groups who meet, have newsletters, conduct e-mail discussions, and so on. Every SIG is different, with its own leadership, special projects, procedures, and activities. I urge you to explore the SIGs and locate the ones of particular interest to you. You will receive e-mails with discussions on topics of interest, you will meet people with shared interests, and you will be able to see the questions that others are asking and answering. Most important, you can participate in these SIG discussions by asking questions, answering others' questions, and learning.

Here is a list of the SIGs hosted by JewishGen along with descriptions of each as indicated on the site:

> Belarus SIG: A forum for researchers with Jewish family roots in the country now known as Belarus and more specifically from the former Russian provinces of Grodno, Minsk, Mogilev, and Vitebsk.

> Bohemia-Moravia SIG: A forum for those researching Jewish genealogy in the areas formerly known as Bohemia and Moravia (now the Czech Republic), plus parts of Austria, especially Vienna, but not Galicia.

> Early American SIG: A forum for those researching Jewish immigrants to the United States before 1880.

> French SIG: A forum for Jewish genealogical research in France and French colonies, as well as other French-speaking areas such as Belgium, Luxembourg, and Switzerland.

> Galicia SIG: A forum for those interested in researching their Jewish roots in the former Austrian province of Galicia (now southern Poland and western Ukraine).

> German-Jewish SIG: A forum that focuses on Jewish genealogy in German-speaking regions, which include not only Germany itself but other areas such as Austria, parts of Switzerland, Alsace, Lorraine, and Bohemia and Moravia.

Hungarian SIG: A forum for those with Jewish roots in the area known as "greater Hungary" or pre-Trianon Hungary, which includes areas that at one time were predominantly Hungarian-speaking.

Latin America SIG: A forum for researchers with Jewish family roots in all countries of Latin America.

Latvia SIG: A forum for researchers of Jewish families of Latvian descent.

Litvak SIG: Encourages preservation and computerization of primary sources of genealogical data for the descendants of the Lithuanian Jewish community.

Rabbinic Genealogy SIG: A forum for those interested in rabbinic genealogy or researching rabbinic ancestry within any geographical area or time period.

Romania SIG: A forum for those with Jewish roots in the Banat, Bessarabia, Bukovina, Dobruja, the Maramures, Moldavia, Transylvania, and Wallachia (all within the modern nations of Romania, Moldova, and southwestern Ukraine).

Scandinavia SIG: A forum for researchers with Jewish roots in Finland, Norway, Sweden, and Denmark—including the former Danish colonies and protectorates of Schleswig-Holstein, the Danish West Indies, Iceland, and Greenland.

Sefard Forum: A forum for researchers of Sephardic genealogies. English is the preferred language.

Southern Africa SIG: A forum to discuss the genealogy and family history of Jewish communities of South Africa, Lesotho (Basutoland), Botswana (Bechuanaland), Zimbabwe (Southern Rhodesia), Zambia (Northern Rhodesia), Swaziland, Mozambique, and the former Belgian Congo (Zaïre).

Ukraine SIG: A forum for researchers with family origins in the former Russian Empire provinces now in Ukraine: Podolia, Volhynia, Kiev, Poltava, Chernigov, Kharkov, Kherson, Taurida, and Ekaterinoslav.

United Kingdom: Jewish Communities and Records (JCR-UK): A project to record genealogical and historical information concerning the Jewish communities of the United Kingdom. A joint project of JGS Great Britain and JewishGen.

Projects and Activities

"Projects and Activities" has a number of amazing and important projects of interest to Jewish genealogists. Here is a listing of these projects as well as a description of each:

SHTETLINKS (http://www.shtetlinks.jewishgen.org). ShtetLinks provides a place for people with an interest in a place where Jews have lived to commemorate that place by creating an individual Web page for that location, with information, pictures, databases, and links to sites that provide additional information on that place. Hundreds of Web pages corresponding to hundreds of towns appear here.

YIZKOR BOOK PROJECT (http://www.jewishgen.org/Yizkor). The Yizkor Book Project was created because the hundreds of Yizkor books or memorial books are some of the best sources for learning about Jewish communities in Eastern and Central Europe. The Yizkor books were published as tributes to these former Jewish communities and the people who were murdered during the Holocaust. The majority of these books were written in Hebrew or Yiddish, languages that many contemporary genealogists cannot read or understand. The Yizkor Book Project was organized in 1994 by a group of JewishGen volunteers led by Leonard Markowitz and Martin Kessel. A translation project was developed by Susannah Juni and implemented by Joyce Field. The purpose of this project, as stated on the site, is "to unlock the valuable information contained in Yizkor Books so that genealogists and others can learn more about their heritage."

The Yizkor Book Project has wonderful material on its part of the JewishGen site, including translations of parts of many Yizkor books, and offers us the ability to search a "necrology" index of Holocaust victims whose names appear in the Yizkor books that have been translated.

It is often difficult to locate Yizkor books, but JewishGen has made it easy by providing information on which libraries own copies of which Yizkor books. This is a remarkable resource. Each of the following libraries has a collection of Yizkor books:

CALIFORNIA

Los Angeles—Hebrew Union College

Los Angeles—Simon Wiesenthal Center/Yeshiva University Library

Los Angeles—UCLA Research Library

Los Angeles—University of Judaism

San Francisco—Holocaust Center of Northern California

FLORIDA

Gainesville—Price Library of Judaica, University of Florida

MASSACHUSETTS

Boston—Boston Public Library

Brookline—Hebrew College

Cambridge—Harvard University Library

Waltham—Brandeis University Library

MARYLAND

Baltimore—Joseph Meyerhoff Library

MICHIGAN

Ann Arbor—Harlan Hatcher Graduate Library, University of
Michigan

NEW YORK

New York—American Jewish Historical Society

New York—Bund Archives (collection at YIVO)

New York—Hebrew Union College, Jewish Institute of
Religion Library

New York—Jewish Theological Seminary Library

New York—New York Public Library, Jewish Division

New York—Yeshiva University Library

New York—YIVO Institute for Jewish Research Library

OREGON

Portland—Congregation Neveh Shalom

GREAT BRITAIN

Cambridge—Cambridge University Library

Finchley—JGS of Great Britain, Finchley Synagogue

London—University of London, School of Oriental and
African Studies

London—Weinser Library

ISRAEL

Ramat-Gan—Bar-Ilan University

Tel Aviv—Ahad Haam Library

Tel Aviv—Hitachdut Yotzei Polin

Tel Aviv—Moadon Ha'Bund

Tel Aviv—Rambam Library

HOLOCAUST GLOBAL REGISTRY (http://www.jewishgen.org/registry/). The Holocaust Global Registry was created for people searching for Holocaust survivors, for survivors searching family members or friends, and for child survivors searching for clues to their identity. As the site states, "As more people add records and search the database, it is our hope that this registry will help bring about reunions with loved ones." The information on this site comes from individuals. "The names are either submitted by the survivors themselves or by people who are looking for survivors. The names are not collected from any other source." The information here includes people who have registered and people who are searching for survivors.

OTHER SPECIAL PROJECTS AT JEWISHGEN. Each of the other special projects at JewishGen are worthwhile to explore and will provide you with information that is useful. These projects include the following:

Burial Registry (http://www.jewishgen.org/databases/cemetery/). An effort to index Jewish burial records.

Web Links (http://www.jewishgen.org/links/). Links to lots of Web sites of interest to genealogists.

Family Links (http://www.jewishgen.org/family/). An effort to link up with Web sites created by people about their families.

Publications (http://www.jewishgen.org/interactive/publi_main.html). An amazing collection of articles posted by people who are recommending their posted material as being of interest to Jewish genealogists.

Hosted Organizations

On the JewishGen Web site, a few important organizations are hosted.

The International Association of Jewish Genealogical Societies (IAJGS) is a nonprofit umbrella organization coordinating the activities of more than sixty national and local Jewish genealogical societies around the world. Its Web site is at http://www.jewishgen.org/iajgs. This site also

provides information about each of the JGS's around the world; go to http://www.jewishgen.org/iajgs/members.html.

The JewishGen site also hosts the following projects:

IAJGS Cemetery Project. The aim of this ambitious project is to collect data from every Jewish cemetery in the world.

Jewish Records Indexing—Poland (JRI-PL). This project aims to index all the Jewish vital records in Poland.

Missing Identity. This project has as its goal the helping of child survivors of the Holocaust find their identities.

The Forgotten Camps. The site gives the history of Nazi concentration camps, work camps, police camps, and transit camps.

The Ellis Island Database One-Step Search Tools. The Ellis Island Database had received a tremendous amount of publicity, and millions of people use its site (http://www.ellisisland.org) or the amazing search tools available on JewishGen (http://www.jewishgen.org/databases/EIDB) that allow researchers to gain relatively easy access to the vast amount of information available about people who entered the United States at Ellis Island. As the Ellis Island site explains, "From 1892 to 1924, more than 22 million immigrants, passengers, and crew members came through Ellis Island and the Port of New York. The ship companies that transported these passengers kept detailed passenger lists, called 'ship manifests.' Now, thanks to the generous efforts of volunteers of the Church of Jesus Christ of Latter-Day Saints, these manifests have been transcribed into a vast electronic archive, which you can easily search to find an individual passenger." The JewishGen search tools make searching quite easy. There is even a tool that searches for Jewish passengers only.

Contributions and Fundraising

JewishGen would not exist today if not for the generosity of many people who have given their money and time. JewishGen is a grassroots effort, and even though the Museum of Jewish Heritage in New York City now supports it, it is still in need of ongoing support, both through financial contributions and through the volunteerism of people who want to help. The JewishGen Web site describes ways to support JewishGen; go to http://www.jewishgen.org/JewishGen-erosity (for financial contributions) or http://www.jewishgen.org/cgi-bin/wanted.pl/Search? (to volunteer).

○

A Conversation with Warren Blatt

Warren Blatt is the editor in chief of JewishGen.org. He is the author of the JewishGen FAQ: Frequently Asked Questions About Jewish Genealogy on its Web site and many other online resources. His published works include *Resources for Jewish Genealogy in the Boston Area* (Jewish Genealogical Society of Greater Boston, 1996) and *Getting Started in Jewish Genealogy* (Avotaynu, 1999), written with Gary Mokotoff. He was the chair of the Fifteenth International Seminar on Jewish Genealogy, held in Boston in 1996. Blatt has been doing Jewish genealogical research for more than a quarter of a century, focusing mostly on Russian and Polish records.

Q. How would you describe JewishGen.org to someone unfamiliar with it?

A. JewishGen is the primary Internet source for Jewish genealogy. Its Web site contains information on how to do genealogical research (the "Frequently Asked Questions" document and the InfoFiles), interactive databases enabling researchers to connect with others with common research interests (the JewishGen Family Finder and the Family Tree of the Jewish People), databases containing transcripts of millions of historical records, translations of hundreds of Yizkor books, Web pages devoted to individual communities (ShtetLinks), and many other tools and features. JewishGen also hosts several discussion groups—mailing lists used by thousands of people to ask questions about Jewish genealogy. JewishGen is a multifaceted Web site with many different features. It's difficult to describe everything—JewishGen currently contains more than twenty thousand Web pages and 7 million database records! I can only suggest that users visit JewishGen.org and browse the site to learn and discover.

Q. What is its history? How and when did it begin?

A. JewishGen started out as a dial-up bulletin board in the 1980s, founded by Susan King. That bulletin board grew and evolved into a mailing list and moved onto the Internet in 1993. We started the JewishGen Web site in 1995 and our first online databases the following year. Other JewishGen projects—the Special Interest Groups (SIGs), Yizkor Book Translation Project, ShtetLinks, and all the rest—quickly followed. JewishGen was built entirely by volunteers.

Q. You are JewishGen.org's editor. What does that mean? How do you spend your time?

A. As editor in chief, I coordinate, administer, and edit Jewish-Gen's Web content, deciding what material is appropriate and what goes where on the site. I spend my time writing and editing Web pages, formatting data, corresponding with data donors and volunteers, and providing the day-to-day technical support to keep the JewishGen site up and running. I am involved in everything from oversight of various JewishGen projects (databases, ShtetLinks, Yizkor book translations) and interacting with other organizations to resolving technical issues and answering genealogical queries.

Q. JewishGen.org is now connected to the Museum of Jewish Heritage in New York. Can you tell us about that connection?

A. On January 1, 2003, JewishGen became affiliated with the Museum of Jewish Heritage in New York. This affiliation has allowed JewishGen to move from being an all-volunteer virtual organization to being part of a major institution dedicated to preserving Jewish culture and heritage. The museum affiliation ensures the financial stability and long-term viability of JewishGen. Although the museum does contribute to JewishGen's basic operating budget, we are still totally dependent on financial donors and volunteers for our data acquisition, transcription, and translation projects.

Q. If you had to give one piece of advice to the beginner, what would it be?

A. Keep an open mind, and never give up. Don't believe everything that you've heard, and don't be surprised to find things in unexpected places. Don't expect your ancestors' names to be spelled the same way that they might be spelled today. Records of your ancestors *are* out there—but you need to learn about the historical and linguistic context in which those records were created in order to research them effectively.

Q. If you had a somewhat realistic Jewish genealogy "wish list" for the next ten years, what would it be?

A. I hope that major Jewish institutions will continue to support and promote Jewish genealogy, providing genealogists with the resources needed for research. I hope that archives around the world will continue to open their doors and allow access to genealogists and that their records will be inventoried, indexed, and preserved

on microfilm. I hope that volunteers will continue to transcribe, translate, and extract records, making them available for others to discover their ancestors.

Q. Do you think there is a core reason why those interested in genealogy are involved with it?

A. Everyone has personal reasons, which vary widely. But I think that most genealogists want to feel connected—and finding out who your ancestors were, where they came from, and what kinds of lives they led is a way to feel connected—connected to a wonderful history and culture. Jewish genealogy fosters Jewish continuity—preserving the memories of our ancestors and their lives, passing information about their heritage on to their descendants from generation to generation.

7

WERE YOUR ANCESTORS
GREAT RABBIS?

IT IS OFTEN POSSIBLE to trace your family back into the early centuries of the last millennium. I can trace my family, on some branches, back before the 1500s. Success usually depends, however, on the possibility of finding a link between a branch of your family and a rabbinic or well-known family. Although you may have doubts as to the feasibility of this endeavor, I need only refer you to my own story in Chapter One to illustrate the point that a most unsuspecting family might descend from illustrious rabbinic lineage.

In Great Britain, old genealogies are most often available for royal families. In the case of the Jews, our "royal families" have been those of the illustrious rabbis. In hundreds if not thousands of cases, the genealogies of the rabbis throughout the centuries exist in great detail and often go back to the Middle Ages.

Again, the point should be stressed that the possibility that you descend, in at least one branch, from a rabbinic family, is not all that remote. The mathematics of it explains it best. In the Kurzweil family, I have traced all of the descendants of my great-great-great-grandparents. They lived in the early 1800s. In all, their descendants number over five hundred people. In other words, from two people in 1800 have come over five hundred people. It is easy to see that with each additional generation, the number will increase greatly. Or we can look at it from the other direction: if each of us counts the number of direct ancestors we have up to our great-great-great-grandparents, we each count 62 people. One more generation, and we each have 126 direct ancestors. One more generation and we have 254 direct ancestors. In other words, each of us has 254 direct ancestors

in just the past couple of centuries. Either way we look at it, from the past forward or from the present backward, we come up with a very large number of relatives. It is not so far-fetched to think that in just one of those cases, an ancestor of ours was either a rabbi or someone who married a rabbi.

Of course, it is not our goal to try to find a rabbi in our family tree. But if we *happen* to find one, it is much easier to trace our own families, generation to generation, back through the centuries. Again, I must repeat the warning: *do not* try to pick a rabbi and prove descent. That would be nonkosher genealogy! But if a family tradition says that you were a descendant of someone who might be better known than the average person, it would be worthwhile to follow up that clue.

Why is it easy to trace the families of rabbis? There are a few reasons, one of which is known as *yichus*. *Yichus* is the biblical word meaning "genealogy," but the term, in more common usage, has come to mean "family background." It was the custom for many centuries (and still is among some families) to try to arrange marriages between one's children and learned families or families with fine reputations as scholars. To marry into a family with this kind of reputation is to marry a family with *yichus*. At the root of this custom is the recognition of the importance of scholarship and reputation.

The result of this custom has been for families to go to the trouble of documenting their lineage to prove illustrious descent. Although the accuracy of these documents, many of which are in the possession of families, is generally reliable, many families went to great lengths to try to document their descent back to King David, which was traditionally the finest lineage a person could have.

There is a fine line between claiming something you do not deserve based on the achievements of your ancestors and recognizing the influence of your ancestors and their achievements on you. This distinction must be made when discussing another source of early rabbinic genealogies. It is often the custom, among some families, to make it known that they were the descendants of earlier rabbis of fine repute. Although this would certainly have some effect on the way they were treated by the community, it is safe to say that a rabbi (or a family) who did not earn his own reputation would not achieve great heights. So even though a rabbi had to stand on his own, it was nevertheless the custom to make it known that he was descended from someone of high esteem, if this was the case. Very often in a document written about a rabbi, or more often in a book written by a rabbi, an introduction will present the respectable lineage of

the author. Since many works of rabbis were published posthumously, there were many opportunities to include introductions containing praises for the author. These introductions, usually written by the children or disciples of the rabbi, included biographies of the author. These biographies frequently included genealogical information.

The most important resource for rabbinic research is the Rabbinic Genealogy Special Interest Group (SIG) hosted by JewishGen.org (http://www.jewishgen.org/rabbinic/index.html). This SIG defines itself as "a forum for those interested in rabbinic genealogy or researching rabbinic ancestry within any geographic area or time period." The current chairperson of the SIG is Neil Rosenstein, one of the world's leading experts in the field. Shirley Rotbein Flaum is the coordinator of the SIG's steering committee. The pages of their SIG are filled with information.

Features of the Rabbinic Genealogy SIG include an online journal, a bibliography of over three hundred resources for rabbinic genealogical research, InfoFiles for tutorials, and reference information on many aspects of rabbinic genealogy (this area of the site is an extraordinary collection of information on the subject), research groups, links to Web sites of significance to rabbinic genealogy researchers, and more. Projects under development include Frequently Asked Questions (FAQs) and the All Rabbis Database.

Another part of these published works are approbations. An approbation is a "certificate of approval" written by a rabbi who either knew the author or read the manuscript and recommended it as a document of worth. Although the approbations were supposed to serve almost as "book reviews," they often contained a great deal of information about the author. It is not unusual for an approbation to contain additional genealogical and biographical information about the author. Very often an approbation of one book will lead the reader to a second book where the reader will discover a marriage in the rabbi's family to another famous rabbinic family, which further extends the genealogy.

Let us assume, for example, that you are able to document descent from a rabbi who lived in the nineteenth century. It is not unlikely that he wrote a book or wrote a manuscript that was later published as a book. The book would certainly have his name on it, and this alone would take you back at least one more generation, since Jewish names include the name of the person's father. It is likely that the book contains one or more approbations (often there are several). A reading of the approbations might enable you to find biographical remarks about the rabbi, tracing his descent from another rabbi in an earlier generation. In this way, combining the information found within rabbinic approbations can give rise to multigenerational genealogies.

הסכמת

הרב הגאון האמ"ת' מופת הדור רשכבה"ג בוצינא ד"יישא חסדא ופרישא נ"י

עה פ ה קדוש יאמר לו כבוד מוה' **חיים האלברשטאם** יצ"ו נ"י

אב"ד דק"ק **צאנז** יע"א :

הנה יד שלומה אלי מסכי סרי אחי הרבני המופלא מוהר"ר **מנשה** נ"י . וסרכבי המופלא מוהר"ד
אפרים נ"י בנים לאומו לדיק המנוח הרב המאתו"ג בו"ק חו"ף מו' **חיים יוסף** אלס"ם
מסי' אב"ד בק"ק סמרלאפקוץ , וסלך למנוחות וקמו בניו הכ"ל ונכמודדו לעשות נחם רוח לאביסס סלדיק
צל שיסי' שפתותיו דובבות ולסוליא לאור מיבור יקר אשר פעל ועשה אביהם המנוח ז"ל ודיו סי' רב לו
בטיב גיטין וקידושין . ובקשו ממני הסכמה על החימור סה וגדליהי לדבריהם ואף ידי תכון
במחם לסוליא לאור מיבור יקר הכ"ל . ומליה גדולה לחיום בצמרהם . וסמכסיע לסס ימצרך בכל מדב
כה דברי המדבר לכבוד הסורה ולומדי' .

יום ד' ע"ו מרחשון **ברכות** לראש לדיק לפ"ק.

פה לאהז . הק' **חיים האלברשטאם**

Approbation by Rabbi Chaim Halberstam for a book by the author's ancestor, Rabbi Chaim Josef Gottlieb. This approbation, like most, includes genealogical information.

A brilliant example of the use of approbations and other similar sources is a book titled *The Unbroken Chain* by Neil Rosenstein, published by CIS Publishers. In this two-volume work, Rosenstein has pieced together genealogical information included in approbations and additional biographical sources and has created a genealogy tracing hundreds of contemporary families back to the 1400s. The remarkable part of this piece of research and scholarship is its presentation of the dramatic way in which the generations since the families' beginnings in the fifteenth century have gone their separate ways. Although his book is quite large, Rosenstein admits that it is not nearly complete, which indicates that many more contemporary families stem from the same lineage. It must also be remembered that Rosenstein's work is one small part of Jewish family history and that there is room for the same kind of work to be done for the vast number of other families in Jewish history.

Rosenstein is setting an important precedent. Although the author himself is a descendant of the original family, his research goes far beyond the documentation of his own lineage. Rosenstein has constructed an enormous Jewish genealogy that includes hundreds of other branches. If more

of this kind of research would be done, it would be easier for contemporary families to make connections with families of earlier centuries. It is absurd for any of us to pick a family in the sixteenth century and hope that if we research the genealogy, we will make a connection with our own; however, it is not far-fetched to do the kind of general Jewish genealogical research Rosenstein has done in an effort to help countless numbers of people trace their family history.

———— o ————

God created Adam rather than creating the whole human race together for the sake of peace among mankind, so that no one could say, "My ancestor was greater than your ancestor."

—Mishnah, Sandhedrin 4:5

If a man casts aspersions upon other people's descent—for instance, if he alleges that certain families and individuals are of blemished descent and refers to them as being bastards—suspicion is justified that he himself may be a bastard.

—Maimonides, *Mishneh Torah*

———— o ————

Rabbinic Dynasties

It is important to stress once again the dangers of going ancestor hunting. It is *not* acceptable to assume that since your last name is the same as that of a famous rabbinic family (or anyone else for that matter), you are related.

On the other hand, if you do trace descent, *accurately,* from a rabbinic family, you will probably be able to accumulate a great deal of information. Many rabbinic genealogies have been documented, and a thorough check at the major Jewish libraries is suggested to locate such material.

The index volume of *Encyclopedia Judaica* (pp. 160–167) contains genealogical charts for the major Hasidic dynasties from the founder of Hasidism, the Baal Shem Tov, to the present.

———— o ————

If three consecutive generations are scholars, the Torah will not depart from that line.

—Johanan B. Nappaha, Talmud, *Baba Metzia* 85a

———— o ————

Rabbinic Sources

Often people assume that an ancestor was a rabbi simply because they were told by a relative who remembers somebody with a long beard. Long beards have been known to grow on people who were not rabbis.

On the other hand, if you were told that your great-great-grandfather was a rabbi, there is no reason to immediately assume that it is impossible. However, even if it is true, it doesn't mean that the rabbi was famous or even that he worked as a rabbi. A traditional ordination or *smichah* was given to many people who simply graduated from a rabbinic course of study. They may have gone on to become merchants or innkeepers.

Most often when a tradition that claims a rabbi in its past is passed to you, the claim is a specific one—for example, "We descend from the Dobno Maggid" or "We descend from the Stropkover Rebbe." When you are searching for information about a certain rabbi, you need to know some clue that you can pursue. Generally, this is either a name or a place. If you know the rabbi's name, you will have to use biographical directories, looking for the rabbi's name. If you know the name of the town, then you will have to do town history research.

The following are some excellent rabbinic biographical sources. Keep in mind that not every rabbi will appear in them. The local rabbi of a small Polish town might or might not be listed. If not, there is still the strong possibility that he will show up in a history of the town.

Otzar Harabanim: Rabbis' Encyclopedia, by Rabbi Nathan Zvi Friedman, Bnei-Brak, Israel. This volume is a biographical directory of twenty thousand rabbis from 970 to 1970. There are a name index, a town index, a book index, and cross-references to the rabbis' fathers, fathers-in-law, sons, and students, if any of them were also rabbis. The book is a fantastic piece of scholarship. Many Jewish bookstores carry this volume. It is written in Hebrew.

HaChasidut, by Yitzchok Alfasi. This book devotes itself exclusively to Hasidic rabbis, from the Baal Shem Tov, founder of Hasidism, to 1977, the year the book was published. The volume includes a name and town index, but the name index is a bit difficult to work with because it is arranged by first name. This might seem impractical, but in fact it is the best way to index a book in which many of the individuals simply do not have last names. The book is organized by Hasidic dynasty, giving the reader a good idea who the teachers and students of the rabbis were. The book is also well illustrated with photographs and drawings of many of the rabbis. Facsimiles of the rabbis' signatures are also reproduced when available. This book also is in Hebrew.

Ohole-Schem, by Scholom N. Gottlieb, published in Pinsk, 1912. This was a directory, with addresses, of rabbis throughout the world in 1912. It is written in various languages, but the names of the rabbis are almost always in the Roman alphabet. The YIVO Institute for Jewish Research has a copy of this book and of all the other rabbinic biographies mentioned here.

Bet Eked Sepharim: Bibliographical Lexicon, by Baruch Friedberg, Tel Aviv, Israel, 1951. This four-volume work is a massive bibliography of rabbinic literature from 1474 to 1950. If a rabbi wrote a book, it is likely to appear here. The set of books includes an index of rabbis.

Meorei Galicia: Encyclopedia of Galician Rabbis and Scholars, by Rabbi Meir Wunder, Institute for Commemoration of Galician Jewry. Four volumes have been published so far (the fourth in 1990). The fifth and final volume will cover the last two letters of the Hebrew alphabet, shin and tav. This important series of books is written in Hebrew, but the author plans "ultimately" to translate all the volumes into English.

Atlas Eytz Chayim, by Raphael Halperin, Department of Surveys, Tel Aviv, Israel, 1978. Through a series of seventy chronological, genealogical, and synchronical maps, tables, diagrams, and graphic illustrations, the author has documented brief biographical information on more than two thousand rabbis and scholars from 940 to 1492. The unique aspect of this book is the way the author has shown the relationships between the individuals mentioned. The diagrams, charts, and illustrations indicate teacher-student, father-son, and colleague relationships. Included with the book is a huge folded poster literally mapping in time the lives of 2,091 individuals in Jewish history. This entire volume is an important addition to the field of rabbinic genealogy.

Although all of these books are in Hebrew, even a mere knowledge of the Hebrew alphabet will allow you to use the indexes to search for names of individuals and towns. If and when you find something of interest, someone who actually understands Hebrew can help you.

If these books are not available in local libraries, once again you must do your best to locate them. The YIVO Institute for Jewish Research has all of these books, as does the Jewish Theological Seminary Library. Many good Jewish bookstores carry some of them. If not, they may be able to order them for you.

○

Lineage is not just a matter of empty self-congratulation. All lineage, and not just that of nobility, carries with it a certain responsibility. A great person discovered among one's ancestors is not just

a cause for bragging but something that must be related to and learned from.

—Rabbi Adin Steinsaltz,
Teshuvah: A Guide for the Newly Observant Jew

○

There are other ways to track down information on rabbis. As noted, the *Encyclopedia Judaica* is always a source to check; memorial books for specific towns are also fine sources.

There has yet to be a definitive volume on the subject of rabbinic genealogy, but over the years a few people have shown impressive results regarding their own investigation into the subject. I have had the pleasure, over the years, of becoming familiar with the work of two particularly impressive individuals.

Dr. Neil Rosenstein, whom I have already mentioned, is a fine gentleman and a surgeon who lives with his family in Elizabeth, New Jersey. His contribution to the field of Jewish genealogy has been most impressive. His several publications are all superb, and it is important to note that the Jewish Genealogical Society phenomenon started at his initiative, with the founding of the first such society.

Rosenstein's most important publication, as noted earlier, is *The Unbroken Chain: Biographical Sketches and the Genealogy of Illustrious Jewish Families from the 15th to 20th Century* (CIS Publishers, 180 Park Avenue, Lakewood, NJ 08701). Be sure to get the second edition. The original publication was a single volume; the newer two-volume edition has been updated and greatly expanded.

Neil Rosenstein has also delivered a number of excellent lectures on the subject of rabbinic genealogy. Recordings of some of his lectures are available on tape from Audiotapes.com at http://www.audiotapes.com/author.asp?author='ROSENSTEIN'.

David Einsidler, a dedicated Jewish genealogist and a special soul, has earned a reputation as an expert on the subject of rabbinic genealogy. He has been published in various places, including *Avotaynu* and the newsletter of the Jewish Genealogical Society of Los Angeles.

○

A man must not rely on the virtues of his ancestors: if he does not do good in this world, he cannot fall back on the merit of his fathers, for in the time to come no man will eat off his fathers' works, but only of his own.

—Midrash, Psalm 146:3

○

Rabbinic Texts

If you have located an ancestor who may have written a Jewish text, there are several libraries that should be checked to see if those books are available:

> Jewish Theological Seminary Library, 3080 Broadway, New York, NY 10027

> Klau Library, Hebrew Union College, 3101 Clifton Avenue, Cincinnati, OH 45220

> Mendel Gottesman Library of Judaica and Hebraica and Archives, Yeshiva University Library, Amsterdam Avenue and 185th Street, New York, NY 10033

> New York Public Library, Jewish Division, Room 84, 42nd Street and Fifth Avenue, New York, NY 10018

> YIVO Institute for Jewish Research, 1048 Fifth Avenue, New York, NY 10028

There may be a large university library near you with a good Judaica collection. It would be worthwhile to check there as well.

I would also highly recommend that you visit the following two Web sites, each of which has hundreds of rabbinic texts available online:

> HebrewBooks.org (http://www.hebrewbooks.org)

> Seforim Online (http://www.seforimonline.org)

————————— o —————————

God prefers your deeds to your ancestor's virtues.

—Midrash, Genesis Rabbah 74

————————— o —————————

Hebrew Subscription Lists

In the past (and sometimes today), Jewish scholars who wanted their books published would do it themselves. They or their representatives would go from town to town trying to sell "subscriptions" to a forthcoming book. The potential reader would pay in advance to support the publication of the volume. In return, the author of the book would

usually publish the subscriber's name in the book—for two reasons. First, as an incentive to subscribe. After all, if your name was to appear in a scholarly Jewish text, you might be more apt to invest. Second, in order for the "publisher" to know who ultimately gets the book, a list of towns and names must be produced for distribution purposes.

The result of all this is that in thousands of rabbinic and scholarly books that have survived to this day, we can find lengthy lists of towns and individuals in those towns. The persons listed are the ones who subscribed to the book before it was published.

The late Berl Kagan put together a magnificent book on the subject: *Hebrew Subscription Lists, with an Index to 8767 Jewish Communities in Europe and North Africa* (published by the Library of the Jewish Theological Seminary of America and KTAV Publishing House, New York, in 1975). The remarkable task that Kagan set for himself and completed is the indexing, by town, of thousands of subscription lists in Jewish books. What Kagan did was go through the thousands of books published during the last few hundred years that had subscription lists in them. Every time a town name appeared, he noted the name of the town, the name of the book, and the number of people who subscribed to the book. In other words, for you to use Kagan's book genealogically, you would look up the name of a town in your family history. Under the listing of that town you would find the titles of Jewish books and a number following the title. The number would indicate how many people in that town subscribed to that book.

Once you discover that certain people in your town subscribed to a particular book, you can go to the original book (to be found at the Jewish Theological Seminary library or other good Jewish libraries) and examine the subscription list. What you just might find is a name familiar to you.

What would such a discovery mean? Well, if you found an ancestor of yours on a subscription list in an old Jewish text, you would now know nothing more—but nothing less—than that your ancestor helped support this particular book in which his name appears. It would not offer you any great new discovery of an unknown ancestor, but it would tell you something significant about that individual.

By the way, the whole process of checking Kagan's book and then checking each old text is a very long one. This step of your research should be saved for a time when you have just about reached dead ends with everything else. But it is a fascinating and educational process.

○

A Conversation with Neil Rosenstein

Neil Rosenstein, a surgeon who lives in Elizabeth, New Jersey, was the founding president of the New York–based Jewish Genealogical Society. He is the author of several important genealogy books, including *The Unbroken Chain*, a compilation of rabbinic genealogies.

Q. How has Jewish genealogy changed since you founded the first Jewish Genealogical Society?

A. The change can be compared to the beginnings of flight by the Wright brothers or the space program that resulted in placing man on the moon. In the 1970s there were only a handful of people actively involved in Jewish genealogy. Foremost in the United States was Rabbi Malcolm H. Stern, with whom I had been corresponding since the early 1960s when I was still living in South Africa. In fact, my letters are part of his archive, which was donated after his death to Hebrew Union College. I met you and Dan Rottenberg, who was able to add a few lines into Rabbi Stern's book about myself and my own book, which was in the process of publication. After *The Unbroken Chain* came out in 1976, I was written up in the *New York Times Magazine* and was soon contacted by many other people with similar interests. Some of these people became part of our founding board. Our original flier already then addressed the concept of databases in anticipation of the age of computers! However, its creation was long in coming.

Q. How did you first get involved with Jewish genealogy?

A. When I was a mere ten years old and enjoyed going to Cheder [Hebrew day school] in the afternoons, my father felt it would be of interest to tell me that our family was descended from a Jewish Polish King for a Day (or a Night). That's all he knew besides the family name, Katzenellenbogen. That really got me going. My teenage years were deeply involved with research, which was nearly impossible in South Africa back then. But I persevered with encouragement from such people as Rabbi Stern and others in the United States and elsewhere. By age sixteen I had begun to develop a Judaica library, which formed the matrix for all my future work in this field. Meantime I was into scouting, photography,

mountaineering, Bani Akiva Zionist Movement, camping, and after high school, medical school in Cape Town.

Q. Why do you think you became so interested in rabbinic research? What is its impact on you personally?

A. It so happened that the Katzenellenbogen family, besides boasting a legendary Jewish king, also boasted a long line of prominent rabbis, scholars, and other men of renown for hundreds of years. The emotional impact of my learning I was a descendant of great rabbis left a deep impact on me and strengthened my belief and faith in our religion and the history of world Jewry. I felt a direct bond and connection to those who had gone before me, and that is how, one night, I hit upon the title *The Unbroken Chain*. A further impact has been on our having raised five Torah-abiding sons, four of whom are married and imparting that tradition to their own children, our grandchildren.

Q. Just how far back is it really possible to document a Jewish family?

A. That is a very broad question. I think it should be divided into Ashkenazic and Sephardic families, as each has some unique genealogical qualities. If one chooses one's parents correctly, the task become much easier. For Ashkenazim, rabbinic families can often be traced back to about the fourteenth or fifteenth century. Prior to that not much exists that can be useful, aside from various traditions in rabbinic sources such as the Talmud and other works you allude to, that is, Rashi, Hillel, and King David. Much of this is part of my new book, *The Lurie Legacy,* which is being published by Avotaynu. Most of my life I have been basing my research on what has been written in primary and secondary sources. More recently, I have come to realize that there are many false or inaccurate assumptions that have misled many scholars who have not had a critical eye. I have now started to have that critical eye, and some points are also discussed in my new book.

Q. If you had to give one piece of advice to the beginner, what would it be?

A. Interview all living relatives, especially those of the previous generations (parents, grandparents, and their siblings), and record (on audio tape or video) all that they tell you.

Q. Do you think there is a core reason why those interested in genealogy are involved with it?

A. I do not believe that there is a single core reason. Besides religious, spiritual, and historical pride, we must remember that it is

a hobby. Different people, for whatever reason, pick up on a specific hobby to enjoy and devote time to. I have often met avid Jewish genealogists who are either unmarried or have no offspring and yet trace their family to share with other relatives.

○

○

The ancestors of the arrogant never stood at Mount Sinai.

—Talmud, Nashim 20a

○

8

THE NAMES IN YOUR FAMILY

OUR NAMES ARE OFTEN revealing links with our past, with history, and with Jewish tradition. We carry them with us every moment. Both our first and surnames represent, when analyzed, pieces of history. Whether it is our first names (which in European Jewish tradition are usually in memory of beloved persons who are deceased) or our surnames (which often contain fascinating clues to help us identify our ancestors and relatives), our names are not merely labels to distinguish us from others but are rather special designations that place us in time and history.

○

A good name is rather to be chosen than great riches.

Proverbs 22:1

○

A Brief History of Jewish Surnames

Our surnames stretch back for generations. Like our heritage, our names have been passed down to us from generation to generation until they arrived in the present. Our surnames provide us with clues about our early ancestors. At some point in time your surname was taken by (or given to) someone in your family, and it then continued through time to you. Of course, we must remember that although each of us has one surname, we are equally the descendants of many families with just as many surnames. Our custom has usually been to take the surname of our father, and he of his father, but we are just as much members of our mother's family and of all the other branches in our lineage. In addition, we are more than just

the product of two families, since each of our parents is the product of two families. Therefore, it is important to keep in mind that when we discuss our surnames, we are speaking of many more than one. In fact, as you discover the names of your ancestors and acknowledge the list of names that are yours, you will be able to understand more of your own personal history by examining the nature of your many surnames.

Although our names are usually generations old, they are not ancient. Use of surnames by Jews is a relatively recent custom, considering the length of Jewish history. In the Torah there are no surnames, nor were there any used in biblical times. It was sufficient to have one name that distinguished each member of a community from the others. In the later books of the Bible we do find the first evidence of surnames, as in Elijah the Tishbite or Uriah the Hittite. But although these names add information to identify the individuals, they are not surnames as we know them today. If Uriah the Hittite moved to Ur, he would probably then be referred to as Uriah of Ur. In the same way, if Uriah the Hittite had a child, the descriptor would not be passed on. Rather the child would be given a patronymic: "ben Uriah" (son of Uriah) or "bat Uriah" (daughter of Uriah). Patronymics were the common way of identifying Jews for centuries before surnames as we know them today were used. But the use of additional names in biblical times, such as place names and patronymics, were precursors of later sources of surnames. A modern surname like Ginzburg is a place name, and a name such as Meyerson is a patronymic.

Another kind of name used in the Bible foreshadows modern surnaming customs. Descriptive names are found in the Bible, such as Ha-kotz in Ezra 2:61. Ha-kotz means "the thorn," which is a descriptive term in the same way that a surname like Klein, meaning "small," is sometimes, but not always, a descriptive surname of modern times. Names in the Talmud reflect the same kinds of customs, although the names of locations, patronymics, and occupations are still not hereditary. Vocational names, which are not found in the Bible, foreshadow modern occupation names. Talmudic examples of this are Abba Jose the Potter and Daniel the Tailor. The names Snyder (from the German) and Portnoy (from the Russian) are the modern occupational identifiers of a tailor.

Patronymics in the Talmud are quite popular. Simon ben Gamliel means "Simon, son of Gamliel." There are even times when we find patronymics representing two generations, such as Raba bar bar Chana, which means that Raba was the grandson of Chana (the terms *bar* and *ben* both mean "son of"). We find nicknames in the Talmud also: Zeira the Younger is an example of this. Also in the Talmud are examples of priestly designations, known to us in modern times by the surnames

Cohen or Levy. In the Talmud we find individuals such as Ishmael the High Priest and Jose Ha-kohen. But again, these names would not necessarily be passed down to children.

For most of Jewish history, Jews did not use surnames as we know them. Sephardic Jews adopted surnames from their Arabs neighbors. who not only used a similar patronymic, with *ibn* designating "son of," but who also added the father's name without the use of *ibn*. But Central and Northern European Jews, even throughout the Middle Ages, generally did not use surnames. Jews were isolated from larger communities and simply did not develop the need for family names. During the tenth and eleventh centuries, surname usage began to become popular due to the rise of cities and of commerce, both of which stimulated the need for family names for practical reasons. But again, it was primarily the Sephardim who were affected by this. They used occupational names, nicknames, and place names. A famous Sephardic occupational name is Abulafia, meaning "father of medicine," and another is Gabbai, which represents a synagogue official. Among place names, we are familiar with Cardozo from Spain and Montefiore from Italy.

The isolation of the Ashkenazim, as I have noted, postponed the use of surnames until much later. It is interesting to note that in the fourteenth century there were only about seven hundred Jews in Frankfurt am Main, and in the sixteenth century Prague had only twelve hundred Jews. Thus it is easy to see that no great need for surnames existed among the self-contained Jewish communities of Northern Europe. When an official register of a city needed to record Jews for whatever reason, the designation "the Jew" was often used. Jews themselves continued to use place names, patronymics, occupation names, and other forms of family names, but these names lasted for just a generation or so rather than being kept as a permanent family surname.

It was actually not until the late eighteenth century that surnames as we know them today were used commonly among Jews. This is why, as we enter the period of Jewish history before this time, it is exceedingly difficult to trace our own specific families back to these years. In all likelihood, if you are an Ashkenazic Jew, the surname that is yours today was not that of your ancestors in the 1600s or even a good part of the 1700s. This is because it was not until 1787 that Jews were first required to register last names, and that was only in Austria. Switzerland, for example, did not require its Jews to register last names until 1863.

Of course, this does not mean that family names did not exist in these places before those dates. It does mean, however, that Jews were given the opportunity to change their names and register them permanently at these

times. In some cases names were assigned to Jews, and at other times they had to be bought. In any case, surnames among Jews are a recent arrival, even though family names might have existed traditionally for much longer.

Some Jews in the Middle Ages did use names to identify their families, and many families grew attached to those names and continued to use them. A fascinating development took place in Frankfurt during the Middle Ages. Jews were forced to live in a special section of the city called the Judengasse, and registration was based on the house that each family occupied. Houses at this time were not numbered but rather were labeled by signs that hung outside. The signs were colorful and represented many kinds of images, including animals, colors, and fruits. A famous surname that reflects a house sign of this time is Rothschild, which means "red shield." The name Loeb might reflect the use of the image of a lion on these house signs, as Gans would reflect the sign of a goose. These sign names were often carved on the tombstones of family members, adding to the permanence of the house signs as surnames. An interesting note pertaining to the use of house signs by Jews is that when the Jews in Frankfurt's Judengasse were ordered in 1776 to use numbers on their houses rather than signs, there was such resistance that the whole Jewish community was fined.

We cannot say, however, that family names tended to be kept within families. Sometimes names were changed by individuals themselves; sometimes surnames changed from parent to child.

The year 1787 is an important date in the history of the Jewish surname, for that is when the Austrian Empire compelled the Jews, for the first time in their history, to adopt surnames. Officers were appointed to register all Jews with these names, and if any Jews refused, the officers were to force a name on them. It was at this time that many meaningless names were assigned to individuals, and this accounts, surely, for some names whose origin we do not know at the present time.

On July 20, 1808, Napoleon issued a decree of a similar nature, insisting that Jews adopt fixed names. The same was done in Frankfurt in 1807 and in Baden in 1809.

Similar laws were enacted throughout Europe at different times: 1812 in Prussia, 1813 in Bavaria, 1834 in Saxony, 1845 in Russia. In each case, Jews were required to register family names. There were several reasons for these enactments. The levying of taxes was made much simpler with permanent surnames, as was the conscription of Jewish soldiers. Another reason was the effort to assimilate the Jews, at least in cases where no specific list of names to be used was issued. When lists of restricted names existed, the exact opposite purpose was intended—to single out Jews among the larger community.

An additional reason for the requirement of surnames was that it was a clever means of obtaining additional revenues for the government. This occurred when taxes were imposed for the registration of the names. It is also known that unfriendly local officials would either impose unattractive names on Jews or threaten to do so unless a nicer name was "purchased." In response to Napoleon's decree, some of the names imposed on Jews included Eselskopf ("donkey's head"), Fresser ("glutton"), and Lumpe ("hoodlum"). In Austria in 1787, the unpopular names included Nussnacker ("nutcracker") and Puderbeutel ("powder bag").

Those names were assigned with cruelty, and nicer names often came at a high price. There were, however, many opportunities to choose whatever name one wanted, and in northeastern Germany, a series of names with "Rose" in them became common, including Rosenzweig, Rosenthal, Rosenblum, and Rosenstein.

Amusing stories of how individuals and communities obtained their names have been preserved. It is known, for example, that in one community a rabbi opened a prayer book and went word by word, assigning names to people from the book. In another case an official asked a person for his name. He said "Yankele." The official asked him again, to which he replied "*Poshet* Yankele," which means "simply Yankele." His name thus became Poshet.

Often I have imagined what it might be like to be forced to choose the surname that will be in your family permanently. It must surely have been a major decision, and this is reflected, perhaps, in the time periods given to the Jews to take a name. Several months were allowed in some cases. Think what it must have been like. Suddenly, you have to choose from any name or word there is (except, of course, in the cases where a limited list was provided—in which case it is a different kind of incredible decision) and be satisfied. When the edicts were enacted, people must have thought that the choice would be a permanent one. Imagine that you were put in this situation: What surname would you choose?

The Origins of Modern Surnames

Our surnames today come from a large variety of sources, and it is sometimes illuminating to know the meaning of the word or the reason the name was attached to the family. It is likely that people with the family name Snyder had an ancestor who was a tailor, but it is impossible to know what the reason behind a name like Schwartz might be. Meaning "black," the word might have been a description of someone's hair or attire, or it could have been chosen simply as the name of the color, or it

could have been adopted for any number of other reasons that will never be known.

Nevertheless, there is much we can learn from our names, and it would be useful to examine the different types of Jewish surnames to help us identify and make tentative conclusions regarding the origins of our own names. Jewish surnames can be divided into several categories, reflecting those discussed in the first part of this chapter.

Patronymics

As we have discussed, the patronymic was an early naming convention, and although patronymics were originally not used as surnames as we now use them, they were eventually adapted to modern surname usage. It is known that when Jews were ordered to take surnames, many people simply used the patronymic form that they were currently using. Thus a man known as Abraham ben Isaac would become Abraham Isaacs.

The patronymic was the simplest way of forming a surname, and such conventions can be found in every language. The Austrian and German patronymic would be a name ending in *-sohn,* such as Abramsohn, Isaac-sohn, or Jacobsohn. Another German patronymic is *-witz;* Polish uses *-wicz,* Romanian has *-vici,* and many Slavic languages use *-vitch,* as in Abramovitch. Other Slavic patronymics include the suffixes *-ov, -off, -eff,* and *-kin,* all of which indicate "descendant of." Examples of these would include Malkov and Rivkin. It is interesting to note that these particular examples are not patronymics but rather matronymics—formed from a woman's name. Malkov would mean "descendant of Malka," and Rivkin means "descendant of Rivka." In Germany and Austro-Hungary, the mother's name was a frequent source of the establishment of a surname. Other examples of this are Perles, Gitles, and Zeldes.

Another form of surname, though not a patronymic, is a name based on the first name of a wife. This kind of name has been formed by adding the suffix *-mann* to a wife's first name, as in Estermann for the husband of Esther and Perlmann for the husband of Perl.

Place Names

Perhaps the largest group of Jewish surnames are based on locations. We are able to learn specific information about our ancestors from surnames derived from place names, for it is fair to assume that an ancestor once came from the location indicated by the name. If, for example, your surname happens to be Berliner, it would be logical to assume that someone in that line of ancestors at one time lived in Berlin.

The Sephardim often took place names as their surnames. We find Spanish surnames like de Cordova and de Lima. From Portugal we have Lisbona; from Italy there is Lucca and Padua; and from the Netherlands we find names like De Vries, "from Friesland."

Every European country has inspired Jewish surnames, reflecting the extent to which Jews migrated around the continent. Sometimes the name was as general as a country name. At other times it was as specific as the sign attached to a house. In fact, we find a whole gamut of Jewish place surnames, derived from countries, regions, towns, streets, and houses. There is some mystery surrounding the derivation of surnames from places. It is not known why there are some towns with no surnames representing them. Even in the cases of towns with large Jewish populations, there are some that did not seem to inspire names.

There are several suffixes that have been added to places in order to turn them into surnames. The suffix -er is a common one, as in Berliner ("from Berlin") or Schweitzer ("from Switzerland"). The suffix -man is also used, as in Osterman, which means "man from the east," adding the notion of direction to our list of place sources for surnames.

We have already discussed house signs, but it is appropriate to mention them again in the context of place names. House signs would have represented on them various images that were later adopted as permanent surnames. We have already mentioned Rothschild ("red shield"); other examples would include Schwarzschild ("black shield"), Blum ("flower"), Buxbaum ("box tree"), Lachs ("salmon"), and Baer ("bear"). One cannot be sure in all cases, however, whether the source of a name is actually from a house sign. Many Jewish surnames have been taken from names of flowers, fruits, plants, animals, and minerals but were chosen for their beauty rather than adopted because of a house sign. There is also an amusing story behind one common name related to house signs. A Frankfurt family of priestly descent had the name of Kahn, which is commonly known as such a name. However, they took as their house sign the picture of a boat, since Kahn is German for "boat." In later years, members of the same family used the sign of a bigger boat, a ship, and so their name became Schiff. The name went from Kahn to Schiff because of a house sign!

Vocational Names

Vocational names are another type of Jewish surname that offers a concrete clue to family history. In fact, it is vocational names that give historians insight into the kinds of occupations either held or permitted to be held by Jews at a certain time. When we examine old tombstones and see

occupational names corresponding to certain dates, we add to our knowledge of what kinds of jobs were done by Jews in certain eras.

Vocational names are less common among Sephardim than among Ashkenazim. We have already offered one example of a Sephardic vocational name, Abulafia, meaning "father of medicine." Other Sephardic vocational names would include Almosnino, meaning "orator" in Arabic, and Mocatta, which is "mason" in Arabic.

Occupational names are taken not only from the exact title of the job but also from the materials used in the activity. A name such as Leder, which means "leather," would indicate a tanner, just as a carpenter might have the name Nagel, meaning "nail." Vocational names are also noted to range from the most common to the most highly respected types of occupations. We find names like Dayan, meaning "judge"; Chazan, meaning "cantor"; and Spielman, meaning "player."

Descriptive Names

A large group of Jewish surnames comes under the heading of descriptive names. These, presumably, were descriptions of the original bearer of the name. These types of names can be separated into two different groups: physical descriptions and personality characteristics.

In the category of physical characteristics, we have names such as Klein, meaning "small"; Kurtz, meaning "short"; and Geller, meaning "yellow," which we assume to be a hair color. In the same way, Graubart, which means "gray beard," is an example falling under another general subheading in this group.

As for personality characteristics, we find names like Selig, which means "happy"; Biederman, which means "worthy man"; Baruch, which means "blessed"; and Gottlieb, which means "God-loving."

Another kind of descriptive name is the nickname, many of which have become surnames. We find names like Purim (perhaps given because of the person's date of birth) and Lustig ("merry") in this category.

My own name, Kurzweil, can perhaps be considered a descriptive name, though it might fall into any of several categories. The word *Kurzweil* literally means "short time" (in German, *kurz* means "short" and *Weile* means "time"), though as a compound the meaning changes to "pastime" or "diversion," something to make the time seem short. The expression *zum Kurzweil* means "just for fun." Some German-speaking people have told me that *Kurzweil* can mean "the opposite of boring." An additional definition of the word, in the sense of "diversion," is a person who entertains others by telling stories. The name could even be

applied to a professional jester. Therefore, although all the definitions have similar meanings, it is interesting (for me) to note that the name could be a simple word, a personal characteristic, or an occupation. All the more fascinating is the fact that the one comment people have made repeatedly when describing members of my family, particularly my ancestors, is that the Kurzweils are often great storytellers.

Names from Abbreviations

One of the most unusual derivations of Jewish surnames is from abbreviations. A popular surname—Katz—is not generally known to be an abbreviation, but it is just that. Although the source of Katz is commonly thought to be the "cat," it is actually shorthand for the phrase *kohen zedek,* or "priest of righteousness." In the same way, the surname Schatz, literally meaning "treasure," is shorthand for "*sheliah tzibbur,* which means "minister of the congregation." Segal (also spelled Segel, Siegel, and other ways) is said to come from *segan leviyyah,* meaning "assistant to the Levites."

Another form of abbreviation that resulted in surnames was that of the letters formed from a man's name or his father's name (or both combined). So, for example, the name Schach is derived from Sabbatai Cohen. The name Bry comes from Ben Rabbi Israel, Brock is from Ben Rabbi Akiba, and Basch is the abbreviated form of Ben Shimeon.

There is another custom in the Jewish tradition concerning the abbreviation of names. During the Middle Ages it was somewhat common to abbreviate names by initials. Although these names were not surnames, they did become the general way of referring to the individual. The three most popular examples of this are Rashi, who was actually Rabbi Solomon ben Isaac; Rambam, who was Rabbi Moses ben Maimon; and Besht, which is the pronunciation of the acronym for Baal Shem Tov.

A final type of surname in this category (though not truly an abbreviation or an actual surname) is the custom of referring to an individual by his magnum opus, his finest literary work. Perhaps the most famous of these is Israel Meir Ha-Kohen, who is known as Hafez Hayyim after his book by that name. Two other examples of this are Roke'ah, who is Rabbi Eliazer ben Judah, and Tur, who is Rabbi Jacob ben Asher. Again, these were not surnames but were shorthand forms of lengthier names.

Matronymics

In the same way that a patronymic is a name derived from a male source (usually the father), a matronymic comes from a female source, usually

the mother. Many Jewish surnames come from this source and include names such as Perl, Rose, Hinde, Freude, and Gutkind.

Some Jewish Surnames and Their Meanings

In general, the origins of surnames can be determined by considering the various sources we have discussed. However, there can be little certainty about this. Despite the fact that a surname can potentially be an excellent clue for insight into a family's history, this is speculation. In the same way that there are many sources for surnames, there are a great variety of circumstances that might have resulted in the establishment or adoption of a family name. Although the name Snyder means "tailor," we cannot be certain that there was a tailor in our past who adopted that name to reflect his profession. The name might have been imposed on him, or he may have chosen it for reasons we will never know.

Another issue regarding surnames in Jewish tradition is the custom of taking the surname of one's father. Although this is common today, there have been times in our past when this was not the case universally among Jews. Often a child would adopt the maiden name of his or her mother and not his or her father. The reason is that when a Jewish child was born, often the parents were not married under civil law but only under Jewish law. Therefore, it was not unusual for the civil law to refuse to recognize the legitimacy of the birth. This resulted in the child's being required, by civil law, to take the name of the mother. This is something to keep in mind when doing family history research. It is not wise to assume that a surname automatically leads to the father of a child.

It should be repeated, however, that the study of surnames is a fascinating part of Jewish history and the history of your family. We are each the descendants of a countless number of families, and each of those families has its own surname. Each of those families has its own history as well, and each of those histories directly affects who you are.

Here are some examples of the meaning of some of my family names as well as some names of people close to me:

Amsel	"thrush"
Aronson	"son of Aaron"
Billet	"banknote"
Blech	"sheet metal; baking tin"
Blum	"flower"
Bulka	"bread roll"
Eisenberg	"iron mountain"

Engel	"angel"
Kaplan	"priest"
Katz	"righteous priest"
Kaunfer	"camphor"
Kurzweil	"amusement, diversion"
Meltsner	"malt maker"
Pomerantz	"orange"
Portnoy	"tailor"
Rothfarb	"red-colored"
Schlaff	"weak, limp"
Schramme	"scratch"
Spack	"sparrow"
Steinsaltz	"rock salt"

Examples of Jewish surnames that were originally nicknames or personality characteristics:

Dienstag	"Tuesday"
Ehrlich	"honest"
Friedmann	"free man"
Frohlich	"happy"
Fruhling	"spring"
Gittelson	"son of good little one"
Gottlieb	"God-loving"
Gottschalk	"God's servant"
Klug	"wise"
Lipgott	"God-loving"
Lustig	"merry"
Shalom	"peace"
Sholem	"peace"
Solomon	"peace"
Sommer	"summer"
Sonntag	"Sunday"

Examples of Jewish surnames from occupations:

Ackermann	"farmer"
Babad	*ben av beth din* ("son of rabbi")
Bauer	"farmer"
Bauman	"builder"
Becker	"baker"
Berger	"shepherd"
Bookbinder	"bookbinder"

Brenner	"distiller"
Breuer	"brewer"
Cantor	"cantor"
Drucker	"printer"
Farber	"painter"
Feldman	"shepherd"
Fleischer	"butcher"
Gerber	"tanner"
Goldschmidt	"goldsmith"
Kauffman	"merchant"
Koster	"doorkeeper"
Kramer	"merchant"
Kunzler	"artist"
Leder	"(tanner of) leather"
Metzger	"butcher"
Nadel	"needle"
Nagel	"nail"
Rabad	*resh av beth din* ("rabbi")
Rabinovitch	"son of rabbi"
Rokeach	"spice merchant"
Sandler	"cobbler"
Schecter	"slaughterer"
Scher	"shears"
Schlosser	"locksmith"
Schneider	"tailor"
Schnitzner	"carver"
Schochet	"ritual slaughterer"
Schuster	"shoemaker"
Singer	"cantor"
Snyder	"tailor"
Waldman	"woodsman"
Weber	"weaver"
Wechsler	"moneychanger"
Zimmerman	"carpenter"

Examples of Jewish surnames from animal names:

Adler	"eagle"
Bar, Beer, Berman	"bear"
Fink	"finch"
Fuchs	"fox"
Geier	"vulture"

Hahn	"rooster"
Hart	"stag"
Hirsch	"stag"
Lowe	"lion"
Ochs	"ox"
Wolf	"wolf"

Examples of Jewish surnames possibly from physical characteristics:

Alt	"old"
Braun	"brown"
Gelber, Geller	"yellow"
Gross	"large"
Jung	"young"
Klein	"small"
Kurtz	"short"
Neu	"new"
Reise	"giant"
Roth	"red"
Schnell	"fast"
Schon	"beautiful"
Schwartz	"black"
Stark	"strong"
Steinhart	"hard as stone"

Personal Names

Ever since the first humans, Adam and Eve, people have had personal names. A great amount of significance has always been given to names, beginning in the Bible, when we witness, among others, Abram becoming Abraham, Sarai becoming Sarah, and Jacob becoming Israel. The change of one's name, in this biblical setting, symbolizes a major change in one's personality and one's being.

Throughout history we find similar examples of customs and beliefs that reflect the seriousness with which we have looked on names. Popular in the Middle Ages and still practiced among many in modern times is the custom of changing the name of a person who is seriously ill in the hope that the Angel of Death would be confused and be unable to locate the person. One of the most popular names given at this time was Chaim, meaning "life," in order to add still another significance to names. The power of this custom is reflected in my own family. As I described earlier in this book, my father was renamed Chaim because he was very ill as a young child. When he grew

up, his parents told him of this, and he has in turn told me. This story of my father's "renaming" became a favorite of mine as a child. It was a deeply powerful story for me, inspiring my imagination to envision the Angel of Death, the renaming ceremony, and a young child (who grows up to be my father) getting well after a prolonged illness. Stories, as well as names, can have a profound effect on a person. This custom, which is known as *meshanneh shem,* is mentioned in the Talmud (Rosh Hashanah 17a).

The same type of belief is found in a custom that was described in *Sefer Hasidim,* by Judah the Pious. He forbade his immediate descendants from bearing his name or the name of his father during their lifetime in the belief that since a man's soul was bound up with his name, the soul would be deprived of its rest if someone else bore it. Although this is not a universally accepted custom, it is generally true that Jewish children are not named after living relatives. Among the reasons for this custom is that the Angel of Death might be unnecessarily confused and might take the wrong person. Finally, the custom of naming children after relatives who are deceased is based on the notion that to do this would be an honor to the deceased. It is also an attempt to "inject" the child with the qualities of the deceased.

It has been customary to name children after deceased relatives or other individuals who are greatly respected. It is common, for example, to name a child after a man's teacher. In European Jewish communities it also became common to name the eldest son after the paternal or maternal grandfather. Because of this, it is curious to examine the repetition of a certain few names over the course of many generations. For example, in one family we find the following: "Meshullam b. Moses b. Ithiel b. Moses b. Kalonymus b. Meshullam b. Kalonymus b. Moses b. Kalonymus b. Jekuthiel b. Moses b. Meshullam b. Ithiel b. Meshullam." The interesting aspect of this genealogy is that among the fourteen people who span three centuries, we find only five names.

Ever since I can remember, the notion that I was named after someone has intrigued me and captured my imagination. I learned at a young age that I was named for my great-grandfather Abusch, and I have been drawn to him in a somewhat mystical way. Through stories that I have solicited about my great-grandfather, I have developed a personal relationship with him that I find difficult to describe.

As we have seen in our discussion of surnames, there was a time when individuals had only one name. Then the surname was introduced, and it became universal. Today many Jews have three names: a first name, a surname, and an additional first name. Many Jews have secular and Hebrew first names. At various points in history, depending on the location, Jews

began to use secular first names. This inspired the custom of giving Jewish children separate Hebrew first names to use during religious ceremonies and for religious purposes. Naming ceremonies have developed for just this purpose.

In modern times, two occurrences of note relating to names have been witnessed among Jews. The first is the changing of names, sometimes without the consent of the individual, during the days of great immigration at U.S. ports. There are many stories, some of them fictitious, of name changes that occurred when an immigration official "renamed" a Jewish immigrant by mistake or on purpose. Of course, it usually happened that immigrants would change their names without such "assistance." The motive for this voluntary change of names might relate to another phenomenon, the adopting of new names by individuals who move to Israel, symbolic gestures that may very well reflect a belief in the power of names. When a name changes, a person changes. It is customary for a new Israeli to abandon his or her original name, often of European origin, and replace it with a new one. Sometimes the new name is a Hebrew translation or interpretation of the European name. For example, I've been told that an Israeli relative of the well-known Yiddish writer Isaac Bashevis Singer has the name Zamir (Hebrew for *singer*). Golda Meir, former prime minister of Israel, came to Israel from Milwaukee, where her family name was Myerson. Sometimes, however, the name chosen is a modern Hebrew name that has no relationship to the original.

For Whom Were You Named?

In my family, I am named after my great-grandfather, my father is named after his great-grandfather, and my grandfather is named after his grandfather. My mother was named after her great-aunt. My brother was named after another great-grandfather, and that great-grandfather was named after his own father's rebbe. My first daughter was named after two great-grandmothers (of hers), my second daughter was named after her great-great-great-grandmother and her great-grandmother, and my son was named after a great-grandfather and a great-great-great-great-grandfather of his!

For whom were you named? What do you know about the person? Why did your parents name you after that person rather than someone else?

Speaking of being named after people, often an older relative will not remember who his or her great-grandparents were until you ask, "Who were you named after?" There's a good chance they were named after the great-grandparent whom they couldn't remember.

You can also try to figure out the names of people early in your family tree by noticing the names that keep repeating. Although you cannot come to any definite conclusions with this method, a repeating name might jolt someone's memory about an early ancestor with the same name.

———————— o ————————

One's name has an influence on one's life.

—Eleazer ben Pedat, Talmud, Berakot 7b

———————— o ————————

What if Your Name Was Changed?

We have all heard stories of how Jewish names were often changed, shortened, or misspelled. If there is no one to ask or no one who remembers what the original name was, how can you find out the original name?

It is, of course, important to discover what your name was in the old country, because without this knowledge it will be impossible for you to bridge the ocean and find out about relatives and ancestors who never came to America.

If your last name is not the same as the one your family used before coming to America, and if there is no one who knows what that original name was, there are some possible ways to discover your original name—assuming that it was changed after your immigrant ancestors arrived in America.

Begin by locating your immigrant ancestors' steamship passenger list, described elsewhere in this book. Follow the directions for the various ways of obtaining the name of the ship and its date of arrival. If you send for a copy of the passenger list for your immigrant ancestor, it will contain his or her original name, since these lists were usually drawn up before the ship sailed—that is, before arrival in America when the name was changed.

Of course, when you get the passenger list, you will not find the name you know. Therefore, you will have to be a detective and try to determine who on the list was your ancestor. There are many ways of doing this because the lists will offer various clues to work with, including the person's place of birth, occupation, and age. Something ought to match—and you will then discover what your name was originally!

Names changes, both voluntary and involuntary, present obvious problems for genealogists. If a person has his or her name changed, it is almost impossible at times to locate the individual. A woman who marries and takes her husband's last name suddenly disappears from the records under

her original name. An immigrant who either changes or shortens his own name or who has his name changed by an immigration official also cuts himself off from the family history

○

Properly, I ought to begin this account by telling when I was born. But—I am ashamed to admit it—I do not know. You see, I was only a Jewish girl, and in my day and time, in the place where I was born, female births were not recorded.

—Rebecca Himber Berg, *Childhood in Lithuania*

○

Names as Clues to Dates

It has been a Jewish tradition for many generations to name a child after a deceased member of the family or a deceased member of a community who is well respected—such as a rebbe or teacher—so names can in fact help you determine dates.

Let me illustrate this by using an example. Look at the following family tree, and notice the dates of birth indicated for the children named Abraham. As you can see, there is no date listed for the children's grandfather, who is also named Abraham.

It is clear from this three-generation family tree that the four families all named a child Abraham, undoubtedly after the grandfather. They all

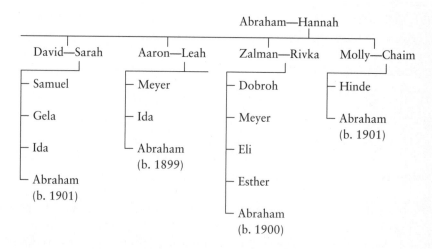

A three-generation family tree.

named a child Abraham about the same time, although the earliest date was 1899. If this example represents a typical family in Europe, all four families probably named their next child after the death of Abraham. Since a child cannot, by tradition, be named after a living person, it is safe to assume that the grandfather died before 1899, and probably in that year or the year before.

Although you cannot know this for sure and cannot know the exact date, it is reasonable to write "ca. 1899" on your family tree. The abbreviation *ca.* stands for *circa*, which means "approximately."

Using this method, it is often possible to figure out older dates from the dates—and names—you already have.

---------- o ----------

What is a good pedigree? A good name.

—Al-Harizi, *Tahkemoni*, c. 1220

---------- o ----------

Last Names from the Maternal Side

As noted before, you should not assume that children always took the last name of their father or that when a couple got married, they took the husband's last name. Often the woman's surname continued to be used. One reason, explained earlier, was the fact that religious marriages were sometimes not recognized as legitimate by civil authorities, so officially both mother and child continued to be known by the mother's maiden name. Another reason is the fact that at various times and places, laws were passed that limited Jewish marriages, making it necessary for Jews to get married secretly. Again, the children of these marriages were considered illegitimate under civil law and were therefore recorded under the mother's name.

Hebrew, Yiddish, and English Names

Most Jews have two names: a secular name and a religious name. The secular name is in the language of the country where the person resides, and the religious name is Hebrew.

Many immigrants had three names: a Hebrew name, an English name, and a Yiddish name. This is because they had two names in Europe (the Yiddish was their secular name), and they adopted an additional secular name on arrival in America. My grandfather, for example, was Julius (English), Yudl (Yiddish), and Yehudah Yaakov (Hebrew-religious).

When charting your family tree, you will come across different names for the same people—sometimes even more than three when nicknames are also used. It has been my practice to record all the names used rather than to "standardize" them. I have seen Jewish genealogies where all Abes, Abbies, and Abrahams became Abraham. It's more important to record a person's name as it was used from day to day than to suddenly become formal when building a family tree. Keep track of all the names used, and when deciding which name to use on a family tree, use the one that was most common or the one that the person himself or herself liked, if you know.

○

One thing is certain: I have no real feeling about my first name. I can only guess why this is. It seems to me that it may be because my parents gave it to me without any particular feeling, simply because they "liked it" (and why did they like it? because at that time it was "different"; only later were there other Franzes in the Jewish community of Cassel). It's as though my parents had seen it in a window shop, walked inside, and bought it. It has nothing traditional about it, no memory, no history, not even an anecdote, scarcely a whim—it was simply a passing fancy. A family name, a saint's name, a hero's name, a poetic name, a symbolic name, all these are good: they have grown naturally, not been bought ready-made. One should be named after somebody or something. Else a name is really only empty breath.

—Franz Rosenzweig

○

Sources for Determining the Meanings of Names

The first serious book written in English to attempt a study of Jewish surnames that included a large number of names with their meanings appeared in 1977. *A Dictionary of Jewish Names and Their History*, by Benzion Kaganoff, was the result of a hobby that Rabbi Kaganoff had pursued for decades. The first half of the book is a history of Jewish surnames; the second half is a listing of nearly one thousand Jewish names with their probable meanings.

In the same year as Rabbi Kaganoff's book appeared, Garland Publishing issued *Jewish and Hebrew Onomastics: A Bibliography*, by Robert Singerman. It is out of print, but it would be a worthwhile book to consult if you were particularly interested in the subject of the origins and forms of names.

There are a number of excellent books on the subject of Jewish names. Alexander Beider, one of the world's leading experts on Jewish names, has written the first three titles on my list. Beider has been studying the etymology and geographical distribution of Russian Jewish family names since 1986. Beider, who has a Ph.D. in applied mathematics, is a Russian émigré who lives in France, where he is a computer scientist. It is relevant to note that Beider was given a standing ovation at the close of his talk in New York City in July 1992 at the Eleventh Seminar on Jewish Genealogy.

Here is my list of recommended sources.

A Dictionary of Ashkenazic Given Names: Their Origins, Structure, Pronunciation, and Migrations, by Alexander Beider (Avotaynu). This book is the most comprehensive compilation and analysis of Ashkenazic given names ever published. In its 728 pages, the author identifies more than fifteen thousand given names derived from just 735 root names. Each root name includes a detailed description of the origin (etymology) of the name, a list of the variant and derivative names displayed in a scheme that reveals how the variants evolved, and references to variations of the root names throughout the centuries—some as far back as the eleventh century. An index to the fifteen thousand variations guides you to the proper root name. Also included in this book is a 300-page thesis on the origins, structure, pronunciation, and migrations of Ashkenazic given names.

A Dictionary of Jewish Surnames from the Russian Empire, by Alexander Beider (Avotaynu). Beider spent six years researching this book in Moscow, Saint Petersburg, and Paris. The result is a 752-page compilation of fifty thousand Jewish surnames from the Russian Pale of Settlement (excluding the Kingdom of Poland). It provides the etymology, along with variants and indications of where in the Russian Empire the name appeared. The ninety-page introduction defines the origin and evolution of Jewish surnames from this area.

A Dictionary of Jewish Surnames from the Kingdom of Poland, by Alexander Beider (Avotaynu). This compilation includes more than 32,000 Jewish surnames with origins in the part of the Russian Empire known as the Kingdom of Poland. The book provides information on where in the Kingdom of Poland the name was prevalent at the turn of the twentieth century, all likely etymologies of the name, and spelling variants and derivatives. A soundex index makes it simple to locate a given surname with its proper Polish spelling. The introductory portion of the book describes the origins and evolution of Polish Jewish surnames.

Russian-Jewish Given Names: Their Origins and Variants, by Boris Feldblyum (Avotaynu). Based on a book published in Russia in 1911, this work presents to the English-speaking reader a comprehensive collection of Jewish given names used in Russia at the turn of the twentieth century—more than six thousand names in all. These names are also included in a dictionary of root names that shows the name's etymology and all variants of the names, identifying them as *kinnui* (everyday names), variants, or distortions. The introduction is a historical essay that reviews the evolution of Jewish given names from biblical times through the late nineteenth century in Russia.

Jewish Personal Names, by Rabbi Shmuel Gorr (Avotaynu). This book presents the roots of more than twelve hundred Jewish personal names. It shows all Yiddish and Hebrew variants of a root name, with English transliteration. The footnotes explain how these variants were derived. An index of all variants allows you to easily locate a name in the book.

○

Names were changed as readily as clothes. From Yacov (Hebrew) or Yankel (Yiddish) to Jacob and finally to Jack. From Hyman to Howard, Leybel to Lester or Leon, Berel to Barnett or Barry, Chai-Sura to Sarah, Breina to Beatrice, Simcha to Seymour, Chatzkel to Haskell, Meyer to Max, Moishe to Mossir, Aaron to Allan.

—Milton Meltzer, *Taking Root*

○

Some Additional Research Suggestions

Here is my list of recommendations regarding the tracing of Jewish personal names.

Back Issues of Avotaynu

I would strongly urge you to search through the index to back issues of *Avotaynu* for the many articles written on the fascinating topic of Jewish onomastics.

The Consolidated Jewish Surname Index (CJSI)

The Consolidated Jewish Surname Index (http://www.avotaynu.com/csi/csi-home.html) searches more than a half million different surnames, mostly Jewish, that appear in many different databases. Combined, these

databases include more than 2 million entries. By accessing the CJSI, you can determine which of these databases have Jewish names of interest.

The following databases searched through the CJSI:

Jewish Records Indexing—Poland (178,935 surnames). An index to more than 1.8 million Jewish birth, marriage, divorce, and death records located in the archives of Poland. An ongoing project, continuously updated. Online database.

Litvak SIG "All Lithuania" Database (29,930 surnames). 300,000 records from many different sources, including revision lists (censuses), vital records, and tax, voter, and cemetery lists. An ongoing project, continuously updated. Online database.

"All Belarus" Database (33,015 surnames). 200,000 records from many different sources, including vital records, voter lists, business directories, and ghetto records. An ongoing project, continuously updated. Online database.

"All Latvia" Database (5,821 surnames). 62,000 records from many different sources, including vital records, voter lists, tax lists, recruitment records. An ongoing project, continuously updated. Online database.

JewishGen Family Finder (82,912 surnames). Surnames being researched by some 60,000 Jewish genealogists worldwide. An ongoing project, continuously updated. Online database.

Family Tree of the Jewish People (63,596 surnames). Names of 2 million individuals who appear on family trees being researched by Jewish genealogists. Based on the microfiche version published in 1998 and then known as the Jewish Genealogical People Finder. CD-ROM.

A Dictionary of Jewish Surnames from the Russian Empire (49,167 surnames). Surnames from the Pale of Settlement. Book.

A Dictionary of Jewish Surnames from the Kingdom of Poland (32,871 surnames). Surnames from the Kingdom of Poland. Book.

Sourcebook for Jewish Genealogies and Family Histories (10,287 surnames). Surnames for which there are published family histories and genealogies. Book.

Index to Russian Consular Records (38,534 surnames). 70,000 persons who transacted business with the Russian czarist consulates in the United States from about 1849 to 1926. Microfiche.

Belarus Surname Index (22,395 entries). Various lists of persons who resided in Belarus. An ongoing project, continuously updated. Online database.

Galicia Surname Index (5,721 entries). Various lists of persons who resided in Galicia. An ongoing project, continuously updated. Online database.

First American Jewish Families (4,762 surnames). Names of 50,000 descendants of Jewish-American families who arrived in America in the period 1654–1838. (Out of print.) Book.

Palestine Gazette (15,169 surnames). Names of 28,000 persons, mostly Jews, who legally changed their names while living in Palestine during the British Mandate (1921–1948). Microfiche.

Gedenkbuch (18,160 surnames). Names of 128,000 German Jews murdered in the Holocaust. Book.

Index to *Memorial to the Jews Deported from France* (26,307 surnames). Names of 70,000 Jews deported from France during the Holocaust. Microfiche.

National Registry of Jewish Holocaust Survivors (14,743 surnames). Names of 35,000 Holocaust survivors living in the United States and Canada. Book.

Sephardic Surnames (7,897 surnames). List of Sephardic surnames. Online database.

Also included in the search are other sources of Jewish surnames:

Emergency Passports (2,383 surnames). Names of 3,000 Jewish applicants for emergency U.S. passports, 1915–1924, processed by the U.S. State Department. Microfiche.

Index to State Department records found in the U.S. National Archives containing Jewish names in the section on protection of interests of U.S. citizens in Russia (3,104 surnames). 5,000 records. Microfiche.

Index to State Department records found in the U.S. National Archives involving the registration of U.S. citizens in Jerusalem, 1914–1918 (863 surnames). 1,000 records. Microfiche.

Index to State Department records found in the U.S. National Archives listing Jewish names in connection with the protection of the interests of U.S. citizens in Romania, Germany, and Poland, 1910–1929 (3,583 surnames). 4,500 records. Microfiche.

Index to State Department records found in the U.S. National Archives listing Jewish names in connection with the protection of the interests of U.S. citizens in Austria-Hungary, 1910–1930 (1,554 surnames). 2,000 records. Microfiche.

Jewish Surnames from Morocco (4,550 surnames). List of 4,644 different Moroccan surnames. Microfiche.

Jewish Burials in Hartford County, Connecticut (8,321 surnames). Records of 13,000 burials. Book.

Jewish Surnames from Prague (1,050 surnames). Ancient Ashkenazic surnames from the fifteenth through eighteenth centuries. Book.

Cleveland (Ohio) Burials (1,413 surnames). Online database.

Birth Index for Buda Jewry, 1820–1852, 1868 (523 surnames). Index to certain Jewish birth records for Buda, Hungary. Microfiche.

Obuda (Hungary) Census of 1850 (591 surnames). Census of all households in this district of Budapest. Microfiche.

Eliyahu's Branches: The Descendants of the Vilna Gaon and His Family (3,292 surnames). Compiled genealogy of more than 20,000 descendants of this great scholar. Book.

Surnames in the Lomza, Poland, Yizkor book (2,274 surnames). Online database.

ROM-SIG Family Finder Surnames (and towns) being researched by members of ROM-SIG, the Romanian Jewish genealogy special interest group (1,957 surnames). Online database.

Poor Jews Temporary Shelter (24,872 surnames). A social service facility in London designed to meet the needs of Jews who were coming to or passing through London founded in 1885. Online database.

Project for the Study of Jewish Names

This scholarly effort has produced conferences and publications. Write to

Professor Aaron Demsky
Director, Project for the Study of Jewish Names
Department of Jewish History
Bar-Ilan University
52900 Ramat-Gan, Israel
e-mail: demskya@mail.biu.ac.il
fax: (972-3) 535-1233

Also learn more about the project at the Bar-Ilan University Web site (http://www.biu.ac.il/Spokesman/scholar/names.html).

----------o----------

There are men whose names are beautiful but their acts ugly.

—Genesis Rabbah

----------o----------

Information on Jewish Names from JewishGen.org

In the section of JewishGen.org called "InfoFiles" (http://www.jewishgen.org/InfoFiles) there is a subdivision called "Names" that contains some terrific sources. Of particular note are the following:

"The Names of the Jews: A Preliminary FAQ," by Joachim Mugdan, Institute of General Linguistics, University of Münster, Germany (http://www.jewishgen.org/infofiles/namfaq0.htm). The author's professional training and passion for the subject serve as a wonderful introduction to Jewish names.

"Bibliography of Jewish Given Names," compiled by Warren Blatt (http://www.jewishgen.org/infofiles/GivenNames/biblio.html). Warren Blatt, who serves as editor in chief of JewishGen.org, has put together a superb bibliography.

Some Final Thoughts About Jewish Names

People with the same last name are not necessarily related. If someone in your family says, "Everyone with our last name is related," the person may very well be mistaken. This goes for even the most unusual last name.

Most Jewish last names were not changed at Ellis Island. In most cases, immigration officials had the immigrant's name in writing, so most of the stories and jokes about how the official couldn't understand the name are fiction! Many immigrants changed their names voluntarily after arriving in this country, often at the encouragement of relatives who were already here or on schoolteachers' advice to new students or some such circumstance.

In Eastern Europe, especially among the more religious families, a child might take the surname of the mother rather than the father. This sometimes explains why you will see that a father and a son had a different last name. As noted earlier in this chapter, the last name of the mother was often imposed by the secular authorities because the public records did not indicate that a marriage had taken place. In other cases,

people voluntarily took the name of the mother rather than the father for one reason or another. In my own family, my great-grandfather, Asher Yshiya Gottlieb, used the name of his mother, probably because it is an illustrious rabbinic name (his grandfather was Rabbi Chaim Yosef Gottlieb, the Stropkover Rebbe).

Sometimes you will find that siblings, especially boys, have different last names. Sometimes this was the result of conscription laws. For example, if the law read that the firstborn son was to be drafted, a child was represented as someone else's child to avoid the situation.

Never assume that there is only one way to spell your last name. You have to look for all sorts of variations. I've seen my last name spelled Kurzweil, Kurtzweil, Kursweil, Kurzwell, Kurzwiel, Curzweil, and Kirzweil, to name a few.

You can't assume from your name that you know where your family was from. My last name is an authentic German word, but my family was not from Germany. Instead, my family was from a part of Poland that was once in the Austrian Empire, and it is for this reason that the name is German.

You can't assume that just because you have the same last name as someone in history, you are a descendant. For example, if your name is Rottenberg, you can't assume that you descend from Rabbi Meir of Rothenberg.

○

A Conversation with Alexander Beider

Alexander Beider was born in Moscow in 1963 into a family whose roots were mainly from the eastern Ukraine. The only exception was his paternal grandmother, Chana Tziva Zeitlin, who was a librarian and whose father was a teacher of Hebrew in a shtetl in eastern Byelorussia (Belarus). Beider's interest in Jewish history and culture grew under her direct influence. In college, at the Russian equivalent to MIT, he studied mathematics and theoretical physics. He has lived in Paris since 1990. In France, he has worked for Enterprise Resource Planning, first as a programmer and later as a trainer and consultant. For nearly two decades, Beider has spent much of his free time studying the etymologies of Jewish names and their ability to shed light on the history of Ashkenazic migrations and the history of the Yiddish language. Several books that he has written on this subject have been published by Avotaynu, Inc. In 2000, Beider received a Ph.D. in Jewish studies from the Sorbonne.

Q. You are recognized as perhaps the leading expert on Jewish onomastics in the world. Do you think that's a fair judgment?

A. During the 1990s I came across two statements in which people were proclaiming themselves as "the world authorities" on the subject of Jewish names. The first came from the pen of one professor of linguistics from Haifa University. The second was signed by the heads of the research department of the Tel Aviv Museum of the Diaspora (Beit Hatefutsot). Generally speaking, I feel uneasy about such judgments. I'm a scholar. My aim is not to sell as many copies of my books as possible but to come to conclusions that can be considered reliable by other people. As a result, any appreciation should necessarily come from outside, not from myself.

A few years ago, a group of people from Oxford University Press was preparing a four-volume study titled *A Dictionary of American Family Names*. When they asked me to be their expert on Jewish names, this indeed was a judgment from the outside. I agreed because (1) their principles for the search of etymologies were very close to my approach and (2) I felt myself able to provide reliable information because a very large portion of American Jews had their roots in Eastern Europe. To be accurate, I would define myself as "an expert"—I prefer the indefinite article—on surnames from the area that belonged to the prepartition Polish-Lithuanian Commonwealth and Ashkenazic traditional first names. In other words, my expertise does not cover large branches of Jewish onomastics. For example, I'm not at all a specialist of Sephardic or Oriental names, and my knowledge of surnames used by German, Alsatian, and Hungarian Jews is rather poor.

Q. What were some of the major shortcoming of the study of Jewish surnames in the past? How have you changed that?

A. Until just a few decades ago, Jews from Eastern Europe and their descendants were not interested at all in their surnames, imposed on their ancestors by Christian authorities two hundred years ago. They considered these appellations to be simple labels used in official, non-Jewish documents. In this context, it is not a surprise that numerous people changed their last names when leaving Eastern Europe. On the other hand, for persons who continued to live in the same general area, and specifically for Soviet citizens, it was rather difficult to perform any study on names or on any other subject related to Jewish matters due to the general anti-Semitic nature of the country after World War II. Avrom Pribluda

compiled the only book written on this topic in Russian in 1971. Despite the absence of any political element in his very accurate study, the book was never authorized for publication. Its main drawback, which also characterizes several general studies that appeared later in the West (I mean the books by Kaganoff and Guggenheimers, as well as the studies by David L. Gold) was the absence of direct links between the suggested etymologies of surnames and their geography. In my studies, I regularly applied the geographic approach, trying to identify the small area where this or that name appeared for the first time. This allowed for determinations as to whether all bearers of the same name were related or not and especially helped explain the origins of numerous surnames derived from the names of villages and small towns. To put this method into practice, before going to the etymologies, I needed to compile large representative lists of names, locating them in the places where they were originally assigned. Fortunately, I was able to discover sources of this kind, mainly in official Russian newspapers from the beginning of the twentieth century. A detailed study of the historical aspects of the mass assignment of surnames (including the texts of the corresponding laws, the circumstances under which they were put in practice, Jewish occupations of that time, and so on) represents another important element of my approach.

Q. Is the situation with the first names similar?

A. The case of first names is different. Contrary to the case with surnames, there are several important studies on this subject that existed before that can without any hesitation be labeled "scholarly." These include the historical method introduced in 1837 by Leopold Zunz in his classical work *Namen der Juden,* the purely linguistic approach suggested in 1969 by Edward Stankiewicz, the deep insights into the etymologies provided by Siegmund Salfeld in 1898, and Max Weinreich's various publications. I have just tried to synthesize these approaches. I have also had a chance to compile and analyze many more representative lists of references to Jewish first names in sources published by historians and archivists of different countries.

Q. Let's show readers just how you work with some personal examples. Please share your thought processes, the sources that you would consult, and your advice to someone like me who is interested but does not have you to ask. Using myself as an

example—my last name is Kurzweil and my family is from Przemysl in southeastern Poland. What can you tell me about the name?

A. In this specific case, the direct source (*etymon*) for the last name is doubtless the identical common noun that exists in German, which means "pastime," "diversion," "amusement"—literally, "short time." It is much more difficult to address the question of why this word was chosen to construct the surname. Without direct genealogical evidence, the answer is totally hypothetical. Since my first book dealt with the Russian Pale of Settlement, I first came across references to this name in the Berdichev and Uman districts of eastern Ukraine. In that area numerous names were constructed from personal characteristics, while the number of artificial names, constructed without any relationship to real characteristics of the first bearer, was rather small. As a result, for the entries Kurtsvajl and Kurtsvejl' (alternative transliterations from German to Russian and later from Cyrillic to Latin characters), I suggested that this name too could be derived from personal nicknames. When working on my second book, which dealt with Polish names, I came across this name only in Warsaw during the twentieth century. This information clearly implied that the surname was unlikely to have originated in the Kingdom of Poland: its bearer most likely came to the Polish capital city from another country. As a result, I said in the entry Kurcwajl (the Polish spelling of the same name) that the name could be artificial or derived from some personal characteristics or even occupational. In the last case I implicitly thought about the occupation called *batkhn,* a word from the Hebrew component of Yiddish, designating entertainers at Jewish weddings. During my recent work on Galician names, I discovered that it was in Galicia that the name Kurzweil was really common. References to its bearers were found during the nineteenth century in all parts of Galicia and specifically in the Krakow, Tarnow, Tarnobrzeg, Nisko, Przemysl, Jaroslaw, Lvov, Dobromil, and Tarnopol districts. Taking into account this geography, I'm now thinking that several families acquired this name independently of one another at the end of the eighteenth century in Galicia. Its bearers in the Ukraine and Poland most likely descended from Galician branches of this family; note that both the Berdichev and Uman' communities were large and certainly included a number of migrants from other regions. As the word Kurzweil is specifically German and has no phonetically close equivalent in Yiddish, the

surname was most likely assigned by Austrian clerks and not chosen by its first bearers, the latter being native speakers of Yiddish
not yet acculturated to German. Of course, in any one particular
family this name could be either occupational (for example, wedding entertainer) or even derived from some personal characteristics: the Jew to whom this surname was given could "entertain" the
Christian official who chose the name. But the same circumstances
could not apply to all independent Kurzweil families from Galicia.
I'm now considering the artificial derivation as the most plausible
hypothesis. This is due to several factors. First, the proportion of
artificial surnames in Galicia was extremely high. Second, in the
same Przemysl we also find a very close name, Kurzweg ("short
way"), for which artificial origin is more than likely. Third, in several towns of Galicia we also find the name Langweil, "boring time"
(literally, "long time"), representing the direct antonym to Kurzweil
and being necessarily artificial as well. Of course, in my books I do
not present all these arguments explicitly; only the geography, the
direct etymon, and the hypothesis about the type (artificial in this
case) are presented. The foregoing discussion just illustrates my way
of thinking.

Q. One of my daughters is named Pesha Malya. What can you
tell me about each of these first names? Are these names dealt with in
your books? Can a Hebrew spelling be determined for each name?

A. Pesha (or Peshe, as it was pronounced in Yiddish) was
known only in Polish Jewish communities. I was unable to find any
reference to this form before the nineteenth century. It is derived
from Pese via the addition of the Polish Yiddish diminutive suffix
-she also found in numerous other (mainly female) names from
Poland: Dvoshe (Deborah), Khashe (Hannah), and Mashe are
examples. Pese, in turn, is related to Peslin, a Jewish form already
popular in southern Germany at the end of the thirteenth century.
It arose in that area due to the confusion between the sounds /b/
and /p/ peculiar to local German dialects. The morphologically
more correct form, Bes(e)lin, and its variant Betzelin are often present at the same period in the communities situated more to the
north: Cologne and Frankfurt. Finally, the last forms were created
by Jews from the biblical Bathsheba (the wife of King David and
the mother of Solomon) via the addition of the diminutive suffix
-lin, standard to the Jewish tongue at that period, this addition
being accompanied by the change of the root vowel from /a/ to /e/,

a morphological phenomenon known in German and Yiddish as *umlaut*. Almost the whole of Ashkenazic history can be seen by just studying this name!

Mala (Male in Yiddish) was a common name in various parts of Poland during the nineteenth century. We also find several references to it in Germany during the eighteenth century and even one reference in Prague in 1407. However, one cannot be sure the Czech, German, and Polish forms are directly related. For example, Mala or Male does not appear at all on the tombstones of the Prague and Frankfurt cemeteries. The unique reference from the fifteenth century could in principle be a nickname, meaning "small" in Czech, and not necessarily a first name. The rare German references could be related to the German Christian name Mala, a short form of Amalia. In Poland, Male is most likely derived from Malke (from the Hebrew for "queen"), in the same way as Rive is derived from Rivke (the Yiddish version of the biblical Rebecca).

As both of these names are not taken directly from Hebrew, their Hebrew spelling is somewhat conventional. For example, Rabbi Abraham Lavot from Ukraine suggested in 1868 to spell the first one as פעשא. I was unable to find any reference to Male in Hebrew sources. All the information given here was extracted from my book *A Dictionary of Ashkenazic Given Names,* published in 2001.

Q. How did you get started with the subject of Jewish names? What do you think it is that draws you to it so strongly?

A. As a teenager, after interviewing my various relatives, I compiled a genealogical tree of my family covering four to six generations and several hundreds of cousins. When I looked at this tree recently, I realized that the only information I put on it was names: first names, last names, and the town names, but no occupations, no dates, nothing else. Clearly the subject already fascinated me. My acute interest in names extended well beyond the Jewish sphere: I remember that from the ages of 11 to 13 I knew by heart the names of numerous Canadian players of the National Hockey League and several leading Soviet hockey teams, as well as hundreds of names of the best soccer players. During the same time I was also totally fascinated with the etymologies of place names. My first "scholarly" work, compiled at the age of 13, was a large notebook where I put the origins of names of various countries and

towns, obviously not discovered by me but extracted from different published sources. I have no idea about the origins of these interests. My third keen interest as a teenager concerned general Jewish history. It resulted from both my grandmothers' influence and my internal protest against the anti-Semitism of the Soviet state. Taking all this into account, it is easy to understand why I rapidly grew so excited when I started in 1986, rather by chance, my first investigations in Jewish onomastics: I finally found a domain in which all my previous "passions" (names, etymologies, and Jewish history) could be combined. Fortunately, at that moment I really had time to devote to my new passion. During the three years that followed, I was officially preparing for a Ph.D. in mathematics and for this reason had access to major Moscow libraries, making my pastime almost totally free. As a result, in 1989, when I received my Ph.D., a large part of my first book was already completed.

Q. Do you think there is a core reason why people interested in genealogy are involved with it?

A. This is a very difficult question, and professional psychologists should address it. Not being such a person, everything I can say on the subject should be taken with great caution: I have never thought about it deeply, and tomorrow my opinion on this subject could be totally different. Generally speaking, many people are fascinated by history. These topics allow you to go well beyond the world in which you live now, toward a world that, moreover, is not make-believe but actually existed decades, centuries, or millennia ago. Genealogy is the most intimate part of this general interest. It relates us not to abstract people but to our own roots, linking epochs and countries via the generations of our own family, that is, people to which our own existence is directly due. It allows us to understand many aspects of our personality, inherited, both genetically and culturally, from our ancestors. Through this study people can start to see themselves not as separate elements that came to this world "fortuitously" but as essential elements of a long chain of human beings who lived on our earth, loved, suffered, thought. . . . However, even though I really believe in the spiritual matters I have mentioned, I cannot keep myself from asking another question. According to statistics, the two domains where the largest number of laypeople are involved are stamp collecting and genealogy. What really fascinates stamp

collectors? I have no answer. This means that my ideas concerning genealogy can also be just explanations ad hoc, without any real basis.

Q. Are there any other books in addition to yours that you would consider part of an essential library on the topic of Jewish names?

A. I very much like the book *Les noms des juifs du Maroc,* by Abraham Laredo (1978) about the surnames of Moroccan Jews. As I have no special knowledge about Sephardic Jews, so I cannot really appreciate the reliability of the etymologies suggested. Nevertheless, the general structure of this work, with large amounts of genealogical information concerning various families, as well as the awareness that the author was knowledgeable in Arabic and Hebrew, make me think it is of good general quality. In the arena of German Jewish onomastics, currently the best references are the books by E. M. Dreifuss, *Die Familiennamen der Juden* (1927), which mainly concentrates on surnames from Baden, and *Stammbuch der Frankfurter Juden,* by A. Dietz (1907), presenting genealogical information about the Jewish families from Frankfurt. I believe it exists in English translation. A few months ago I was able to see parts of the manuscript being prepared by Lars Meck, which covers all of Germany. I was very impressed by the comprehensiveness of the collection of sources taken into account by its author in compiling the book. It will soon by published by Avotaynu, Inc., and to my mind it has the capacity to immediately become the standard English-language book on German Jewish family names.

For those interested in Jewish first names, I would recommend *Les noms des Juifs de France au Moyen Âge,* by Simon Seror (1989), which complements my own study of Ashkenazic first names by way of an excellent dictionary of appellations used by French Jews in the Middle Ages. A number of valuable scholarly books, Jewish and Christian, cover the names from the Bible. Among popular sources written for laymen, I particularly appreciate *The Complete Dictionary of English and Hebrew First Names,* by Alfred J. Kolatsch, which generally provides accurate information about names of Semitic origin.

It might seem strange, but I would also recommend the book on last names written by Benzion Kaganoff. In contrast to the other reference books I have mentioned, it has the merit of being

written in an easy-to-read style. Of course, the information it pos-
sesses can't really be considered reliable—the error rate is rather
high. Nevertheless, this kind of popular literature, merely by virtue
of the themes it addresses, can be an excellent avenue for getting
laypeople interested in the topic of Jewish names and encouraging
them to study these or other aspects of Jewish cultural history
more deeply.

○

9

HOLOCAUST RESEARCH

CHANGING NUMBERS INTO NAMES

IT OFTEN SEEMS TO ME that the phrase "Six million Jews were murdered in the Holocaust" slips out of our mouths too quickly, too easily, and too often even thoughtlessly. We speak the number as if we know what six million human beings really means. As if we can understand such proportions of death through murder. The number seems unfathomable.

Even the word *murdered* seems to be spoken without much difficulty, as if we can grasp those murders, as if they are calculable. We say "murdered," but we do not mean simply murdered. Not like the killings we see so often depicted on television and on the movie screen, where life is taken every few moments without pause.

And that word *Holocaust*. Its nine letters are supposed to add up to the six million murdered, as if a word, any word, can grasp, can include, can measure the loss, the tragedy, the meaning of what happened.

---
o

Six million Jewish people is one Jewish person six million times.

---
o

Six million Jews were murdered in the Holocaust.

Yes. But it was more than that.

There are no graves for the victims. No markers stand as their memorials. Yes, throughout the world there are monuments, museums, posters, plaques, statues, and sculptures commemorating their lives and paying tribute to them. But who were they? Who were the "six million murdered in the Holocaust"?

We have labeled the murders, added them up, written about them as if they were a phenomenon, but do most of us know the names of the members of our families who were stolen from us and killed?

And what should we tell our children? How should we explain to those who do not remember the event or, as time goes by, are farther and farther removed from it? In what way should we keep the memory alive?

Elie Wiesel taught a course on the Holocaust that he invited me to attend at City College in New York. One day a student asked, "What shall we tell our children?"

"And what if they don't believe us?" a girl in the class added.

"They won't," a third student answered. "I'm convinced that in a few years, a few generations, it will all be forgotten."

"I am not sure I can agree," Wiesel said. "I have heard a theory, a fascinating, intriguing theory. Irving Greenberg told me this. He said that when one considers the Exodus of the Hebrews from Egypt, to those Hebrews, their exodus did not have much of an impact. But consider the impact it has had since. Consider the impact of the Exodus on Jews today. This observation might be applied to the Holocaust. Who can know? It may be the same."

"But since we weren't there, what should we say to the next generation?" a young man asked. "You have said that we will never understand what happened. If so, how can we tell people about it?"

Eti and Gizi Gottlieb, in Bistritz, Romania, 1929. Relatives of the author, they were both murdered during the Holocaust.

"Yes," Wiesel said. "You will never know. But you will know that there was something. You will know one incident. One tear. That will be yours to tell."

Wiesel went on. "In my books, I don't like to repeat stories. Once I did. One story I told in two books."

He then told the legend, a Hasidic tale. It was a tale that contained many of the Hasidic Masters. It began with the founder of Hasidism, the Baal Shem Tov, the "Master of the Good Name," known as the Besht. It seems that when there was a disaster about to strike, the Besht went to a certain spot in the woods, lit a candle, and said a prayer—and the disaster was prevented. Then a disciple of his was faced with a disaster. He knew where the special spot in the woods was located, he knew how to light the candle, but he did not know the prayer. But the disaster was averted. Then another disciple was faced with calamity. He knew where the spot in the woods was located, but he did not know how to light the candle, and he did not know the prayer. But the disaster was prevented. Then a final disciple was faced with a disaster. He did not know how to light the candle, he did not know how to say the prayer, and he did not know where the spot in the woods was located. *All he knew was how to tell the story.* And in his case, too, the disaster was averted.

The Hasidic tale was instructive to the class, but Wiesel wanted to be even more explicit in response to the question. So when a student asked, "What is the story we should tell?" Wiesel responded, "In a few years, a very few years, there will not be one survivor left. Not a single survivor will be alive. Their numbers are decreasing at a very fast rate. Soon there will be no one who was there.

"What can you tell your children? Tell them that you knew the last survivors. As the survivors were alive when it happened, you were alive to hear their story. Tell them that—you knew the last survivors.

"They will listen. And they will ask the same question: What shall we tell our children? They will tell them: We knew people who knew the last survivors. We heard the story from people who heard the last survivors. The very last.

"And the question will again be asked. And the story will be told. Again and again, it will be told."

Wiesel looked with complete seriousness at his students.

"This is what we hope for," he said. "That it will be remembered. It is up to you."

The easiest way for the Holocaust to become nothing more than one more chapter in Jewish history is to be satisfied with an impersonal approach to the understanding of it. If we allow the murders of our people

Pinchas Gottlieb, a relative of the author who was murdered during the Holocaust.

to be "written up" in the history books, to be put on a shelf for future reference, we will be helping to forget. It is incumbent on us to remember. As Jews, we are a people of memory, a people whose history should be part of each of us. We cannot let the Holocaust become just another subject for books and articles and for monuments in cemeteries.

We have to make a personal connection with the Holocaust. Each of us must understand the Holocaust in the most personal of terms. Who was murdered? Where were they? What are their names? How old were they? Who were in their families? Where did they die? How did they die? What is their relationship to me?

It is not enough to know that "the Jews" were killed or that "six million were murdered" or even that "my people were slaughtered." We must try to find out who they were, these people of ours. We must know their names and their fates.

There are no gravestones for them. Our knowledge of them might be their finest memorial.

How do we discover who the victims were? How do we determine what their names were, when they were last heard from, or where they died? How do we find out what their relationship was to us?

The first step is to ask. Begin to make inquiries in your family as to who remained in Europe rather than immigrating to the United States,

Israel, or some other country. You will probably discover quite quickly that close members of your family were taken to death camps or murdered in their towns.

Often the best sources for this kind of information are survivors of the Holocaust. Inquire as to who in your family was there and survived, and arrange to talk to these relatives, or write to them if distance is too great. Don't delay. Often we are hesitant about talking to people who lived through the experience. We think that we will stir up old memories—as if survivors of the Holocaust have themselves forgotten about it. This is obviously not the case. Often survivors are silent for other reasons. As Elie Wiesel has said, "They are silent either because they are afraid you will not understand or because they are afraid you will understand."

Survivors of the Holocaust are also sometimes silent because they have not been asked. They feel that they do not want to volunteer the information but are waiting to be asked. Always remember the difficulty of speaking about the subject, but keep in mind its importance as well.

When you arrange to speak to a survivor in your family, ask if you can bring a tape recorder. Needless to say, a recording of the memories of a Holocaust survivor is important for future generations. If you become the one who helps keep the memory of the Holocaust alive, you will be performing a fine deed.

You will discover that people in your family who have survived the Holocaust will be knowledgeable about the people in your family who did not survive. The question "Why did I survive while they did not?" will surely have passed through many minds. Remember to record or write down the names of the Holocaust victims in your family and to determine their relationship to you. I suggest that you do this in the form of a family tree. Not only will this permit you to see more clearly the relationships among relatives, but the family tree will also become a memorial to these people.

Not only survivors, but also other family members, will remember people in your family who were killed. Often after the Holocaust, families in the United States made inquiries to try to locate family members. It was at this time that people began to discover who did not survive. Try to locate the people in your family who were involved with these inquiries. They will be your best resources for discovering the answers to your questions. You will watch the branches of your family tree grow as you are doing this research. Never forget, however, that if not for your inquiries and your research, the names that you are gathering would be lost. You are making an effort to keep the memory of these deaths and

The Kurzweil family in Dobromil, Poland. Of the twenty-one individuals shown, fourteen were murdered during the Holocaust.

of the Holocaust alive. It is one thing to know about "the six million" and quite another to have the names of the people who were in your family and were murdered.

I once naively thought that my family had escaped the Holocaust. It was my belief that since I was born in the United States and my parents were in the United States and even my grandparents were not in Europe during the war, our family "got out in time."

It was not until I found an old family photograph and asked my great-uncle to identify people in the picture that I realized how wrong I was. The photograph, taken in Poland, showed twenty-one people, including my great-grandfather, who also came to America, as well as my father, aunt, uncle, great-uncle, and grandmother. That added up to six people of the twenty-one whom I could recognize from the photograph. Who were the others?

I didn't think much about the other people in the photograph when I first found it. After all, my grandmother and her children were in it, and I knew all of them. Perhaps I was also preoccupied with the fact that my grandfather was not in the picture. He was already in America at the time, earning enough money to send for the rest of the family.

Yes, "the rest of the family." Since my grandmother and her three children were finally sent for five years after my grandfather came to America, I always assumed, as I said, that we "missed it."

Today I know the truth: in addition to the six people whom I recognized in the photograph, only one other person survived the Holocaust. The other fourteen people were murdered. Out of twenty-one family members, two-thirds were killed.

When I asked my great-uncle Sam who the other people in the picture were, he said, "This is my brother Elya, his wife Dobroh, and their two children. This is my brother Hersh, his wife Anna, and their five children. And this is my sister Reisl, her husband Shimon, and their two children. Only Mechel, the oldest son of Hersh and Anna, survived. You know him. The others were all killed."

As I looked at the photograph, I thought again of my grandfather in America, working to earn the money that would bring his wife and three children, one of whom was my father, to this country. Had my grandfather stayed, had he continued his life with his brothers and sisters in the town in which they were born and raised, his family, like the others, almost certainly would have been killed.

In all, at least 103 people in the Kurzweil family alone were murdered in the Holocaust. That's just one branch of my family.

And I thought we'd escaped it.

Holocaust Research: The Search for Victims and Survivors

Several years ago, for a few semesters, I taught a class at Queens College in New York City called "Research Methods in Jewish History." Basically, I had my students do Jewish genealogical research. On the first day of the semester, I asked the students to raise their hands if they knew of people in their families who were murdered during the Holocaust. Usually, not a hand went up. On the last day of class each semester, after a number of weeks of research, I asked the question again. Usually every hand was raised.

If you had a great-grandmother who had brothers and sisters, and if those brothers and sisters got married and had children who in turn had children, then you could have hundreds of second and third cousins who were murdered during the Holocaust.

The International Tracing Service

In 1943 the Committee on Displaced Populations of the Allied Post-War Requirement Bureau, located in London, observed the obvious: as

Belzec, Poland. Location of death camp where most of the Kurzweil family were murdered during the Holocaust.

a result of the war, and particularly because of persecution, extensive displacement of populations had occurred. The committee decided, therefore, to establish the National Tracing Bureau in different countries with the aim of locating people who were missing or who had been deported. In 1944 the Supreme Headquarters of the Allied Expeditionary Forces, known as SHAEF, gave orders to register all displaced persons on index cards, to aid in the location process. By 1945 SHAEF had established a tracing bureau that was given the task of collecting lists of names of displaced persons as well as persons incarcerated in concentration camps. This effort was aided by the United Nations Relief and Rehabilitation Administration (UNRRA) and was located in Versailles. Together, however, UNRRA and SHAEF relocated to Frankfurt am Main.

In July 1945, SHAEF was dissolved and the Combined Displaced Persons Executive, known as CDPX, established a collecting center for documents as well as a tracing bureau. This Central Tracing Bureau had as

its goals to trace missing persons—military and civilian—of United Nations member countries, as well as to collect and preserve all documents concerning non-Germans and displaced persons in Germany. It was also given the task of assisting in the reuniting of families that had been separated by the war.

In 1946 the Central Tracing Bureau moved from Frankfurt to Arolsen, Germany. It was renamed the International Tracing Service (ITS), as it is still called today. At present, and since 1955, the International Tracing Service has been directed and administered by the International Committee of the Red Cross.

Initially, this organization was involved mainly with displaced persons. However, when the ITS came into possession of concentration camp documents, the function of the organization changed. Suddenly, the ITS became involved with furnishing proof of deaths that occurred in the death camps. It is mainly this function of the ITS that concerns us here.

I have provided the historical background of the ITS to help explain why the major source of information on concentration camp victims is located in Germany. The ITS continues to receive hundreds of thousands of inquiries from all over the world and provides a free research service to all interested parties.

Basically, the ITS has the most acceptable information of concentration camp victims and displaced persons in the world. Yad Vashem, in the years 1955–1957, filmed the records that were available then and exclusively about Jewish victims of the Nazi regime. Since then, the ITS has acquired a lot of records (if placed in a single stack, the new documentary material would stand more than 800 feet high), especially after the political changes in Eastern Europe, so the information at Yad Vashem no longer corresponds to that of the ITS.

When you are in Israel, at Yad Vashem, you can use the ITS materials, including the Master Index, which is perhaps the most important item in the ITS archives. This index is a file, by name of individual, of all names appearing on all the documents in the archives. The reference cards include the name, personal data available, and a description of the document in which the name is mentioned. At present, this Master Index contains 45 million cards. It is interesting to note that the index is not filed alphabetically but rather in phonetic-alphabetical order to account for different spellings of the same surnames. Another rather remarkable resource used by the ITS in this regard is a two-volume set of books listing first names and their many variations. This is obviously useful for locating individuals. The list of first names contains about 55,000 forms of names.

The Master Index is, however, just the axle about which the collections within the archives revolve. A closer look at the contents of the archives will show how useful ITS can be.

The following materials are contained in the ITS archives:

- Indexes and name lists of concentration camps
- Indexes and name lists of Gestapo (secret police) and Sipo (security police) offices
- Name lists of persons
- Deportation lists of Jews
- Index cards and name lists of towns and communities, district magistrate offices, labor offices, health insurance firms, and so on, concerning foreigners who were registered during the war in Germany
- Index cards and name lists concerning children who had been separated from their parents or close relatives during the war or immediately after the war

Although the holdings of ITS archives are vast, the material is far from complete. For example, the concentration camp material in the archives is the largest, but it is not a collection of all concentration camp material that existed. The ITS rates the completeness of its concentration camp collection as follows:

Buchenwald	almost complete
Dachau	almost complete
Flossenburg	incomplete but quite numerous
Mauthausen	incomplete but quite numerous
Mittelbau	incomplete but quite numerous
Natzweiler	incomplete but quite numerous
Stutthof	incomplete but quite numerous
Niederhagen-Wewelsburg	incomplete but quite numerous
Ravensbrück	incomplete
Auschwitz	very incomplete
Gross-Rosen	incomplete
Sachsenhausen	incomplete
Neuengamme	incomplete
Lublin	incomplete
Krakow-Plaszow	very incomplete

According to the ITS, there are literally millions of individual documents in the collection just described.

Another collection of the ITS is the Post-War Documents, which generally concern displaced persons who were registered from 1945 to 1951. Included in these documents are lists of the inhabitants of the displaced persons camps.

The Historical Section of the ITS archives is also of great value. It contains documents of a more general nature, including materials on concentration camps, Jewish towns, Nuremberg trial records, and information on the persecution of Jews in different countries. If you are interested in certain Jewish communities in Europe during the Holocaust, you will find these archives at the ITS to be excellent.

The ITS is currently in the process of establishing a subject index to its concentration camp material for use by researchers. The "Register of Concentration Camps and Their Outlying Commandos Under the Reichsführer-SS in Germany and German-Occupied Territories, 1933–1945" has been compiled, but it is for internal ITS use only.

One might think that the "tracing" function of the ITS has outlived its usefulness, but in its 1999 annual report, the ITS noted that "in 1999, over 250,000 responses were given to former victims of persecution. That number is slightly lower than the 1998 figure on account of the efforts made to prepare for digitalization, but the shortfall should be largely offset by the advantages digitalization will provide." After more than thirty years, people are still looking for lost relatives—and are sometimes finding them. It is sad to note, of course, that often the ITS provides verification of the deaths of individuals in the concentration camps.

The ITS is also proving to be important for survivors who are in need of documentation of their Holocaust experiences, for reparation suits or other reasons.

Finally, the ITS has a staff who can make translations into German from Croatian, Czech, Danish, Dutch, Greek, Hungarian, Italian, Latvian, Polish, Romanian, Russian, Serbian, Spanish, and Ukrainian.

If you know the name of a relative and you want to find out his or her fate during the Holocaust, write to the ITS and provide as much information about the person as you can. The ITS requires more than just a name, since its files contain so many duplicate names. The ITS usually asks for a person's name and birthdate, but if you do not know that (even an approximate date will help), try to supply any other information that will narrow the field for the researcher.

What the ITS *will not* do is send you information on everyone in their files with a certain surname. Remember: it is a service for tracing *individuals*.

The ITS has all the available records kept by the Nazis at the concentration camps, but as I have noted, its collection is not complete. It also has a great number of other types of records. This means that its files include not only Holocaust victims who were killed but also others who survived.

As I have mentioned, the ITS also has information concerning the fate of towns during the Holocaust. Along with your inquiry pertaining to individuals, you might want to ask about certain localities.

When you write to the ITS, simply state that you are interested in knowing whatever can be found in its files on your family members and then list those individuals along with any additional information that might be helpful. The ITS, operating under the auspices of the International Red Cross, does not charge for its research—nor should it. Write to

> International Tracing Service
> Grosse Allee 5–9
> D-34444 Arolsen
> Germany

The Holocaust and War Victims Tracing Center

The American Red Cross will also help you in your search and in contacting the International Tracing Service. For many years I dealt directly with the ITS, but in 1990 the American Red Cross arranged to help searchers in the United States make contact with the ITS.

Go to the Web site of the Holocaust and War Victims Tracing Center of the American Red Cross at http://www.redcross.org/services/intl/holotrace. The site states:

> The Holocaust and War Victims Tracing Center is a national clearinghouse for persons seeking the fates of loved ones missing since the Holocaust and its aftermath. We assist U.S. residents searching for proof of internment, forced/slave labor, or evacuation from former Soviet territories on themselves or family members. This documentation may be required for reparations.
>
> • All of our tracing services are confidential and free of charge.
>
> • We pioneered a process with the International Tracing Service, which results in expedited replies to searches.
>
> • We use the worldwide network of more than 177 Red Cross and Red Crescent societies and the Magen David Adom in Israel.

- We also consult museums, archives, and international organizations to further facilitate tracing requests.

- Cases remain open, and if new information becomes available, it is immediately shared with the inquirer.

○

The one million Jewish children murdered in the Nazi Holocaust died not because of their faith, nor in spite of their faith, nor for reasons unrelated to faith. They were murdered because of the faith of their great-grandparents. Had these great-grandparents abandoned their Jewish faith, and failed to bring up Jewish children, then their fourth-generation descendants might have been among the Nazi executioners, but not among their Jewish victims. Like Abraham of old, European Jews sometime in the mid-nineteenth century offered a human sacrifice, by the mere minimal commitment to the Jewish faith of bringing up Jewish children. But unlike Abraham they did not know what they were doing, and there was no reprieve. This is the brute fact which makes all comparisons odious or irrelevant. This is the scandal of the particularity of Auschwitz which, once faced by the Jewish believer, threatens total despair.

—Emil L. Fackenheim

○

Yad Vashem

Yad Vashem is a national institution in Israel dedicated to perpetuating the memory of the victims of the Holocaust. Its stated goal is "to gather in material regarding all those Jewish people who laid down their lives, who fought and rebelled against the Nazi enemy and their collaborators, and to perpetuate their memory and that of the communities, organizations, and institutions which were destroyed because they were Jewish."

In addition to administering a museum devoted to the Holocaust, Yad Vashem is a research institution that collects material and publishes books and periodicals in Hebrew and English. Yad Vashem also aids in bringing Nazi war criminals to trial through the information it provides to legal authorities throughout the world.

The Yad Vashem Web site is http://www.yad-vashem.org.il.

Although Yad Vashem will not do research for individuals with general requests, one division is of great interest to those who wish to find information about Holocaust victims: the Hall of Names/Pages of Testimony

Division. Since 1955 Yad Vashem has been actively collecting "pages of testimony" in Israel and around the world. The primary goal of the Hall of Names at Yad Vashem is to receive, file, and store pages of testimony. The Hall of Names currently has 3 million pages of testimony written by individuals who were able to provide information regarding the fate of Holocaust victims. It is the sacred goal of the Hall of Names to eventually have on file a page of testimony for every Jewish person who perished in the Holocaust. If you can supply the names of persons whom you believe were murdered by the Nazis, or if you do not know the fate of individuals who were in Europe during the Holocaust, the Pages of Testimony Division might have information on these persons.

Regarding the Page of Testimony department, Yad Vashem's Web site states, "The martyred dead are remembered not as cold, anonymous numbers, but as individual human beings. The Pages of Testimony are an attempt to give them back their personal identity, and dignity, which the Nazis and their accomplices tried so hard to obliterate."

To send pages of testimony with information about Holocaust victims in your family to Yad Vashem, you can use the forms, in English or Hebrew, provided at the Web site (http://www.yad-vashem.org.il/download/temp_download/temp_index_download_remembrance.html).

To obtain information that Yad Vashem has in its files, either visit in person or write. The Web site notes that "Yad Vashem has over 3 million names computerized from Pages of Testimony and other sources. The names database is not accessible via the Internet. If you have a specific query about a Holocaust victim, please contact holocaust.resources@yadvashem.org.il."

In 1992 the Hall of Names began computerizing the pages of testimony. Individual searches for names of Holocaust victims commemorated on the pages of testimony can be performed freely on workstations set up for public use in the Hall of Names. Printouts can be obtained for a small fee.

--------- o ---------

Everything new must have its roots in what was before.

—Sigmund Freud

--------- o ---------

An Indispensable Guidebook

Gary Mokotoff once again demonstrated his leadership in the field of Jewish genealogical research with the publication in 1995 of his excellent

YAD VASHEM

The Holocaust Martyrs' and Heroes' Remembrance Authority

יד ושם

רשות הזיכרון לשואה ולגבורה

Hall of Names

היכל השמות

Page of Testimony דף עד

Page of Testimony for commemoration of the Jews who perished during the Holocaust; please fill in a separate form for each victim, in block letters.

The Martyrs' and Heroes' Remembrance Law 5713-1953 determines in section 2 that: "The task of Yad Vashem is to gather into the homeland material regarding all those members of the Jewish people who laid down their lives, who fought and rebelled against the Nazi enemy and his collaborators, and to perpetuate their names and those of the communities, organizations and institutions which were destroyed because they were Jewish."

Victim's photo Please write victim's name on back. Do not glue	Victim's family name:	Maiden name:
	First name (also nickname):	Previous/other family name:
	Title:	Gender: M \ F	Date of birth:	Approx. age at death:
	Place of birth:	Region:	Country:	Nationality:

Permanent residence:	Region:	Country:

Residence before deportation:	Region:	Country:

Victim's father's family name:	First name:

Victim's mother's name:	Maiden name:

Victim's spouse:	Maiden name:	Family status:	No. of children:

Member of org./movement:	Place of work:	Profession:

Places, events and activities during the war (prison / deportation / ghetto / camp / death march / hiding / escape / resistance / combat):

Date of death:	Country:	Region:	Place of death:

Circumstances of death:

I, the undersigned, hereby declare that this testimony is correct to the best of my knowledge.

First name:	Family name:	Previous/other family name:

Street:	House no.:	City:	State/zip code:

Country:	Tel.:	I am/I am not a survivor:	Relationship to the victim (family/other):

During the war I was in a camp / ghetto / forest / the resistance / in hiding / had false papers (circle relevant options)

Date: _____	Place: _____	Signature: _____

Distributed by DoroTree Technologies Ltd. - www.dorotree.com

"...And I shall give them in My house and within My walls a memorial and a name...that shall not be cut off"   Isaiah 56:5

Blank "Page of Testimony" from Yad Vashem in Jerusalem. Yad Vashem asks individuals to "testify" on these forms regarding victims known to them.

overview of the major sources of Holocaust research, *How to Document Victims and Locate Survivors of the Holocaust* (published by Avotaynu).

Memorial Books as Sources for Learning About Holocaust Victims

If you can find a memorial book devoted to a town from which your family has come (see Chapter Four), you might find a listing of Holocaust victims from that town. Many memorial books contain lists of individuals murdered during the Holocaust as a way of keeping their memory alive. Even if you think your family left its ancestral home before the Holocaust, these listings might provide names of family members who stayed. You cannot assume that people with the same surname as yours appearing on these lists are related, but there is a good chance that they are—especially if it was a small town. If you find names in memorial books that are familiar, you should ask your relatives, particularly your older relatives, if they remember them.

Landsmanshaften can also be a good source for learning about the fate of your family and your ancestral towns during the Holocaust. Often the members of landsmanshaften are survivors and have much to share regarding this part of your family experience.

Locating Survivors

I write this with great hesitation. Although six decades have passed since the Holocaust ended, I have met many people who still have hopes that one day they will find their relatives who have been missing since the war. Every once in a while a news item will stimulate more of this hope. "A brother and sister, separated by the Holocaust, find each other decades later." Although these stories are true, they are few and far between. Nonetheless, if the hope is there, a distant dream might one day be fulfilled.

Yet I write this section with hesitation because I do not want to raise false hopes or give the impression that one can easily find lost relatives. I do not want to add to the thought that "they might be alive," only to bring on greater disappointment when they are not found.

So I ask that you understand the situation: the likelihood of finding a lost relative is slight. Yet if the possibility exists and if you have the strength to pursue the question, you may want to attempt the research. Finally, before I describe this next source, you should understand that

the odds are great, sadly, that your missing relative is not alive and was murdered.

But despite my caution, I know that miracles do happen. Just read a few of the "reunion stories" that appear on the Web site of the American Red Cross Holocaust and War Victims Tracing Center (http://www.redcross.org/services/intl/holotrace/stories.html).

Survivor Lists

After the Holocaust, a major activity of Jews around the world was searching for missing relatives. The question in everyone's mind was, "Who was killed and who survived?" Immediately after the war, Jews were asked to return to their hometowns. This was perhaps the best way to find out the fate of one's family and friends. If everyone returned "home," even for a short time, the survivors could learn the fate of their loved ones. In addition, if any of the family's personal effects were still there, this would be an opportunity to claim them.

There are an enormous number of postwar horror stories relating to this very subject. How often a surviving Jew returned to his or her village only to be murdered—after the war—by anti-Semites in the town. In my family, there are eyewitness accounts by many people of just this situation. A cousin of mine returned to our shtetl searching for his missing relatives and was killed by the local people.

For the Jews who returned to their homes, their experience was a mixture of joy and sadness. In many cases a survivor's wildest dreams were fulfilled: others in his family survived. But in most cases, perhaps every case, the death of many loved ones was discovered.

Not everyone returned home, however. Some refused ever to go back to the town where they were originally from—not even for a day. Others were physically unable to travel great distances to return home or were too ill to make the journey. Other circumstances also prevented many Jews from going "home." In addition, usually a person had family in several different towns. A survivor could not be in all places at once. Yet the survivor was desperately anxious to learn news about his or her family.

Various agencies attempted to aid in the search for missing relatives because of this situation. The Jewish Agency for Palestine in 1945 established the Search Bureau for Missing Relatives. The World Jewish Congress established the Division for Displaced Persons. Other organizations such as the Czechoslovak Jewish Committee, the Relief Committee of Jews from Czechoslovakia, the American Federation for Lithuanian Jews, and many others also joined in to help Jews find survivors.

The major effort of these organizations was to gather and publish information about survivors in the form of alphabetical lists of names. The Jewish Agency for Palestine's Search Bureau for Missing Relatives published a 300-page book in 1945 called *Register of Jewish Survivors*. It was a list of 58,000 Jews in Poland in June of that year. This book can now be searched online at JewishGen.org (http://www.jewishgen.org/databases/Holocaust/0058_PinkasNitzolimII.html).

Here is a list of titles of some of the published lists:

Surviving Jews in Warsaw as of June 5th, 1945

Surviving Jews in Lublin

List of Persons Liberated at Terezin in Early May 1945

List of Children at Terezin

Displaced Jews Resident in the Czechoslovak Republic 1948

List of Jews Residing in Riga

Jewish Refugees in Italy

Jews Liberated from German Concentration Camps Arrived in Sweden 1945–6

Surviving Jews in Yugoslavia as of June 1945

A List of Lithuanian Jews Who Survived the Nazi Tyranny and Are Now in Lithuania, France, Italy, Sweden, Palestine, 1946

Jews Registered in Czestochowa

An Extensive List of Survivors of Nazi Tyranny Published So That the Lost May Be Found and the Dead Brought Back to Life

These are just some of the lists that were published. The titles of many of the lists are in themselves quite moving.

Where are these lists located? The YIVO Institute for Jewish Research has an excellent collection of survivor lists and related material. YIVO's address is

YIVO Institute for Jewish Research
Center for Jewish History
15 West 16th Street
New York, NY 10011
e-mail: yivomail@yivo.cjh.org
phone: (212) 246-6080
fax: (212) 292-1892

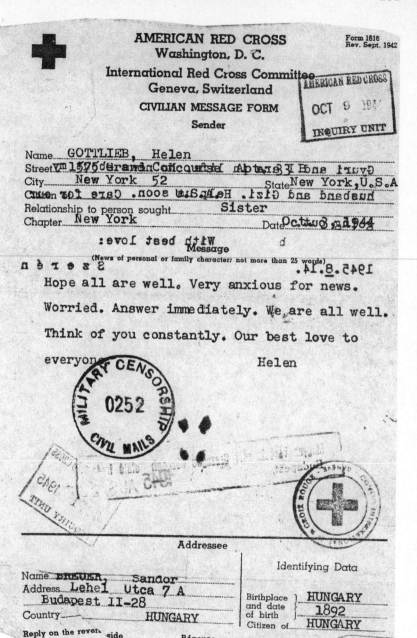

AMERICAN RED CROSS
Washington, D. C.

Form 1616
Rev. Sept. 1942

International Red Cross Committee
Geneva, Switzerland

CIVILIAN MESSAGE FORM

Sender

AMERICAN RED CROSS
OCT 9 194?
INQUIRY UNIT

Name   GOTTLIEB, Helen
Street 1575 Grand Concourse Apt. 1 E
City   New York 52   State New York, U.S.A
Relationship to person sought   Sister
Chapter New York   Date October 3rd 1944

Message
(News of personal or family character; not more than 25 words)

Hope all are well. Very anxious for news.
Worried. Answer immediately. We are all well.
Think of you constantly. Our best love to
everyone.   Helen

MILITARY CENSORSHIP
0252
CIVIL MAILS

Addressee

Identifying Data

Name   BREUER, Sandor
Address Lehel utca 7 A
         Budapest II-28
Country   HUNGARY

Birthplace and date of birth   HUNGARY
                                 1892
Citizen of   HUNGARY

Reply on the reverse side   Réponse au verso

American Red Cross message from the author's grandmother inquiring about relatives during the Holocaust.

JewishGen.org's Holocaust Database

Through the use of JewishGen.org's Holocaust Database (http://www.jew-ishgen.org/databases/Holocaust), you can do some amazing searches through a large amount of very moving and important material. Jewish-Gen's Holocaust Database is a gathering of databases containing information about Holocaust victims and survivors. It includes the following databases, which contain 320,000 entries:

The *Aufbau* Database. Names of over 33,000 Holocaust survivors, published in the German-language newspaper *Aufbau* in New York, 1944–1946.

Jews who Resided in Krosno, Poland, before 1941. Over 2,000 Jews who resided in this Galician town before June 22, 1941.

Norway Compilation. Data on nearly 900 Norwegian Jews, compiled from eleven different sources.

Danish Deportees Database. Over 400 persons deported from Denmark to Theresienstadt.

Arrivals to Buchenwald on Jan. 22, 1945. 2,470 new arrivals in Lager II (Buchenwald, Germany).

Deaths in Mühldorf, Nov. 1944–April 1945. 1,857 persons who died at this forced labor camp in Bavaria.

Auschwitz-Sachsenhausen Transfers, 27 Nov. 1944. 356 prisoners on one transport between these two concentration camps.

American Military Government Compiled List of Jews. 987 survivors and victims of concentration camps.

Buchenwald Death List—Polish Men, 1939. An unpublished list of 864 Polish men murdered at Buchenwald before World War II.

Silesian Jews in Mixed Marriages, October 1944. A list of 73 Jews married to non-Jews in Silesia, compiled by the Nazis.

Jews Who Died in Berlin, July 1943–Mar. 1945. Data on 480 Jews who died in Berlin, from Gestapo files.

Austrian Jews in Concentration Camps. Information on over 800 Austrian Jews, from various sources.

Confederation of Jews in Germany. 1,662 names from the *Reichsvereinigung der Juden in Deutschland* collection.

Polish-German Children in Zabiczyn. 111 children without parents expelled from Germany to Poland in 1938.

Jewish Partisans and Fighters of Volyn. Names of 822 from *Partizanim v'Lochamim Yehudim MeiVolhyn L'zichram*, 1997.

Deportation of Bialystok Children from Theresienstadt. Names of 1,200 children deported from Theresienstadt to Auschwitz, October 5, 1943.

Jews Who Died at Dachau After Liberation. 555 who died in the Revier Clinic at Dachau after liberation.

Jewish Inhabitants of Krosno, Galicia, Poland. 3,298 entries, compiled from multiple sources.

Dachau Inmates—Possessions upon Entry. A list of more than 2,800 inmates of the Dachau concentration camp and their possessions.

Czech Inmates at Bergen-Belsen and Theresienstadt. 610 Czechoslovak Jewish women liberated at Bergen-Belsen.

Czech Inmates at Bergen-Belsen and Theresienstadt. 333 Czechoslovak women nationals in hospitals.

Czech Inmates at Bergen-Belsen and Theresienstadt. 445 Czechoslovak Jewish women at Bergen-Belsen who were repatriated.

Czech Inmates at Bergen-Belsen and Theresienstadt. 384 Czech Jews still in Terezin on February 5, 1945.

Jewish "Training" Centers in Germany. Names of 1,800 Jewish youth, 1934–1938.

Germans, Swiss, and Austrians Deported from France. Information about 825 deportees, 1942–1944.

Westphalian Jews and the Holocaust. The fate of over 8,000 Westphalian Jews.

German Jews at Stutthof Concentration Camp. Names of 2,750 German Jews at this concentration camp near Gdansk.

Lvov Ghetto Database. Names of over 10,000 Jews in the Ghetto of Lwów Poland, 1942–1945.

Kraków Ghetto Database. Names of over 19,000 Jews in the Ghetto of Kraków, Poland, in 1940.

Pinsk Ghetto List, 1942. Data on over 18,000 Jews in the Pinsk ghetto in late 1941 or 1942.

Vilna Ghetto: Lists of Prisoners. Over 15,000 Vilnius Ghetto prisoners, from a census of Lithuania conducted in May 1942.

The Extraordinary Commission Lists: Riga. Over 2,000 individuals residing in Riga who are recorded as having perished at the hands of the German forces, most during 1941.

Brest Ghetto Passport Archive. Identity papers of over 12,000 people in the ghetto of Brest-Litovsk, from Soviet archives.

Sugihara Passports. Names and visa dates of 2,140 mostly Polish Jews, who were saved by passports from the Japanese diplomat Chiune Sugihara in 1940.

Kovno Ghetto Cemetery, 1941–1943. Transcripts of 840 burials from the register of the *Chevra Kadisha* of Viliampole Slobodka, Lithuania.

Children from Prague. 1,216 Jewish children living in Prague, Czechoslovakia, 1943–1944.

Jews Deported from Spisska Nova Ves, Slovakia. Information on 1,054 Jews deported from Spisska Nova Ves, Slovakia, on May 28, 1942.

Jews of Szombathely, Hungary, 1944. Registration of 3,116 Jews in Vas County, 1944.

Jews in Debrecen, Hungary, 1945. 4,000 survivors registered in Hajdu County, 1945.

Borislav-Drohobycz Delinquent Water Bills, 1941–1942. Data on 5,000 residents of Boryslaw and Drohobycz, now in Ukraine.

Sachsenhausen Arrivals and Departures, Oct. 1940–June 1941. Data on 5,000 arriving and departing prisoners at this camp, north of Berlin.

Temporary Passports for Jews in Germany, 1938–1941. Exit passports for 500 persons, from Gestapo files.

Dachau Concentration Camp Records. Data on over 78,000 prisoners, from captured German documents.

Jews Deported from Würzburg. 276 persons deported from this town in Lower Franconia.

Auschwitz-Stutthof Transfers, 26 Oct. 1944. 500 Jewish men sent to Stutthof on October 26, 1944.

Pinkas HaNitzolim II—Register of Survivors. Names of nearly 58,000 survivors in Poland, published in 1945.

Austrian, Czech, and German Jews in Riga. Data on 876 forced Jewish laborers in Riga, Latvia.

Breslau Deportations. Three transports of 1,845 persons sent to Silesian towns in 1941–1942.

Auschwitz Forced Laborers. Documents on 5,310 who entered Auschwitz, including parents' family names and maiden names.

Czestochowa Forced Laborers. 4,610 prisoners at the Hasag Pulcery labor camp in Czestochowa.

Pinsk Records from the Soviet Extraordinary Commission. Compilation of testimonials about 11,704 Holocaust victims from Pinsk.

Galician Forced Laborers from Lvov. Data on 1,110 workers, from a collection of the Lvov State Archives.

How Can These Lists Serve You?

The International Tracing Service has all available data on Holocaust victims and survivors, but I have already explained that the ITS is a *tracing* service. In other words, if you give ITS researchers the name of a person (and additional identification), they will check to see if the ITS has information on the person. However, what if I am looking, for example, for information about people with the name Kurzweil? The ITS cannot and will not supply me with information on every Kurzweil in its files, although I have been informed in correspondence that the files contain information about more than two hundred Kurzweils! The ITS cannot send me all of that information, but it can check its files if I ask regarding specific names. Again, the mission of the ITS is to trace individuals.

This is one circumstance where the lists come in. If I check the survivor lists for the surnames I am interested in, I might find people with the same surnames. The names of the towns where they registered are also listed. These towns are the ones where the people were at the time the list was compiled. Since most Jews registered in their hometowns, this is often the town where they lived before the Holocaust. If the town matches one in your family history, you *may* be on the right track in locating a relative. Once you find a listing of interest, you can photocopy the page and ask family members if they recall this person. Then you can send it to the ITS, which will check its files for the name. Finally, you can check phone books (discussed later in this chapter), and you might match the name on the list with a listing in an Israeli phone book or some other phone directory.

So these lists provide a possible way to locate missing people. They were published more than four decades ago, but they might help in discovering

or piecing together some valuable information. However, I must repeat that the chances of actually tracking down a missing relative are slight, and you must not allow your hopes to be raised too high.

The Jewish Agency Search Bureau for Missing Relatives in Israel

In 1945 the Jewish Agency for Israel established the Search Bureau for Missing Relatives to help reunite family members who had been separated by the catastrophic events of World War II. At one time the Search Bureau had a staff of forty-five people working to help find missing relatives. Until recently, the work of the Search Bureau was done solely by its extraordinary former director, Batya Unterschatz (with the help of a part-time secretary). The Search Bureau receives ten thousand to forty thousand requests per year from individuals searching for missing relatives. These requests for help increase greatly every time there is a new wave of immigration, with new émigrés hoping to find their Israeli relatives. Fifteen percent of the requests the Search Bureau processes come from Americans and other foreigners who are researching their family history.

Contact information is as follows:

> Bureau for Missing Relatives
> Jewish Agency for Israel
> 48 King George Street
> P.O. Box 92
> 91000 Jerusalem, Israel
> Web site: http://www.jafi.org.il/ph/relatives.htm
> phone: (972-2) 620-2652
> fax: (972-2) 620-2893

The Web site states:

> The Bureau has over 1,250,000 people listed on its data base; these names are supplemented by Ministry of the Interior records, telephone directories, and records of the International Red Cross. The Bureau also helps Holocaust survivors, whose records were destroyed, verify legal issues dealing with age, pension rights and the like. In recent years, thousands of immigrants from the former Soviet Union have approached the Bureau, hoping to find family members—either relatives with whom they lost contact 30, 40 or even 50 years ago, or relatives whom they have never met. The Bureau currently serves some 30,000 people every year. Enquiries may be made by phone, fax, mail or in person.

○

Mid-nineteenth century European Jews did not know the effects of their actions upon their remote descendants when they remained faithful to Judaism and raised Jewish children. What if they had known? Could they have remained faithful? Should they? And what of us who know, when we consider the possibility of a second Auschwitz three generations hence. (Which would we rather have our great-grandchildren be—victims or bystanders and execution-ers?) Yet for us to cease to be Jews (and to cease to bring up Jewish children) would be to abandon our millennial post as witnesses to the God of History.

—Emil L. Fackenheim

○

Hebrew Immigrant Aid Society (HIAS) Location Services

For more than a century, the Hebrew Immigrant Aid Society has had an extraordinary impact on millions of Jews. For generation after generation, HIAS has provided essential lifesaving services to world Jewry through its mission of rescue, reunion, and resettlement.

The HIAS Location Service was founded in the early part of the twentieth century to help émigrés reestablish contact with family and friends with whom they had lost touch. The HIAS Location Service faced its greatest challenge after World War II, when it helped thousands of displaced persons contact their U.S. relatives. HIAS continues to receive requests from people around the world who are trying to locate their relatives and friends. Additional inquiries come from those who are engaged in genealogical research into their ancestors who immigrated to the United States early in the last century.

To initiate a HIAS Location Service search, you can go to the Web site and fill out a search form. You may also request a form by calling HIAS at (212) 613-1409 or (800) HIAS-714 or by writing to

HIAS Location Service
333 Seventh Avenue
New York, NY 10001

You can also submit your request via fax to (212) 967-4383 or e-mail to location@hias.org. See the HIAS Location Service Web site (http://www.hias.org/Find_Family/overview.html) for full details on how to use the search services.

The Benjamin and Vladka Meed Registry of Jewish Holocaust Survivors

In 1981 the American Gathering of Jewish Holocaust Survivors established a national registry to document the lives of survivors who came to the United States after World War II. It includes over 185,000 records related to survivors and their families. In April 1993 the registry was transferred to the United States Holocaust Memorial Museum in Washington, D.C.

On its Web site (http://www.ushmm.org/remembrance/registry), the Museum explains, "The Registry of Holocaust Survivors is not made available over the Internet in order to maintain the privacy of the survivors and their families. However, if you will send us the names you are looking for, we will gladly check the Registry for you. Please also send us your postal address so we can mail you copies of any matches we may find."

The registry is also available in both book and CD-ROM formats and was sent to Holocaust organizations, libraries, universities, and Jewish community groups across the United States and around the world. Consult the Web site for a location near you.

> Registry of Holocaust Survivors
> United States Holocaust Memorial Museum
> 100 Raoul Wallenberg Place, S.W.
> Washington, DC 20024
> e-mail: registry@ushmm.org
> phone: (202) 488-6130

Deportations from France During the Holocaust

A remarkable book was published in 1978 that should be of great interest to anyone researching Holocaust victims. Titled *Le mémorial de la déportation des Juifs de France* and written and compiled by Serge Klarsfeld, this book lists all the Jews deported from France during World War II. The book, which is the size of a New York City telephone directory, contains the names, birth dates, and birthplaces of nearly 80,000 Jews who were deported. The deportees from the main transit camp at Drancy alone came from thirty-seven countries including 22,193 victims from France, 14,459 victims from Poland, and 1 victim from Tahiti.

Surname	First name	Date	Place	Code
KLEPANT	ESTERA	1886	SIEDLEC	P
ENDEL	MARIE	1883	RENOGA	P
ENDEL	MELCHIOR	09.07.80	MZGOUD	P
E RICH	ALFRED	02.08.76	PFORZHEIM	A
EPHRON	HENRIETTE	16.05.03	VIENNE	IND
EPSTRIN	ANNA.	1882	ELISABETHGRAD	R
ERDBERG	ZYSSA	1882	KUTNA.	R
EBDELYI	ANNIE	25.01.41	BLOIS	F
ERDELYI	BETTY	31.01.38	ST AIGNAN	F
ERDELYI	GEORGES	11.04.08	CZENZEHAGOS	H
ERDELYI	MICHEL	17.03.37	ROUEN	F
ERDELYI	MISCA	20.12.11	CHISINAU	RO
ERDER	CHAIM	16.04.22	KOLN	R
KRHENSTEIN	ALEX	01.08.97	BUDAPEST	H
ERLICH	CHAJA	27.03.82	LUBLIN	P
ESKENAZI	ALBERT	1935	ROUEN.	F
ESKENAZI	ALLEGRE	07.03.32	ST AIGNAN	F
ESKENAZI	LEON	04.03.36	ROUEN	F
ESKENAZI	MAIXI	1901	CONSTANTINOPLE	T
ESKENAZI	MISSIM	06.06.28	PARIS	F
ESKENASI	NAHAMU	1883	SALIKLIE	T
ESKENASI	RAYMONDE	10.01.37	PARIS	F
ESKENASI	ROBERT	05.09.32	PARIS	F
ESKENAZI	ROSE	23.01.30	ST AIGNAN	F
ESKENAZI	CADEM	.11	SMYRNE	T
ESTREICHE	BEILA	16.06.02	VISANT	P
ESMAN	MOISE	09.01.93	VARSOVIE	IND
FADDA	DORA	30.11.10	PARIS	P
FAGURE	RENE	07.07.24	BUCAREST	RO
FAINSTEIN	SOPHIE	20.07.92	EKATENNOSLAW	R
FAZTELBAUM	CHANA	1893	VARSOVIE	P
FELLEMAN	ADRIAN	04.03.02	ANVERS	HOL
FELLEMAN	BERTHE	22.11.99	ANVERS	HOL
FELLEMAN	JACQUES	17.03.29	ANVERS	HOL
FELLEMAN	PHILIPPE	19.01.26	ANVERS	HOL
FELZENSWALBE	REGINE	25.12.21	VARSOVIE	P
FICHE	MARIUS	24.04.83	ELISABETHGRAD	R
FINCHELSTEIN	FANNY	06.12.04	BUCAREST	RO
FINGERHUT	MINNA	28.12.18	OFFENBACH	IND
FINKEL	MILA	20.03.78	EZERGE	T
FISCHEL	ELLY	23.02.89	COLOGNE	IND
FISCHEL	SIEGFRIED	09.03.80	TILSIT	IND
FISCEL	JACQUES	1938	IDEL	IND
FISZMANN	ELLA	01.01.99	HIDEL	P
FLAPAN	HERSA	13.06.09	TOMASZOW	P
FLESSEMAN	ELIE	16.01.84	ROTTERDAM	HOL
FLESSEMAN	MARIUS	17.02.31	AMSTERDAM	HOL
FLORENT	AIZIK	14.11.80	VARSOVIE	R
FLOUM	ICEK	24.05.96	SMOVITZ	R
FLUGER	CHAIM	14.10.12	KWASENINA	P
FOGEL	BURUCH	01.06.92	BENSA	F
FOESHIT	NATHAN	28.11.00	JASSY	RO
FRAENKEL	GEORGES	22.10.80	ZASLAVOL	R
FRAJMAN	MOISE	15.02.00	SZIDLOWICE	P
FRANK	KEINTZE	25.10.81	GROENINGEN	HOL
FRANK	SIMON	26.05.76	GROENINGEN	HOL
FRENKIEL	MAJER	17.04.20	VARSOVIE	P
FRENKEL	MAX	05.03.09	COLOGNE	P
FRENKEL	MAYER	07.04.20	VARSOVIE	P
FRENKEL	DWOJRA	18.09.95	VARSOVIE	P
FRENKEL	PAJWEL	20.05.96	VARSOVIE	P
FRENKEL	SURA	16.04.25	VARSOVIE	IND
FREUNDENSTEIN	NICOLAS	24.10.94	PETROGRAD	R
FRIEDMANN	BERTHA	15.11.76	EELWANGEN	A
FRIZKINE	JERIDA	01.10.03	NEGRINI	DIN
FRIEDIGER	MIKA	14.10.81	BEUTHEN	R
FRIEDLAND	JACQUES	16.02.12	MOSCOU	R
FRIEDMAN	DAVID	30.07.01	GLESZ	IND
FROMBAUM	NISSYM	01.10.85	VARSOVIE	P
FRUKMANN	FANNY	1870	VOLTYEREN	RO
FRIDMAN	MENDEL	10.01.04	PRZYTYK	P
FUHRER	LILA	20.02.88	PARIS	RO
FUNKELSTEIN	ESTHER	08.03.99	PLODOK	R
FURMAN	CHAIM	15.05.82	KALDSZIN	P
GABBAI	BERNARD	11.04.94	SMYRNE	HOL
GABBE	CWJA	22.05.11	PLOCK	P
GAJER	SABAH	12.04.87	BLEINDROW	P
GANON	EDMOND	20.01.18	SMYRNE	H
GANON	LEVTO	18.12.13	ARDIN	T
GARBAI	BERNARD	11.04.94	SMYRNE	IND
GASER	LINDA	17.10.78	SYDEL	T
GDANSKY	JACKI	18.08.29	BERLIN	P
GELBERT	WOLF	23.02.83	PRZWORKS	P
GELKOFF	PERLA	22.02.80	CRZUSZYN	F
GELLER	GERARD	13.10.05	KERTEGYSAZA	F
GERACT	JOSEPH	14.07.83	PHILIPOPOLI	P
GERSENOWICZ	BERNARD	03.07.07	VARSOVIE	P
GEZUNTHEIT	JENTA	1880	VARSOVIE	P
GINSBURGER	ERNEST	15.04.76	HERICOURT	F
GLAPINSKI	CLARA	09.07.95	PODOLSKA	P
GLASER	FRED	18.05.01	BERLIN	A
GLATTEAU	MAURICE	13.09.82	VIENNE	IND
GLEZER	ROBIN	23.01.87	REIMS	F
GLIKZELIGER	TAUBA	.86	VARSOVIE	P
GOARGUIR	ESTERA	.74	SMYRNE	P
GORENTS	NOZES	07.05.08	BUSSUM	HOL
GOBEL	ISIDORE	03.09.18	PARIS	P
GOLDA	ANNA	15.08.69	SAHADOW	P
GOLDBERG	CHANA	.91	KALUZYN	P
GOLDBERG	BETTY	03.10.00	ZDUNY	A
GOLDBERG	HERSCH	18.08.05	KAHVODYKA	P
GOLDBERG	PERLA	.01	TUCHOW	P
GOLDBERG	SUPA	.90	SYDLOWICE	P
GOLD ERINE	HAJA	19.02.81	ZLNOTIR	R
GOLDCHTAIN	KLARA	.94	CONTANZA	BU
GOLDFARB	BAROUCH	09.08.95	VARSOVIE	IND
GOLDFARB	KAIMAN	.87	SCHENIKA	R
GOLDFARB	SZYJA	17.11.98	RAKOW	R
GOLDIKIND	SELMA	06.03.01	STASZA	P
GOLDRING	JANKIEL	09.11.79	LODZ	P
GOLDSTEIN	ESTHER	05.08.85	LODZ	RO
GOLDSZTAJN	FRANCOISE	14.02.42	PARIS	P
GOLDSZTAJN	MICHELINE	06.01.41	PARIS	P
GOLDSZTAJN	PERLA	15.04.12	OZAROW	P
GOLDSZTAJN	CHAJA	.10	NOVE MIASTO	P
GOLFARB	RICHARD	01.02.29	RADOM	P
GOLKINE	FRIEDA	.66	TCHERNIGOW	R
GOLDSTEIN	DAVID	17.12.15	VARSOVIE	P
GORDON	GITLA	JANV.76	WILNA	P
GORDON	PAUL	22.01.18	PARIS	F
GORTCHAK	MAURICE	30.07.98	VARSOVIE	IND
GOTTSTEIN	ANNA	05.07.12	FRANCFORT	P
GRABER	ESTERA	17.07.01	OSTROW	P
GRANEK	LEJA	.58	PIOTRKOW	IND
GRASSIAN	MICHEL	26.01.12	ISTAMBUL	T
GRASSIAN	YOSSEF	26.11.14	ISTAMBUL	T
GRIMBERG	LAZARE	04.12.87	GALATZ	RO
GRIMBERG	PAULINE	28.07.87	EKATERINOSLAW	RO
GRODJZDYK	IDESSA	06.04.02	NOW MINSK	R
GRODJZDYK	MOZEK	29.08.99	MINSK	R
GRONNIS	SAMUEL	01.03.81	EKATERINOSLAW	R
GUIRCHOVITZ	RACHEL	18.01.81	FRIEDRICHSTAD	R
GUZIK	MAJA	23.06.78	DOBROISYN	P
GRUMBERG	RUCHLA	.97	VARSOVIE	P
GRUMBERGER	VICTOR	.36	PARIS	F
GRYN	SAMY	05.04.33	NANCY	F
GRYN	YETTE	05.12.11	MANNHEIN	P
GRYNER	CHAJA	.25	SIEDLICE	P
GRYNER	SHUL	21.02.05	SIEDLICE	P
GUELFAND	SAMUEL	13.11.78	DVINSK	R
GUINI	MOISE	25.02.88	SMYRNE	T
GUTWATZ	GUCNI	16.09.70	ST. PETERSBOURG	R
GUZIK	HERZ	.81	NOVY DWOR	P
GYORGI	EUGENIE	.93	BUDAPEST	HO
GYORGI	JOSEPH	09.12.93	BUDAPEST	H
HABER	JOSEPH	08.01.35	NANCY	F
HABER	PERLA	25.05.00	GLAVACZOW	P
HABER	SAMUEL	02.02.93	OPATOW	P
HAHN	MARGUERITE	07.03.78	BERLIN	A
HAHN	PAUL	11.10.76	BERLIN	A
HAIM	ACHER	15.01.77	SALONIQUE	G
HAIM	SEROULA	.70	SALONIQUE	G
HAMBURGER	JOHANA	15.12.78	BERLIN	A
HARACH	SOPHIE	17.12.89	WILNA	R
HARAST	SIRETANA	10.04.89	CONSTANTINOPLE	T
HEIFELD	ISRAEL	.78	BALTA	RO
HERSCHBERG	SAMUEL	11.07.84	WOJNILOW	P
HERNYNGSET	JEAN	20.10.20	NANCY	F
HERZ	JACQUES	31.10.98	BOCHOLT	IND
HERZBERG	KURT	04.01.07	MAGDEBOURG	A
HESSE	JEAN	04.10.07	ST. PETERSBOURG	A
HESSE	MAURICE	16.02.06	ST. PETERSBOURG	F
HESSE	ROSE	28.10.79	PETROGRAD	F
HILLINGER	JOSEF	10.02.99	GLOGOW	P
HOCHBERG	DORA	.80	VARSOVIE	P
HOCHBERG	MATHILDE	10.05.22	VARSOVIE	P
HOCHBERG	ROSE	.06	VARSOVIE	P
HOCKMANN	BELKA	.64	WOJNEBISINSK	R
HOFFMANN	OTTO	20.10.86	VIENNE	APA
HOFRYCHTER	MICHEL	.92	MOCHELLOFF	P
HOFRYCHTER	LINDLA	03.07.20	IND	IND
HOLCMAN	WOLF	25.03.11	JADOW	P
HOLDNER	ANALYA	.85	KITRAPADIIKI	IND
HORCHOVER	MOISE	03.01.82	CONSTANTINOPLE	P
HOROWICZ	ESTHER	02.12.18	VIELLOUNG	P
HOROGICZ	SCYA	23.11.14	PABIANIC	P
HEYMANN	ERICH	26.04.82	DORTMUND	A
HUBERT	EMILE	16.12.30	ANVERS	F
IGIELNIK	HERZ	07.09.23	SCHIELNICK	P
IGIELNIK	JANNA	28.03.23	CHRIELNICK	P
IGLA	HELENE	10.01.13	VARSOVIE	P
INNEDJIAN	HAZA	20.05.11	JASSY	RO
JABLONSKI	MINA	11.11.28	BRUXELLES	R
JACOB	GASTON	14.03.75	LORIENT	F

From alphabetical lists of Jews transported on trains from France to death camps.

This large volume costs $75 and is available from the American Inter-faith Institute, 321 Chestnut Street, Philadelphia, PA 19106. It can also be ordered online at http://interfaith-scholars.org/order.html.

Mauthausen Death Books

The National Archives in Washington, D.C., has two rolls of micro-film that contain seven volumes known as the *Mauthausen Death Books*. These books recorded the deaths of about 100,000 victims at the Mau-thausen death camp. The volumes are arranged chronological by date of death and include such personal data as name, birth and death dates, and other comments. These volumes were introduced by the U.S. prosecution staff before the International Military Tribunal, commonly known as the Nuremberg Trials.

There is no index to these death books, so it is quite difficult to find specific names. However, if you have reason to believe that family mem-bers were killed in Mauthausen and you care to do the research, these rolls of microfilm are available. You can also view the microfilm if you want to witness a frightening example of Nazi sickness.

These and other National Archives holdings are available on inter-library loan. The code number for the death books is T 990.

Other Death Books

At the YIVO Institute for Jewish Research in New York, along with the collection of lists of survivors, are a few examples of lists of murdered Jews. There are no gravestones for the millions murdered. These lists, in effect, become their memorials.

Examples of such books are two volumes published by the Jewish Labor Committee in 1947: *Memorial Dates of the Martyred Jews of Dachau—Jews Born in Lithuania, Latvia, Estonia and White Russia* and *Memorial Dates of the Martyred Jews of Dachau—Jews Born in Poland*. Both books were compiled by Jesef Lindenberger and Jacob Silberstein, themselves Dachau survivors.

These kinds of lists, although possible sources for research, also serve as a further inspiration. We must try our best to learn about those mem-bers of our families who perished during the Holocaust. We ought to know their names and to write them down on our family trees. We ought to print these family trees and distribute them to our family members so that everyone knows who perished and how we are connected to them. Their memories must live.

○

Whoever teaches his son teaches not only his son but also his son's son—and so on to the end of generations.

—Talmud, Kiddushin 30a

○

Pre-Holocaust European Phone Books

The New York Public Library Research Division attempts each year to obtain current phone books from all over the world. They also save the old phone books.

One day I wondered how far back the oldest Polish phone book went in the library collection. The New York Public Library Annex on 43rd Street keeps these books. At the annex I found two volumes of the 1936 Polish telephone directories.

Since most of my family who came to America arrived in the early part of the 1900s, and since even those who came later arrived before the Holocaust, one might wonder why these phone books would be of use to me. In addition, you might ask, "What Jews had telephones in Poland in 1936?"

In answer to the second question, the fact of the matter is that many Jews in Poland in 1936 had phones. The myth is that every Eastern European Jew was as poor as Tevye the Dairyman. As for my family being in the United States before 1936, it turns out, as I noted earlier in this chapter, that many of my relatives did not come to America—and were murdered in the Holocaust.

The 1936 Polish phone books were arranged by town. Some towns had only two telephones; others had more. In one of the towns in my family history, there was a listing of about twenty phones. Two of the names, to my great surprise, were slightly familiar to me. I photocopied the page and brought it to a man in the family who was from the same town and in fact had the same last name as the people listed. When I asked him if he knew who the two people listed were, he said, "Of course. One is my uncle, and the other is my father."

They were both killed during the Holocaust, but in 1936 both had telephones. My cousin was then able to tell me about some of the other people who were listed as having phones in the same town. It was an excellent way to discover new people as well as to stimulate a memory to recall stories about people who had not been seen for thirty-five or more years.

The following is a listing of some of the pre-Holocaust telephone books that can be found in the New York Public Library Annex, located at 521 West 43rd Street between 10th and 11th Avenues in New York City:

AUSTRIA

Vienna, 1928–1930, 1932–1934, 1936–1938

Burgenland

Karnten

Niederösterreich

Oberösterreich

Salzburg

Steiermark

Tirol

Vorarlberg

CZECHOSLOVAKIA

Prague, 1932–1938, 1940

Bohemia, 1934–1935, 1935–1936, 1936–1937, 1938–1939

Moravia and Silesia, 1932, 1933, 1936

Slovakia and Russian Lower Carpathia, 1934, 1935

GERMANY

Berlin, 1913, 1926–1938

Düsseldorf, 1931–1936

Frankfurt, 1928–1937

Hamburg, 1927, 1930–1935

Leipzig, 1932–1934

München, 1932–1937

Stuttgart, 1936

HUNGARY

Budapest, 1913, 1928–1934, 1936–1938, 1940

POLAND
Warsaw, 1931–1935, 1936–1937
All districts except Warsaw, 1936

YUGOSLAVIA
Belgrade, 1934

The New York Public Library also has post-Holocaust phone books that may aid in tracking down missing relatives.

———○———

All our ancestors are in us. Who can feel himself alone?

Richard Beer-Hoffman, *Schlaflied für Miriam*, 1898

———○———

YOUR IMMIGRANT ANCESTORS

WE OFTEN LOOK AT Jewish history in terms of broad categories of time. The arrival of Jewish immigrants in the United States, for example, has been broken into stages, each spanning many years. Perhaps the best-known era in American Jewish history occurred just before and after the turn of the twentieth century, when vast numbers of Jews streamed through the Port of New York. Steamships carrying Jews from Europe arrived daily, pouring Jews into the United States.

That period of history, when the Lower East Side of New York filled up with immigrants, when other cities in the United States saw their Jewish population increase rapidly because of this immigration, when the United States emerged as a center of world Jewry, has become almost legendary. The phenomenon of Jewish immigration has been written about, studied, and celebrated literally since it began. Books continue to appear on the subjects of the Lower East Side, Jewish immigration, and related topics.

Although it can be useful to view history in terms of eras, stages, or time spans such as this, it is perhaps even more useful to go from the general to the specific to see where, in fact, we fit into those broad swaths of history. We know that steamships arrived in American ports daily during the active periods of immigration, but which ships brought us—our ancestors—to those ports? What were the names of the ships that carried our family to America? What did they look like? What route did they travel? When did they arrive? How long did it take to make the journey? Who traveled with whom? How old were your ancestors when they arrived? Where did they go when they got off the ship? Where did they live?

Again, we can understand the general history of different eras, or we can move in closer and examine details. We can see the crowd, or we can examine the individuals.

As you read this, chances are you are sitting at home or near your home. How long have been living where you currently reside? How long has your family lived in the area where you are now? Whatever the answers are to those questions, if you are like most Jews in America, you have not been here for too many generations. Just as the United States is a nation of immigrants, you and your family are part of the collection of people whose ancestors arrived here sometime in the recent past. Most of us live our lives as Americans, rarely remembering that the United States is a relatively new experience for our families.

Do you know when your family arrived in America? Perhaps you yourself are an immigrant, in which case you are well aware of the date and circumstances of arrival. Or perhaps your parents were immigrants, in which case you may also have a good idea of the story behind your arrival on these shores. Let's take a look at the Jewish immigrant experience in the United States and see where we fit into the large picture. Our examination of this aspect of Jewish history will be like a gradually moving close-up in a motion picture. We will begin with a wide-angle shot of the phenomenon of immigration. Slowly we will focus in on a more and more narrow portion of the picture until we arrive at a single detail in the original scene: you.

Immigration to the United States

Jewish immigration to the United States can be divided into five different stages, and different branches of your family may well fit into each of these time periods. Remember that unless you yourself are an immigrant, the arrival of your family in America will vary. Branches of your mother's family may have arrived in 1908, whereas your father's family—or parts of it—may have been here since before the Civil War.

The five stages of Jewish immigration are as follows: 1654–1825, 1825–1880, 1880–1929, 1929–1945, and 1945 to the present. Let us briefly examine each of these periods.

1654–1825

The year 1654 is a famous one in Jewish history, for in that year the first Jewish settlement was established in North America. It consisted of twenty-three individuals and was located in Dutch New Amsterdam. Much research has been done on this group in the years of the colonial period in America. The number of Jews during that period was small, and

assimilation was great. Jewish settlements were founded throughout the early colonial period, however, and we find them quite early in Virginia, Rhode Island, and Maryland. By 1733 all thirteen colonies had Jewish populations. During this wave of settlement, most of the Jews were of Spanish descent, but after 1700 we find German Jews arriving in small numbers. By 1750 the German Jews had outnumbered the Sephardic Jews. Nevertheless, the Jewish population of the United States in 1790 was a mere fifteen hundred.

When the American Revolution broke out in 1776, most Jews were Whigs, that is, supporters of the Revolution. Having little or no tie to England, they were much more interested in independence. A great deal of historical material exists on this early period of Jewish history in North America, including the Jewish role in the Revolution. Although the history is often fascinating, we are still aware of the fact that assimilation was the most common experience among the Jews in this period, and the reason that the Jewish population remained fairly stable was because of the balance between the Jews who faded out of the Jewish community and the trickle of Jewish immigration that continued throughout this time. By 1826, the Jewish population had reached approximately six thousand. Most of these Jews, by this time, were native-born and completely acculturated. Intermarriage remained common.

1825–1880

The second period of American Jewish history is one of enormous growth. In fact, it is during this period that the American Jewish community evolved from a small group of little significance to a major Jewish community. A quick look at population figures tells the story:

1826	6,000
1840	15,000
1860	150,000
1880	280,000

The increase in population was mainly the result of foreign immigration. Most of the immigrants were Germanic Jews, coming from Bohemia and Bavaria. Large numbers also came from Hungary. An interesting aspect of this migration was that many of the Jews who arrived in America did not remain on the East Coast. In fact, one of the great contributions of the Jews in America at this time was the continued opening up and development of the West. The older Jewish communities in

places such as Charleston, South Carolina; Newport, Rhode Island; and Norfolk, Virginia, saw a decline during this time as Jews moved west. Other cities began to develop Jewish communities, including Cincinnati, Louisville, New Orleans, Chicago, Saint Louis, Cleveland, Newark, Albany, Syracuse, Buffalo, Detroit, Milwaukee, and Minneapolis. Many Jews who arrived at the time of the Gold Rush, which began in 1849, traveled to California and were among the first to settle in San Francisco. And as a result of the European revolutions of 1848–1849, the early 1850s evidenced the greatest wave of immigration of this entire period.

This was also the great era of the Jewish peddler and traveling salesman. Because of the lack of retail outlets to be found in a still-developing nation, the Jewish peddler contributed to the growth of the American economy by traveling to cities throughout the country. In fact, many major department stores, including Macy's, Gimbel's, and Abraham & Straus, had their beginnings in this period as tiny retail outlets, sometimes in the form of a horse-drawn wagon.

The middle of the nineteenth century in American Jewish history was dominated by the German Jew. With the arrival of so many German Jews came the establishment of German theater, newspapers, cultural societies, and other groups. These were often devoid of much Jewish content; however, the development of Reform Jewry as a major force in Jewish thinking took place at the same time. Major figures in the history of the Reform movement emerged at this time, and synagogues as well as schools reflecting Reform Jewish ideology and ritual appeared.

Because many Jewish communities were intact by the 1860s, Jewish participation in the Civil Wars was significant. Jews lived in both the North and the South and tended generally to support the war effort of the region in which they resided. After the Civil War, industrial expansion in the reunited nation was great, but Jews were generally excluded from most of the industries that developed at this time, such as oil, railroads, shipping, and banking. The area of business that remained wide open was retailing, and in large part this is the reason for Jews in the United States being associated with retail commerce.

1880–1929

At the start of this period the Jewish population of the United States was 280,000; by 1925 it had increased to 4.5 million. Those figures tell the story of the few decades that constituted a major event in Jewish history. Between 1880 and 1925, some 2,378,000 Jews arrived in the United States.

The reasons for this huge migration of Jews, primarily from Eastern Europe, are simple and yet complex. The simple reason is that life in Eastern Europe was becoming more and more unbearable. Pogroms were widespread during the late 1800s, Jews were periodically expelled from different regions, and anti-Semitic violence was a constant threat. Underlying those more immediate reasons, however, were other factors: the Jewish populations in Eastern Europe grew at a pace that often made it impossible for a community to survive economically. In addition, the exodus from Eastern Europe was building momentum. As more people arrived in the United States, the notion of America as a land of the free made its way back to the villages of their ancestry. Eastern Europe was literally abuzz with the idea of America as a sort of new Promised Land, and this considerably spurred the migration of the masses to the United States. The immigrants to America were mostly from Russia, Poland, Romania, and Austro-Hungary during this period. It is during these years that most of our ancestors came to this country.

During this era, the pace of immigration increased with each decade. Between 1881 and 1892 approximately 19,000 Jews arrived, on the average, each year. Between 1892 and 1903 the annual average was 37,000. Between 1903 and 1914 the yearly average was 76,000. By 1918 the United States contained the largest Jewish community in the world.

Most of the immigrants arrived in New York. Many went to Philadelphia, Boston, Detroit, Cleveland, Chicago, and other places, but the Lower East Side of New York City became the center of the world for the largest number of newly arrived Jews. With the start of World War I in 1914, immigration came to a temporary halt. After the war, a series of bills passed in the U.S. Congress also served to slow immigration considerably.

This period in American Jewish history is perhaps the richest and best known. It constituted a milestone in the history of the Jews, transplanting families from one side of the world to the other. Jews left their ancestral homes of generations to establish new roots in America. The quantity of material written during and about this period is vast, and entire libraries could be filled with the stories of this era.

1929–1945

The time period from the beginning of the Great Depression to the end of World War II can be seen as another era in American Jewish history. However, it is here that we can see that dividing history into distinct eras has its problems. So much can happen within just a few years that to lump several years together does not serve much of a purpose. Although this is particu-

larly true of this era, the same can be said of the other time periods already discussed. History is a complex unraveling of time, and hardly a generalization can be made without there being an exception quickly found.

We do see that there was very little immigration during these years, particularly in comparison with the years of the period before this one. The key date during this era is 1933, the year Nazism came to power in Germany. With vicious anti-Semitism increasing in Germany as well as in Poland and Romania, the number of Jews driven to leave increased. Those seeking immigrant status in the United States came up against difficulties in this period that were unknown just a few years before. The economic situation in the nation, coupled with anti-immigrant sentiment on the part of U.S. consuls empowered to grant visas, held the immigrant numbers down. During the years 1933–1937, total immigration did not exceed 33,000. The rate increased between 1938 and 1941, however, to 124,000. The increase was the result of the extreme worsening of the situation for Jews in Germany as well as in the lands taken over by Germany. But by the end of 1943, Jewish immigration to the United States had virtually stopped.

1945 to the Present

During the years 1947–1951, just under 120,000 Jews immigrated to the United States. The large majority of these were Holocaust survivors, more than 63,000 of them entering the country under the Displaced Persons Act of 1949. Between 1960 and 1968, about 73,000 Jewish immigrants arrived, made up of Israelis, Cubans, and Near Easterners. In recent decades, many Jewish immigrants to the United States have come from the former Soviet Union and Israel.

Immigration to Canada

Although the Jewish history of Canada parallels that of the United States in many ways, it would be useful to take a glimpse of Jewish migration to Canada.

The year 1759 begins the Jewish history of Canada. It was then that a permanent settlement was founded. In the early years the Jews were concentrated in the city of Montreal. The community was quite small, however, and by 1831 there were still only 107 Jews in Canada. By 1851 the Jewish population had increased to 248, and ten years later there were 572 Jews in the country. By 1871 the population was 1,115, split fairly evenly between Quebec and Ontario. Finally, on the eve of the period of mass migration that began in 1881, there were 2,393 Jews in Canada.

Immigrants to Canada came from the same regions as those who came to the United States In the mid-nineteenth century, most Jews arrived from Western and Central Europe, with a minority coming from Eastern Europe. As in the United States, it was after 1881 that the bulk of the Jewish population arrived in Canada. The present-day Jewish population of Canada consists mainly of families descending from the post-1881 migrations. By 1891 the Jewish population of Canada was up to 6,414, and by 1920 the figure was more than 125,000.

When the United States introduced a quota system for immigration after World War I, Canada saw an increase in immigration, but with the arrival of the Great Depression, restrictions tightened in Canada as well, limiting immigration severely. As in the case of the United States, the rise of Nazism in 1933 in Germany led to another increased effort at immigration by Jews. Pressure in Canada by its Jewish leadership attempted to keep the doors open for oppressed European Jews. But restrictions and anti-immigrant and anti-Semitic sentiment kept the figure low.

Between 1930 and 1940 some 11,000 Jewish immigrants arrived in Canada. After World War II an additional wave of Jewish immigration occurred, the number totaling 40,000 between 1945 and 1960.

The major Jewish centers in Canada have been and still are Quebec and Ontario, with Montreal, Quebec, Toronto, Hamilton, and Ottawa the leading Jewish cities.

Aliyah to Israel

Not all European immigrants went to North America. In fact, there were years during which transatlantic migration was at a standstill and other countries were sought out by Jews looking for a better life. Israel, or Palestine, was not merely an alternative to America; a "return to Zion" had been a part of Jewish tradition for centuries, and whether or not individuals who migrated to Israel saw it as a biblical return to Zion, it was and remains a major destination of many Jews.

Throughout history, several reasons have been advanced to explain migration to Israel. The first is the ancient notion of a return, as just mentioned. A second reason has been the desire to study Torah where the Sanhedrin and the great academies were located. There has also been a belief that a person who is buried in Israel will reap benefit from this in the "next world."

Another motive for migration to Israel, or *aliyah,* as it is called, has been the belief that only in Israel can mitzvot be fulfilled. There has also been the belief that Israel will cure illness as well as barrenness. A belief

that an increased population in the Land of Israel will hasten the Messiah has been another motivation for aliyah. Finally, we find that large numbers of people went to Israel—even since the thirteenth century—to escape persecution in Europe.

In modern times, migration to Israel has been motivated by combinations of these reasons in addition to national and ideological factors that inspired great numbers of Jews to "make aliyah."

During the period after 1881, which as we know was the height of Jewish exit from Europe, there was considerable migration to Palestine. Migration to Palestine and Israel has also been divided into stages, known as "First Aliyah," "Second Aliyah," and so on. The dates of the First Aliyah are considered 1882 through 1903. By 1903 approximately 10,000 Jews had settled in the region. The Second Aliyah was the period from 1904 through 1914, the start of World War I. The First and Second Aliyot combined saw about 70,000 Jews migrate to the region, though it must be noted that many of them left because of the hardship of life there. There is no question but that the United States was the major attraction of Jews relocating during this period. Of all the Jews who were intercontinental migrants between 1881 and 1914, only 3 percent arrived in Eretz Israel.

As immigration to the United States slowed after World War I, aliyah picked up. Between 1919 and 1926 nearly 100,000 Jews made aliyah. When the 1930s arrived, Palestine became enormously important as a destination for Jewish migrants. Anti-Semitism was worse than ever because of the rise of Nazism, and the United States and Canada had slowed the acceptance of immigrants drastically. Therefore, Palestine took on even greater importance. Between 1932 and 1939, during the Fifth Aliyah, almost half of the intercontinental migrants went to Palestine. In that same period, the United States and Canada received but a fifth of the intercontinental migrants. The period of World War II is, of course, the most tragic. Most Jews were unable to leave Europe, though between 1940 and 1945 nearly 45,000 of them reached Palestine—where the British turned many back. The British also denied entrance to Palestine to many Jews in the years following the Holocaust, right up to Israeli independence in May 1948. Fewer than 70,000 Jews were able to enter Palestine after the war under the British mandate. In May 1948, much of the Palestine mandate became the independent nation of Israel, and ever since that time, Israel has been the most popular destination of Jewish intercontinental migrants. Many migrants continued to go to the United States, Canada, and France (especially in the 1960s), but Israel was clearly the leader. From May 1948 through 1951, almost 700,000 Jews went to Israel. It was only in the mid-1960s that migration to Israel began to slacken.

Your Immigrant Ancestors: Who Were They?

The Jewish migrations and population growth in the United States, Canada, and Israel form the backbone of Jewish history for the time periods covered. Basic to the understanding of a particular history and a particular people are the answers to three questions: Where were they from? How did they get there? What did they do?

As I have noted, if you examine the general periods of recent Jewish history, you should be able to place your own personal family histories in these eras. So, for example, if your great-great-grandfather was a German Jew who arrived in this country in 1852, you can easily see that this particular branch of your own family background was a part of a special era in Jewish history. Of course, to know this, you must know the history of your own family. It is not enough to think that your ancestors were immigrants and that they came to America once upon a time. Your own personal history is wrapped up in the choices made by your ancestors. To lump them together in a category called "the past" is a disservice to them, their risks, their strengths, and their lives. Again, the question remains: Where do you fit into Jewish history?

One of the results of tracing your family history and creating a family tree is that at one point, for each of the branches in your direct ancestry, you will discover your immigrant ancestor. Eventually, when you follow each branch back, your mother and your father, your four grandparents, your eight great-grandparents, your sixteen great-great-grandparents, and so on, one individual in each line will be an immigrant. For some of us, it may be found very soon: our own parents might be the immigrants. Or it may be that just two generations back, our grandparents were the immigrants. In any case, no Jew born in America is without immigrant ancestors.

Although each person in your family history is special for his or her own contributions to your life, your immigrant ancestors surely have a unique distinction among the others. We know that it was often hardship, anti-Semitism, and fear that pushed immigrants to America, but that final decision—to make the journey—must have taken immense courage. All you have to do to know what the experience may have been like is to imagine for yourself leaving your home, family, friends, familiar environment, and everything that you have known for a lifetime, never to see it again. The result of that kind of imagining is dramatic. To envision your grandfather at age fifteen leaving his parents, his brothers and sisters, and his entire known life to journey by himself to America, never to return, is a powerful experience and an education. It strains the mind to realize the number of divided families, the number of children who said farewell to

parents, the number of sisters who said goodbye to brothers, the husbands who left behind wives and children to save enough to send for them.

Another frightening image is to think about what the fate of your family might have been (in most cases) had your ancestor not made the decision to take the risk and leave home. As you build your family tree, you will often notice that your direct ancestors—grandparents, great-grandparents, and so on—had brothers and sisters whose decisions were quite different from theirs. You will also come to understand that it was the decisions made by your direct ancestors that are in large part responsible for your very existence. If yours is like most Jewish families, you will undoubtedly find siblings of some of your direct ancestors who made different kinds of decisions—and their descendants were never born. This is understandable, of course. When you think of the radically different kinds of decisions that brothers and sisters make all the time, it is easy to comprehend why some lines of your family still exist and why some did not survive. But what you ought to understand above all else is how the choices made by your ancestors are so profoundly linked to your own life. If any one of your sixteen great-great-grandparents had chosen a different life from what he or she did, you would not be where you are today. You might not exist at all. Imagining this is not a senseless game; it is, rather, a serious invitation to attempt to understand the lives of your ancestors and the paths they traveled.

It is possible to enter Jewish history in a dramatic way through the history of your family, as I have said many times in this book. One of the most important points in the history of your family as well as in the history of the Jewish people is in the recent migrations. In the last 150 years nearly every Jewish family in the world has made a radical move geographically. The Jewish population pockets of today are remarkably different from those of 150 years ago or even 100 years ago. In Eastern Europe, where world Jewry was centered for hundreds of years, the Jewish community today is almost nonexistent. The United States, whose Jewish population was minuscule 100 years ago, is one of the two centers of world Jewry today.

It will probably not be difficult for you to determine, for each of your family lines, who your immigrant ancestors are. Jewish migrations to this country were recent enough to make this task easy in most cases. If your family stems at all from a German Jewish family that migrated in the 1850s, the chore might be more difficult than others but will still be generally easy since records often exist even where memories of family members fail. Along with your search for the names of your immigrant ancestors, you will want to concern yourself with other questions as well. When did each

immigrant ancestor arrive in this country? What towns and countries did they come from? Let us treat each of those questions separately.

When did your immigrant ancestors arrive in this country? The answers to this question relate directly to the summaries of the different eras of Jewish history and migration we have discussed. When you know the year that an ancestor of yours arrived on America's shores, you can then link up to general Jewish history and understand your part in it. For example, let us assume that your grandfather arrived in the United States in 1907. From that simple piece of knowledge, you will know, from your understanding of American Jewish history, of what era and what phenomenon your grandfather was probably a part: the major wave of Jewish immigration to this country.

The date of arrival of a direct ancestor of yours is a special event in your own personal history regardless of how long ago it took place. It does not take much imagination to understand the profound impact that the decision to leave and the arrival in America had, not only on your ancestor but on you as well. There are many dates that we all have been taught are significant in history. The date of arrival of an immigrant ancestor should be among such dates for each of us. Unlike the famous dates of history shared by all, these dates are personal and meaningful to us as individuals. We each have a personal history as well as a common history. It is important to know both.

What towns and countries did they come from? This is another question of importance when pursuing our family histories. How many of us know the names of the towns left behind by our immigrant ancestors? How many of us know what the conditions were like in those towns that forced or provoked our ancestors to leave? General history tells us about the anti-Semitism, the economic hardships, and other conditions that plagued Jewish communities throughout Europe. But what, specifically, was it like in the places where our families lived for generations? This is a question that we discussed at greater length in Chapter Eight.

Once the decision was made to journey to America, money had to be saved and a steamship ticket had to be purchased. Although steamships made their way back and forth across the Atlantic throughout the years, it is hardly enough to know that the type of vehicle used to transport Jewish immigrants was a steamship. How much more alive Jewish history and your own personal history become when you know the name of the ship traveled on by your ancestors, what the ship looked like on the outside, and what it was like living on the ship for the days of the long journey.

When the ship arrived, it landed in a port. Most often, that port was New York, though Boston, Philadelphia, and other seaports were also vis-

The author's paternal grandfather, Yehudah Yaakov Kurzweil (right), with a coworker and child, leaning on his metal-bending machine, shortly after arriving in the United States from Poland.

ited. Do you know where your immigrant ancestors arrived? Do you know, in addition, where your ancestors went after they arrived in America? Did they stay in the city of their port of arrival? Did they travel to some inland city to reunite with a relative who had arrived in America earlier? Did they go to some unexplored location? Maybe they were sent by an organization set up to aid and relocate immigrants to some rural community or to a job opportunity. The encounter that your immigrant ancestor had with his or her new country must surely have caused what we now call "culture shock." The United States was very different from the old country. The people were different; the language was odd; the customs seemed strange. Where did your ancestors go? How did they deal with the shock of an alien culture? What organizations might they have joined, or helped found, that made life in the United States more manageable?

There are many questions that can be asked and, ideally, answered regarding the experiences of your immigrant ancestors. Suppose you discover

that an ancestor settled in Richmond, Virginia, but you have lived all your life in New York. You will want to learn more about the Jewish community of Richmond at the time that your ancestor was there. Here is one more example of Jewish history coming alive through your family history: though the history of the Jewish community of Richmond might have once been the farthest thing from your mind, it is now important for you to learn about it in order for you to understand yourself. When was the Richmond Jewish community founded? Was there a Jewish section of the city? What synagogues existed when your ancestor lived there? Is there a Jewish cemetery there in which family members may be buried? What occupations did Jews have at that time in Richmond? What made people go to Richmond to live, and what made them leave? Are there any old photographs of the Richmond Jewish community for that time period from which you can get an idea of what life was like? Is there a photo of the street on which your ancestor lived? What other information can you discover about the city to add to your understanding of your ancestor's life?

The question of where your ancestors lived is not one of concern exclusively regarding your immigrant forebears. This is particularly true for families who have been in America for several generations. If some branches of your family have been in this country for many generations, you will have the same kinds of questions for each of them. Where did they live? What were their occupations? When did they arrive in the places they lived? When did they marry? What did their homes, their streets, and their neighborhoods look like? Which synagogues did they belong to? For each generation before you, back to your immigrant ancestors, you will want to approach the same questions with interest and research. You will want to enter their lives as much as possible, knowing the streets on which they walked, the occupations that earned their living, and the choices that molded their lives—and yours.

Landsmanshaften

Immigrants often joined and formed organizations known as landsmanshaften. A landsmanshaft, as explained in Chapter One, is an immigrant benevolent organization formed by the former residents of a particular city, town, shtetl, or region. For example, if you were an immigrant from Pinsk, you might belong to the Pinsk Society.

Before 1880, landsmanshaften were generally synagogues, each formed by individuals and families from the same European locality for the purpose of having a place to pray among one's "people." However, the spate

of Jewish immigration after 1881 brought more secular organizations of this kind into being. These later benevolent societies often had synagogues as well, but their purposes were expanded to include other functions. Often the landsmanshaften, as their first order of business, would raise money to buy a burial plot for the use of families of the membership. Membership would also offer other advantages, such as sick benefits, interest-free loans, and aid to families during a mourning period and to residents of the town who were still in Europe. The landsmanshaften were also often instrumental in arranging for individuals and families to come to America.

Several American cities had landsmanshaften. New York City and Chicago, two of the largest Jewish communities in the United States, had hundreds of landsmanshaften. In 1914 there were at least 534 of them in New York, for example. As time went on, the ancestral home of immigrants faded from their minds. This and the deaths of members over the decades has brought the era of the landsmanshaften almost to a close. Although many such organizations continue to function in Latin America, the United States, Western Europe, and Israel, the numbers are minute in comparison with the days when landsmanshaften were major societies. The decline of these groups was well under way by the beginning of World War II, although there was a slight revival of activity after the Holocaust when many groups published memorial books in honor of the destroyed towns.

To locate landsmanschaften and their records, see page 311.

The total experience of your immigrant ancestors, including their homes in the old country, their decision to travel to America, their journey aboard a steamship, their arrival wherever else they landed, and their lives in their new home all should have meaning for you. Most important, there are many ways in which you can learn about and document those journeys and those lives, to begin to see the experiences of your family as Jewish history and to see yourself as a part of it as well. Enter Jewish history through the lives of your ancestors and make your own personal connections with your past and your people.

Tracing the Journey

It is difficult for me to imagine the complex mix of emotions that my mother's mother must have felt, at the age of fifteen, as she set off across the Atlantic Ocean in the early part of the twentieth century. My effort to understand that pivotal moment in my family history, however, has been aided by my ability to uncover the details of the trip she took.

How to Find the Ship That Brought Your Ancestors to America

The steamships on which your ancestors traveled to America and the dates of their arrival are important in the context of your family history. In the same way that the *Mayflower* was the celebrated ship that brought early settlers to the American continent, the steamships in your family history should be noted as turning points in your own history.

It is not always easy to find the names of ships or their arrival date, but with a little detective work, you should be able to do it.

The first step, of course, is to ask your relatives, if they are available, if they remember the names. If your family has been in this country for generations, you cannot expect anyone to recall these things, but in families with more recent arrivals, it is possible that they do recall. I tried to track down the steamship of my grandmother Helen for a long time with no luck. My grandmother was one of those people (whom you will surely encounter) who did not care to talk much about family history, but one day I decided to ask her if she knew the name of the ship on which she came to America. It did not take her a second to answer, *"The Fatherland."* This was the same woman who refused to tell me her place of birth for months! All of my research time could have been saved if I had begun by asking the immigrant herself. Since then I have asked many immigrants if they knew the name of the ship that brought them to America. Most people remember as if it were yesterday.

If your immigrant ancestor is alive and does not remember the name of the ship, ask if he or she traveled alone or with other people. If you get names of others and they are alive, ask them. You have to become a detective, trying to locate leads wherever you can find them.

If you have partial information about the ship and its arrival, you might be able to narrow the field by using the *Morton Allen Directory of European Passenger Steamship Arrivals*. This volume, which is a standard book in large public and research libraries, and especially genealogy collections, features a year-by-year listing of arrival by steamship companies, including dates of arrival, ports of arrival, and the exact names of the steamships, for all vessels arriving in New York between 1890 and 1930 and arriving in Baltimore, Boston, and Philadelphia between 1904 and 1926.

How can you use this directory? Let's assume that you have been told the exact date of arrival (someone might remember the date but not the ship) and the port. The *Morton Allen Directory* has an easy-to-find listing of the ships that arrived in port each day. This will surely narrow the field to just a few. Or you may know the ship and the approximate date but not an exact date. Again, you can narrow the possibilities consider-

ably by using the directory. In either case, this might be helpful if you are forced to use microfilmed passenger lists (to be described shortly).

The Genealogical Publishing Company publishes a reprint of the *Morton Allen Directory*; go to http://www.genealogical.com.

One of the pieces of information often given on petitions for naturalization or declarations of intention is the name of the steamship and date of arrival for the individual who applies for citizenship (see "Naturalization Records" a bit later in this chapter).

If you can locate the passenger list of the steamship on which your ancestors arrived in America, you can obviously identify the name of the ship (this too is discussed a bit later in the chapter).

Steamship passenger lists are on microfilm at the National Archives and various genealogy libraries. If you know the approximate time of arrival and the port of arrival, you can search through the microfilm looking for the names of your ancestors.

Passenger list of the author's grandmother, father, uncle, and aunt.

Finally, and most important, there are new ways to locate the names of your ancestors' ships and their passenger lists on the Web.

How to Find Steamship Passenger Lists with Your Ancestors on Them

One of the most intriguing documents relating to the history of your family is the actual passenger list of the steamship on which your ancestor traveled. The National Archives has more than eleven thousand reels of microfilm containing immigration records for various ports for the years 1800–1959.

It is possible to research immigration records in person at The National Archives Building, 700 Pennsylvania Avenue, N.W., Washington, DC 20408. Go to Room 400, the Microfilm Reading Room. Staff are available to answer questions.

If you know the name of the ship and the date of arrival for an ancestor, the National Archives will, for a fee, check its collection and make copies of the lists for you. Or if you are in Washington, D.C., you can do the research yourself, provided that the ship arrived more than fifty years ago. Lists of ships that arrived since then are confidential. They can be searched, however, by the staff of the National Archives, who will provide you with the information pertaining to your family alone.

In some cases the passenger lists have been indexed by name, thereby relieving you of the problem of locating the name and date of the ship yourself.

To obtain copies of passenger lists, you must fill out National Archives Trust Fund (NATF) Form 81 and send it to the National Archives and Records Administration, 700 Pennsylvania Avenue, N.W., Washington, DC 20408, marked "Attention: NWCTB." You can obtain NATF Form 81 by providing your name and mailing address at http://www.archives.gov/global_pages/inquire_form.html. Be sure to specify "Form 81" and the number of forms you need.

Although the information provided on the passenger lists varies from ship to ship and year to year, some of the lists contain quite a bit of information, including name, age, occupation, closest living relative at last residence, place of residence, place of birth, and destination in the United States. These and other facts will be of interest and might serve as clues for additional information.

For example, many passenger lists give place of birth. You might only know the last place where an ancestor lived. This will give you an additional town where your family lived.

For full details of what the National Archives has in its passenger list collection, go to its Web site at http://www.archives.gov/research_room/genealogy/immigrant_arrivals/passenger_records.html.

Passenger Lists Online

Several Web sites are extremely useful for people hoping to find their ancestors on steamship passenger lists. An excellent guide is Internet Sources for Transcribed Passenger Records and Indexes at http://home.att.net/~wee-monster/onlinelists.html.

ELLIS ISLAND RECORDS ONLINE. As the Ellis Island Online Web site (http://www.ellisislandrecords.org) explains, "From 1892 to 1924, more than 22 million immigrants, passengers, and crew members came through Ellis Island and the Port of New York. The ship companies that transported these passengers kept detailed passenger lists, called "ship manifests." Now, thanks to the generous efforts of volunteers of the Church of Jesus Christ of Latter-Day Saints, these manifests have been transcribed into a vast electronic archive, which you can easily search to find an individual passenger."

You will need to register, with a user name and password, but membership is free. Your registration will also allow you to conveniently save your searches. The Web site also has some other features of interest to family historians.

JEWISHGEN.ORG'S ELLIS ISLAND DATABASE ONE-STEP SEARCH TOOLS. JewishGen.org offers an extraordinary alternative to searching the Ellis Island database through its Ellis Island Database One-Step Search Tools at http://www.jewishgen.org/databases/EIDB. It has some features that make it quicker and often easier for Jewish family searches.

I also suggest that you review the Ellis Island Database FAQ and Tips regarding the Ellis Island data at JewishGen's FAQ Web page: http://www.jewishgen.org/infofiles/eidbfaq.html.

HAMBURG PASSENGER LISTS (1850–1934). The Mormon Church has a microfilm collection of a rather unusual set of passenger lists that are worth noting. Lists were kept in Hamburg of all passengers who left from that port. The lists provide each passenger's name, occupation, place of birth and residence, age, sex, name of vessel, captain's name, destination, and departure date. The lists were kept from 1850 to 1934 and are indexed by year and first letter of the surname. In other words, if an ancestor of yours went through the port of Hamburg on the way to

America, he or she should appear on these lists. If you know the date, you can look in the index under the first letter of the last name and find it. Other indexes are also available. For example, a fifteen-year index covering the Direct Lists for 1856 through 1871 was compiled on typed cards by Mormon volunteers in 1969. If you do not know the year, checking various dates would be necessary, of course. This resource is more valuable than it might seem at first since many Jews who did not originate in Germany came through Hamburg.

The Hamburg State Archives, for a fee, will do searches of these lists. See the Web site at http://www.hamburg.de/fhh/behoerden/staatsarchiv/link_to_your_roots/english/index.htm.

Avotaynu Articles Concerning Immigration Records

Two articles published in *Avotaynu* are very instructive:

> "How to Find a Post-1906 U.S. Immigrant Ancestor," by Edward David Luft (Spring 1998). "Certificates of Arrival and the Accuracy of Arrival Information Found in U.S. Naturalization Records," by Marian L. Smith, Historian, U.S. Immigration and Naturalization Service (Summer 1998).

------------ o ------------

Sometimes the decision to change names was not the immigrant's own. Immigration officials at the ports of entry refused to be bothered with exact transcriptions of a new arrival's difficult name. Down on the forms went totally new or easy names—Smith, Jones, Johnson, Robinson, Taylor, Brown, Black, White, Green. And then there were Jews who named themselves after old streets on the Lower East Side—Clinton, Rivington, Delancy, Rutgers, Stanton, Ludlow. Or when children went to school, teachers who found a name unpronounceable put down on the records something close enough but easier to say. After a time the parents would accept the new name the children brought home.

Milton Meltzer, *Taking Root*

------------ o ------------

Canadian Immigration Records

The National Archives of Canada holds immigration records from 1865 to 1935. It maintains microfilm copies of passenger manifests for ships arriving at six Canadian ports, including Quebec (from 1865) and Hali-

fax (from 1881) up to 1935. Chronologically arranged, the lists have no name index.

There is an online index to the half-million arrival records for 1925–1935: http://www.archives.ca/02/020118_e.html.

You can contact the National Archives of Canada at 395 Wellington Street, Ottawa K1A 0N3; phone: (613) 996-7458.

An excellent article in *Avotaynu* is essential reading for all researchers whose search includes Canada: "Immigration Records at the National Archives of the Canadian Jewish Congress" (October 1986).

How to Obtain Photographs of Your Ancestors' Steamships

The ships that took our ancestors to America were often overcrowded, uncomfortable, and in poor condition, yet they are a profoundly important part of our history. Therefore, an interesting and unusual addition to your family history would be photographs of the steamships themselves. Here are some sources for photographs of the steamships that brought our families to America.

If you locate a ship's manifest of interest from the Ellis Island records, you can purchase photographs (framed or unframed) directly from the Web site.

The Mariners Museum in Newport News, Virginia, has a huge collection of steamship photographs, indexed by the name of the ship. Call for more information: (757) 591-7767. The Web address is http://www.mariner.org.

An equally excellent source for these photographs as well as for additional information about steamships and their history is the Steamship Historical Society, 414 Pelton Avenue, Staten Island, NY 10310. Its Web site is at http://www.sshsa.net. If you want information about the society, write to the street address. However, if you want to obtain photographs of steamships from its huge collection, contact the University of Baltimore Langsdale Library, Steamship Historical Society of America Collection, 1420 Maryland Avenue, Baltimore, MD 21201. The Steamship Historical Photo Bank located at the University of Baltimore contains more than sixty thousand photos. The Website is http://archives.ubalt.edu/steamship/table.htm.

Naturalization Records: An Important Genealogical Source

Finding naturalization records is not like looking for a needle in a haystack. It can sometimes be worse. First you have to find the haystack. (It's not easy to find the "haystacks" of naturalization records, since they are scattered all over the place, look different, and are often hidden under

haystacks of other kinds of documents.) Once you find the haystack, looking for the needle (the papers *you* want) requires you to have certain
amounts of knowledge, skill, or luck. The final problem is this: however
difficult it might be to find a needle in a haystack, the saving grace is your
assumption that the needle is in there somewhere, but in searching for naturalization records of an ancestor, you can never know if you will find
what you are looking for. In fact, you can never be sure that the documents even exist.

Despite that pessimistic introduction, we have to attempt to tackle the
problem of naturalization records, because they are often profoundly
important sources of information—genealogically. One personal illustration will suffice. After sending for my great-grandfather's naturalization
records, I received a reply from the Immigration and Naturalization Service that gave me my great-grandfather's birth date, place of birth (in
Europe), place of last residence (in Europe), first wife's name (she died in
Europe and never came to America), date of arrival (this allowed me to
get a copy of the passenger list of the ship), and the names and birth dates
of all his children—some of whom were killed in the Holocaust and
whom I would never have been able to learn much about.

How did I get the document that provided me with so much information? I simply sent a letter to the Immigration and Naturalization Service,
stating what I wanted. The INS sent back a form. I filled it out, and in a
few weeks I received the information.

If it's that easy, what was the "needle in a haystack" business all about?
The answer is that it can be easy, and it can be terribly difficult, depending
on when your immigrant ancestor arrived in America and petitioned to
become a citizen.

Let's start at the beginning. We are looking for naturalization records,
better known as citizenship papers. On your family tree, only your immigrant ancestors might have naturalization records on file. Ancestors of
yours who never came to America would not have become citizens, obviously, and those ancestors (or family members) who were born in the
United States were automatically citizens and therefore never had to fill
out papers. For your immigrant relatives, however, citizenship papers
might very well be on file somewhere in the country. As a genealogist, you
should be interested in finding those records.

There are three different types of naturalization records. The first is the
declaration of intention, which was filled out by an immigrant who
wanted to become a citizen. This declaration of intention was commonly
known as one's "first papers." Then there is the final petition, which was

Declaration of intention to become a U.S. citizen for the author's maternal grandfather.

Certificate of naturalization for Abusch Kurzweil, the author's paternal great-grandfather.

completed just prior to becoming a citizen. Finally, there is the certificate of naturalization, which is the document given to the new citizen declaring that citizenship has been granted.

Among old family papers you can often find the certificate of naturalization, but this is the least valuable document in terms of information about the individual. The declaration of intention and the final petition are more valuable because they often reveal the answers to several personal questions of genealogical interest, such as occupation, date and place of birth, name of ship and date of arrival, and details on spouse and children.

There are a few more things to know before we discuss the locations of naturalization records. Although we may assume that immigrants became citizens (unless we know for sure that someone did not), it is possible that an immigrant ancestor of yours never applied for citizenship. Indeed, you may have a grandparent still alive who was an immigrant and who is not a citizen.

Also be aware of the fact that between 1855 and 1922, wives and children became citizens when the husband or father did. A woman became

a citizen automatically if she married a native-born or naturalized citizen. After 1922, women had to file their own papers.

The key date in the story of naturalization records is September 26, 1906. It was on that date that citizenship procedures became a federal function. If you are looking for the naturalization records of someone who was naturalized on or after September 26, 1906, you will usually have an easy time of searching. How do you know if your ancestor was naturalized on or after this date? You don't. But by asking a few questions in your family, you will probably have a good sense of when the immigration occurred and therefore when the naturalization could possibly have taken place.

If you have reason to believe that the naturalization of interest to you took place after this date, write to the Immigration and Naturalization Service, FOIA/PA Section, Room 5304, 425 Eye Street, N.W., Washington, DC 20536; phone: (202) 514-1554. Ask for a few copies of Form G-639 (Freedom of Information Privacy Act request). You can also obtain this form online at http://www.immigration.gov/graphics/formsfee/forms/g-639.htm.

Don't write a long letter describing your great-grandmother and her trip to America or any other information of a personal nature. No matter what you write, however long, short, or interesting, if it has to do with naturalization records, you will be sent a copy of Form G-639. So you might as well ask for it right from the start. And again, ask for a few copies; it will save you time when you want more.

Fill out the form as best you can. Do not be alarmed if you find that you cannot fill out the entire form. The INS has the nice policy of working with whatever information you can provide. If *all* you have is your ancestor's name, fill that in and leave everything else blank. The more you can fill out, the better your chance of locating the document—or the right document. (Once, when all I knew was the person's name, I received the papers of someone with the same name but who was an entirely different individual.)

The INS has been flooded with requests for information because of all the recent interest in genealogy. Although the agency is required by law to acknowledge receipt of your request, it can take as much as a year before you receive the information you are looking for. One thing I have yet to figure out is the INS policy on sending information. Sometimes I receive photocopies of the desired documents, and sometimes I receive a letter that contains a transcription of the information on the original documents.

What if you are sure that a person was naturalized but the INS tells you it has nothing? Either the person was naturalized before September 26, 1906, or a clerk made a mistake (which wouldn't be the first time). As far

as a clerical error is concerned, all you can do is try again (unless you want to—and are able to—examine the documents yourself, which we will discuss in a moment). The fun begins if the person was naturalized before our key date.

Before September 26, 1906, naturalizations were a local function, and naturalization proceedings could take place in just about any court, federal, state, or local. Although naturalizations took place in courts around the country after our key date, it was only then that the courts were required to send the information to the federal government for processing and filing.

Besides the lack of centralization of these documents before 1906, the procedures also varied. Therefore, different questions were asked of the potential citizens, and different records were kept. So although the type of information on post-1906 naturalization records is basically standard, the pre-1906 information varies, from next to nothing but the person's name and former country on up.

Let's say you are looking for the naturalization records of someone who arrived in the United States well before September 26, 1906. I say "well before" because if the immigrant arrived shortly before that cutoff date, there is still a good chance that the naturalization took place after the 1906 date. It is here where excellent detective work is essential. What you must try to determine is at which port the immigrant whose papers you are looking for entered the United States and where he or she resided right after arrival.

Once you have determined this to any degree of accuracy, you must try to determine to which court the immigrant might have gone to file "first papers." Of course, there is no guarantee that the immigrant filed for citizenship immediately upon arrival. He or she might have waited ten years (at which time the immigrant could have been living in another city), or he or she could never have gotten around to becoming a citizen.

We have to assume that the immigrant became a citizen, however, and we must also begin somewhere in our search. The best bet is to start at the location where the person entered the country and first resided. Finding the right court is not easy. It takes patience, time, and lots of letter writing—unless you can travel to the city in mind, in which case you might either get the search done quickly or you might reach a dead end. If this all sounds very negative, it is meant to.

The process of searching for pre-1906 naturalization records can be difficult, especially if you have little information to go on. Of course, if someone entered the United States in Boston and then spent all of his or her life there, the search would not be too difficult. You would have the field narrowed, and it would just be a limited amount of legwork. But the more vague your information is, the more difficulty you will have.

Indexes of naturalization records can save years of work, depending on the location you are dealing with. During the Great Depression, the Works Progress Administration (WPA) put people to work doing various interesting and unusual tasks. One of them was the photocopying and indexing of pre-1906 naturalization records for certain locations. If the naturalization that you are looking for took place in the states of Maine, Massachusetts, New Hampshire, or Rhode Island, or in New York City, you're in luck. The National Archives in Washington has the soundex indexes and photocopies for these states. These indexes consist of all six New England states and all five boroughs of New York City for the years 1790–1906. These indexes are also available on microfilm at LDS Family History Centers.

Since New York City was not only the entry point for most Jews who came to the United States but also the home of the greatest number of Jews, it would be justified to go into more detail here regarding naturalization resources for New York City.

The National Archives' Northeast Region Branch in New York City has an excellent collection of naturalization records for the New York City area:

> National Archives—Northeast Region (New York)
> 201 Varick Street
> New York, NY 10014
> e-mail: newyork.archives@nara.gov
> Web site: http://www.archives.gov/facilities/ny/new_york_city.html
> phone: (212) 337-1300
> fax: (212) 337-1306

The holdings there are a large but incomplete collection of New York City naturalizations. For example, the county clerk of each county in New York has the records of naturalizations that occurred in the state supreme court of that particular county. Other records are scattered elsewhere as well. In fact, this situation of the noncentralization of these records is a good example of what a researcher often has to face when trying to track down naturalization records.

A trip to this National Archives regional branch would be worthwhile for all people doing searches of these documents for the New York City area.

There is one important reason why a trip to this records center (or any archives) is worthwhile. A clerk will try to answer a specific question. However, in my opinion, only you alone can do an adequate search. You can look for a dozen alternate spellings of a name, whereas a clerk will usually only check the spelling provided. In addition, every researcher knows that you always learn more than what you are looking for—*if* you do it yourself.

Finding naturalization records is not easy but is certainly worthwhile. Be aware, if course, that the earlier the naturalization took place, the less information there is likely to be. However, you can never know what you might find until you try.

The best book on the entire subject of naturalizations in the United States is John J. Newman's *American Naturalization Records, 1790–1990: What They Are and How to Use Them* (Bountiful, Utah: Heritage Quest, 1998).

O

> With our despised immigrant clothing we shed our impossible Hebrew names. A committee of our friends, several years ahead of us in American experience, put their heads together and concocted American names for us all. Those of our real names that had no pleasing American equivalents they ruthlessly discarded, content if they retained the initials. My mother, possessing a name that was not easily translatable, was punished with the undignified nickname of Annie. Fetchke, Joseph and Deborah issued as Frieda, Joseph and Dora, respectively. As for poor me, I was simply cheated. The name they gave me was hardly new. My Hebrew name being Maryashe in full, Mashke for short, Russianized into Marya, my friends said that it would hold good in English as Mary; which was very disappointing, as I longed to possess a strange-sounding American name like the others.
>
> Mary Antin, *The Promised Land*

> The future of Judaism belongs to that school which can best understand the past.
>
> Leopold Lowe, Hungarian rabbi

> Research into the past, as an aim in itself, without the present, is not worth a bean.
>
> Chaim Nachman Bialik

O

The Legitimacy of Sending for Family History Documents

As you send for all of the different kinds of documents available that will help you to research your family history, you might wonder whether the U.S. government and local government agencies see your requests for information as important enough for them to help you. *Never worry.* Not

only are you entitled to see the kinds of records that are described in this book, but you will also be paying for almost everything. Government documents cost generally between $2 and $10—and considering the simple process required for most document searches, it becomes a rather lucrative business for government agencies.

So never feel that your family history is not "important" and that you will get a response only if you are on "official" business. Genealogy in pursuit of one's family history is a legitimate and accepted endeavor.

Everything that typified the old country, in family names as well as first names, had to go. The Russian -skis and -vitches were dropped. Levinsky became Levin, Michaelowitch, Michaels. Russian and Polish names were Anglicized: Bochlowitz to Buckley, Stepinsky to Stevens, Shidlowsky to Sheldon, Horowitz to Herrick, Willinsky to Wilson. Davidowitz became Davidson, Jacobson became Jackson. The Germanic names too were readily translated into English: Weiss-White, Preiss-Price, Reiss-Rice, Rothenberg-Redmont.

Milton Meltzer, *Taking Root*

"These Are the Generations"

As we continue to travel backward in time through Jewish history, we find it increasingly difficult to discover our individual ancestors and the lives they led. Some of us will find it impossible to trace branches of our family histories farther back than three generations. In part this is because of the recent adoption of fixed surnames as we discussed in Chapter Eight. In part, your inability to find people who remember the histories of your families will also contribute to the difficulty of the task. But it is important that we continue to see Jewish history in terms of individuals and families. Jewish history is the story of individual Jews, not simply the "important" people. Although those "important" people had sweeping effects on our Jewish ancestors, we want to continue to examine the lives of our ancestors and how they might have lived them.

Jewish history can be seen as several overlapping layers. First there are the individuals. Individuals are connected to each other through their immediate families. Immediate families come together to form the Jewish people, and if we take our progression one step farther, the Jewish people belong to the "family of humankind."

It is easy for us to view the first stage of our progression. Each of us is an individual, as are our parents, and so on. We want to view the lives of as many persons as we can and to see how their lives fit into Jewish history. For example, when we view the life of your grandmother who journeyed to America in 1908, we see her as a significant part of Jewish history. When we learn about a cousin of ours who was murdered in the Holocaust, we see that as a significant part of Jewish history. Despite the fact that those experiences happened to millions of people, we enter those experiences ourselves through the lives of the people in our families.

We can also observe the history of our families. Since we, ourselves, are a part of many families, we can see the differences among them. One of our families might be more religious, another might be more Zionist, another might be more literary, and so on. Our purpose is not to generalize about people but rather to see where they fit into the larger story of Jewish history. In my father's family, for example, there is one branch of the family tree almost all of whom went to Israel when it was still Palestine. Another branch, almost in its entirety, stayed in Europe and was killed in the Holocaust. Hardly a representative of that branch left Europe. In still another branch, nearly the whole family escaped the Holocaust and came to America. It is fascinating to examine these family branches to see how differences and decisions just like these resulted in modern Jewish history.

Can you make these same kinds of observations in your families? Can you see certain entire branches of your family tree having gone in one general direction while others took different courses? What about your branch? When viewed from the outside, what choices were made by your family during the last several generations that have affected you and your life—as a person and as a Jew?

There are countless stories of American families who have discovered family in Israel whom they never knew existed. Sometimes branches of a family traveled to Israel a few generations ago. In other cases, survivors of the Holocaust went to Israel and their American cousins did not know that they survived. There could be branches of your family in other countries as well. In my own family, there are branches in Israel, Australia, Poland, Hungary, South America, and the United States.

Again, however, there will come a point when it will be impossible for you to trace the tracks of your early ancestors, in which case you can focus on the history of their community. Let's say that a branch of your family can be traced to the town of Jaroslaw in Galicia. Perhaps you can even trace a few generations back in Jaroslaw with names, dates, and stories. But then you can go no further; no one remembers anyone that far back,

and research was unable to turn up anything about your specific family. This should not stop you from continuing to understand the Jewish community of which your family was a part. Where is Jaroslaw? What was it like? When did the Jewish community establish itself there? What is its history? Although you cannot trace individual members of your family in Jaroslaw, you can certainly begin to get an idea of their lives as members of the Jewish community there and in that way enter Jewish history.

To continue with our example, we have to remember that the history of Jaroslaw had to have affected the lives of your Jaroslaw ancestors. As a part of the community, its history and its events touch its members' lives. By quickly checking a source such as the *Encyclopedia Judaica,* we can get a glimpse of the history of Jaroslaw back to the 1600s. We learn about the famous fairs that took place there and the meetings of the Council of the Lands of Poland, which were held there. These meetings were important for all of Polish Jewry. We also learn that in 1738 there were one hundred families living in Jaroslaw. If this was a town of yours, perhaps one of those families was yours. In 1737 a case of "blood libel" occurred, giving us a further idea of the history of this town. This just scratches the surface of the history of the Jewish community of Jaroslaw—but if it was a town of your ancestors, you would want to continue to learn about it and thereby enter Jewish history.

In other words, when you have traced your family history as far back as you can go, expand your understanding of your history by examining the circumstances of daily life in the towns and regions whence you have come. For example, if you know that your family came from Germany in the 1840s, an understanding of the jumble and jostle of city-states that was Germany in the decades before that date will contribute to your sense of the history of your ancestors and the fabric of their lives.

Although it is not possible to take every family history back through the Middle Ages, it is possible to begin to understand the history of the Jewish people through the history of a particular Jewish community. Again, let us take the example of the town of Jaroslaw. Two items in the brief history that I reviewed are of particular interest. The first is the Council of the Lands of Poland, and the second is the "blood libel." To understand the history of your ancestors' community, you would need to know about the Council of the Lands of Poland and also the history of "blood libel." In both cases, these questions will take you to other aspects of Jewish history, and again you will find that you have entered Jewish history through the history of the community of your ancestors. This method of understanding Jewish history can be compared to setting up a long row of dominoes and then tipping over the first one. One by

one, the entire row of dominoes will fall over. In the same way, once you have touched any piece of Jewish history, you will arrive quickly at the next one until you have gone through history yourself and begun to understand the experiences of your family. Your ancestors are the focus of this process; in tracing their steps, you are tracing the steps of the Jewish people. In tracing the steps of the Jewish people, you will eventually arrive at the beginning of time, and you will also arrive back in the present—at yourself.

A next step would be to begin to get an understanding of the migration patterns within Jewish history. Again, if your family came from Jaroslaw, they were certainly not there since the beginning of time. The Jewish community in Jaroslaw had a beginning—before that time, there were no Jews there. Whence did the Jews of Jaroslaw come? There are general answers to this type of question, and a familiarity with migration patterns—the routes taken by Jews throughout Jewish history—allows us to get a better idea of where our families came from. For example, we know that in 1492 the Jews of Spain were expelled from that country. Historical research informs us of many places where Spanish Jews fled. If the places where they fled included areas we know our families to be from, it is reasonable to assume that parts of our families may have originated in Spain. Although we cannot be sure of this, it is reasonable speculation, and we can continue to approach Jewish history from that perspective. A branch of my family, as I mentioned earlier, whose earliest known location in Europe was the city of Przemysl, claims a family tradition that had us originate in Spain. Although our names are not Spanish (we were probably in Przemysl when surnames were first required) and we do not look Spanish, it is interesting to note that the first synagogue in Przemysl was built by two Spanish immigrants in 1560. This means that Spanish Jews did reach the east end of Galicia at that time and that our family tradition is conceivable. Suddenly, the expulsion of the Jews from Spain in 1492 becomes a real part of my history.

The details of Jewish history, from the destruction of the Second Temple to modern times, are filled with tremendous variety and complexity. Although short histories of the Jewish people have been written that include the major events and areas of our history, they cannot, by definition, tell the stories of individuals and their communities in the detail that they deserve. And it is the detail that is often the most colorful, the most instructive, and the most interesting.

It is a curious fact that most of us have a good idea as to the events of biblical history, a familiarity with the Talmudic era, and a general knowl-

edge of recent Jewish history during the last century or so. But in between those eras, from the early days of the Diaspora to the 1800s, most of us have no more than a vague idea of Jewish life. We are familiar with biblical personalities, dramas, and heroes, as we are familiar with the Holocaust and the birth of the state of Israel, but what was life in Prague like in the 1600s? How did our ancestors in Germany live in the 1700s? What was life like for our forebears in the centuries between the Talmud and the present?

────── ○ ──────

He has a great future, for he understands the past.

Heinrich Heine

────── ○ ──────

DISCOVERING THE OLD COUNTRY

AS YOU TRACE YOUR Jewish family history, you will come to see that your focus is generally on people and places. As your family tree grows, like branches and leaves on a tree, the names of your relatives will fill up the space and will become the outline of your history. Along with names, of course, will come marriages, children, occupations, dates of birth and death, family stories, and other details. But the backdrop of it all will be the towns and communities from which your families have come.

In this chapter we will look closely at the sources available to locate your towns, to learn about them, and to plan your possible visit.

○

Remember the days of old.

—Deuteronomy 32:7

○

Where Once We Walked

Every now and then a reference book is published that fills a gigantic void for researchers. The award-winning *Where Once We Walked* (WOWW), by Gary Mokotoff and Sallyann Amdur Sack with Alexander Sharon, published by Avotaynu, is just such a book. Originally published in 1991, the 2002 edition has been completely revised and updated to reflect the changes in the political geography of Central and Eastern Europe. WOWW identifies more than 23,500 towns in Central and Eastern

Europe where Jews lived before the Holocaust and includes 17,500 alternate names, due to the numerous changes to many town names and the varieties of spellings for each town name (including Yiddish names, names under former political systems, and synonyms). WOWW is the most ambitious and remarkable Jewish gazetteer ever produced.

WOWW is a massive work. It pinpoints each town's location by providing the exact latitude and longitude of the town as well as its direction and distance from the closest major city. It also provides Jewish population figures from before the Holocaust. Finally, for those who want more information about the Jewish history of the towns, each entry includes citations to other sources that refer to that town.

WOWW also includes an index to town names using the Daitch-Mokotoff Soundex System, which allows the researcher to locate a town's entry based on how it sounds rather than how it is spelled.

Gary Mokotoff and Sallyann Amdur Sack did a brilliant job in creating this most valuable reference source.

JewishGen ShtetlSeeker

An extremely useful and enjoyable tool provided by JewishGen.org is the ShtetlSeeker (http://www.jewishgen.org/ShtetlSeeker). Type in the name of the town that is of interest, and ShtetlSeeker will display the latitude and longitude for each location, the distance and direction from the country's capital, and a link to a map. Once you know the coordinates, you can get a list of towns within a certain distance of that given latitude and longitude.

Central Archives for the History of the Jewish People

The Central Archives for the History of the Jewish People, officially founded in 1969, was actually established in 1938 as the Jewish Historical General Archives. Its goal, as stated on its Web site (http://sites.huji.ac.il/archives/page18.htm), is "the reconstruction of an unbroken chain of historical documentation, reflecting the collective past of the Jewish people: a Jewish National Archives."

The Central Archives are located in Jerusalem at 46 Jabotinsky Street. The Web site explains:

> The chief genealogical sources are birth, marriage, death and burial registers. These were maintained chronologically in most communities

from about the end of the 18th century onwards. The *Central Archives* have a large collection of such registers from Germany, as well as sporadic registers from other countries, such as France, Italy and Poland. Other sources are circumcision registers, voting lists, tax lists, etc. All, however, are catalogued geographically, by communities and not by the names of the people listed in them. It is therefore necessary to know precisely where your parents or grandparents were born/married/died in order to initiate a search in the *Central Archives* for material on additional generations. In some cases, the *Central Archives* have no relevant material, but are able to provide addresses of archives in other countries holding such material.

It would be best to write to this archive, which houses the largest collection of Judaica in the world, and ask for a listing of its holdings for specific locations. For example, if you are interested in Minsk, write to the archives and ask for a listing of material in its Minsk holdings.

––––––––– O –––––––––

To preserve the past is half of immortality.

—Benjamin Disraeli

––––––––– O –––––––––

Encyclopedia Judaica

If you are not familiar with *Encyclopedia Judaica* (EJ), you should be. This beautifully produced sixteen-volume set of books is a wellspring of Jewish knowledge. Though various criticisms have been lodged against the encyclopedia, it remains the finest source, in my opinion, with which to begin research on most Jewish subjects.

Although the smallest of villages and towns will not appear in the EJ unless something quite unusual happened there, you can find brief articles about hundreds of Jewish settlements throughout the world. Volume 1 is the encyclopedia's index. Always check the index because it can lead you to discussions of subjects that do not have their own entries in the encyclopedia.

When looking up towns of interest in the EJ, I have noticed that practically every entry provides the names of the significant rabbis who served in that town. When a topic in an entry of the EJ also has its own entry, this is indicated by an asterisk (*) next to the term or name. Inevitably, the names of the rabbis have such an indicator. This allows me to go to

the entry devoted to the rabbi of the town where my family lived. And inevitably, that article indicates who the rabbi of that rabbi was, marked with an asterisk, sending me to yet another entry. It is astonishing how far back you can eventually go. In this way I have traced the chain of Torah teaching, from rabbi to rabbi and from generation to generation, all the way to the towns of interest to me.

Each entry in the EJ has a bibliography as well, which is useful in directing you to even more useful information.

_____ ○ _____

There is an uninterrupted chain of generations that makes it possible for us to reward ourselves as having descended from Abraham, Isaac, and Jacob. We may question this statement biologically; nevertheless, they were our ancestors for all intents and purposes. We are members of one *mishpahah*, even though our cosmology, our conception of the universe, our way of living, our whole hierarchy of values may differ radically from theirs. Our relationship to our earliest childhood as a people is analogous to the relationship we have to our own childhood. We think and live differently from the way we did when we were children. Yet when we think of our childhood, we maintain that we are the same persons we were before, even though there may not be a single cell in our body that has remained unchanged since we were children; but there is a continuity of personality that consists of memories, associations and habits.

—Rabbi Ira Eisenstein

_____ ○ _____

Locating Landsmanshaften

Before explaining how to track down a landsmanshaft, I want to explain the usefulness in doing so. If your family came from a certain town that still has a landsmanshaft, there is a good chance that members of the organization knew your family and can tell you about them. In addition, landsmanshaft members can give you a personal perspective on the European town of your ancestors. They might also have pictures of the town.

I have tracked down the landsmanshaften of two towns in which my ancestors lived, and I've gone to their meetings. In one case I was able to purchase a copy of the town memorial book and to meet people who

knew my family. In the other case my luck was even better: I met a man who had photographs of family members of mine who were killed in the Holocaust! If not for that man and his photographs, my family would never have known what those cousins looked like. I also met a man at a landsmanshaft meeting who was a musician. He was about ninety years old, charming and friendly. He had played the fiddle at my grandparents' wedding in Europe! From members of this landsmanshaft I learned the names and addresses of landsmen in Israel who knew my family from Europe. I wrote to them and received letters with still more stories about my family and their life in the shtetl.

It is often extremely difficult to track down landsmanshaften. Most of these organizations have ceased to exist. For the few that remain, some have but a handful of active members; even if they do meet, they do so infrequently. A few of the groups are still quite active and still meet regularly, but they are difficult to locate. There is no central headquarters for this kind of information. Nonetheless, you can make the following attempts:

○ Contact the office of the cemetery where the landsmanshaft has a plot. The office will often know how to get in touch with a contact person.

○ Inquire of the YIVO Institute for Jewish Research. YIVO has published a booklet called *A Guide to YIVO's Landsmanshaften Archive,* by Rosaline Schwartz and Susan Milamed. This index reflects the content of YIVO's landsmanshaft archives, a collection of material of great potential interest to Jewish family historians. Since YIVO has been actively seeking material from landsmanshaften over the years, it may have some information on how to contact them.

○ The United Jewish Appeal (UJA) Federation, I've been told, has a superb list of landsmanshaften, which the UJA uses for fundraising. The federation is protective of its lists, but it can't hurt to try.

○ Another method of locating landsmanshaften, or even landsmen, is to place an ad in a Jewish newspaper. People have been known to take out an ad in a big-city Jewish paper saying, "Anyone belonging to or having knowledge of a *(name of town)* landsmanshaft, please write or call me." An ad like this can bring interesting results.

○ An excellent article on the subject of landsmanshaften appeared in *Toledot* in the summer 1978 issue. Written by Zachary M. Baker, former head librarian at the YIVO Institute for Jewish Research and currently a librarian at Stanford University, the article is titled "Landsmanshaften and the Jewish Genealogist."

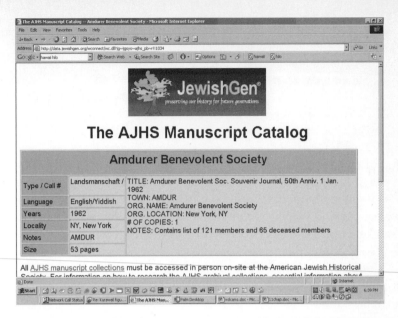

A typical entry in the JewishGen.org Landsmanshaft Manuscript Collection database.

Sources for Landsmanshaft Records

There are a number of sources for landsmanshaft records.

○ The JewishGen.org site offers a database providing information on its Landsmanshaft Manuscript Collection. To see this material, you must visit the AJHS Archives. The address of this Web page is http://www.jewishgen.org/databases/ajhsv.htm.

○ ShtetLinks (http://www.shtetlinks.jewishgen.org), a project of JewishGen.org, is a wonderful source for information about selected towns. Entries often include information about landsmanshaften.

○ The Association of Polish Jews in Israel maintains a Web site that lists landsmanshaften functioning in Israel (http://www.zchor.org/POLISH10.HTM). It can also be contacted at the following address:

Association of Polish Jews in Israel
158 Dizzengof Street
63461 Tel Aviv, Israel
phone: (972-3) 522-5078
fax: (972-3) 523-6684

○
_____

The past is our cradle, not our prison, and there is danger as well as appeal in its glamour. The past is for inspiration, not imitation, for continuation, not repetition.

—Israel Zangwill, *Fortnightly Review,* April 1919

_____
○

Your Shtetl or Town During the Holocaust

Earlier in the book I discussed the International Tracing Service (ITS) in Germany. Another very important source of Holocaust information is Yad Vashem.

Yad Vashem in Israel used to publish a series of books called *Guide to Unpublished Materials of the Holocaust Period*. These books offered a listing of the towns represented in the Yad Vashem archives. Usually this material was taken from postwar testimony offered by survivors. You might find some moving and fascinating information about your towns here.

In 1965 Yad Vashem published the *Blackbook of Localities Whose Jewish Population Was Exterminated by the Nazis*. This book contains a list of almost 34,000 localities in Europe with Jewish residents. Some of these localities contained thousands of Jews, and others contained just one or two Jews living among non-Jewish neighbors.

During the Holocaust, almost every city, town, and village listed in the *Blackbook* was purged of its Jewish population.

The reader of the *Blackbook* will find listings of the tiniest hamlets in Europe. If your ancestors came from a small village that has long disappeared from the map, chances are good that the *Blackbook* will list it. Often you will be told the names of towns your family lived in but you will be unable to find any references to them, but you may find it in the *Blackbook,* which will also indicate the number of Jewish residents in that town sometime before the war. The book will tell you the date of the census on which the population figures were based.

I once gave a lecture in which I mentioned the *Blackbook*. I rather boldly stated that the book listed *every* Eastern European town. A young woman raised her hand and said, "The town my family was from, in Hungary, had only four people in it. They were all my family. That town will not be listed!" Well, the book, as we said, lists town names and their prewar population figures. We looked up the town that the woman had

in mind—and we found it! And the population *was* four! A skeptic was suddenly a believer.

Although this book is out of print, the information contained in it is included in *Where Once We Walked*.

———————— o ————————

No individual can be constructed entire without a link with the past.

—Ahad Ha'am

———————— o ————————

How to Locate Your Shtetl

It is not always easy to locate a shtetl, town, village, or city. There are several possible problems:

- o The location may no longer exist, having been wiped off the map with its inhabitants during the Holocaust. This is rare, but it happens.
- o The name may have changed since your family last resided there.
- o You may know the location by a name in a different language from the one in current use.
- o You may know the location by its Jewish name, but not by its more commonly used name.
- o The way the name sounds is not necessarily the way it is spelled on maps.
- o Since borders change throughout history, you may be looking for your town in the wrong country.
- o The town may have been hardly a town at all and may simply not be found on most maps. Frequently, a town was no more than a few houses.

If you have tried, without success, to locate a particular town, do not give up. There are several additional possibilities.

Most libraries have an atlas collection, and large public and university libraries often have extensive map departments. One of your first steps to locating your towns and shtetlach is to consult a gazetteer. A gazetteer is a geographical dictionary. You use it just like a dictionary, looking up the word by the various ways you think it might be spelled. A gazetteer will

provide the "definition" of a location. It will tell you the country that it is in, its proximity to other well-known locations, the longitude and latitude, and even a little about the current and historical situation.

One of the finest gazetteers available is *The Columbia Lippincott Gazetteer of the World.* This book was published after World War II, so it will often not be helpful for towns that were completely wiped off the map. In that case, you should check the earlier edition, known as *A Complete Pronouncing Gazetteer or Geographical Dictionary of the World,* published by the J. B. Lippincott Company in 1906.

A gazetteer in the German language that is also excellent is *Ritters Geographisch-Statistisches Lexikon.*

A final suggestion is this: whenever you learn the name of a town, try to find out where it was near. If you can locate a familiar spot on a map, you can then examine a detailed map of the area and try to locate the place by scanning the map. One of my ancestral towns is Przemysl, but I had never seen it written; I had only heard its name, which is pronounced "Pahshemishel." It took me a while to find it on a map, but after using some of the resources just mentioned, I was able to do so rather quickly. My one key was that I knew its general vicinity. From that point on, finding it was simple.

When you have exhausted the few sources pertaining to geographical locations mentioned here, as well as the many others discussed elsewhere in this book, I would urge you to read Zachary M. Baker's fine study on locating Eastern European towns, published in the winter 1978 issue of *Toledot,* titled "Eastern European 'Jewish Geography': Some Problems and Suggestions (Or, How to Get from Amshinov to Mszczonów Without Moving an Inch)." Baker's article is quite useful and inspirational if you are having difficulty spelling, pronouncing, or locating your ancestral towns. But you should first consult *Where Once We Walked.* It can solve most spelling problems when looking for towns and is the best source for locating Jewish towns that exists.

Soundex Systems

It is often difficult or impossible to find names of towns or surnames due to spelling errors or variations. Researchers have been dealing with this problem for a long time, and the so-called soundex systems have been developed to try to solve problems like these. I would suggest that you familiarize yourself with the whole phenomenon of soundex systems by reading Gary Mokotoff's excellent study of them on the Web at http://www.avotaynu.com/soundex.html.

○

"Why are you crying, Mother? Because the house is burning?"

"Yes."

"We shall build another, I promise you."

"It's not the house, son. If I cry, it is because a precious document is being destroyed before our eyes."

"*What document?*"

"Our family tree; it is illustrious, you know."

"Don't cry. I'll give you another. I'll start anew, I promise you."

At the time, Dov-Ber was five.

—Elie Wiesel, telling of the Maggid of Mezeritch,
a Hasidic Master, in *Souls on Fire*

○

Genealogical Sources in the Old Country: How to Do Long-Distance Research

Once you have determined where your family came from, you will want to figure out how to get information from those places. One way, of course, is to travel to your ancestral towns. One need not, however, travel to Europe or the former Soviet Union in order to get records from those places.

Having said that, it is important to make the point that the path is not easy, nor is it consistent. For years, genealogists thought that records behind the Iron Curtain would never be within reach. Today things are different. We have more contact with archivists in Eastern Europe and the former Soviet Union than ever before. At the same time, it seems that things are changing in that part of the world quite rapidly: one day a Russian archive is answering genealogical requests for a low fee and rather quickly, and the next day the rates have jumped up and the service is slow. Or a records center asks for a fee before doing research for you and finds and sends a lot of material, but then someone else sends money, receives a canceled check, and never hears from the center again.

I have been careful in this book to make sure that I send you in productive directions. I have seen many books on genealogy that fill their pages with names and addresses of overseas archives that hardly ever prove lucrative. The following are some pieces of general advice as well as some sources that some of us have found to be useful.

1. Don't underestimate the usefulness of comparing notes with other genealogists. Discoveries are being made every day. Wouldn't it be nice to

hear of the successful experience a fellow genealogist had writing to organizations in Poland before you do your own letter writing? Join a Jewish
Genealogical Society; plug into the ever-growing network of people who
are doing Jewish genealogical research.

2. Subscribe to *Avotaynu* and purchase some back issues. As you look
through the index, notice that there are articles on just about every country in the world, written by people who have had firsthand experience
with genealogical research.

One thing you will notice when reading the articles is that the situation
keeps changing. The clearest example of that is for locations in the former Soviet Union. There is no question that things have opened up considerably and that lots of people have received information that we only
dreamed about just a few years ago. But it is also true that many of us
have had radically different experiences, with great successes and great
stumbling blocks.

Nevertheless, a growing number of people are involved with contacting archives overseas, and with the increased experience has come some
important sources.

3. The Mormon interest in genealogy is perhaps the most significant
factor helping those of us who cannot travel to the countries of interest
and don't want to rely on the often dubious process of writing to local
archives in Europe. The LDS Family History Library has the largest collection of Jewish records in the world. For example, I had no difficulty
locating the birth, marriage, and death records for my grandmother's family from Hungary because the Mormons have records for her little Hungarian town going back a few hundred years.

The Mormon collections are remarkable and should not be underesti-
mated. The Mormons have microfilmed records worldwide, and their collections grow daily. Simply put, anyone doing serious Jewish genealogical
research must keep alert to the Mormon holdings.

4. An effective way to work with foreign countries is through the aid
of professional researchers who live in those countries. It is important to
keep in mind that a hired researcher might spend lots of time without success. It may take many, many hours of research before something interesting is found. It can get expensive.

On the other hand, many of us have had great success when contacting reliable freelance researchers in other places around the world. Once
again, *Avotaynu* is a useful source. You will often see advertisements there
placed by researchers looking for customers. In addition, there are articles written by freelance researchers in *Avotaynu*.

○

I never realized, when I was very young, how much I missed by never having met either of my grandfathers. Not having known a grandfather, I had to go out looking for him, and what I will try and set out here is simply the story of the search. The trouble is that, given my own type of mind, this is bound to take me further than a few nostalgic family tales. However, if it is a little grown up for the *einiklach* [grandchildren] at this stage, they'll get round to it one day. Above all, they will understand, I think, that I was not just looking for my grandfather but for myself.

—Chaim Raphael, "Roots—Jewish Style," *Midstream*

Tradition must be a springboard into the future, not an armchair for repose.

—David Ben-Gurion

○

Visiting the Old Country

Sooner or later, every Jewish family historian considers planning a trip to the places in the old country from whence they or their ancestors came. For years I harbored the fantasy of walking the same streets in Poland that my great-grandfather walked as a child and as a young married man. I wanted to see the shops that were once ours; I wondered if the Jewish cemetery still existed. Were there any Jewish records in the town? Were there any Jews still there? Did the citizens of the town remember my family? These questions and others ran through my mind hundreds of times.

I eventually made the trip to Poland and did visit my great-grandfather's town. Before I share that experience and discuss the things you ought to consider before making such a trip, it would be best to explore the cons of the argument as to whether or not to travel to the old country.

Several family members were upset with me for considering and planning such a trip. "How could you even step foot on the places where our people were murdered?" they asked. Other people said, "You have better things to do with your money than support those countries." Still others said, "If you want to go to find your roots, go to Israel!" People used all kinds of reasons to dissuade me from making the journey.

"What do you expect to find there?" many asked. "Everything was destroyed." Or "They won't let you see anything. You are wasting your time." Or "I know someone who was there shortly after the war. Nothing is left."

I've heard all the arguments, and while I can appreciate them all, I nonetheless had my own private reasons for going. I had to see for myself.

Let me try to answer all of the questions and objections as best as I can. Although I know that the decision of whether to travel to the old country is a personal one, I think it would be useful to share my own feelings on the subject.

I try to understand the bitterness felt by survivors toward the non-Jewish population in the countries where our people were murdered. I can understand their not wanting to have contact with people, many of whom just stood by watching while Jews were killed. Others, of course, did not just stand by but actively participated. But I was born after the war, and as the member of a new generation, I feel I must have faith in humankind. I cannot harbor the same feelings as the generations before me. Although I am, for example, quite suspicious of Germans who were adults in Germany during the war, I cannot declare them all guilty, and I surely can hold nothing against their children. The same is true for other countries in Europe.

As for the comment (which I have heard several times) that my "roots" are really in Israel and I should go there instead, I have two responses. One is that I have visited Israel and feel that every Jew who has the opportunity should do the same. But my "roots" do not lie only in Israel. Maimonides was from Spain, Rashi from France, the Baal Shem Tov from Eastern Europe, and even the Babylonian Talmud was not written in Israel. Certainly my roots go *back* to Israel, but they travel far and wide outside of Israel as well. I want to discover *all* of my past.

I was quite influenced before my first trip to Eastern Europe by the people who told me that everything was destroyed and that there was nothing left to see. If this were true, I thought to myself, then surely I would be wasting my time and money. I thought about it for a long time. What if the town was completely leveled and a new town built on top of it? What would be the point of seeing this? But finally I decided: I was going to Eastern Europe not only to see what was left but also what was gone! I had done enough research about the town and seen enough photographs of the places where my ancestors lived to know what it looked like when they were there. I wanted to see what had stayed the same and what had changed. Seeing *nothing* would also be important to me.

Josef Schlaf and his daughter, Anya, cousins of the author, 1978. A Holocaust survivor who remained in Poland, Josef was discovered by the author through genealogical research.

There was one additional factor in my decision to visit Eastern Europe: I had cousins who lived there. My father's cousin, Josef Schlaf, lived in Warsaw until his death several years ago (he is survived by his wife and daughter), and my mother's first cousin Gyorgy Barta, may he rest in peace, lived with his family in Budapest. I wanted to visit them. This was the most important element in my decision. I finally decided to go.

The day finally came. I arrived in Warsaw. After spending a few days in that historic Jewish city with my cousin, I went to Przemysl. One of the first things I wanted to see was the Jewish cemetery. Everyone knew where it was. When I saw it, I was astounded for opposite reasons. I was shocked at how bad it looked and by how good it looked. It was interesting to learn that the major problem with Jewish cemeteries in Poland is not vandalism but neglect. The stones were not toppled over and crumbling from deliberate desecration. It was the bad winters, the overgrown trees and bushes, the tall growth of weeds and roots, and the total neglect of the whole area that caused the cemetery to look so bad. On the other hand, there it was, sitting there peacefully. Many of the stones could be read with ease. Others were quite worn but could still be made out. Still others were not visible at first, but after we pulled up giant weeds and pushed aside bushes and overgrowth, they too appeared. Some of the

Zsuzsa Barta, second cousin of
the author, in Budapest, Hungary.
She now lives in Australia.

stones were 150 years old. Others were certainly older, but a good percentage of the old stones were totally illegible. Some were just slabs of rock with no inscription. Obviously, they once had words engraved on them, but time has worn them clean. I stayed in the town for five days. Three times I visited the cemetery, taking photos on each visit, recognizing names each time I uncovered new tombstones under the overgrowth. Visiting that cemetery was one of the most moving moments of my life. Each time I went, I prayed and somehow felt the presence of a Jewish community that once was so filled with life and now is present only in the remains of the cemetery.

One of the many surprises in Przemysl was the number of people I found who spoke English. English is taught in the schools and is apparently a popular subject. I had almost no problem communicating with people. The people who spoke English were happy to show me around and serve as my interpreters.

I was anxious to see where the synagogues were. I knew from my research that there were several synagogues before the war. Today, two of the buildings still exist. One is now the Przemysl Public Library. The other is a bus garage. This was obviously an upsetting discovery. I did not expect the buildings still to be synagogues (there are only a handful of Jews left in Przemysl); however, it was horrible to see this beautiful building turned into a garage. Somehow the library did not bother me as much. Actually, the reason is evident. Although I visited both buildings, I was most interested in the one that is now the library. This synagogue was a short distance from where my family lived, so I was fairly certain it was in this synagogue that my family prayed. Walking into the library, I was obviously a stranger. Only one member of the library staff spoke English, and I was introduced to her. She was a young, pretty woman, very bright and warm. After an interesting conversation and a glass of tea, which I was served right in the middle of the library, the young librarian invited me to her home for that evening. I had a wonderful time, learned a lot about Przemysl from her and her husband, and I continued to write to them for years. They sent me information about Przemysl, and I sent them magazines about tennis, their favorite pastime.

I could go on for pages about my first trip to Eastern Europe. Suffice it to say that it was a deeply moving and profound experience for me. Again, both what I saw and what I knew I could never again see had a great impact on me. I visited death camps and former ghettos. I visited synagogues that were hundreds of years old and cemeteries that were even older. I met Jews who survived the Holocaust and stayed in Eastern Europe, and I met some of their children. They are all eager to make contact with American Jews, and in this way I think my trip served a valuable purpose in showing a few lonely Jews that they are not totally alone.

Did I discover anything of specific genealogical value in Eastern Europe? I certainly did. When I was in Przemysl, the city of my great-grandfather's birth, I went to the city hall and asked the man behind the counter (through the aid of a Jewish man who still lived in the town and spoke some English) if he had my great-grandfather's birth record. He asked me when my great-grandfather was born. I said 1867. The man climbed up a tall ladder and reached up to grab a volume that was covered with dust. When he set the book down on the counter, I saw that it was a birth register of Jews from the 1800s! This particular volume was dated 1860–1870. Within a few minutes I found the name of my great-grandfather, along with his parents' names, their address in Przemysl, and other information as well. It was the birth record of my great-grandfather, Abusch Kurzweil.

A former synagogue in Przemysl, Poland. It is now a bus garage.

I was told the myth so many times that all Jewish records were destroyed. The fact of the matter is quite different. There, in Przemysl, Poland, was the birth record of the man after whom I was named. It was waiting for me all these years.

I have had the opportunity to do more genealogical traveling since my first trip. In addition to the wonderful time I had in Poland and Hungary visiting my relatives, I made other discoveries. One of my most extraordinary moments was locating the gravestone of one of my great-great-grandmothers in a tiny town in Hungary.

How to Plan Your Trip

Things have changed considerably since my first trip to Eastern Europe. They also changed drastically after my second trip. (When I entered the former Soviet Union, restrictions on travelers there were severe: only a limited number of towns could be visited; the others were off limits. I waited for hours in Lvov, hoping for permission to travel to Dobromil, my father's birthplace. After waiting for seven hours, permission was denied.) Today, in the former Soviet Union and in Eastern Europe generally, travel is much easier than it was only a few years ago. Many travel

The author (right), with the archivist in the city hall in Przemysl, Poland, in the late 1970s, holding a book containing the birth record of his great-grandfather, Abusch Kurzweil.

agents specialize in trips to specific countries; I suggest you try to work with one of them.

More important, I strongly urge you to hook up with one of the Jewish Genealogical Societies. Undoubtedly there are people in these groups who have recently made the kind of trip you are thinking about. There's nothing like good advice from recent travelers.

On the other hand, don't let the remarks of others about their experiences have too great an impact on you. For example, many people have had no success doing archival research when traveling to Poland. Others, myself included, have been able to walk into an archive, ask for information, and get almost instantaneous results. So keep an open mind, be daring, and stay optimistic. I believe that attitude is perhaps the most important ingredient.

Of course, you should not travel to your ancestral hometown without having done your homework. You must learn about the general history and Jewish history of the places you intend to visit. Otherwise you will not be able to fully appreciate your visit. Try to locate as many photographs of the towns as possible so that you can recognize the places when you get there. Make copies of your family history notes and papers to bring with you. You might meet someone with whom you can have a rewarding family history conversation.

This photo, taken during one of the author's trips to Poland, shows a street on which a branch of the author's family lived in Przemysl.

Often I am asked, "For how long should I visit my ancestors' town?" That depends on how big the town was. If it is Warsaw or Prague, you can stay for days. If it is the average little village, one day is more than enough time (after which you will want to explore other places in the area). A small city might interest you for a few days. But do not think that your visit to a tiny old shtetl need take a week. Chances are you can walk every street and take every photograph and talk to every person within a few hours. Most of these places are rural, and there is not much to see. Nevertheless, your day or two might be among the most memorable moments of your life.

Jewish cemeteries and certain other sites of Jewish interest are often still intact. Of particular interest for me, in each town I visited, were the answers to three questions: Where is the Jewish cemetery? Where are the buildings that used to be synagogues? Are there any Jews still in the town? Often I found cemeteries and buildings that were once synagogues, and sometimes I even found Jews.

Memorial books are a must to check before your trip. If there is a memorial book for your town, it will provide you with pictures, names, history, and sometimes even a map of the town. With a map, you can find

sites of interest more easily. For example, since the synagogues have almost all been converted into other kinds of buildings, an old map from a memorial book can serve as your guide to finding it. By the way, there are four things most synagogue buildings are now used for: libraries, warehouses, garages, and movie theaters.

The *Encyclopedia Judaica,* mentioned often throughout this book, can be a good source of information about the current situation in the town of interest.

Landsmanshaften can also be good sources of information, but I must warn you that members of the landsmanshaften I have encountered were both the most eager to discourage me from making the trip as well as the most eager to hear about my experiences and seeing my photos when I returned.

Speaking of coming home, when I returned from my first trip, I did two things: I wrote an open letter to family and friends describing my trip. I could not write a separate note to each person, but I found it useful to write up a letter that I photocopied and sent to interested people. The second thing I did was to make slides of my photographs (in some cases I took slides too) and invite the family to see them while I narrated. I did *not* put in all of my tourist shots—I did not want to bore my family with one more travelogue—but only the photos relating to the family history (along with a few general shots of Eastern Europe to provide context). My slide shows always turned into successful "parties," appreciated by the family. And through my trip, they obtained a better sense of family history, which was of course the whole purpose behind my travels.

A Jewish travel guide that might prove useful when planning your trip is *The Jewish Traveler: Hadassah Magazine's Guide to the World's Jewish Communities and Sights,* by Alan M. Tigay (Aronson, 1994).

Remove not the ancient landmark which the fathers have set.

—Proverbs 22:28

Advice Before Traveling to Eastern Europe and the Former Soviet Union

As noted earlier, many people objected to my trips to Eastern Europe. "Don't go to those horrible places." "Poland is soaked with Jewish

This house, still standing, was home to a branch of the Kurzweil family in Jaraslov, Poland.

blood." "Don't bring them money." "There's nothing left to see. It was all destroyed." "Don't you have anything better to do with your time and money? Take a vacation!" First of all, there are still Jews in Poland, Hungary, the former Soviet Union, and other parts of Eastern Europe. They want and need contact with us. Second, if there is something drawing you to those places, you must trust your own instincts and intuition. Despite the fact that many people told me there was "nothing to see," I found that they were wrong. There is *plenty* to see—the way towns look; Holocaust memorials; relatives (there are eighty thousand Jews in Hungary today—they have to be *somebody's* relatives!); historic sites; people who still recall people in the family; and much more. Plan that trip and go!

You don't need to speak the language. English is probably the most widely spoken language in the world. I found English speakers almost everywhere I went. As long as I was sincere and friendly, there was always someone to help. Young people in Eastern Europe and the former Soviet Union are actually eager to meet English-speaking friends and visitors.

Keep your expectations low. In some cases you will find more than you ever dreamed you'd find. In other cases you will not find what you are looking for. I'd suggest you don't have any specific expectations that will make or break the trip. If you have as your goal one small piece of information and you don't find it, that is no reason to call the trip a failure. Keep your eyes open, make friends, be curious, take pictures, and do your best.

Take single dollar bills with you. They make great gratuities. The American dollar is strong in Eastern Europe and the former Soviet Union. A small amount means a lot. A few dollars given to a local archivist is often the thing that opens doors.

Do your homework before you travel. Do some research about the town you plan to visit and the region it is in. Ask the country's tourist bureau for maps and other information. Don't just arrive in Warsaw one day, thinking you'll figure out the details of your travel plans once you are there.

Be in touch with people who are in Jewish Genealogical Societies and explore the resources on JewishGen.org. You'll be able to locate many people who have already taken trips either to your very places of interest or places that are nearby. Many Jewish genealogists have already made trips to the places in which you are interested. They will have good advice. (Take *all* advice with a grain of salt: just because someone went to your town and found nothing does not mean you will also find nothing. Your interests and your goals will be entirely your own.)

Government regulations in Eastern Europe keep changing. Be flexible. And patient.

When you meet people who help you, try to stay in touch with them— or at least send a thank-you note. Not only is it a nice habit, but it will also benefit the next person who travels through.

During my trips, I went from town to town looking for several things. First, I was looking for living Jews. In some towns I found one Jewish person or two or just a few. These people are usually extremely grateful for the contact. I was also looking for the Jewish cemetery. Cemeteries in Eastern Europe suffer more from neglect than vandalism. Stones have toppled over; trees and whole forests have grown up around the stones. (I found one family cemetery in the middle of a cornfield; the farmer had simply planted around the stones.) Ask people where the old Jewish cemetery is; often the older people know. Sometimes you can locate old guidebooks in libraries that will indicate where things were. For example, I have a collection of old Baedeker's travel guides that date back to

the turn of the twentieth century. These guidebooks have provided me with locations of Jewish cemeteries, synagogues, and other destinations of interest.

Don't expect local town archives to be either well staffed or well organized. Don't expect to walk into a Polish archive, announce your great-grandfather's name, and plan to be handed a family tree. Sometimes you have to make a request one day and then return the next day (or week) for the results. This is obviously not always practical. I suggest that you write for an appointment before you leave home.

12

JEWISH CEMETERIES

YOUR HISTORY CHISELED IN STONE

APART FROM THE PERSONAL significance that a cemetery has for the survivors of someone who has died, cemeteries also represent the history of people. There is something special, something strange yet basic that you feel when walking among the graves in a cemetery. I have said this to people who have responded by calling me morbid. But a cemetery is not morbid. On the contrary, somehow a cemetery, on a quiet day, is filled with life. Scanning the stones, you can read "Died at age 87," "Died at age 68," "Died at age 74," and you begin to have the sense that each of the stones that surround you represents lives that were filled with complexity, love, struggle, hardship, pleasure, celebration, faith, pain, and exploration of life. Each stone is a lifetime, a family, a world.

In a cemetery, you cannot escape facing your own life. You are alive. This is what each stone says to you. You are alive. You are able to read the words engraved in the rock. You can read the names, the dates, the epitaphs. In fact, those words on the monument were put there for you, for that very moment when you wander over to it and wonder what this person's life was really like.

I would like you to go to a cemetery at a time other than when you must for a funeral because I want you to know what it is like to walk between the paths of graves in silence, with no one near you to distract your thoughts. I want you to know, as I have known, what it is like to read gravestone after gravestone, wondering about each person and the life he or she led.

But how can you know, from a few words chiseled on a stone, what a person was like? And what would it mean if you could? These people are strangers.

I cannot answer that in full; but in part, what a cemetery affords you the opportunity of doing is to see the world, for just a moment, frozen in time. Outside, in the busy streets and noisy rooms, the world seems to move too fast. It is difficult to see that this planet of ours is made of individual lives, each of which has feelings, sensitivities, and his own concerns. But in a cemetery, the lives are still, and each grave stands there to be witnessed, each representing the end of time for an individual. Standing in front of the grave of a stranger—the same kind of stranger I might pass on the street on any given day—the vivid sense comes over me that we are all so mortal, so unique, so special in our ways. Individual lives—this is what our world consists of.

But walking through a graveyard must be more than that, more than simply the ideas I have been trying to express. Otherwise, it would be enough to read this—and it surely is not.

Some people make it a point to visit a cemetery when they go on vacation. They put it on their sightseeing list, along with museums, parks, and historic spots. Why would a graveyard be a place to visit on a vacation? Why would one visit such a place when sightseeing? Again, it has to be experienced to be known. But in part a cemetery is a symbol (and the reality) of the history of a community and a people. When you stand on a piece of ground and read a stone that says "1803," you suddenly know, perhaps more than if you were told it or read it, that life went on at that very spot generations ago. And you know, as you stand before each grave and read the date of death, that it was just a day or two later that a group of people stood where you are standing, to bury a loved one. Each grave represents a life and the world left behind. A cemetery contains the monuments representing the people who made history: not just the famous individuals who make the history books and the headlines, but also each person who, in his or her way, brought time forward a few more years, to this very moment.

But this still is not all that a graveyard represents. There is more to this custom that we have of burying those who have died. The custom itself goes back to the earliest days of human history. The particulars have changed, but the custom and its importance have been a part of humankind and the Jewish people since the beginning. The Bible records burial customs, as does the Talmud and other writings. Sometimes the burial was done in caves, other times in scattered graves, but always there was a great concern for this point in our lives.

○
_____

Cemeteries must not be treated disrespectfully. Cattle may not be fed there, nor a watercourse turned, nor grass plucked.

—Talmud, Megilla 29a

_____
○

Our cemeteries, as sacred as they are to us, have often been desecrated. History records the desecration of Jewish cemeteries as early as the Middle Ages, and today we still hear of Jewish graveyards attacked by vandals.

During the Middle Ages, when Jews were forced out of a community, the cemetery was frequently destroyed, the tombstones used for other purposes. Some old buildings in Europe can still be found with slabs of stone taken from Jewish cemeteries. In more recent times, such desecrations in Israel by Arabs have been witnessed on a large scale. Jewish tombstones have been stolen and used for a variety of calculated purposes.

We know that the desecration of Jewish cemeteries has always been widespread. It is important to note that there are no ancient Jewish burial grounds in existence, save for a few scant traces. Furthermore, an old Jewish cemetery such as the Prague Cemetery contains no graves earlier than the fourteenth century, for the Jewish cemetery before that time was totally destroyed in April 1389. In addition, it is tragic to note that popes Calixtus II, Eugenius III, Alexander III, Clement III, Celestine III, and Innocent III had to specifically protect Jewish graveyards by means of papal declarations. Duke Frederick II of Austria declared in July 1244, "If a Christian attempts to destroy a Jewish cemetery or to break into it, he shall be put to death after the manner of the law, and all his property, no matter what it may be, shall be confiscated by the Duke."

There were other rulers who also extended protection, for a time at least, to Jewish cemeteries, including Frederick the Great of Prussia (1786–1840), who put up a sign at the entrance of the Jewish burial grounds warning that anyone who harms the cemetery would have his head chopped off with an ax.

Unfortunately, these attempts at protection of the Jewish graves were few and far between. Desecration of Jewish cemeteries coincided throughout history with the persecution of living Jews as well. Neither the living nor the dead were left in peace.

After World War I, desecration of Jewish cemeteries was widespread in Germany and continued throughout the Holocaust. During and after World War II, Jewish graveyards continued to be desecrated, and the

destruction of Eastern European Jewry resulted in the absence of Jewish communities who could even maintain these sacred spots. Although many Jewish cemeteries in Europe now have Holocaust memorials placed in them, the task of maintaining these sites becomes a greater problem with each passing day.

Cemeteries as Family Bonds

Often we will go to a cemetery on the sad occasion of a death and we will find ourselves standing with members of our family and friends of the family whom we have not seen for a long time. We sometimes think to ourselves that it is odd to see these people at graveyards and nowhere else. But in fact a funeral is not just an occasion to bury the dead but also an opportunity to renew our ties with the living and also with our past and our tradition.

When we attend a funeral, we have the opportunity to reflect on the past and on the people in our families who were members of past generations and whose lives were the links between our own and history. A funeral is a time to go to a cemetery, to read the epitaphs of family members who have departed from this earth, and to remind ourselves of who we are and where we have come from.

Ironically, funerals and burial grounds often serve to renew our relationships with those people, whom we have perhaps not seen since the last funeral. There may have been no contact since the last death in the family, but maybe this time there will be future contact "at happier occasions." A funeral is a time of sorrow, but it is not inappropriate or irreverent to think of the funeral or the presence at the cemetery as a deeply important opportunity from which to reap benefits. It is a time to think about one's childhood, to remember the last generations and their contributions to our lives, and to see the people whom we have not seen in a long time. Often those people remind us of happy times in our past and offer us a strong sense of who we are.

It is for these reasons, in part, that graveyards and funerals are so important in the Jewish tradition. Cremation (forbidden by Jewish law) or other methods of treating the dead often prevent the coming together of people at a funeral, unveiling, or cemetery. Even when there is a funeral but no burial, the absence of a grave means the absence of the opportunity for a visitor at a grave to read the words on a tombstone.

Standing before the grave of an ancestor or a relative and reading the words on the stone is a unique and priceless experience. One has to stand

The author standing next to
the grave of his great-great-
grandmother, Szofi Grün-
berger, in the Jewish cemetery
in Mateszalka, Hungary.

in silence among the graves of a burial field to be in touch with a sense of
one's own history in such a vivid way.

For many years my father and his brother and sister came together
annually to visit the graves of their parents. Although the three of them
saw each other often during the year, there was something special about
the annual visit to the cemetery. If they went separately, it would have been
different. If there were no grave, it would be different. If they got together
and spoke about their deceased parents for hours, it would be different.
By coming together and standing in silence surrounded by the graves of
their parents—and their grandfather, who is buried in the same family
plot—they shared moments that could never be replaced or equaled. Their
silence at the graves said more than words could ever express. When three
children stand as grown adults at the grave of their parents, it is as if, in a
sense, their family is together again. And of course, it is not imagination
but reality, for their family *is* together for those moments at the graves.
As they leave until the next time, they know that they come away from
the cemetery with much more than they had when they arrived.

A Walk Through a Jewish Cemetery

A walk through a Jewish cemetery is a walk through Jewish history. Find the Jewish graveyard closest to your home, or travel to one that has members of your family within its gates, and spend an hour or two wandering up and down the paths, comparing the monuments, reading the inscriptions, and absorbing the decades (or perhaps centuries) around you.

You will encounter, on your walk, the brief though often moving personal histories of many people. You will notice children who died before reaching their first birthday and great-grandparents who left this world after ninety-five years. Be on the lookout for unusual or instructive items. Perhaps you will wander over to a family plot and notice the more recent generations shortening the European last name. Speaking of names, a cemetery is an excellent place to observe the different naming customs from era to era. Names that were common sixty years ago will be unfamiliar today.

Do not think it bizarre to walk through a burial ground. The stones were engraved with words for people to read. Each monument was chosen to keep a memory alive. Certainly the family of the deceased would not mind if you stopped at a grave, read the inscription, and pondered the life of the person so commemorated.

Notice the different shapes and sizes of the gravestones. Some will be tall and massive; others will be smaller and more modest. Some will be lavishly engraved with Jewish symbols and decorations, and others will be simple, without any frills. The inscriptions, too, will be quite different. Some will be entirely in Hebrew, others totally in English. Some will include just the name of the person and the dates of birth and death, and others will include lengthy sayings and quite a bit of information about the person. Many gravestones even include photographs that are embedded in the monument.

Read the inscriptions carefully. You will usually find the name of the deceased and then, in Hebrew, the name of the person's father. For the family tree researcher, this is, of course, an excellent source of genealogical information.

An inscription on a gravestone can offer more information about the life and the time of the person buried in the grave. You can discover the length of the person's life, for example. Often on a double gravestone, where there is room for a husband and a wife, one side is still empty, telling you that a spouse is still alive. Or both sides might be filled and you will know how long one person lived after his or her spouse died. You cannot help but wonder what the survivors of the family must be feeling when these graves are visited.

Family plots are popular, and you will surely find one that will tell a story about several generations of a family. You will find the graves of the great-grandparents; their children, the grandparents; and their children. It is easy to pick out family plots, not only by the family name being repeated but also by studying the inscriptions carefully. Since gravestones of Jews usually provide the name of the father of the deceased, it is a rather simple task to pick out the relationships, both by the names and by the positions of the stones. In this way, you can visualize entire families, imagine the lives of these people, study the names and see who was named for whom, who carried on the tradition in whose name, who lived to a ripe old age and who died tragically in his or her youth, who never married and who had many children.

A cemetery is rich in tradition and history. Jewish symbols abound on the stones that memorialize simple, common people. Their ancient names inscribed in stone stand as a tribute to lives of happiness, sadness, struggles, and celebrations. You look at a stone and read a few words about a man; when he was born, when he died, what his name was, and what his father's name was. You glance to the right and see his wife's name and her father's name. You see how long they lived and wonder whether they were born here or across the ocean in a Jewish community that no longer exists. You look to see where the graves are located and notice that this is not a family plot but the plot of a landsmanshaft, consisting of people from the same town who are now "resting in peace" among people from their community, their lifelong friends who journeyed to America too and established their families here. Suddenly this is not the grave of one person at all; it is, rather, a brief history. It is the history of a man, his family, his community, and his beliefs. He was born a Jew, and he died a Jew. He was born in his community, and he lies at rest in his community. He lived with his wife and now, as the inscription on the grave itself says, he is with his beloved forever.

As you walk through the narrow paths of the Jewish graveyard, the names and the lives of the people who a few moments ago were strangers are no longer foreign. By stopping by a grave and reading the few words on the stone, you touch the life of the person who is represented to you by the inscription. A moment ago you did not know her name; now you know her name. A moment ago you did not know her father's name; now you know this too. A brief moment ago you did not know her husband's name or her age or her English and Hebrew names or the fact that she died a wife, mother, grandmother, and great-grandmother. Now you know that too. Next to her grave you notice the grave of a child. The first name is the same as her father's, so you know that the child was named for a

great-grandfather. Then you realize that the child is the woman's grandson. She went to her grandson's funeral.

Visiting Jewish Cemeteries

A walk through a Jewish cemetery is an encounter with lives and generations, a stroll through history. You will not learn about kings and battles; you will not encounter politicians and political upheavals; but you will meet the people who made Jewish history—by living and dying as Jews.

Tombstones

As noted, tombstones offer a variety of information. Some include lengthy epitaphs, others have photographs embedded in the stone, and still others include biographical information about the person.

Since the Jewish tradition includes a father's name along with a person's name (and sometimes includes a mother's name, though not often), tombstones can help you add a generation or two to your family tree.

You may find that a tombstone offers differing information from what you have learned from other sources. Keep in mind that tombstones are often inaccurate. This is so for a few reasons: (1) there may have been no one available to give accurate information to the engraver, (2) it is difficult to correct a mistake made during the engraving, and (3) false information was sometimes given deliberately to make a person seem younger or older at the time of death. Many people approach the question of age with peculiar biases. In any case, do not be surprised if you find a tombstone that conflicts with the information you have.

No monument gives such glory as an unsullied name.

—Eleazer ben Judah, *Rokeah* 13c

Cemetery Plots

There are several types of cemetery plots.

Some plots are owned by entire families and contain the graves of family members. Often a large stone or archway can be found at a family plot with the name of the family on it. Family organizations such as cousins'

clubs or family circles will own a plot. This would obviously be helpful to a family historian.

Synagogues often have plots for their members or for those members who have purchased a plot.

Landsmanshaften and other fraternal organizations also have cemetery plots. In fact, many of these organizations originally formed for the very purpose of buying a plot for its members.

Finally, some people have individual plots with no affiliation, special location, or relation to other plots in the cemetery.

    Walk reverently in a cemetery, lest the deceased say, "Tomorrow they will join us, and today they mock us."

                              —Talmud, Berakot 18a

Tombstone Transcribing

When you visit a cemetery for family history purposes, make sure you transcribe all the information on the tombstone into your notebook. Don't just jot down the names and dates; record the inscription in its entirety. Although you should seriously consider photographing the stones as well, sketches of the tombstones are also worthwhile.

If you are visiting a family plot containing many tombstones of personal interest, you should draw a map of the entire plot and note the location of each stone with its inscription. Finally, do not forget to label your notes, indicating the exact location of the plots within the cemetery. Cemeteries are often quite large, and an exact record of the plot location may be helpful in the future.

How to Read a Jewish Tombstone

If a tombstone of interest is written in Hebrew (as most Jewish tombstone are—in part, if not completely), a few pointers will be helpful if you cannot read the language.

    After every funeral I used to stay on at the cemetery and copy tombstone inscriptions.

                —Jacob Shatzky, Jewish historian, in memoirs about his youth

---

At the top of most Jewish tombstones are some abbreviations:

פ׳נ   for a man   פ׳נ   stands for
                             פה נקבר   meaning "here lies"

פ׳ט   for a woman   פ׳ט   signifies
                             פה טמונה   meaning "here is
                                         interred"

At the close of most Jewish tombstone inscriptions you will find the abbreviation

תנצב׳ה, which stands for תהי נפשר צרורה בצרור התיים
This is a verse from 1 Samuel 25:29, "May his soul be bound up in the bond of eternal life."

The tombstone may contain an epitaph in Hebrew, in which case you would simply have to copy the letters or take a clear photograph of the inscription and get it translated.

Calculating a date from the Hebrew on the tombstone will also be necessary. Actually, it would be useful for you to learn how to convert a Hebrew date into an English date for tombstones as well as any other Jewish document written in Hebrew. The system is quite simple.

The letters of the Hebrew alphabet each have a numerical value, as follows:

א	= 1	ל	= 30
ב	= 2	מ	= 40
ג	= 3	נ	= 50
ד	= 4	ס	= 60
ה	= 5	ע	= 70
ו	= 6	פ	= 80
ז	= 7	צ	= 90
ח	= 8	ק	= 100
ט	= 9	ר	= 200
י	= 10	ש	= 300
כ	= 20	ת	= 400

When a Hebrew date is written, you must figure out the numerical value of each letter and then add the values together. This is the date. But remember that this is the Hebrew date, not the date we use in daily life. Hebrew dates are calculated from Rosh Hashanah (which occurs on the modern calendar in September or October) in the year 3761 B.C.E.

September 27, 2003, therefore marked the start of the Jewish year 5764. Armed with this information, you need only do a little arithmetic to change a Hebrew date to a secular date.

There is just one minor complication. Often a Hebrew date after the year 5000 on the Hebrew calendar will leave off the number 5 in the thousands column. In other words, taking the example of 2003 being 5764, you will usually see the Hebrew date written as 764 rather than 5764. To arrive at a Common Era date, simply add 1240 to the shortened date: 764 plus 1240 is 2004. Why 2004 rather than 2003? Because the Jewish date changes, as I have said, in September or October. Consequently, most of the year 5764 will be in 2004, not 2003.

Of course, a tombstone, as well as other documents, may indicate the month too, probably the Hebrew month. Here is a list of the Hebrew months:

תסרי	Tishre		September
הסון	Heshvan		October
כסלר	Kislev		November
טבת	Tevet		December
שסבט	Shevat		January
אדר	Adar (Adar II in leap year)	אדר ב	February
ניסן	Nisan		March
אייר	Iyar		April
סיון	Sivan		May
תמוז	Tamuz		June
אב	Av		July
אלול	Elul		August

Because the Hebrew calendar is not the same as the calendar that we use in secular life, the months do not correspond exactly. In a given year the corresponding months can be off by several days or even weeks.

Here is an example of how to convert a Hebrew date into an English date: If the year is תרפ, the letter ת is 400, ר is 200, and פ is 80. This totals 680. As I pointed out, the 5000 is usually left off, so actually the date would be 5680. Using our formula, 680 plus 1240 is 1920. That is the date we are familiar with.

The JewishGen.org Web site has a terrific page called "Reading Hebrew Tombstones" (http://www.jewishgen.org/infofiles/tombstones.html) that explains everything you need to know when you encounter a gravestone.

Another great resource is on the Jewish Genealogical Society of New York's Web site called "Translations of Common Hebrew and Yiddish Words in Landsmanshaftn and Burial Society Names" (http://home.att.net/ %7EJGSNYCem/translations.htm). This list will help you translate names of organizations, synagogues, and other things inscribed on tombstones. For example, if the name of a synagogue of interest is Anshei Chesed and you are not familiar with either word, this Web page will tell you that *anshei* means "people of" and *chesed* means "grace."

Tombstone Rubbings

Tombstone rubbing is the art of transferring the design and inscription of the surface of a tombstone to a piece of paper or fabric using a special wax or crayon. The procedure is simple, does not harm the tombstone, and provides you with an exact, life-size reproduction of the stone.

Although the art of rubbing is used to reproduce other images besides tombstones, old graveyards are probably the most popular sites for this ancient pastime. Rubbing tombstones is particularly effective for old stones with unusual shapes and lettering styles.

To obtain the supplies you need to practice this art, write to Oldstone Enterprises, 1 Deangelo Drive, Bedford, MA 01730; phone: (781) 271-0480. This is the largest supplier of rubbing materials in the United States.

Perfect love, brotherhood and mutual assistance is only found among those near to each other by relationship. The members of a family united by common descent from the same grandfather, or even from some more distant ancestor, have toward each other a certain feeling of love, help each other, and sympathize with each other. To effect this is one of the chief purposes of the Law.

—Maimonides, *Guide III*, 49

Photographing Tombstones

It is not in bad taste to photograph tombstones. A photograph of a tombstone or a cemetery can be meaningful and moving.

If you are visiting cemeteries for your family research, it would be a good idea to photograph the stones as well as to transcribe the engraved message. Pictures of your family's tombstones would be a significant addition to your family history collection.

The grave of Rabbi Chaim Josef Gottlieb, the Stropkover Rebbe, great-great-great-grandfather of the author. Relatives of the author have recently constructed a structure that covers the grave.

Of course, taking photographs should not prevent you from visiting the graves again, for personal reasons as well as to make sure that the graves are in good condition.

○

We always found out at a funeral whoever was great or distinguished in Jewish Warsaw. I used to attach myself to every funeral procession that seemed to me important—according to the number of mourners. Often I did not even know who the deceased was, but hearing the eulogies at the cemetery, I felt that it was a privilege to be there in such lifeless proximity to a living past. Instinctively I inherited that impersonal attitude toward one whose life had graced Warsaw's Jewish life, a life which first revealed itself to me at the cemetery.

—Jacob Shatzky, Jewish historian

○

Locating Cemeteries

If no one in your family knows where a burial plot is located, try to obtain a copy of the person's death certificate. A death certificate usually gives the location of the cemetery. When you arrive at the graveyard, inquire at the office for the exact location of the plot.

All burial offices will tell you the location of a specific plot, but they vary when it comes to giving you additional information about the individual and his or her family. They also have information in their files that might be helpful (such as the name of the spouse and the address at time of death), but cooperation varies from office to office.

A superb source for information is International Jewish Cemetery Project (http://www.jewishgen.org/cemetery), a joint project of the International Association of Jewish Genealogical Societies (IAJGS) and the JewishGen Online Worldwide Burial Registry (JOWBR). Its stated mission is to catalogue every Jewish burial site throughout the world. Don't underestimate the value of this Web site. It contains information about Jewish cemeteries everywhere in the world, country by country, and includes a lot of additional data. If you know the name of the town from which your family emigrated, check out the entry for that town on this site. You will find a vast amount of valuable information about that town in addition to cemetery information.

○

A generation goes and a generation comes, but the earth stands forever.

—Ecclesiastes 1:4

○

Death Certificates

The registration of deaths varies from place to place and year to year, but there is usually a death certificate on file for deaths that have occurred in the United States. A death certificate can be helpful in your family history research because most of them include information such as full name, name of father, maiden name of mother, name of spouse, date of death, place of death, cause of death, place of burial, name of funeral home, place of birth, address at time of death, and number of years in the United States.

Any one of these pieces of information can lead you to more information. For example, if you know how many years a person was living in

the United States, you can narrow the field when searching for immigration papers and steamship passenger lists. If you know an ancestor's mother's maiden name, you can begin a new branch of your family tree. If you know the place of burial, you can locate the grave and obtain more information from the gravestone.

The best guide to help you locate death certificates is a thirty-eight-page booklet called *Where to Write for Vital Records,* available from the U.S. Government Printing Office, Washington, DC 20402–9325.

---
o

Happy is he who grew up with a good name and departed this world with a good name.

—Johana, Talmud, Berakot 17a

---
o

Wills

A last will and testament that is filed with the state is usually a public record and is often filled with family history data. In many cases, wills include names of children, grandchildren, and other relatives. Also, you can learn a lot about a person by what he or she is giving to others in a will, as well as to whom the bequests are being given. I have found wills indicating sums of money to go to yeshivas and other religious organizations, for example, which give me an insight into the religiosity or affiliations of the deceased.

Wills are located in a variety of places. Sometimes they are kept in surrogate's court, probate court, or elsewhere. You should check the county clerk's office for whatever location interests you and see where the wills are kept. Keep in mind that you are entitled to see these documents, except in specific cases for various legal reasons. I mention this because I have often gotten the feeling that wills are confidential. I have also met with resistance on the part of some clerks in a few places. Be insistent. You have a right to examine most wills.

Obituaries

Newspaper obituaries can often be key sources of family history information. The difficulty, however, is that there is no systematic way of finding an obituary, for several reasons:

Death certificate of the author's great-grandfather. It notes that he died in the synagogue on the holiday of Passover.

○ There are no indexes to obituaries that would be useful to the general population. (The *New York Times* has issued an index, but it is selective.)

○ There are two kinds of obituaries: articles written by the newspaper and announcements provided by individuals. To find the obituary of a specific individual, you must first be able to locate the right newspaper. Then you must know the exact or approximate date of death. Then you must hope that either an article was written or that an announcement was published.

○ Back issues of newspapers are often available on microfilm in the geographical area where the newspaper is published. This is true for defunct newspapers as well as those that are still publishing.

○ Do not forget to consider Yiddish papers. Again, this can present a problem, since there were many Yiddish newspapers circulating at times, and you may not know which paper was read by the people who might have published a death announcement. Check with the YIVO Institute for Jewish Research regarding how to locate back issues of Yiddish newspapers.

The American Jewish Periodicals Center, Hebrew Union College, 3101 Clifton Avenue, Cincinnati, OH 45220, also has an excellent collection of Jewish newspapers. More than 875 titles, with over 12 million pages, are maintained there.

Despite the problems surrounding obituaries, they can still be of great use and should be considered when you are doing your research.

---------- ○ ----------

Moses received the Torah at Sinai and handed it down to Joshua; Joshua to the elders; the elders to the Prophets; and the Prophets handed it down to the men of the Great Assembly.

—Talmud, Pirke Avot 1:1

---------- ○ ----------

European Jewish Cemeteries

Many Jewish cemeteries in Eastern Europe were partly or entirely destroyed during the Holocaust. Yet a surprising number of them have survived and are intact. Some are quite old and are filled with family history.

Old Jewish cemeteries in Western Europe are also good sources of information, and a trip to ancestral locations should include such

Yahrzeit (anniversary of date of death) calendar for the author's maternal great-grandfather.

research. The International Jewish Cemetery Project Web site (http://www.jewishgen.org/cemetery) is your best source for locating Jewish cemeteries in Europe (and elsewhere).

Other Valuable Jewish Cemetery Sources

There are several additional sources that you may find useful in your cemetery research.

- o "Jewish Cemeteries in Hungary" (http://www.geocities.com/winter_peter_4) is a Web site with ambitious plans. If you are interested in Hungarian Jewish cemeteries, try it.

- o "New York Area Jewish Cemeteries" (http://members.aol.com/jgsny/cemeteries.htm) is a Web page on the site of the Jewish Genealogical Society of New York. It includes a map with the locations of the cemeteries in the NYC area.

- o "Jewish Cemeteries in the Eastern Slovakia" (http://cemeteries.wz.cz) is an interesting Web site for those interested in this region. There

are a few hundred photographs of Jewish cemeteries and other information.

○ The Jewish Genealogical Society of Great Britain (http://www. jgsgb.org.uk) has a section for Jewish cemeteries in Scotland (http://www.jgsgb.org.uk/bury03.shtml).

○ ShtetLinks (http://www.shtetlinks.jewishgen.org), a project of JewishGen.org, provides lots of information about a large number of Eastern European Jewish towns, including the location and status of Jewish cemeteries.

○ Many of the special interest groups (SIGs) hosted by JewishGen.org (http://www.jewishgen.org/JewishGen/sigs.htm) have information on their Web pages concerning Jewish cemeteries in its regions.

RELATIONSHIP CHART

HOW ARE WE RELATED?

HOW MANY TIMES have you had conversations with relatives of yours when you tried to figure out how you were related? There is often confusion regarding the names of the relationships between people. For example, do you know the difference between a second cousin and a first cousin once removed? What does "once removed" mean? Is it possible for you to be your own cousin? The following chart will clear up any confusion you might have with the definitions of relationships. This is an easy system for you to use to answer the question: How are we related?

First we need to define some terms.

Common progenitor. The closest ancestor two people have in common is their common progenitor. So, for example, you and your sister have your parents as your common progenitors. You also have your grandparents and great-grandparents in common, but for the purpose of this chart, we are concerned only with your *closest* common ancestor. To give another example, the common progenitor of you and your first cousin is one of your grandparents. In other words, you and your first cousin do not have the same parents, but you have the same grandparents.

Removed. When we speak of a cousin being once removed, we are referring to generations. For example, if you know your father's first cousin, you are that person's first cousin once removed. In other words, you are one generation away (removed) from the first-cousin relationship. If you know your grandfather's first cousin, you are that person's first cousin twice removed. You are two generations away from that relationship.

HOW ARE WE RELATED?

	0	1	2	3	4	5	6
0	CP	S	GS	GGS	GGS	GGS	GGS
1	S	V	N	GN	GGN	2 GGN	3 GGN
2	GS	N	1C	1C 2R	1C 2R	1C 3R	1C 4R
3	GGS	GN	1C 1R	2C	2C 1R	2C 2R	2C 3R
4	2 GGS	GGN	1C 2R	2C 1R	3C	3C 1R	3C 2R
5	3 GGS	2 GGN	1C 3R	2C 2R	3C 1R	4C	4C 1R
6	4 GGS	3 GGN	1C 4R	2C 3R	3C 2R	4C 1R	5C

CP   Common progenitor

C   Cousin

V   Brother or sister

BR   Times removed

S   Son or daughter

N   Nephew or niece

GS   Grandson or granddaughter

GGS   Great-grandson or great-granddaughter

Relationship chart.

Cousin. Your cousins are the children of your aunts and uncles, great-aunts and great-uncles, and so on. Thus your second cousin is the son or daughter of your first cousin once removed.

With those terms understood, you will now be able to understand and determine your relationships with your relatives.

———— o ————

Emperor Hadrian was walking one day when he saw an old man digging holes to plant trees. Hadrian asked the old man, "How old are you this day?" Said he, "I am one hundred years old." Said Hadrian, "You are a hundred years old and you stand there digging holes to plant trees! Do you expect to eat their fruit?" The old man replied, "I shall eat the fruits if my merits are sufficient. If not, I toil for my descendants, as my fathers toiled for me."

—Midrash Rabbah, Leviticus 25

———— o ————

As you see on the chart, there are numbers from 0 to 6 across the top and down the left side. These numbers represent the number of generations from a common progenitor. The square in the upper left corner labeled "CP" stands for common progenitor.

The first thing you must do is figure out who is the common progenitor between two people. For example, suppose you want to know the relationship between yourself and your first cousin's son. The first question to ask is: Who is the closest ancestor to both of us? The answer is your grandfather (or grandmother, but for simplicity, the chart shows only male descent, though it is the same for males and females).

In the left-hand column, notice that the square next to number 2 says "GS," which stands for *grandson.* That is *you* (in our example). On the row across the top, you can see that the square below number 3 says "GGS," which means *great-grandson.* That is your first cousin's son. Again, your grandfather and your first cousin's son's great-grandfather are the same person. On the chart, you are number 2 and he is number 3.

The square at which rows 2 and 3 meet tells you the relationship. That is, the square that says "1C1R" is the square where row 2 and row 3 meet. "1C1R" means *first cousin once removed.* That is your relationship to each other.

By the way, "once removed" works both ways. You are his first cousin once removed, and he is your first cousin once removed.

Try the chart with a few examples from your family to get used to determining relationships.

Finally, to the question "Can you be your own cousin?" the answer is yes. If, for example, your great-grandparents were first cousins when they married each other (as in the case of my great-grandparents), you are your own fourth cousin!

THE AUTHOR

ARTHUR KURZWEIL'S own personal quest eventually led him to explore his spiritual identity, which resulted in his seminal book on Jewish genealogical research, *From Generation to Generation: How to Trace Your Jewish Genealogy and Family History.* Realizing that there were relatively few serious Jewish books available to the English-language reader, he has directed what has been described as a visionary plan to transform the experience of the Jewish seeker looking for nourishing Jewish books. During his career as an editor and publisher, he has commissioned and published more than seven hundred volumes of Jewish interest.

Kurzweil's passion for books has been lifelong. Trained as a professional librarian, editor in chief of the Jewish Book Club for seventeen years, past president of the Jewish Book Council, Judaica acquisitions editor and literary agent, he came to a personal conclusion that the ultimate book for him is the one often described as the cornerstone of Jewish culture, the Talmud.

With the guidance of his teacher, the renowned Rabbi Adin Steinsaltz, Kurzweil has inspired many people across the United States to discover and get involved with the Talmud. As the coordinator of the Talmud Circle Project, under the direction of Rabbi Steinsaltz, his mission has been to introduce the Talmud to Jewish spiritual seekers. He has been the catalyst for many individuals as well as synagogue groups who now study Talmud regularly. He is also the editor of two collections of essays by Rabbi Steinsaltz, *The Strife of the Spirit* and *On Being Free.*

Arthur Kurzweil is also an accomplished magician. A member of the Society of American Magicians (founded by Harry Houdini) and the International Brotherhood of Magicians, he often blends his spiritual interests with magical effects, adding his own insights and weaving together an enchanting presentation for his audiences.

Frequently described as America's foremost Jewish genealogist, Arthur Kurzweil's name has become synonymous with Jewish genealogical research. His highly praised book, *From Generation to Generation,* the

new edition of which you hold in your hands, is acknowledged as the definitive guidebook in the field of Jewish genealogy. Kurzweil has addressed hundreds of Jewish groups on a variety of topics related to Jewish genealogy. He was a cofounder of the very first Jewish Genealogical Society in the 1970s; there are now nearly seventy Jewish Genealogical Societies throughout the world.

Kurzweil is also the author of *The Encyclopedia of Jewish Genealogy* and *My Generations: A Course in Jewish Family History. My Generations* is a popular textbook that has been used for almost twenty years in many synagogue schools throughout North America.

Kurzweil's writing has appeared in *New York,* the *Los Angeles Times,* the *Miami Herald, Newsday,* and most of the national Jewish periodicals. For two years he wrote a weekly column for *Jewish Week* of New York.

Kurzweil is the recipient of the Distinguished Humanitarian Award from the Melton Center of Ohio State University for his unique contributions to the field of Jewish education. He also received a Lifetime Achievement Award from the International Association of Jewish Genealogical Societies. For many years he has been one of the most popular teachers at the annual conference of the Coalition for the Advancement of Jewish Education. He also serves as Judaica consultant for Jossey-Bass, a division of John Wiley Publishers.

A popular, engaging, humorous, and moving lecturer and entertainer, Kurzweil has spoken and performed before hundreds of audiences of all ages.

INDEX

The Best Jewish Writing 2003
Arthur Kurzweil
Paperback
ISBN: 0–7879–6771–8

"Kurzweil presents an impressive list of prominent authors and allows them to speak for themselves . . . he has done readers a fine service by bringing together a stellar, diverse collection for their enjoyment."
—*Publishers Weekly,* **August 11, 2003**

The latest edition of this annual collection marks the debut of a new editor, Arthur Kurzweil, a man widely known as a major thinker, teacher, leader, and publisher in the Jewish community. He has selected the best work from a broad range of Jewish interests, including articles, essays, short stories, poems, polemics, personal memoirs, and sections of novels. The contributors represent some of the most important established Jewish authors as well as powerful voices from the next generation of spiritual leaders, artists, teachers, and activists. Selections include Elie Wiesel's "Letter to George W. Bush," Ed Koch on Woody Allen, Amos Elon on "Israelis and Palestinians: What Went Wrong," Cynthia Ozick's "The Heretic," Jonathan Rosen on "Waking Up to Anti-Semitism," and outstanding works by writers such as Alan Dershowitz, Phyllis Chesler, David Grossman, Adin Steinsaltz, Marge Piercy, Herb Gold, and others.

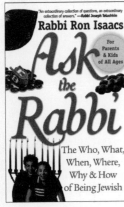

Ask the Rabbi: The Who, What, When, Where, Why, and How of Being Jewish
Rabbi Ron Isaacs
Hardcover
ISBN: 0–7879–6784-X

"An extraordinary collection of questions, an extraordinary collection of answers, Ron Isaacs is indeed the rabbi who can be asked anything. His knowledge is encyclopedic, and this book is a pleasure to read."

—**Rabbi Joseph Telushkin, author,**
Jewish Literacy **and** *The Book of Jewish Values*

"If you've ever wanted a resource to turn to when your children ask you questions about Judaism or if you've got a whole bunch of left-over questions from your own childhood, *Ask the Rabbi* will fill the bill beautifully."

—**From the foreword by Dr. Jonathan Woocher,**
president, Jewish Education Service of North America

From the mundane to the perplexing, Rabbi Ron Isaacs answers all your questions about the Jewish faith in a manner that is warm, wise, and witty. Isaacs brings his many years of experience as a rabbi and scholar to create a family-friendly resource that you and your children can use again and again to answer questions as they arise in your day-to-day lives–such as questions about worship services, blessings, famous people in the Bible, miracles, fast days, Rosh Hashanah, Hanukkah, the Seder, circumcision, Bar/Bat Mitzvah, marriage, keeping kosher, sex, death and dying, medical ethics, Jewish beliefs, Hasidim, Jewish denominations, rabbis and cantors, black Jews, Jewish professions, what others think of the Jews, Israel, ritual garments, the Torah, the mezuzah, anti-Semitic documents and statements, Sephardic and Ashkenazic Jews, language, Jews and cults, kabbalah, and classic Jewish books.

Opening the Tanya: Discovering the Moral & Mystical Teachings of a Classic Work of Kabbalah
Rabbi Adin Steinsaltz
Hardcover
ISBN: 0–7879–6798-X

Written by internationally acclaimed author, scholar and teacher Rabbi Adin Steinsaltz, *Opening the Tanya* is a groundbreaking book that offers a definitive introduction, explanation, and commentary upon the Tanya. A seminal document in the study of Kabbalah, the Tanya explores and solves the dilemmas of the human soul by arriving at the root causes of its struggles. Though it is a classic Jewish spiritual text, the Tanya and its commentary take a broad and comprehensive approach that is neither specific to Judaism nor tied to a particular personality type or time or point of view.

As relevant today as it was when it was first written more than two hundred years ago, the Tanya helps us to see the many thousands of complexities, doubts, and drives within us as expressions of a single basic problem, the struggle between our Godly soul and our animal soul. *Opening the Tanya* guides us to achieve harmony of body and soul, of earthliness and transcendence.

Make Your Own Passover Seder: A New Approach to Creating a Personal Family Celebration
Rabbi Alan Kay and Jo Kay
Hardcover
ISBN: 0–7879–6766–1

"The Kays have transmitted their own love—and knowledge—of the Passover seder onto the printed page in a way that's catching for novices and seder entrepreneurs alike."

—Dru Greenwood, director, Outreach and Synagogue Community Union of American Hebrew Congregations

"Simplifies the challenging prospect of figuring out how to make a meaningful seder while providing spiritual insight and support. . . . Helps all to transform the seder experience—the central experience of Jewish family life—into a sacred memory."

—Kerry M. Olitzky, executive director, Jewish Outreach Institute, New York

"Jo and Alan are outstanding Jewish family educators who have written a practical guide to making a Passover seder into a participatory and meaningful experience. A treasure trove of great ideas for every seder leader!"

—Ron Wolfson, author, *Passover: The Family Guide for Spiritual Celebration, Second Edition*

*M*ake Your Own Passover Seder gives you the information needed to create a customized seder that expresses your and your family's particular spiritual, political, and personal values and sentiments. No matter what your religious persuasion—Orthodox, Conservative, Reform, Reconstructionist, Renewal, or not Jewish at all—this guide provides a wise and learned approach that is filled with warmth and creativity. *Make Your Own Passover Seder* offers new ideas and myriad options based on the authors' own experience and hundreds of other examples of seders throughout the world.